STEVIE SMITH

Frances Spalding first discovered Stevie Smith in
Erin Pizzey's bookshop in Caterham, Surrey, where
as a teenager she came across the intriguing title,
Novel on Yellow Paper. On reaching university she was
dismayed to learn that its author was a cult figure, and
only some years later, after she had trained as an art
historian, and written books on art as well as two
biographies *Roger Fry: Art and Life* (1980), and
Vanessa Bell (1983), did she decide to write a life of
Stevie Smith.

Stevie Smith

A CRITICAL BIOGRAPHY

FRANCES SPALDING

faber and faber
LONDON·BOSTON

First published in 1988
by Faber and Faber Limited
3 Queen Square London WC1N 3AU
Reprinted 1988
This paperback edition first published in 1990

Photoset by Wilmaset Birkenhead Wirral
Printed in Great Britain by
Richard Clay Ltd Bungay Suffolk

British Library Cataloguing in Publication Data

Spalding, Frances
Stevie Smith: a critical biography.
1. Poetry in English. Smith, Stevie –
Biographies
I. Title
821′.912

ISBN 0–571–14223–0

Contents

Acknowledgements

My thanks go first of all to Stevie Smith's literary executor, James MacGibbon, for granting my request to write this book. I am further indebted to the following for generous assistance: Mr Walter Allen; Miss Diana Athill; Mr Paul Bailey; Mrs Vera Baird; Mr Jack Barbera; Miss Rosemary Beattie; Mr Mark Bence-Jones; Mrs Peggy Blackburn; Dr Marjorie Boulton; Mr and Mrs John Bradford; Miss Margaret Branch; Mr and Mrs Neville Braybrooke; Miss Maria Browne; Mr and Mrs Michael Browne; Professor Norman Bryson; Mr George Buchanan; Miss Jessie E. Buckfield; Mr Robert Buhler; Mrs Racy Buxton; Mrs Freda Calstern; Mrs Lilian Carpenter; Mrs W. E. A. Chatfield; Mrs Sally Chilver; the late Douglas Cleverdon; Mrs Nest Cleverdon; Mrs Barbara Clutton-Brock; Mr Stephen Coan; Mrs Becky Cocking; Mr Robert Cook; Miss Lettice Cooper; Miss Rosemary Cooper; Mr Nicholas Cottis; Miss Jeni Couzyn; Professor Maurice Cranston; Mrs Eleni Cubitt; Dr James Curley; Mr A. J. Davey; Mr Ian Davie; Mr Michael De-la-Noy; Mr Nigel Dennis; Mrs Doreen Diamant; Miss Kay Dick; Mr Patric Dickinson; Mr John Drummond; the late Donald Everett; Mrs Molly Everett, Miss Kathleen Farrell; Mrs Vicki Feaver; the late Wallace Finkel; Brigadier and Mrs Laurence Fowler; Miss Peggy Fox; Miss Margaret Gardiner; Mr Richard Garnett; Mrs Lucy Gent; Miss Stella Gibbons; Miss Helen Glatz; Miss Deidre Good; Mrs Celia Goodman; Mr John Guest; Mr Michael Hamburger; Mrs Sally Hardy; Sir Rupert Hart-Davis; Mrs Gertrud Häusermann; Mr John Heath-Stubbs; Miss Judith Hemming; Mrs Kitty Hermges; Mr David Heycock; Dr Polly Hill; Mr F. C. Hodgkin; Mr John Horder; Lord Horder; Mr Ladislav Horvat; Mr Michael Horovitz; Sir Fred Hoyle; Miss Audrey Insch; Revd Gerard Irvine; Mrs Susannah Jacobson; Miss Helen Jessop; Mr Rory Johnston; Mr Leo Kahn; Mr Peter Kiddle; Mr Terence Kilmartin; Professor Ruth Landes; the late Philip Larkin; Miss Marghanita Laski; Mr James Laughlin; Mr and Mrs George Lawrence; Sir John and Lady Lawrence; Miss Rosamond Lehmann; Miss Naomi Lewis; Mr Eddie Linden; Professor William McBrien; Mrs Jean MacGibbon; Miss Cecily Mackworth (La Marquise de Chabannes la Palice); Miss Judith Maravelias-Eckinger; Mr Derwent May; Mr Christopher Middleton; Dr Jonathan Miller; Miss Margaret Miller; Miss E. Margo Miller; Miss Sarah Miller;

ACKNOWLEDGEMENTS

Mr Adrian Mitchell; Professor Charles Mitchell; Mr David Mitchell; Mr T. H. Mobbs; Mr John Morley; Miss Lin Morris; Lord Moyne; Mrs June Nethercut; Mr Peter Newbolt; Mrs Margaret Newman; Miss Juliet O'Hea; Miss Armide Oppé; Mr Ronald Orr-Ewing; Mrs Olive Pain; Mrs Trekkie Parsons; Mrs Frances Partridge; Mr Brian Patten; Mrs Kathleen Peacock; Mrs Elizabeth Popley; Mr Anthony Powell; Miss Joan Prideaux; Mrs Eleanor Quass; Miss Margaret K. Ralph; Dr Priaulx Rainier; Mrs Joan Ransom; Miss Helen Rapp; Miss Naomi Replansky; the late Dame Flora Robson; Mr Jeremy Robson; Mr C. H. Rolph; Mrs Joan Rowell; Mr Piers Russell-Cobb; Mr Trevor Russell-Cobb; Mrs Natasha Shokoohy; Mr Norman Shrapnel; Mr Arthur Shrimpton; Mr Bill Shrimpton; Mrs Mary Siepmann; Mrs Nickola Smith; the late R. D. Smith; Miss Phebe Snow; Miss Muriel Spark; Mr Colin Spencer; Professor Ernest Stahl; Mr Quentin Stevenson; Miss Jane Stockwood; the late George W. Stonier; Mr Walter Strachan; Mr Robert Sykes; Mr and Mrs Stefan Themerson; Mr and Mrs Anthony Thwaite; Mr T. E. Utley; Mrs Jane Wailes; Mrs Antoinette Watney; Mrs Susan Watson; Dame Veronica Wedgwood; Mr Christoph Werner; the late Eric W. White; Mr Richard White; Mr Jonathan Williams; Mr David Wright; Mr Ian Whybrow; the Misses Nina and Doreen Woodcock; Mr Francis Wyndham.

I am also indebted to various institutions and their staff, for access to Stevie Smith letters or related material: to Mr Graham Dalling and Palmers Green Library local history collection; to Mrs Anne Piggott and *The Times* newspaper archives; To Mr Jeff Care and the *Observer* for access to files and microfiche; to Miss Anne Galloway and the *New Statesman* archives and to Mrs M. Hancock and the City University for *New Statesman* correspondence; to Miss Amanda Mares and the BBC Written Archives; to Mr Jonathan Vickers and the National Sound Archive; to the staff of Palmers Green High School; to the former headmistress of North London Collegiate School, Miss Madeleine McLauchlin and to its archivist Robin Townley; to Dr Michael Halls and King's College, Cambridge; to Mr Michael Bott and Reading University Archives; to Professor G. D. Zimmermann and the University of Neuchâtel; to the university libraries at Birmingham, Dublin, Durham and Hull; to the National Library of Scotland and the National Library of Wales; to Washington University Libraries; Smith College Library, Northampton, Massachusetts; Humanities Research Center, University of Texas at Austin; Lilly Library, Indiana University; the State University of New York at Buffalo; to Abbot Leo Smith and the monks at Buckfast Abbey; to Mr Edwin Green, archivist of the Midland Bank Group; to the Public Records Office; the British Library and its newspaper branch at Colindale. I am also indebted to the publishers, Jonathan Cape, André Deutsch, The Bodley Head, Longman, New Directions and Alfred Knopf for access to archival material. In addition I would like to express especial gratitude to John Kirby and his excellent staff at the Faculty of Cultural Studies, Sheffield City Polytechnic, and to Mrs Caroline Swinson and her staff in the Special Collections, McFarlin Library, University of Tulsa, for all the help and hospitality they provided during my visit to Tulsa. Their Stevie Smith collection at that time contained her library, manuscripts of her poems and *The Holiday*, a large collection of drawings and Smith family memorabilia.

I am grateful to the following for permission to quote from copyright material: to Helen Fowler who generously lent me her unpublished memoir on Stevie Smith; to Celia Goodman for extracts from Inez Holden's unpublished diaries; to Neville Braybrooke and Francis King for an extract from Olivia Manning's unpublished memoir, 'Let me tell you, before I forget . . .'; to Neville Braybrooke for an extract from a Barbara Jones letter to Jonathan Williams; to Norman Bryson for an extract from a letter to myself; to Judith Maravelias-Eckinger for letters from her father, Karl Eckinger, to Elfriede Thurner; and to James MacGibbon, Penguin, Virago, Longman and New Directions for extracts from Stevie Smith's poetry and prose.

Especial thanks go also to my editors at Faber and Faber, Frank Pike and Jane Robertson, to Maureen Daly for typing assistance, and to Sheila Walker, Kathleen Moynahan and Julian Spalding for making this book possible.

Illustrations

The drawings at the chapter openings are by Stevie Smith.

Abbreviations

When a quotation from one of Stevie Smith's poems is used a reference is given only if neither the title nor first line appear in the text. In the case of the three novels I have chosen to refer, not to the original editions, but to the Virago reprints, currently available.

NYP	*Novel on Yellow Paper* (Virago, 1980, since reprinted)
OTF	*Over the Frontier* (Virago, 1980, since reprinted)
TH	*The Holiday* (Virago, 1979, since reprinted)
CP	*The Collected Poems of Stevie Smith* (Allen Lane, 1975, since reprinted by Penguin)
MA	*Me Again: Uncollected Writings of Stevie Smith*, edited by Jack Barbera and William McBrien (Virago, 1981, since reprinted)
BBC WA	BBC Written Archives
U of H	University of Hull
U of T	University of Tulsa, Special Collections, McFarlin Library
U of N	University of Neuchâtel
U of R	University of Reading
WUL	Washington University Libraries
KCC	King's College, Cambridge
PGP	Palmers Green Papers, letters and documents in Stevie Smith's possession at the time of her death and now belonging to her literary executor, James MacGibbon

Introduction

Stevie Smith is an unusually difficult subject for biography. She enjoyed few personal relationships of any intimacy and those she veiled with a privacy that has been extended beyond her death by a telling absence of revelatory material. In addition, hers was a life composed of few external events which, by themselves, do not explain or support the trajectory of her career. More relevant are the internal lines of development, 'the ties', referred to in *The Prelude*, 'That bind the perishable hours of life / Each to the other, and the curious props / By which the world of memory and thought / Exists and is sustained.' If these can be discerned, as we move back and forth between her life and work, then meaning is given to the humdrum and often tragic facts of her existence, and we can perceive more clearly the matrix of thought and feeling which enabled her to rescue 'the poetical', as she termed it, in her own life and the world around her from formlessness.

The riddle she presents extends also to her work. Critical opinion on her achievement remains unsettled, lacks consensus. Her poetry has been extensively reviewed and enjoys popularity. But it has so far received limited critical attention of the weightier kind, and all of it, with one exception,[1] has offered an overview rather than an examination in more detail of some aspect of her poetics. It is perhaps apposite that the only full-length book on her poetry that has so far appeared is by an amateur, an enthusiast and self-named eccentric,[2] and not by a professional critic writing from within the literary establishment. Stevie Smith, always an outsider, appeals to the same. Even feminists have been slow to acclaim her, this despite her relish for parody which inscribes her disaffection with aspects of the tradition she inherited. Recently, however, her fascination with myth and fairy tale has been related to the feminist interest in recasting familiar narratives.[3] Her use of the Grimm Brothers' fairy tales sets a precedent for Anne Sexton's *Transformations* (1972), which retells sixteen stories from Grimm, and Liz Lochhead's *The Grimm Sisters* (1981), and the extent of her influence on contemporary women poets has yet to be assessed.

It has been remarked that her poetry is easier to patronize than to engage in debate.[4] It is certainly difficult to categorize her work or to explain how it achieves its effects, at times teasing and flippant, at others, powerfully serious. Although there are poems in which the influence of Eliot can be detected and in which syntax is fragmented and compressed, modernism was not her chosen inheritance. Instead her poetry ranges freely over associations connected with older traditions, forms and genres. With a teasing playfulness she picks up rhyme schemes and metrical contracts, only to abandon them when she shifts her tone or idiom with arresting effect. Similarly her diction switches abruptly from the biblical or portentous to colloquialisms, cliché and slang. Moreover, a recurrent ambiguity in her work makes it sometimes difficult to know whether a literary influence or convention is being leaned on or parodied. She knowingly exploits a diverse range of tactics, and can give us a poem that is dense with poetic diction and another that has a childlike simplicity. Often an absence of complex metaphor is combined with a diction that is simple, flat and poignant, the words positioned in such a way as to give them an extraordinarily large and suggestive power. This may be why her work has appealed to musicians, to Elisabeth Lutyens, Stanley Bate, Gordon Crosse, Peter Dickinson, John Patrick Thomas, Robin Holloway, and John Gardiner, all of whom have set poems by her to music. Stevie, herself, frequently had a tune in mind when she composed her poems, some of which she sang in performance. And though she never upheld euphony over meaning, she referred to her poems as 'sound vehicles'.[5]

Her aim was to write poetry that comes to the lips as naturally as speech. In this she is an inheritor of a tradition that looks back to the *Lyrical Ballads* and beyond. But her liking for simplicity, her refusal to overdecorate her themes, is only one aspect of her poetics. Another is her constant use of quotations, half-quotations, travesties, echoes and allusions drawn from the work of other poets whose voices infiltrate her own. 'The accents are those of a child,' Christopher Ricks has written; 'yet the poems are continually allusive, alive with literary echoes as no child's utterance is.'[6] Learning poetry by heart at school developed her auditory imagination which, in turn, fed her highly literary, referential poems. As John Bayley has argued, 'these poems have in their own way as much disciplined digestion behind them as those of Yeats or Valéry'.[7] She wears this learning lightly and makes shrewd use of her sources. Some of her poems are translations, strictly or freely rendered; others rework famous tales, legends or plays, in which meaning turns upon a reversal of convention. Her Frog Prince, for example, is content to be under a spell and fears disenchantment; her Persephone, also indicating a fear of life, prefers the underworld.

Stevie Smith's metric is also hard to pin down, and at times might or might not be there. Partly because she aimed in her poetry at 'memorable speech', she more often than not avoids the formality of a too consciously present metre. She relies instead on rhyme, cunningly and variously deployed, and on rhythm, that of speech and of thought itself. Hermione Lee has listed internal rhymes, alliteration, startlingly concentrated monosyllables and repetition of simple key words as some of the things that buttress Stevie Smith's lines from within.[8] Punctuation is not a key tool and is often absent. Stevie wrote to a friend in 1959: 'Punctuation continues to bother me, so if you find anything odd about it in these poems, do say so, please! Oddity, I assure you, is never intentional.'[9] Considerations of syntax and punctuation, Michael Schmidt argues, are overridden by her handling of rhythm which is for him her most striking characteristic.[10]

Though much in her work is autobiographical she is not a confessional poet. Instead, she adopts a variety of personae, some of them animals, through which to voice her thoughts, fears and feelings. These do not cohere to construct a single, authoritative voice but remain multivocal and contradictory. Her writing upholds the importance of inconsistency and paradox. 'In Lear's mind run also the Fool's iconoclasms,' she once wrote,[11] this duality appearing also in her own work with its blend of the tragic and comical. The interrogative aspect of her work has been stressed by Martin Pumphrey: 'The elusive "self" of the poems is not found in any one mask or image but rather, obliquely implied, in the endless play of construction and deconstruction the poems demonstrate.'[12] From a feminist perspective, her playfulness asserts her 'difference' from the tradition she inherits, appropriates and extends. By teasing our expectations, as she so often does, she throws into question accepted literary values. Moreover the anger in her work, which takes the form of fierce social satire, is not submerged beneath or disguised by a false detachment. It emerges as freely as it does today in the work of those women writers who reject the detached formality often associated with masculine authority. But what chiefly aligns her with the feminist cause is her refusal to turn aside from pain, for as Adrienne Rich argues, 'only the willingness to share private and sometimes painful experience can enable women to create a collective description of the world which can be truly ours'.[13] One of the most appreciative critics of this aspect of Stevie's work was Richard Church. 'I admire her work,' he wrote, 'both in prose and verse, because it is a garment worn with courage by a tragic spirit. The tragedy is there because in almost every phrase she utters, not excepting the many witty and hilarious ones, her purpose is to explore the cavities of pain and to find a way out of their horror and darkness.'[14]

This is an authorized biography in that it has received the encouragement and full support of Stevie Smith's literary executor, James MacGibbon. I would like to acknowledge my predecessors in this field, Jack Barbera and William McBrien, who began the recovery of the facts surrounding Stevie Smith's life. Any two biographies of the same subject will display dissimilarities and readers will find here a more restricted use of anecdote in order to focus more consistently on the vital relationship between Stevie Smith's life and work. New information also makes possible different emphases and fresh interpretation. I, too, have chosen to adopt throughout the name by which Stevie Smith was familiarly known, partly because it is too laborious to employ her full name throughout and too impersonal to use only her anonymous surname. I have also been advised against the pomposity that clings to the latter by Stevie's remark that the use of just surnames for male contemporary poets makes it sound as if they have all been raised to the peerage.

Georgia O'Keeffe once said: 'Where I was born and where and how I have lived is unimportant. It is what I have done with where I have been that should be of interest.'[15] It is a remark I have tried to keep in mind. There still exists the suspicion that biography is intrusive and not entirely justified, and for this reason I would like to appropriate a passage by Yeats, changing the gender to suit my purpose: 'A poet is by the very nature of things a woman who lives with entire sincerity, or rather, the better her poetry, the more sincere her life. Her life is an experiment in living and those who come after her have a right to know it.'

CHAPTER I

From Hull to Palmers Green

Reading her poems at the Edinburgh Festival in 1965, Stevie Smith received warmer and more immediate applause than that given to W. H. Auden. There was a startling incongruity between her small person, prim dress and apparent helplessness (she had to beg a pair of spectacles from her audience) and the steely, ironic entertainment she delivered. Recognition had come slowly to her, snowballing during the last decade of her life as she became part of the 1960s poetry boom, a star of the poetry-reading circuit. By then the character she had created for herself, beginning with the appearance of Pompey in *Novel on Yellow Paper* in 1936, had become indelibly fixed. One fact that she promoted was her unchanging address. 'Born in Hull. But moved to London at age of three and has lived in the same house ever since.' So she told Peter Orr when he was editing transcripts of recorded interviews with poets. 'I started on the biographical note, which you asked for. But it didn't get very far, as you see.'[1]

It surprised her friends that, living with her aunt in Palmers Green, Stevie Smith could find material for poetry in such restricted circumstances. She recounts the history of her home and its inhabitants in a late poem, 'A House of Mercy', which is accompanied by a drawing of a habitation, apparently in imminent state of collapse. In the first four stanzas the poem likewise teeters between the anti-poetic and a language evocative of ballads, fairy tales and romance.

It was a house of female habitation,
Two ladies fair inhabited the house,
And they were brave. For although Fear knocked loud
Upon the door, and said he must come in,
They did not let him in.

There were also two feeble babes, two girls,
That Mrs S. had by her husband had,
He soon left them and went away to sea,
Nor sent them money, nor came home again
Except to borrow back
Her Naval Officer's Wife's Allowance from Mrs S.
Who gave it him at once, she thought she should.

This blurring of genres allows mythical overtones to accrue: facts concerning Stevie Smith's life take on a fictional air. 'Who and what is Stevie Smith?' asked Ogden Nash. 'Is she woman? Is she myth?' As the poem moves towards an affirmation of strength in the last two stanzas, there is a noticeable increase in formal control and a display of rhythmic felicity.

Now I am old I tend my mother's sister
The noble aunt who so long tended us,
Faithful and True her name is. Tranquil.
Also Sardonic. And I tend the house.

It is a house of female habitation
A house expecting strength as it is strong
A house of aristocratic mould that looks apart
When tears fall; counts despair
Derisory. Yet it has kept us well. For all its faults,
If they are faults, of sternness and reserve,
It is a Being of warmth I think; at heart
A house of mercy.

Paradoxically Stevie Smith's rooted existence allowed her to become a poet of alienation, orphanhood and loneliness; to imbue her work with, Seamus Heaney argues, 'a sense of pity for what is infringed and unfulfilled'.[2] The tragic note sounded in her work is, however, made buoyant by a humour that keeps despair at bay; breezy commonsense, shrewdness and stoicism combat melancholy. Nevertheless her stark moral sense denied her comforting illusions and drove her to confront stupidity and cruelty, loneliness and loss. 'Here is no home, here is but wilderness,' is a line by

Chaucer to be found in her *Batsford Book of Children's Verse* (1970). Her poems are full of characters who are not at home in this world, who 'walk rather queerly' or give signals that are not answered. 'We carry our own wilderness with us,' remarks Pompey in *Over the Frontier*.[3] 'Celia,' says another, in *The Holiday*, 'you have always said that we are in exile in this world and must long for home.'[4] Reviewing the memoirs of Prince Serge Obolensky, Stevie Smith remarked that he became 'almost too much at home, and in a world really where one should not feel at home; too blunted, too destroyed'.[5] With laughter always in close attendance upon her thoughts, she herself remained indestructibly sharp, painfully alive. 'Learn too', she once wrote, 'that being comical / Does not ameliorate the desperation.'[6]

Florence Margaret Smith was born in Hull on 20 September 1902. Not until the 1920s, when riding over a London common, did she acquire the name 'Stevie': some boys called out 'Come on, Steve', alluding to the well-known jockey, Steve Donaghue, whose fringe stood on end when he rode, and the friend with her thought the name apt. Steve became Stevie, a sobriquet that took over from 'Peggy', the name by which up till then she had been known to family and friends. She had one sister, Molly, who was almost two years older. Whereas Molly was christened Ethel Mary Frances in Hull's most prestigious Anglican church, Holy Trinity, Peggy was baptized at home on 11 October 1902 owing to her critical health. 'The doctor had given up all hope,' her mother recorded, 'but she began to improve this very night and thank God continued to do so.'[7]

Delapole Avenue, where the Smith family lived, is a long narrow street in West Hull composed of two-storey, terraced houses. No. 34 is a modest but substantial house, having four bedrooms and a small back garden. The elaborate mouldings still visible in the hall attest to the fact that Hull was then a prosperous city which had, during the second half of the nineteenth century seen an enormous increase in trade. Between 1850 and 1876 the tonnage of ships entering Hull docks had increased from 81,000 to 2,258,000, an increase that caused considerable congestion in the docks and warehouses and led to the opening of the Alexandra Dock in 1885 and the breaking of the monopoly of the North Eastern Railway with the introduction of the Doncaster to Hull line. This increase in trade had attracted to the city a large immigrant community, creating problems of overcrowding and, in slump periods, unemployment and destitution. By the end of the century, however, a generation of reformers had effected improvements in all spheres of life and, owing to the work of the architect,

Alfred Gelder, the city was being transformed into a place of pomp and circumstance. The year after Stevie was born Victoria Square was opened by royalty, Queen Victoria's statue unveiled and the foundation stone laid for the present-day City Hall.

Stevie Smith never knew her maternal grandfather, John Spear, for he died the year before she was born. Nevertheless his presence was felt through the legacy he left and which funded her childhood and paid for her schooling. Born in 1844, the son of a Devonshire yeoman Christopher Spear and his wife Ann Hearn, John Spear almost certainly began his career by going to sea before becoming a shore-based civil servant, a surveyor with the Board of Trade, first in Newcastle-upon-Tyne where his elder daughter, Margaret, was born in 1872, and that same year moving to the Posterngate office at Kingston-upon-Hull. In addition, he was chief engineer to the Royal Naval Reserve, probably in the Humber section. His job as a surveyor entailed the overseeing of vessels, particularly their engines, to determine whether they were seaworthy. He also acted as examiner of engineers. By 1882 he was well enough established to live in one of the fine Victorian houses that lined Park Street, with his wife, Amelia Frances, and two children, Stevie's mother, Ethel Rahel, having been born in 1876. By 1885 he had become principal surveyor at the Board of Trade offices. Four years later he left, after seventeen years' service, to take up a post elsewhere. His colleagues presented him with a gilded testimonial which, all Stevie Smith's life, hung in the hallway at Palmers Green.

John Spear left the Board of Trade to become superintendent engineer with the shipping company Thomas Wilson and Sons. 'Hull is Wilsons and Wilsons are Hull' was the then popular Yorkshire expression. The firm had begun importing Swedish iron ore in the 1820s; after the death of its founder in 1869, Thomas Wilson's sons expanded its fleet and trade routes, even westwards to America though geographically Hull is less well placed for these routes than other British ports. When John Spear joined the firm in 1889 it had a fleet of more than fifty ships and was on its way to becoming the world's largest privately owned shipping company. Spear would again have been responsible for repairs and maintenance and for the appointment of seagoing engineers. He probably attended when new ships were being built and would certainly have been on board when they underwent trials. A man with considerable responsibility, he was regarded by his family with pride; up until Stevie's death a photograph of him in dress naval uniform ornamented the sitting room at Palmers Green.

John Spear had a sister, Martha Hearn Spear, who married Isaac Clode of Sidmouth in Devon. After his wife died, Spear appointed Martha Hearn

Clode one of three trustees of his estate, in the event of him dying before his daughters came of age. She is named in Stevie's poem, 'A House of Mercy' and is probably the original for 'Great Aunt Boyle' in *The Holiday*. In this book Stevie recounts tales of her ancestors by reporting conversations that 'Celia', the narrator, has with her aunt. It remains our sole source of information on relationships within the Spear family, and though presented as fiction can be taken as fact, for Stevie's autobiographical writing is always true to the situation, if selectively and obliquely told.

In *The Holiday* Great Aunt Boyle urges Celia's grandfather to remarry. John Spear was only forty-three when his wife died and, having worshipped her, he refused to marry again. 'But he was a moody sad man after her death,' *The Holiday* tells us, 'she was so wise, and with a sure touch could draw the right people around her, and keep the sad moods away from him.'[8] He apparently lost confidence in himself and felt that if he walked into a room others walked out of it. His loss of equilibrium allowed 'a poor sort of acquaintance' to congregate in the family home, to drink whisky, play whist and smoke until two in the morning. At the same time he grew irritated with his younger daughter whose melancholy matched his own: 'she was silent when he rounded on her, and grew so sad and dreamy that he could not bear it.'[9] He antagonized her further by laughing at her fancies and at her paintings. Though the elder sister took on the care of the house and the management of the two servants, the sisters were still in need of parental advice which they did not get.

'And if your mother and I asked him: "Shall we go to this place or to that? Or have these people to dinner, or those?" he would say: "You must decide for yourselves." But we were too young to decide wisely. And so your mother met your father and married him.'[10]

Stevie, influenced by her aunt, retained the notion that her parents' marriage was the result of unfortunate circumstances. It is touched on, its drama reduced to light romance, in her first prose work, *Novel on Yellow Paper*.

'When my mama was a girl she was being rather romantic, and so she made an unsuitable marriage. My aunt used to say: If your grandmother had lived your mother would never even have met your father.'[11]

Ethel Spear was twenty-two when she married Charles Ward Smith on 1 September 1898. He was twenty-six, and a forwarding agent in his father's offices in Fish Street in the 'Old Town' part of Hull, down towards the ferry pier and the riverside. This part of town still had many medieval, half-timbered buildings; its market place boasted a gilded equestrian statue of William IV as well as Holy Trinity Church where Charles and Ethel were married. As seen at night, this area has been memorably recorded in the paintings of Atkinson Grimshaw. Along the edge of the Old Town the tidal river Hull flowed into the Humber and was crossed by North Bridge, which remained up at high tide so that ships arriving from Russia and Scandinavia could sail right into the heart of the city.

Charles Ward Smith's father, Charles Smith, was born in Louth, Lincolnshire and had been a part of the large migration from the North Midlands and other parts of Yorkshire to Hull in the second half of the nineteenth century. There he married Mary Ward and found employment as a shipping agent's clerk. He then set up on his own as a shipping and forwarding agent, work that involved arranging the import and export of goods carried by sea, compiling ships' manifests and arranging custom fees. In 1876 he bought the lease on 54 Lister Street, a fairly fashionable address where he is shown living with his wife in the 1881 census records. Five children are listed as present in the house at the time the record was made, when it would seem that the two eldest children, Charles Ward Smith and another, were elsewhere. Charles Smith appears to have profited from the rapid growth in certain mercantile sections, accompanying the improved dock facilities, because while still living at 54 Lister Street he acquired two further properties, 17 and 18 Paradise Place. These he disposed of in 1887, which is perhaps the first evidence that his business had begun to decline. However, he continued to act as a shipping and forwarding agent and in 1901 added insurance and coal export to his firm's description. The insurance of ships' cargoes would have been a logical addition to his work as a forwarding agent, the other addition made possible by the large quantities of coal coming through Hull as a result of the development of the Yorkshire coalfield and the expansion of the railways.

Charles Smith's son, Charles Ward Smith, knew from childhood that he wanted to go to sea. As a boy he did well at languages. It was agreed that he would enter the Navy on leaving school, but when one of his brothers, as Stevie recounts in *Novel on Yellow Paper*[12] (if not two, as she told Kay Dick[13]), was drowned at sea, his mother forbade it. He was directed instead into his father's business which, by 1903, was registered as Charles Smith and Sons. According to his daughter Molly,[14] he let the business run down and go bankrupt owing to his lack of interest and the adverse effect of an economic depression. His father was unable to help. Charles Smith still owned 54 Lister Street though in 1897 he had moved to Westwood, one of the large semi-detached villas overlooking Pearson's Park. But by 1901 he

6

had moved to Bridlington, to a house he did not own, and in July 1906 he mortgaged 54 Lister Street to the York City and County Bank as security for debts. By 5 February 1907 these debts had clearly not been paid as a deed of foreclosure gave the bank possession of this security. The bank's records show that by the end of 1906 Charles Smith owed £507. 12s. od. and that the 'estimated value of securities and dividends to be realized' was £300. Accordingly the bank provided for a loss of £207. 12s. od. on the account, and the manager explained in his December report that the loss was 'caused by depreciation of property formerly worth £600, now sold for £300'.[15] The bank's records do not refer to bankruptcy, but as it was prepared to accept such a relatively large loss on the sale of the security, it seems safe to assume that by the end of 1906 the firm Charles Smith and Sons was no longer trading.

This date tallies with Molly Smith's claim that her father ran away to sea when she was five and Stevie three.[16] He had wanted to join the Navy during the Boer War but family pressure prevented him from doing so. Frustrated, unhappy, and with little sense of responsibility, he left home. Stevie was convinced she was partly to blame. 'Poor Daddy took one look at me and rushed away to sea,' she told Kay Dick,[17] an idea she promotes in her poem 'Papa Love Baby'.

> What folly it is that daughters are always supposed to be
> In love with papa. It wasn't the case with me
> I couldn't take to him at all
> But he took to me
> What a sad fate to befall
> A child of three
>
> I sat upright in my baby carriage
> And wished mama hadn't made such a foolish marriage.
> I tried to hide it, but it showed in my eyes unfortunately
> And a fortnight later papa ran away to sea.

After Charles Ward Smith disappeared (he joined the White Star Line as pantry boy and rose to the position of assistant purser), his wife and children had to survive on John Spear's money. Molly Smith recollected that they moved south because they could no longer afford the house in Hull.[18] But the difference in size between 34 Delapole Avenue and 1 Avondale Road is not so great as to explain fully this move, or the haste with which it was made. Perhaps the desire to escape the gossip of neighbours and friends was a motive. Almost certainly the marriage had broken down before Charles

Ward Smith went to sea, and his departure was merely a way out. More than sixty years later, when she summed up the situation for Kay Dick, Stevie recollected: 'Not happily married – he wanted a career at sea. When I grew up I realized it was what's called an unsuitable marriage, but he used to come home on leave. My mother was immensely loyal; no word was ever said against this creature, and appearances were kept up.'[19] As can be seen, Stevie gave her affections to her mother but in her poetry was to identify herself, if only subconsciously, with her father, making the theme of journeying an important one. Charles Ward Smith maintained his presence in their family life by sending postcards, of the briefest sort. 'Off to Valparaiso love Daddy', was the one Stevie instanced, adding: 'And a very profound impression of transiency they left upon me.'[20]

In some ways, his absence was easily filled. 'So then it was, and how it was,' Stevie explains, 'that my Aunt the Lion of Hull came to live with us.'[21] Margaret Annie Spear, known to her friends as Madge and to her nieces as Auntie Maggie, had, at the age of fifteen, taken over the running of her father's house; now she did the same for her sister, Ethel. Photographs reveal a marked difference in appearance between the two sisters: Ethel Smith was pretty and slight, probably already slightly debilitated by poor health; Madge Spear was stalwart, more handsome, her face composed around a strong bone structure. A person of sterling character who all her life retained a Yorkshire accent, she was not an intellectual but shrewd, intelligent, dutiful and commonsensical. In Molly Smith's autograph album in 1915 she inscribed a line from Dryden: 'We first make our habits then our habits make us.'[22] Whether it was the philosophy this expressed or the neatness of the chiasmus that appealed, she contributed a similar motto to the St John's Church, Palmers Green birthday book printed in 1932: 'If you cannot do what you like, try to like what you do.'

Despite her no-nonsense attitude, Aunt in sentimental mood would sing, 'In the gloaming, / Oh my darling, / Think not bitterly of me,' thus commemorating, as Stevie's persona, Pompey, remarks, 'the suitors, already no doubt devoured in wrath and digested at leisure'.[23] Madge Spear displayed a natural capacity to do without men. In *The Holiday* Stevie compares her with a Begum: 'there was no He-Begum in your life, no there was not, Alec Ormstrode [whose real name, Oscar Troostwyck, appears in the manuscript of *The Holiday* and in postcards sent to the aunt] loved you, but you would have none of him . . . you are the Begum Female Spider who has devoured her suitors and who lives on and makes these crocodile-like pronouncements, and who is like a lion with a spanking tail who will have no nonsense.'[24]

Her favourite book, Stevie tells us, was *The Relief of Chitral* (1895), written by two brothers, Captains G. S. and F. E. Younghusband, both of whom had served in this campaign and acted as correspondents to *The Times*. Ostensibly an objective account of the rising of the Chitralis against the British, its underlying jingoism loses no opportunity to uphold the British Army as honourable and unquestionably right. It is hard to imagine the woman who took such pleasure in this book, with its maps, diagrams and careful amassing of factual detail, ever indulging in a romantic novel. Her fascination with *The Times* law reports also suggests a taste for the cut and dry, though it must also be said that reading these reports was at this time the only way that a lady could acquaint herself with the seamy side of life.

It was Madge Spear who found 1 Avondale Road. Once a move had been decided upon, she had gone to London ahead of her sister and nieces, leaving them in Hull waiting to hear what their change of address would be. Not until the last minute did a telegram arrive, and by then the new owners of 34 Delapole Avenue were anxious to move in and the Smith furniture already packed, the men waiting to drive it away. Arriving in the north London suburb of Palmers Green one afternoon in September 1906, the children were pleased to discover, as they finished their journey by tram, that they had in fact exchanged the town for the country, for Palmers Green was still attractively rural and a motor car a very rare sight. 1 Avondale Road, a modest, red-brick, end-of-terrace house, trimmed with white facing and with a small garden in front and behind, greatly pleased Molly and Peggy Smith. It had, however, obviously been found in haste: Miss Spear refused to sign the lease on it for longer than six months assuming it would be merely a temporary home.

Shortly after they arrived three-year-old Peggy Smith was taken round to a neighbouring plumber in order that she could be weighed. When she told him, in a thick Yorkshire accent, how she had travelled on a train and then on a tram, he replied, 'Why you're a furriner, you're a foreign package'.[25] Speaking more accurately than he knew, he then lifted her down from the scales.

Palmers Green was originally a tiny hamlet, a mere collection of houses and cottages clustered together at the point where Hazelwood Lane runs into Green Lanes, the main road leading out of London, from Islington to Enfield and which, during the early nineteenth century, had become a popular excursion route, as its name implies, for Londoners in search of beautiful countryside. Apart from the building of some large villas to the west of Green Lanes, between Fox Lane and Hoppers Road, Palmers

Green remained virtually unaltered right up until the end of the nineteenth century. Even the advent of the railway had brought little change, for the area was protected by owners of large estates who refused to carve up their land and therefore kept the speculative builder at bay. Some building did begin in the 1890s. Then in 1902 Captain J. V. Taylor of Grovelands sold large tracts of his land for development. After this more and more land came on to the market and suburbia spread.

Already by 1906, when Stevie and her relations arrived, Green Lanes was entirely lined with shops and houses. The surrounding fields, country lanes and toll gate that gave the area its charm were steadily diminishing with the spread of bricks and mortar, pavements and privet hedges. Long-standing residents in the larger villas began to express fears in the local magazine, the *Recorder*, that as a result of all this building a poorer class of resident would be attracted to the area. Shopkeepers in Alderman's Hill complained about the muddy state of the road and the need for more pavements, for it soon became apparent that the existing road system was far from adequate. In just ten years, between 1901 and 1911, the population in the district of Southgate, which includes Old and New Southgate, Palmers Green and Winchmore Hill, rose from 14,993 to 33,612. The rapid influx of population put pressure on existing services; by the summer of 1908 the Metropolitan Water Board was having difficulty in maintaining adequate pressure in the mains for Winchmore Hill and Palmers Green. And though the district was still without electricity, negotiations for gas began that year.

Very quickly Palmers Green developed a reputation for being one of the most snobbish of London's outer suburbs. It was attractive to those wanting to move to a better class of district than Hackney or Wood Green. Advertisements in the local press for 'artistic villas' in Palmers Green stress the healthiness and convenience of life in the suburbs. The political flavour of this up-and-coming residential area was already noticeably right wing. A Palmers Green Conservative and Unionist Association was formed in 1907, and when a Liberal MP, James Branch, a Nonconformist shoe manufacturer from Hackney who had narrowly won his Enfield seat in the 1906 election, spoke at Palmers Green in 1909, he had a bag of rubbish thrown at him. The tone of the area is reflected in the correspondence columns of the local press, where a persistent demand for better services from Southgate Urban District Council is coupled with a violent antipathy to paying for these services in increased rates.

The residents of Palmers Green took pride in their wide-fronted shops and in the dignity of its larger villas, some with garages and carriage sweeps. Despite the rapidity with which a quiet, rural area was transformed into a bustling suburb, the area quickly established a settled, rather self-congratulatory air. In 1921 it was gently satirized by Thomas Burke in his book, *The Outer Circle*, which records his travels, by bus, through outer London, as he passed from Wood Green into Bowes Park and from there into Palmers Green:

'If Bowes Wood is Wood Green in Sunday clothes, Palmers Green is a Bowes Park that has "got on" . . . There is an austere flavour about it: a fine serenity, almost serendipity. In its streets one becomes chastened, yet not humiliated. No little half-hearted shops here . . . No barbers at all – hairdressers only. No drapery stores or baby-linen shops; but veiled, contemplative establishments with empty windows, labelled Odette or Julie or Yvonne – ladies whose presence in a suburb is a cachet of social rightness. Folk don't let themselves go in Palmers Green. The word "jolly" is never used; its synonym is "charming" or "delightful". Children on scooters proceed along its pavement with almost Chinese placidity. Everybody proceeds. Even the butchers' carts proceed.'[26]

In an area where social differences were sharply observed, the straitened circumstances at 1 Avondale Road, where there was no maid or servant of any kind, would not have gone unremarked. Yet Palmers Green snobbery, Stevie later averred, gave zest to life and was fairly harmless. There was sufficient money from John Spear's legacy for Stevie and Molly to attend a fee paying local school. It was a cut above the County School in Fox Lane and the Board School in Hazelwood Lane and placed them, not unhappily, among children on the whole better off than themselves.

Even in this benign area, Stevie as a child soon learnt a sense of dread out of key with the surrounding social brightness. Two elderly ladies lived next door and one of these kindled her imagination with talk of the White Slave Traffic. She also took the small child on afternoon walks to a nearby cemetery. 'These graveyard excursions,' Stevie recollected, 'fired me later on to write a very solemn poem.'[27] It begins:

> The ages blaspheme
> The people are weak
> As in a dream
> They evilly speak
>
> Their words in a clatter
> Of meaningless sound
> Without form or matter
> Echo around.

For the most part, however, Stevie associated her childhood with the mellow warmth of September sunshine:

'This sunny time of a happy childhood seems like a golden age, a time untouched by war, a dream of innocent quiet happenings, a dream in which people go quietly about their blameless business, bringing their garden marrows to the Harvest Festival, believing in God, believing in peace, believing in Progress (which of course is always progress in the right direction), believing in the catechism and even believing in that item of the catechism which is so frequently misquoted by the careless and indignant . . . "to do my duty in that state of life to which it shall please God to call me" (and not "to which it has pleased God to call me"); believing also that the horrible things of life always happen abroad or to the undeserving poor and that no good comes from brooding upon them.'²⁸

The building of churches helped establish the community life of the area. St John's, Palmers Green, the Anglican church to which Mrs Smith and Miss Spear belonged, was built in stages between 1904 and 1909. Not long after its completion a large Roman Catholic church, St Monica's, went up in Green Lanes. Both played an important social role, St John's in particular, for its church hall hosted society meetings and, during the First World War, a great many concerts, plays and bazaars in aid of charity. As a child attending regular services at St John's, Stevie grew familiar with the Psalms, *Hymns Ancient and Modern* and biblical tags. She might not always sing the same hymn as everyone else, but she knew her catechism and the Bible stories, having been trained in both by Miss Fanny Schubert who ran the Sunday School. She also retained a conviction that 'there is cheefulness and courage in the church community, and modesty in doing good'.²⁹

With the religious needs of the area catered for, secular entertainment swiftly followed. The first cinema in the Palmers Green area opened in 1912. Much entertainment was home-grown; societies and clubs flourished. The area had its own branch of the Fabian Society which on one occasion was visited by Mrs Pankhurst and her daughters Christabel and Sylvia, probably because they had a link with these parts through Mrs Pankhurst's brother, Herbert Goulden, who lived in Winchmore Hill. Even in Palmers Green the issue of women's suffrage could not be ignored. Near to Stevie's home, in Stonard Road which cuts across the top of Avondale Road, lived two suffragette sisters, one of whom went to prison after a window-smashing expedition in Oxford Street and who must have been the talk of the district. In addition, Lady Constance Lytton came to speak on the women's question to Palmers Green Literary Society, to which Stevie's mother belonged. In April 1910 Mrs Smith entered a short-story competition and won a prize. This Literary Society met once a month, on the Monday night nearest to the full moon. One of its visiting speakers lectured on the moon, with Stevie, still a young child, in the audience, listening enthralled.

She also enjoyed playing in the nearby Winchmore Hill woods. These lay on the other side of Hoppers Road which runs parallel with Avondale Road, and though Stevie and Molly were forbidden to cross the railway line that edged the woods, they soon found a culvert under the line and crawled through. Here a great many games were invented and trees climbed. Stevie became the leader of a small gang; they enjoyed outwitting the keeper whose business it was to keep children out, for these woods were then still privately owned and trespassers forbidden.

There was also a calmer pleasure to be had in Winchmore Hill woods. Here began Stevie's lifelong love of trees and water. 'Paradise', she recalled, '. . . was that part of the wood which lay just behind the railway cutting, an open pleasant place it was with a little stream, all open and sunny as the day itself. But behind that again lay the dark wood, with the trees growing close together, the dark holly trees, the tall beeches and the mighty oak trees.'[30] This oasis, reminiscent of the approach to Milton's Paradise, gained in preciousness as parts of the wood became parcelled out and the trees marked for cutting down. All her life Stevie had reason to be grateful to Southgate Urban District Council for stepping in when part of Captain Taylor's estate was withdrawn from a sale at which it had failed to reach a satisfactory price. In 1911 the Council bought sixty-four of these acres, later increasing their holding to ninety-one acres, thereby creating the public park, Grovelands.

Though the park contains a coppice wood and a large lake, is roomy and varied, it is not distinguished. But here Stevie found that 'loamish landscape' evoked in *Novel on Yellow Paper* and admired by her in the poetry of Tennyson and Thomas Hood. She liked the park best when the weather was wild and the only other people in it were anglers. 'Nobody', she once asserted, 'who does not know and love the English weather will understand the complicated feelings that come to those who walk alone in the damp.'[31] Elsewhere she described how the park in wet weather salved claustrophobia·

'When the wind blows east and ruffles the water of the lake, driving the rain before it, the Egyptian geese rise with a squawk, and the rhododendron trees, shaken by the gusts, drip the raindrops from the blades of their green-black leaves. The empty park, in the winter rain, has a staunch and inviolate melancholy that is refreshing. For are not sometimes the bright-ness and busyness of suburbs, the common life and the chatter, the kiddy-cars on the pavements and the dogs, intolerable?'[32]

Stevie never tired of extolling the virtues of Palmers Green, a true suburb, according to her, because it is an outer suburb and not one of the inner ones which have been captured by London. In her own lifetime it grew shabby and down-at-heel and has since her death deteriorated still further. But even before its decline few could share her view: Grovelands which for Stevie was 'a happy place even when it is raining'[33] is a very average park, dull and dreary in bad weather; nor did the colours of Palmers Green, with its windy shopping corners and people attached to dogs or prams, seem to her friends quite so fresh and exquisite. But Stevie doted on the area:

'In the high-lying outer northern suburb the wind blows fresh and keen, the clouds drive swiftly before it, the pink almond blossom blows away. When the sun is going down in stormy red clouds the whole suburb is pink, the light is a pink light; high brick walls that are still left standing where once the old estates were hold the pink light and throw it back. The laburnum flowers on the pavement and trees are yellow, so there is this pink and yellow colour, and the blue-grey of the roadway, that are special to this suburb. The slim stems of the garden trees make a dark line against the delicate colours. There is also the mauve and white lilac.'[34]

It was not just the environment of Palmers Green that pleased her: there was also its promotion of 'briskness, shrewdness, neighbourliness, the civic sense and *No Nonsense*'.[35] She respected the caring, if humdrum, life of the suburbs, and the stalwart reliability of her neighbours. She argued that its community spirit owed much to the fact that the area had its roots in the country: because the inhabitants of Palmers Green had been considerate to the countryside, keeping large oaks and areas of parkland, the countryside, she felt, had in turn been kind to them. For herself, Stevie required of nature, even when chastened into a park, a larger, more impersonal role. It set a challenge –

> Alone in the woods I felt
> The bitter hostility of the sky and the trees[36]

– and could create a 'dark wood' in which, as in Dante's, all sense of motivation and direction is lost. The image of the wood in her poetry is often a metaphor for life, both attractive and fearful. More particularly, the 'dark wood' is an enchanted realm, where a life of the imagination is pursued at the expense of ties that bind us to a more everyday existence, and from whence there is no return. 'Those gentle woods of my remembered childhood', Stevie once reflected, 'have had a serious effect upon me, make no doubt about it . . . Only those who have the luxury of a beautiful kindly bustling suburb that is theirs [sic] for the taking and of that "customary domestic kindness" that De Quincey speaks of, can indulge themselves in these antagonistic forest-thoughts.'[37]

Charles Ward Smith's brief reappearances at 1 Avondale Road did little to absolve him in Stevie's eyes. As a child, she was sharply aware of his irresponsibility and never forgot how he arrived one bank holiday when the shops were shut, with a parrot as a present but nothing to feed it with. The absence of a father, Stevie thought, had a marked effect on her character.

'. . . most women, especially in the lower and lower-middle classes, are conditioned early to having "father" the centre of the home-life, with father's chair, and father's dinner, and father's *Times* and father says, so they are not brought up like me to be this wicked selfish creature, to have no boring old father-talk, to have no papa at all that one attends to . . .'[38]

She was also affected by the advantage of fragile health. If the poem 'Infant' is autobiographical, as the reference to her father tarrying in Ostend suggests, she was born two months premature. At the age of three she had the habit of suddenly turning cold and stiff. The hold this gave her over her elders, combined with her father's absence, made her domineering and spoilt as a child. However, the nickname 'Miss Baby', as she never forgot, 'cut the ground from under my imperious stamping feet' and 'shredded the imperial purple of my infant rage'.[39] Even so, her infant face could express such cynical hauteur that her elders sat her in the pram facing away from them to avoid it.

At the age of five she contracted tubercular peritonitis. This disease, most often caused by unpasteurized milk, would have brought bowel disorders, sickness and a disinclination to eat. A local physician, Dr Woodcock, convinced Mrs Smith that her younger daughter ought to be sent away, and, later, Stevie more than once declared she owed her life to this man. She was sent to a children's convalescent home at Broadstairs, endowed by the shipbuilder, Sir Alfred Yarrow, and which had extensive grounds. Yarrow's intention had been to provide a charity, but in order to ensure that its recipients appreciated their benefit, a small charge was made, as this was thought to stimulate co-operation on the part of children and parents. Many years later Stevie recollected that she had been fed on raw eggs and made to drink three pints of milk a day; that sitting with the boys on a table set aside for those on a special diet she had felt grand and privileged. She also established a lasting friendship with a girl called Hester Raven-Hart whose father, Canon William Roland Raven-Hart, may be the original of Canon Heber in *The Holiday*.

Stevie remained at Broadstairs for three years, returning home, it is said, only in the summer holidays. She was certainly with her mother, aunt and sister at Lowestoft in the summer of 1908 where a postcard arrived from her father: 'Darling Peggy, I hope you are still continuing on the meat and when I do see you I shall find you strong and well and eating a lot.'[40] It was the Smith family custom to take themselves off each summer to small houses or cottages by the sea. Mrs Smith made the bookings by answering advertisements and they set off, taking the cats and parrot, not knowing what they might find and enjoying the adventure. Particularly memorable was a holiday spent at Saltfleet in the summer of 1911: the weather was exceptionally hot, they stayed for about two months and the children dug up bones in the sand dunes. Stevie not only re-evokes this holiday in *Over the Frontier*, but later combined her memory of it with another Norfolk experience in 'Archie and Tina', a poem redolent of undimmed pleasure.

These holidays remained some of her most treasured memories, perhaps because they were framed by long periods of confinement at Broadstairs, where the pain of seeing her mother turn to wave goodbye was on one occasion so great that the doctors feared for her chances of recovery and forbade further visits.

At one point during her time at Broadstairs Stevie experienced a loss of innocence. She describes in *Novel on Yellow Paper* how one of the maids used to take her on her knee, would kiss and hug her, displaying maternal feelings which the young child recognized were frighteningly arbitrary and superficial. 'It was so insecure, so without depth or significance . . . It very profoundly disturbed and dismayed and terrified me.'[41] When in 1958 Stevie wrote her poem 'The Last Turn of the Screw' she reinterpreted the Henry James story in the light of her own childhood experiences at Broadstairs. In her version the boy Miles likes to sit on his governess's knee ('Yes, it was warm, poetical and cosy'), but is at the same time divided inside himself, one half of him aware of the fickleness of this woman's love. This poem was for Stevie about 'the price of intelligence'.[42] Her Miles is slightly contemptuous of the governess's love; he senses her false values and the cruelty that underlies them. But his cynicism and contempt are also a smudge on him and he is therefore doubly sickened by his knowledge.

Unwilling to pay this high price, the child in the poem denies his intelligence. This Stevie, as a child, could not do.

One thing that preyed on her mind while at Broadstairs was her mother's poor health. Towards the end of her stay this anxiety, combined with the misery of homesickness, became intolerable. Because there were few people she could talk to, she began to soliloquize, as she was to do in her novels. Helpless in the grip of an institution and its relentless routine, subject to the whims of others, the eight-year-old child contemplated suicide. Only then, when her existence seemed most at the mercy of external forces, did she paradoxically take hold of her life through the realization that the ability to end it lay in her control: this sovereign power was hers. But this non-Christian belief, that if circumstances could not be borne we can give ourselves the gift of death, had other consolations: it restored self-esteem, for in the dissymmetrical relationship between life and death the potential to kill evidences the power to live. As Stevie recollected in *Novel on Yellow Paper*: 'It was also a great source of strength so that I came out of that experience very strong and very proud,'[43] for she retained this richly anarchic realization that death lay within her control, an idea that was to inspire some of her best poems. And later, when the bitterness of the experience that underlay this revelation was a thing of the past, she could return to it with airy lightness: 'I actually thought of suicide for the first time when I was eight. The thought cheered me up wonderfully and quite saved my life. For if one can remove oneself at any time from the world, why particularly now?'[44]

It is doubtful if Stevie had much formal education before the age of nine when she left Broadstairs and entered Palmers Green High School. Known locally as 'Miss Hum's', it had opened in 1905 with twelve pupils in a small private house on the corner of Osborne Road and Green Lanes and soon spread into the house next door. At first the school was co-educational, taking children from the ages of four-and-a-half to sixteen, though boys were expected to leave at the age of eleven. Alice Hum, its founder, who had decided on the vocation of teaching at the age of three, entered into partnership in 1912 with her cousin Miss Elsie Roberts and her friend Miss Esther Tempest, who had for some time been teaching at the school. It very quickly developed such a good reputation that families moved to Palmers Green in order to be near it.

Miss Hum enjoyed huge respect. She was a small, red-cheeked woman invariably dressed in brown: velvet in winter, silk and cotton in summer. She was bright, cheerful, energetic and a silent martyr to ill health. Though small in stature and nicknamed 'Cow's Eyes' by her pupils, she exerted complete authority and was capable of making the largest girl feel very small. Each morning she stood on a soap box and led assembly, giving the school a pious quotation to reflect on. She always spoke of her pupils as 'my girls' and was very strict on discipline, dress and etiquette. She revered Miss Frances Mary Buss, the founder of North London Collegiate School and established unofficial links with the school. She herself took responsibility for the teaching of English Literature. These classes took place in her small sitting room with the girls sitting on stools or on the floor. Her bible was Palgrave's *Golden Treasury* and she taught her pupils to learn passages by heart, to be aware of different metres and to adopt an analytical approach. She also instilled a sense of her subject's worth. The actress and contemporary of Stevie, Flora Robson, has recalled: 'Miss Hum had a great gift for imparting her love of literature, it was not just a lesson. My hands shook with joy when I picked up the *Golden Treasury of Verse*, my Tennyson, and the works of William Shakespeare ... Miss Hum had around her many excellent teachers ... they excited our curiosity, they inflamed our interest, it was not just a swallowing of facts and figures; like a pebble dropped into still waters, the circles widened till we began to love what we studied, and went on with our studies after we left school.'[45]

So high-minded was the school it banned Angela Brazil's schoolgirl tales, thereby ensuring that most pupils somehow managed to read every new and exciting book this author published. Miss Hum's authority, though, was never shaken, perhaps because she inspired affection as well as respect. 'By Love Serve One Another' was the school's motto, chosen by her, and its flower the wood anemone that grew in abundance in Winchmore Woods. When war broke out Miss Hum read anti-war poems to her pupils to counteract the prevalent jingoism. She was 'a very wise and original lady,' Stevie later reflected, 'and rather brave too, because when the war came ... she said that not absolutely *every* German was "a fiend incarnate" as was the general opinion in our suburb'.[46] In September 1916 Miss Hum became a Quaker and was welcomed as a member of the Society of Friends at the Tottenham monthly meeting.

At Palmers Green High School Stevie was considered to be one of its brighter pupils. She revealed a penchant for drawing, her incessant scribbling entertaining her classmates, especially when she portrayed each pupil as an animal. Her auditory imagination was equally strong: she once claimed that she could remember the first hymn that she sang at this school word for word. Miss Hum's habit of getting her pupils to learn poetry by heart meant that Stevie acquired more poetry than she understood, could recite almost the whole of Macaulay's 'Horatius' and admired passages in

Shelley. Her interest in words, their sound and unexpected combinations, extended even to the names of fellow pupils: Glory Wellswood, Adela Livermore, Roma Cork and Florence London.[47] Perhaps not surprisingly, when she left this school in July 1917, at the end of the Lower V, she took with her a prize for literature, an edition of Thomas Carlyle's *Sartor Resartus* and *On Heroes and Hero-Worship*.

Both in and out of school Stevie took part in many plays. Once a year the school performed Shakespeare, both Stevie and Molly appearing in *As You Like It* in 1913, Stevie as the courtier, Monsieur Le Beau. In addition there were children's plays organized each year by Mrs Zoë Cooper, the mother of Stevie's friend Olive, and again the two Smith sisters appeared regularly in these, Stevie on one occasion throwing herself into the part of the wolf in *Red Riding Hood* to such an extent that she frightened the smaller children present. Photographs exist recording her appearance with Flora Robson in *Ali Baba*. She also starred in a play written by Grace Richardson, the actress and aunt of another of Stevie's friends, Margaret Cockman. The play – *The Wishing Well* – was one of three performed in aid of the League of Pity, the junior auxiliary of the Society for the Prevention of Cruelty to Children. Stevie, wearing an Eton collar and looking smart enough for Palmers Green, as the local press commented, played the impoverished cripple 'Bob'. If these plays fostered her sense of drama and laid the foundation for her later transformation into a performing poet, they also drew her into another world, making that imaginative leap on which her fairy-tale poems also depend. Then, too, as a child she adored pantomimes, their humour especially and 'moments of green lights and devilry, to which I was happy to pay the tribute of being very much afraid'.[48]

The happiness of Stevie's childhood grew out of many things. She loved dodging the overhanging trees and shrubs as she ran along the wall that traversed the back of the gardens in Avondale Road. She was daring and gregarious, very much the leader of her small gang of friends. But even when absorbed in a game, she could become suddenly aware of difference: this spinning of her talents in front of others was sometimes accompanied by, as she describes, 'a sudden dangerous capture . . . made of oneself by a person who is outside',[49] an experience she reckoned to be dangerous, leaving her scorched and unhappy.

Home life was happy, if emotionally sometimes strained and financially rocky. When the war began Charles Ward Smith entered the Royal Navy as temporary assistant paymaster and in January 1916 was transferred to the position of Acting Interpreter in French; in *Novel on Yellow Paper* Stevie claims he was, 'among many other duties, in charge of the coding department'.[50] On his rare appearances at 1 Avondale Road he asked for, and was given, Ethel Smith's Naval Wife's Allowance. Perhaps it was for this reason, as Molly Smith said, that Mrs Smith did not welcome him and Stevie hated his visits.[51] Molly, on the other hand, loved him unreservedly. Madge Spear, too, had a soft spot for him, despite his inability to pass a pub. He served mostly in the Arctic, between Greenland and Iceland on the Northern Patrol, and Ethel Smith's letters from this period reveal anxiety on his account. He sent home photographs of his ship with the great guns shrouded in snow and the figures of the men scarcely discernible in icy fog. Because of the danger to which he was exposed, family affection rallied and a certain pride was taken in what he did. When he accompanied them to church one Sunday morning dressed in naval uniform, his appearance caused a sensation.

Another cause for concern during the war was Ethel Smith's poor health. Lack of strength made her querulous, and sometimes unable to cope with her high-spirited daughters, for Molly Smith was not only thought to be more intelligent than her sister, she was also more domineering and more temperamental. Olive Cooper, Stevie's contemporary, remembers Mrs Smith complaining about her children who seemed never to do the right thing, though they, in turn, were very protective of her. Dr Woodcock's daughters, Nina and Doreen, remember her sitting in an armchair with a rug over her knees, with hands that were clearly those of an invalid folded in her lap. She was much prettier than her sister, with large, soft brown eyes and hair parted in the middle and swept back in two puffs on either side. Whereas Auntie Maggie remained strong, sensible, unworried and decisive, Ethel Smith grew more and more fragile and anxious, falling into a fairly perpetual state of misery about her health. In October 1913 she had added a codicil to her will, leaving everything to her sister because she had 'generously shared the expense of bringing up and educating my two children, and thus fitting them to earn their own living'.[52]

Ethel Smith's ill health would have created a barrier between her and her daughters and limited her emotional reserves. She and Stevie were certainly close, as Molly Smith attested in conversation with Helen Fowler, and as Mrs Smith's letters confirm. She had a liking for Ruskin and Walter Scott and would have shared with her younger daughter a love of books. Nevertheless it is not surprising that a note of irritation appears in some of Stevie's poems dealing with the mother–child relationship.

> I have a happy nature,
> But Mother is always sad,

> I enjoy every moment of my life, –
> Mother has been had.

In another poem Persephone uncharacteristically complains:

> My mother, my darling mother,
> I loved you more than any other,
> Ah mother, mother, your tears smother.[53]

But either through observation or experience, Stevie also knew of a more straightforward love which she celebrates in 'Human Affection':

> Mother, I love you so.
> Said the child, I love you more than I know.
> She laid her head on her mother's arm,
> And the love between them kept them warm.

'Reading is an appetite which grows as it feeds, and if you give it weak and second-rate stuff it will never grow strong.'[54] So Stevie advised in an article on childhood reading. Her own diet nurtured feelings and interests out of which sprang many of her poems. It was as a child that she first became familiar with the myths of ancient Greece and Rome. Their legendary figures mingled in her mind with characters from the fairy stories which she read. She was familiar with the classic tales, read Hans Andersen, Charles Perrault and Andrew Lang, and once declared the last of these to be 'the sort of fairy-story writer from whom one can pick up a lot of useful information'.[55] When she was seven years old her mother gave her for Christmas a copy of *Grimm's Fairy Tales*. The climate of these chilling fantasies, in which fate is simple and peremptory, had a profound influence on Stevie's mental landscape. All her life she was to return to *Grimm's Fairy Tales*, a copy of which, in German, was found beside her bed at Avondale Road after she died. The copy which her mother gave her was illustrated by Arthur Rackham and may have sharpened her taste for illustrations. As an adult, she expressed admiration for Tenniel's illustrations in *Alice in Wonderland* and *Through the Looking Glass*, and in her article on childhood reading advised: 'no modern illustrator is worth putting up with so far as Alice is concerned . . . If you are firm about getting the right books, and the right drawings to go with them, you will never be muffed by the second-rate.'[56]

With poems, her liking as a child was for those that had a strong narrative or didactic content. 'As our English mistress read the poems aloud to us,' she recalled, 'a line would strike across to me, a story grip, a picture take colour.'[57] Browning was an especial favourite, and the imagery in 'Childe Roland to the Dark Tower Came' remained deeply ingrained. She also enjoyed 'Bishop Blougram's Apology' which would have demonstrated to her what stuff could be made from, not external action, but a drama of mind and thought. Tennyson was also admired and remained for her a great poet far above alterations in fashion. What caught her attention as a child was not his *Idylls of the King* but 'Mariana in the Moated Grange' and the bitter pessimism in 'Locksley Hall'. If Tennyson fostered, among other things, her interest in assonance and sound music, Byron's ambitious epic poem *Don Juan*, 'with its flashing cynical wit and its critical clever words'[58] taught her how sharp poetry could be. Meanwhile her fondness for lyrics was well served by Palgrave's *Golden Treasury* and by the *Oxford Book of Ballads*.

This childhood enthusiasm for poetry was, perhaps, less remarkable then than it would be now. In the pre-1914 period good versifiers were much in demand. Magazines such as *The Strand*, *Nash's*, *Pall Mall Gazette*, *Tit-Bits* and *Pearson's Weekly*, were flourishing and benefiting from the fact that great writers such as Wells, Shaw, Chesterton, Hardy, Conrad and Kipling were not averse to contributing to popular periodicals. The audience for poetry was broad, its taste largely shaped by Palgrave's *Golden Treasury* of which a 'pocket' edition came out in 1891. As a child Stevie would have encountered not only the 'greats' but also much light verse. The swift changes of tone in some of her poems, from the portentous or grandiose to the mundane or comical suggest an interest in marrying the demotic appeal and craft of light verse with serious themes. Certainly she explored beyond the limits of the school curriculum. Her advice to children describes the method she herself was to pursue when, on leaving school, she adopted a process of self-education in the place of a more formal university training.

'Reading is a living thing, a thing for pleasure and experiment. Read with an open mind and a wary eye. You will soon learn your way about. Do not be fobbed off with rubbish, but do not let other people judge for you. Make your own experiments. It is far better to read rubbish from time to time than to go about burdened by other people's opinions and the fear of reading the wrong book . . .'[59]

When Stevie first wrote a poem, her aunt pronounced it 'unnecessary'.[60] It bore no relation to need, whereas much of Madge Spear's life was occupied with tasks that had to be done. The Smith household had no servant, therefore there was the house to clean, the food to cook, the shopping to organize. In addition, she took responsibility for the cassocks and surplices worn by the choirboys at St John's. Twenty minutes before the ten o'clock Sunday service she arrived at the church ready to cast a sharp eye over each boy in order to assess how fast he was growing and when a hem would need lengthening. Owing to her stoutness, she always arrived a little out of breath, making a slight hissing noise. Ken Pain, who was to marry Stevie's friend Olive Cooper, thought of her in terms of a battleship with black hair who put the fear of God into her charges. But another ex-choirboy, Tom Mobbs, recalls that her maternal interest in all thirty-two boys earned her much affection.

Though devoted to the church, a member of the Southgate Conservative Association and a person of strong character, Madge Spear was shy of the parish's social life. She and her sister nevertheless supported the vicar at St John's, the Revd Roland d'Arcy Preston whose Anglo-Catholic leanings were criticized by many of his parishioners. There was something about his manner that also aroused irritation and distrust. When preaching he threw himself about in the pulpit; even when addressing children, he employed a highly theatrical mode of delivery, creating the utmost drama with his questions and waiting only a few moments before adding, 'Well, Ruby?', for Ruby was always certain to know the answer. This slightly eccentric man became the subject of much gossip. His sister Alice, with whom he lived, did much to improve his relations with the parishioners, for she was a sensible, practical woman who ran the church bazaars, helped with the Mother's Union and called her brother Rolly. In addition, he was adored by the organist Ethel Cosier. The fact that for twenty-one years her devotion was ignored may explain why she was sometimes seen weeping at the organ by the communicants as they returned to their pews, and was not always ready to start the hymns. While the Revd d'Arcy Preston remained at St John's he became the subject of amusing anecdotes at 1 Avondale Road and a source of spiritual help. But after a severe illness in 1928, possibly a stroke as it altered his appearance and left him with a hangdog expression, he was persuaded to retire. In 1931 he wrote a sad letter of resignation: 'At the last meeting of the Council it was made quite clear to me that some members, not by any means all, wished me to resign, and would not be satisfied with what the doctor and Bishop suggested – a year's leave of absence . . . I beg you to forgive any rudeness of which I may have been guilty, and to believe that this was quite unintentional.'[61] Miss Cosier's long devotion was now rewarded, for soon after d'Arcy Preston resigned and moved away, he married her.

Outside the Palmers Green community, Mrs Smith and Miss Spear received a certain amount of support from relatives. For a while they kept in touch with relations in Hull, with the accountant Alfred Whitehead who had married Charles Ward Smith's sister Florence and whose daughter, Grace, was close in age to Stevie. Another Smith cousin, a boy called Bobby, spent a part of his childhood at 1 Avondale Road; he is listed in St John's parochial accounts as having contributed to the Farthing Fund in May 1908, but nothing more about him is known. Stevie once claimed in print that she had 'a boy cousin and a dear one' whose name was Caz,[62] the name she gives to a character in *The Holiday*. This was probably Charles Smith who, her address book records, sailed for Alberta on 3 June 1922, at the age of twenty. Little more is known about her relations on her father's side, the name Smith cloaking them in anonymity.

The closest of their relatives was probably John Spear's sister (Stevie's great aunt), Martha Hearn Clode, who spent the last years of her life at 1 Avondale Road, from around 1916 until her death in 1924. Certain financial advantages would have been gained by this, which may explain why Madge Spear was able to buy the leasehold on the house in 1920. Auntie Grandma, as Martha Hearn Clode was called, had no children of her own and took an especial interest in Molly and Stevie. More shadowy are the many cousins on the maternal side of the family, one of whom was Richard White, an architect–surveyor who married Louisa Toyne in 1905 and settled at Westcliff-on-Sea where he developed a passion for boats. His two children, Richard and Joan, recollect that Stevie and Molly, Miss Spear and Mrs Smith, made occasional visits to Westcliff for a day by the sea. Stevie's awareness of anti-Semitic feeling may have begun here: not infrequently Richard White voiced disgust at the sight of the East End Jews lining the beach with their deckchairs. The photograph albums of both the White and Smith families record the marriage of another cousin, Alice White, to Robert Fastnedge in 1912. It was their daughter, Mary, who became a nurse and worked in Cairo and to whom Stevie refers in *Novel on Yellow Paper*, naming her Joan after Richard White's daughter. Another of her mother's cousins, Emily White, married Alfred Hook who also appears in *Novel on Yellow Paper* as Uncle James. A man of considerable ability and no small sense of prestige, he wrote books on tax, politics and psychology, was a member of the Fabian Society, acted as Chief Inspector of taxes in Ireland at the time of the troubles and later became Principal Inspector at Somerset House. He is said to have given Stevie and her aunt financial service.

One of Mrs Smith's cousins lived in Palmers Green. This was Richard White's sister Florence who married C. P. Moss and had two sons. When the young Joan White visited the Moss family her aunt, Florence Moss, took her round to 1 Avondale Road. Miss Spear greeted them kindly and provided afternoon tea but Stevie, who was upstairs with a headache, did not appear. It is a small but telling recollection, for Stevie, even as a teenager, continued to suffer poor health. Her friend Olive Cooper recalls that after her parents moved to a house in Winchmore Hill which had a tennis court in the garden it was Molly, not Stevie, who most often went up for a game. Poor health and a lack of energy fostered her childlike dependence on others, a situation that brings both frustration and unexpected strength. To carry the child into adult life is, as Stevie's poem observes, to be handicapped and defenceless yet powerful.

> You would say a man had the upper hand
> Of the child, if a child survive,
> I say the child has fingers of strength
> To strangle the man alive.

If in her teens she felt within herself a growing power, it had as yet no outlet.

> But oh the poor child, the poor child, what can he do,
> Trapped in a grown-up carapace,
> But peer outside of his prison room
> With the eye of an anarchist?[63]

CHAPTER 2

North London Collegiate

Stevie did well at Palmers Green High School; she got top marks in the Oxford Local Examinations in the Enfield area in the summer of 1916 and the following year won a school prize for literature. But it was Molly who won the scholarship to North London Collegiate, Stevie following her in September 1917, at her mother's wish. Here she displayed the irritating knack of being able to get to the heart of the matter with the minimum of work or effort. Despite this, she performed badly at her second school which she found unsympathetic.

North London Collegiate School, founded in 1850 by the pioneering Frances Mary Buss, was renowned for its academic excellence. After its transformation in 1870 into a public school with a governing body, it began to attract funds from City companies and in 1879 moved into imposing new buildings in Sandall Road, Camden. Under its second headmistress, Mrs Sophie Bryant, academic standards were maintained and improved. Mrs Bryant herself was a formidable scholar, the first woman Doctor of Science, author of some ten books, campaigner on behalf of Women's Suffrage and Home Rule for Ireland, a member of various educational committees and capable, in her spare time, of composing philosophical articles for the erudite periodical, *Mind.* Her obituary in the school's magazine quotes her belief that 'women's lives would be happier and sounder if they had, as a matter of course, the fair share of the sterner intellectual discipline that had been such a joy to me'.

The school was situated in an area once popular with the professional middle classes but by the turn of the century run down, chiefly owing to the building of three termini, Euston, St Pancras and King's Cross, and the large, shifting work-force of navvies this had brought with it. By the 1910s many of the pupils at North London Collegiate came not from the immediate vicinity but outlying parts. Molly and Stevie took the train from Palmers Green to Finsbury Park and then a tram that went past Holloway Prison. The journey was tiring and one reason why Stevie performed badly. Talking to Phebe Snow, Stevie claimed she 'was too exhausted to keep up academically and . . . so . . . decided to be tiresome as she would rather be thought tiresome than stupid'.[1]

It surprised her contemporaries that she did not do better. One of her classmates was the future author of *Cold Comfort Farm*, Stella Gibbons. She recollects that, unlike herself, Stevie did Latin and seemed cleverer than most; that she tended to keep herself aloof and was outwardly distinguished by the beauty of her dark eyes. Another pupil, Janet Phillipson, also noticed that Stevie, or Peggy Smith as she was still called, belonged to no group but watched the behaviour of others with interest and detachment. Molly Smith seemed to her co-operative, orthodox and gregarious: 'Peggy something of a loner, with just one or two intimate friends'.[2]

The school, which then had some five hundred pupils, was larger and more impersonal than Palmers Green High School. It was also academically more rigorous. Apart from a fifteen minute break, lessons ran from nine until one-thirty, with extra-curricular activities in the afternoon. In addition, the older girls were expected each day to do at least four hours homework which was carefully monitored. One pupil during Mrs Bryant's regime was Alice Head, later to enjoy an outstandingly successful career in journalism. For her, none of the exigences experienced as editor ever compared with those undergone at 'North', as the school was affectionately termed: 'Over and above everything else we were taught the necessity of *thoroughness* in everything we undertook; no half-measures were ever allowed. The disciplines and rigours of life there were such that the hardest day's work I have done since has been child's play compared with any normal day at school.'[3] The school's inflexible timetable must have been anathema to someone like Stevie who needed time to think her own thoughts:

'. . . it was certainly at school, in my grand second school after I left behind my dear kindergarten, that I first learnt to be bored and to be sick with boredom, and to resist both the good with the bad, and to resist and be of low moral tone and non-co-operative, with the "Could do Better" for ever upon my report and the whole of the school-girl strength going into this business of resistance, this Noli-me-tangere, this Come near and I shoot.'⁴

Elsewhere she describes how she rebelled:

'Why were they so cross with me? . . . I was more than cross, I out-Heroded them all, drawing myself with that infuriating ability of childhood into complete aloofness disgust and disdain. They do not put this on the report. They do not put, Is aloof and disdainful. They put, Could do better. But all the time it is this hateful non-co-operative feeling indeed it is very aggravating for them.'⁵

Discipline was enforced by a system of punishment known as 'signatures'. If a girl behaved carelessly, spoke on the stairs or in the corridor, or in some other way, no matter how small, neglected the rules, she was commanded to 'take a sig', which meant she had to record her crime in the 'Appearing' book and sign it with her name. Signatures were inflicted mercilessly. On rainy days prefects were stationed at the door to give 'sigs' to those girls who, inadequately protected against the weather, arrived with wet skirts. As this shows, precision on matters of decorum was taken to an extreme. Once a girl asked a teacher if she 'could go upstairs'. Given an affirmative answer, she did so and on her return was commanded to take a signature. It was pointed out that 'could' had a different meaning to 'may' and had she used correct grammar her request would have received an answer in keeping with the rules. (A similar distinction is made in Stevie's poem 'The Poet Hin' who reflects his author's training in his use of 'shall' rather than 'will'.) If a girl collected more than a certain number of signatures she received an imposition which usually meant the learning of a poem or Latin text. (Stevie was on one occasion given a Catullus poem, and later loosely translated it under the heading 'Dear Little Sirmio'.) If a girl received more than a certain number of impositions, the name of her class was removed from the 'Golden List' which was read out at the end of each term. Such an unremitting penal system did little to lighten the scholastic atmosphere. For many girls the school was too repressive to be an entirely happy place. Despite this, it had a knack of inspiring lasting affection, even among those whom it had placed under constant strain and stress.

Stevie chafed under the regulations and with her friend, Margaret Macdonald, made frequent sorties into the centre of London, visiting museums and galleries and exploring places which Margaret told her sister she would never have discovered on her own.⁶ There was less need for escape when, in the autumn of 1918, Miss Isabella Drummond took over from Mrs Bryant as headmistress and the school's climate altered. Gently but persistently Miss Drummond introduced change: she took a vote on the colour of the school uniform and, without disclosing the result, got rid of the navy blue serge in favour of neat brown tunics; some penalties also disappeared and there was a slight relaxation of the rules. Mrs Bryant had thought nothing of giving a ten-year-old girl two hours homework every day: Miss Drummond, arguing that the air raids were having an adverse effect on children's sleep, tactfully reduced the load. She continued, however, to uphold the tradition that made social service a component of school life. She also did as her predecessors had done, and insisted that no adverse distinction was to be caused by race, class or creed. The needs of Jewish children were recognized and Jewish prayers were taken every morning in a separate room by a Jewish teacher, the children afterwards entering the gallery to join the general assembly in the school's Cloth-workers' Hall and to hear the notices read. Every Wednesday morning after prayers an address was given, sometimes by the headmistress but more often by outside speakers on a range of subjects. One of these must have been the original for Stevie's Miss Hogmanimy in *Novel on Yellow Paper* who visits the school in order to talk on how babies are born. From Stevie's account it appears that the technicalities of childbirth were not primarily what this lady had come to impart. She had come to extol teetotalism, to condemn the effect of alcohol on sexual behaviour and to imply that 'babies were lovely when they were legitimate' and terrible when not.[7] Stevie, who had just been learning a speech in praise of wine delivered by a messenger in Euripides' *The Bacchae* was amused by this divergence in thought, and never forgot this lady's smile, polished face, bright eyes, unprovocative blouse and clumsy hands.

During Stevie's time at North London Collegiate the Smith family received occasional visits from three soldiers who were convalescing at Grovelands, the large house in the park of the same name, that had been given over to the war-wounded. One of these was Sydney (Basil) Scheckell, a Lieutenant in the Lincolnshire Regiment wounded in the Battle of the Somme, whose family came from the east coast, and who may have known the Smiths when they lived in Hull. In *Novel on Yellow Paper* Stevie calls Scheckell 'William' and tells us that it was a letter from his sister that sent Pompey's mother and aunt up to Grovelands to visit him. This may have been the same sister mentioned in the manuscript of *Yellow Paper* who, employed as a nursemaid, gave all her loyalty to Pompey's mother and left no one in doubt that Pompey's father, Mr Casmilus, 'was the villain of the villa'. 'The indiscretions of Elsie/Elizabeth', the manuscript continues, 'form a chapter which, no which [sic] I say I shall not write.'[8] Very little on Elsie/Elizabeth is found in the published novel, but her brother is described at length. 'William', as he is here called, is found at Grovelands sitting up in bed looking a little like George III, 'very fair, with a round face',[9] and suffering from what Stevie calls 'arrangement dementia' in that he had to have the contents of his locker arranged exactly so. Still more fascinating for the teenage girl was the look that came into his eyes when the arrangement dementia passed, and a line of Virgil came into her mind.

'. . . a look of sadness and fortitude, and perhaps a little of patience. And his eyes would disengage themselves and withdraw. But this withdrawal was perhaps a withdrawal into the outside of himself and of time, a withdrawal into the *Ewigkeit.*

And the person of William, and the lineaments of his face in their pain and weakness, might be allowed to say: It is the tears of things and our mortality touches us.'[10]

Basil Scheckell is also commemorated by Stevie in the poem 'A Soldier Dear to Us' written after his death in 1968. In this she recalls how, either fetched in a Bath chair or hobbling on crutches he made visits to 1 Avondale Road, sometimes in the company of two friends, to relax by the fireside and indulge in gossip surrounding the Anglo-Catholic movement, in particular the crisis of conscience faced by Ronald Knox who became a Roman Catholic in 1917 and recorded his troubled route in his autobiography, *A Spiritual Aeneid*, published the following year. What was not discussed during Scheckell's visits was his experience in the trenches. This ghastly landscape, though absent in their conversation, was present in Stevie's mind as she listened to Scheckell talk, for she had been reading Browning's 'Childe Roland to the Dark Tower Came' at school. She never lost her conviction that, as one of her characters in a short story says, ' "Childe Roland" is such an exact spiritual description of the detail of the Flanders battlefield . . . the bits of broken machinery, and the mud and the dampness and the greyness and the longness and the horse'.[11] Browning's imagined landscape, blended with intimations of historical fact, haunted her all her life. Commenting on 'Childe Roland' on the radio in 1961 she remarked: 'Great fear, rich and true, knocks at the heart as Robert Browning's landscape of desolation, of hopeless courage and resistance without belief, unfolds upon the reader's eye . . .'[12] Reflecting on Scheckell and his friends in her poem 'A Soldier Dear to Us', Stevie recollected her strong feelings at the time and perceived that from Scheckell, in particular, she learnt 'a secret you did not perhaps mean to impart', that painful things could be brushed off lightly without diminishing them.

Scheckell and his friend, 'Tommy' Meldrum, acted as witnesses to the fresh will Ethel Smith made in July 1918. Her health had for some time been a cause for concern. While Stevie was holidaying with an aunt and uncle at Knaresborough in May 1916, she sent a postcard to her mother with the remark: 'It was very kind of the doctor to take you home in his motor wasn't it?'[13] Mother and daughter shared a mutual concern. Mrs Smith's letters to her younger daughter contain much practical advice, on clothes, train fares and school work. 'I hope you have prepared the holiday work you had to do,' she wrote, ' – don't forget next term is the Examinations and we shall expect you to do wonders after such a lovely and bracing holiday!'[14] She herself was still able to make excursions, but by 1916, a trip into the centre of London to see the Australian and New Zealand troops returning from the Dardanelles and *en route* to a memorial service at Westminster Abbey, required her to spend the previous day in bed reserving her strength. Already she was unable to walk far and went shopping in a Bath chair pushed by Molly. She seems never to have doubted the necessity of the 1914–18 war and shared in the widespread patriotic fervour. Her attitude to the war may explain Stevie's pride in her father's naval position, for the family followed his postings with anxiety. 'Daddy is in Glasgow,' Mrs Smith informed Stevie while she was in Knaresborough, 'so it is some relief to know that he is safe and well.'[15]

A photograph of Ethel Smith taken in 1918 shows her strained, thin and gaunt, looking much older than her forty-two years. When travelling with this tragic figure, Stevie must have felt considerable anxiety. In *Novel on Yellow Paper* her persona, Pompey, mentions that when journeying by tram with her mother, the fierce shaking of the vehicle left her feeling furious and powerless. She also describes how her mother had attacks of suffocation and how once returning home from school she rang the doorbell and waited longer than usual to be let in, for her mother, who was alone, was having a heart attack.[16] Her condition became critical at the start of 1919, a year in which Molly Smith kept a diary.[17]

Mrs Smith's illness disrupted the flow of schoolgirl events that made up Molly's and Stevie's lives. On 7 January they had been taken to a nativity play by their aunt, Florence Hook, having previously visited a department store as well as the Times Book Club, Stevie losing a ten-shilling note which, in Molly's slang, was 'awfully feeding'. Two days later the sisters returned to school and on 12 January Mrs Smith fell seriously ill. 'Mother taken ill,' Molly's diary reads. 'Gasped for breath from 1.30 to 6.30. Dr

Armstrong came as Dr Woodcock was away. He doesn't think she'll get over it.' Two days later her condition was still critical and Dr Woodcock, who had returned, was 'very grave'. Another two days passed and the doctor advised them to wire for Charles Smith. He arrived 'in a fearful state late at night', as Molly recorded. The next day neither Molly nor Stevie went to school, though it was kept from Mrs Smith that her younger daughter was at home. The same may have happened the following day; certainly Molly remained at home and went for a walk round Southgate with her father and another aunt, Emily Hook. On 18 January, Charles Smith left, perhaps because his wife's strength had begun to return. By 21 January she appeared to have rallied, but this recovery was short-lived. On 24 January Molly noted in her diary, 'Mother still very bad.' She adds that her mother now slept a lot, and that her feet and nose were swollen and discoloured. By Saturday, 1 February her condition was again so bad that Molly and Stevie were forbidden to attend a Candlemas service at their Aunt Florence Hook's church the next day. On 3 February a second cylinder of oxygen was brought in for Ethel Smith whose feet were now so swollen the doctor feared gangrene had set in. Two days later she almost died, then rallied. The same happened in the early hours of 6 February but again, by mid-morning, the crisis seemed momentarily to have passed. Molly went out and did some shopping; Charles Smith returned, just before his wife finally died at four o'clock in the afternoon.

When re-evoking this death in *Novel on Yellow Paper* in the mid 1930s, Stevie, having learnt from Scheckell's example, dealt lightly with the suffering she had witnessed:

'And for a week this last suffering leading to death continued. Oh how much better to die quickly. Oh then afterwards they say: Your mother died quickly. She did not suffer. You must remember to be thankful for that. But all the time you are remembering that she did suffer. Because if you cannot breathe you must suffer. And the last minute when you are dying, that may be a very long time indeed. But of course the doctors and the nurses have their feet very firmly upon the ground, and a minute to them is just sixty seconds' worth of distance run. So now it is all over, it is all over and she is dead. Yes it is all over, it is all over, it is.'[18]

The final phrase is ambiguous, at once affirming that the death is finished and yet keeping it in the present. In 1969, thirty-three years after the publication of *Novel on Yellow Paper*, Stevie, in a television interview, broke down and was unable to answer when asked if she had been present at her mother's death.

The day after Mrs Smith died Molly and Stevie went to buy mourning: black straw hats, gloves, blouses, and possibly the black-and-white check dresses with black bows which they wore when they reappeared at North London Collegiate. That afternoon the undertakers arrived and Stevie and Molly were taken by Auntie Mabel, who lived at Purley, to Auntie Florence Moss who lived near by with her husband and two sons. Over the next few days letters and wreaths poured in and more relatives arrived. On 12 February the funeral took place. 'Rather terrible,' Molly wrote in her diary. 'Lots of people there. Dad and I kept together . . . Dad fearfully cut up.' Charles Smith stayed on at 1 Avondale Road another eight days and continued to reappear at weekends for some time afterwards. In December 1919 he was demobilized. Many years later Molly Smith recalled that her father had 'retired to the country with a male friend who decamped with his Naval Gratuity'.[19] He subsequently married a woman called Hylda Lingen and with her began a poultry farm in Worcestershire. Molly occasionally visited them, but not Stevie whose dislike of her father remained constant.

Around this time both Molly and Stevie were going through a 'Roman Fever', as Molly termed it,[20] which had begun before Ethel Smith's death. In *Novel on Yellow Paper*, Stevie recounts how William (Basil Scheckell) lends Pompey's mother a book by Khomjakoff on the mystical philosophy of the Russian Orthodox Church. Pompey also reads it and copies out the prayer by Demetrius of Rostoff that William has inscribed into this book. Stevie's religious fervour appears to have lasted for a period of several years and involved her in a considerable struggle. One of her contemporaries recollects her saying at Palmers Green High School that she 'couldn't wait for the glory.'[21] In *Novel on Yellow Paper* Pompey voices the memory that 'at this time I was trying very hard. Yes at this time I was pushing and forcing myself to get into the inside-of this Christian religion. But all the time at this time I was feeling cold, very cold and outside-of, and not at all ever warm and inside-of'.[22] Already the Christian God was, for her, being challenged by another:

'. . . and all the time, at the back of my mind was the idea of death, like it was the idea personified, like it was the idea of Thanatos the god, that was yet to come at a call, but not a god you could pray to certainly to make you a better man.'[23]

If, for Stevie, the seeds of doubt were already there, Molly, in 1919, was on the point of embracing Roman Catholicism. She recorded in her diary how her Aunt Florence Hook visited and argued with their neighbour Miss Prior about Roman Catholicism. She brought home pamphlets on Roman

Catholic doctrine and convents, and made secret visits to the Catholic Church, St Monica's, where she prayed to the Blessed Virgin on behalf of her mother. When the opportunity arose, she visited Westminster Cathedral, lighted a candle to honour the Virgin Mary and, again, brought home more literature. Evidently Aunt Florence Hook encouraged her leanings towards Catholicism and wrote that she would give her and Stevie rosaries. When Madge Spear read this letter she was extremely annoyed. 'She is awfully bigotted,' Molly sulked in her diary, for she found much opposition in Auntie Maggie. Her obsession continued, fuelled by strong emotionalism and intensive reading. One night she dreamt that she had been converted and received into the Roman Catholic Church. The next day, at a service at St John's, she doubted whether the Revd d'Arcy Preston could lawfully administer the Sacraments.

Stevie was familiar with the Anglo-Catholic's temptation to 'pope', to submit him or herself to Catholic arguments and undergo conversion. She had been taken by Scheckell to the High Anglican Church, All Saints, Margaret Street, and was, at the time of her mother's death, in correspondence with Scheckell's friend, 'Tommy' Meldrum. One of his letters to her displays the religious fervour with which Stevie was involved.

'I knew during that dark time that Miss Spear would stand out magnificently and be a tower of strength. I sincerely hope you will try to avoid going through increasing stages of pessimism . . . This is what has happened to me during the past two years . . . However for a month I have been simply ravenously hungry for Catholicism. I long to be in an intensely quiet chapel like the one at S. Matthew's, Westminster. I feel the gap in life which lack of Catholicism makes . . . It was a sweet thought of yours to say the "Anima Christi". How fine it is to say the same devotions as the Saints and Martyrs said of old and how their shining examples put me to shame.'[24]

Much of the Anglo-Catholic debate at this time concerned the practice of ritual. Listening to such talk, Pompey comes to feel 'that by and by . . . you are going to understand something that is much more than that, so you listen, you prick up your ears, you listen, you are full of hope'.[25] When at the end of February 1919 'Tommy' Meldrum sent Stevie a copy of Ronald Knox's *A Spiritual Aeneid*, along with a copy of Rupert Brooke's poems, she read it with interest. Knox's skill as a writer, his intelligence, humour and love of limericks contributed to the sensation that Pompey describes: 'But those times with their unquietness and bewilderment were very much alive.'[26]

Ronald Knox had first been drawn to High-Church ritual while a schoolboy at Eton where, precociously brilliant, he had published his first book, verse in English, Latin and Greek. It was there he became interested in the mystical meaning symbolized by such things as amices, incense and the sign of the cross. At the age of seventeen he took a vow of celibacy, went on to Balliol College, Oxford and became an *habitué* of Pusey House where he pursued friendships that drew him ever more firmly into the Anglo-Catholic movement, a fact that distressed his father, Edmund Knox, Bishop of Manchester, a stalwart supporter of the evangelical cause and who persecuted ritualistic clergymen in his own diocese. The core of *A Spiritual Aeneid* concerns the period when Ronald Knox prepared for ordination, became deacon and priest of the Church of England, served as Chaplain at Trinity College, Oxford and became a leading writer and preacher within the extreme Anglo-Catholic party. Reading the book one learns nothing about contemporaneous debates affecting other spheres of thought, about Women's Suffrage, Post-Impressionism, Home Rule for Ireland or industrial unrest; but what is impressive is the vehemence and detail with which Anglican principles concerning Church doctrine and practice were then being discussed, in railway carriages and senior common-rooms.

Ronald Knox's attraction lay partly in his scrupulous sense of taste, reflected in *A Spiritual Aeneid* in its precise and elegant prose. He not only helped stimulate a particular brand of humour, furthered by John Betjeman's poems, that has become associated with High Anglicanism, he also indulged in a certain line in snobbery. While drawing up a list of arguments for and against conversion to Roman Catholicism, he observed: 'Your fellow-priests won't be married: but they'll be much more vulgar.'[27] A central paradox within his character was that beneath his brilliance and versatility, his effortless fluency of expression and reputation for being flippant, lay a profoundly troubled soul and a melancholy which, though he took pains to conceal it, became noticeable with age. Another irony was that though Oxford had left him with 'a fierce love of sifting the evidence and the power of not being fascinated into acquiescence when superior persons talked philosophy at me',[28] he resisted the growing influence of the modernists and came to champion the sacramental church because it represented absolute spiritual authority, a truth handed down in an unbroken line over which it was forbidden to theorize or speculate. When finally he was ordained a Roman Catholic priest in 1919 he took the anti-modernist oath 'against all liberal interpretations whether of scripture or history'.

The importance of Knox for Stevie is that we find in him a paradigm for her attitude towards belief. As Father Thomas Corbishley has written: 'He was to become one of the most persuasive advocates for the fullness of Christian faith, with a simplicity and directness of argument.'[29] This Stevie also wanted, a faith entire and unequivocal, which did not unpack difficult biblical passages in such a way as to remove difficulties. All her life Stevie admired his combination of polished eloquence with erudition, warm humanity with spiritual perceptiveness. Reviewing a volume of his sermons in 1960, she wrote: 'They are polished in the best sense, that is they breathe the spirit of achieved simplicity.'[30] It has also been observed of him that the air of casual superiority in his writings made his readers feel that membership of the Church was vaguely analogous to an entrée into the best social circles. No wonder, therefore, that after reading *A Spiritual Aeneid* and talking with her High-Church friends, Pompey finds the word Anglo-Catholic 'takes you slap up into a little clique'.[31]

Stevie came close at this time to an orthodox belief in Christianity. She had been confirmed on 12 March 1918 and was given a hymn book and prayer book, bound in black leather, that together fitted into a leather case. It is evident from the condition of her prayer book that it was at one time regularly used. The habit of church-going had a crucial influence on her auditory imagination, as it did on D. H. Lawrence. Many of her poems use the rhythms and metre of hymnody as their base, while familiarity with the Psalms developed her sensibility, as she many years later described in a *Spectator* review:

'The Psalms are a document in human feelings, especially in the feelings of the heart that is oppressed from outside by the behaviour of the heathen and from inside by not being at home in the world and by sin. There are the gay ones. too, that sing the gaiety the soul feels in relation to the natural world of fish, trees, animals and earthquakes, and in relation to the Being the soul looks towards. Even if this Being is an emanation, a creature of the leaping soul . . . still the leaping feelings are true and in the Psalms most truly cited . . . seldom have agitated souls cried out more truly than in the Psalms; and souls ought, in a holy way, to be agitated, especially modern souls.'[32]

The Anglican Church was a powerful force at this date. The writings of Bishop Gore, the fervent apologist for High-Church principles, attracted a huge audience. Stevie read him and, through Pompey, voiced her admiration for the bishops of the Church of England and for Dean Inge.[33] The Church was still at the centre of cultural life. 'In those early post-war years,' Mervyn Stockwood has written of this period, 'Church, unlike most places, suggested gaiety and colour.'[34] And from the Anglo-Catholic point of view, the 1914–18 war had helped break down a number of shibboleths, including the traditional Protestant objection to the Catholic habit of saying prayers for the dead. Malcolm Muggeridge recounts in his autobiography how, when he went up to Selwyn College, Cambridge, in the autumn of 1920, he found the Anglo-Catholic movement in full swing, its former struggles a thing of the past and looked back on with pride.

Stevie's involvement with Christianity in her late teens and early twenties sensitized her conscience. 'I am not at all surprised,' one of her teachers wrote to her, soon after Stevie had left school, 'to hear you have a conscience. I am still thinking about your yearnings to do something really useful.'[35] The temptation to become an orthodox Christian remained strong for several years. In 1926 she bought a copy of John Shorthouse's famous novel, *John Inglesant, A Romance*, originally published in 1881. By making his hero the seventeenth-century Inglesant, Shorthouse, who spent almost ten years writing this book, was able to examine Roman Catholic, Anglican and Puritan beliefs. In this way he thought through his own nineteenth-century religious confusion to a firm pronouncement in favour of the English Church. The book, which includes a portrait of Nicholas Farrer and his Little Gidding community, frequently attains a mood of quiet intensity. Stevie makes Pompey remark:

'Oh the really great Christians are very admirable, very quiet. So later on I was reading *John Inglesant* and if ever I came near to getting into the inside-of the Christian religion it was then.'[36]

She found in this book a passage extolling the need to confront and absorb pain, not in order to prove moral worth, or goodness through strength, as in the philosophy of the Stoics, but in order to attain maturity. Because this idea remained a cornerstone to her philosophy, even after she became a committed agnostic, this passage from *John Inglesant* is quoted at length in *Novel on Yellow Paper*. Part of it reads:

'We must suffer with Christ whether we believe in him or not. We must suffer for the sins of others as for our own; and in this suffering we find a healing and purifying power and element. That is what gives to Christianity in its simplest and most unlettered form, its force and life.'[37]

In conversation with Phebe Snow, Stevie recalled that she had reached a pitch of exhaustion and tension at the time of her mother's death. A contributory factor was perhaps that she sat her matriculation that year. Once this was a thing of the past, she went on to enjoy her last year at North

London Collegiate, for she was able to give up the subjects she disliked and found school work a pleasure. A fellow pupil, Peggy Angus, remembers Stevie in the sixth form as a person always full of glee.[36]

She seems not to have suffered from comparison with her outwardly more able sister. Whereas Molly played in the First Eleven Hockey Team, Stevie remained steadfast with the Beginners' Eleven. She did, however, share Molly's enthusiasm for acting and during her last year at school gave two notable performances: the school magazine praised Peggy Smith's 'clever and farcical character study of old Hardcastle' in *She Stoops to Conquer* as well as her performance as one of the two messengers in *The Bacchae* whose acting was 'excellent, strikingly vivid and yet natural'.[39] *The Bacchae* was performed in Greek; Stevie learnt her lines phonetically and never forgot her 136-line speech which she enjoyed declaiming, both at school and alone in the woods at Palmers Green. The play was produced by Miss Holding, whose remark that they could not perform *Medea* as it needed a married woman of at least twenty-five to do justice to the part amused Stevie. 'So instead we did the sweet peaceful girlish *Bacchae* . . .'[40] Though she claimed she had not realized how cruel the play is until she saw it many years later, she understood enough to recognize the absurdity of Miss Holding's logic.

It is indicative of Molly's potential ability as an actress that in *The Bacchae* she played Agaue with such dramatic effect that her schoolmates found her performance unforgettable. Her ability and enthusiasm left her in a sorry predicament: she was utterly stage-struck yet had promised her mother, before she died, that she would not go on stage. Some compensation was to be found in following the career of Sybil Thorndike, then leading lady in the Old Vic Repertory Company. Molly lost no opportunity to see her act and even managed to establish a slight acquaintance with the actress who treated her kindly and invited her to tea. When Aunt was told of this she refused to let Molly go. A few weeks later, after watching three performances of *Everyman* in which Sybil Thorndike appeared, Molly again managed to achieve contact as her 1919 diary records: 'I went behind afterwards, as per stage door man's directions, asked for her and she came in her white Everyman things with wig, make up and all. Held my hand and arm and talked. She was superb. I worship her. She wants me to drop her a line and go round and see her . . . and she knows and did know it wasn't my will that refused before . . . How I love her!'

Molly's infatuation with Sybil Thorndike was sustained by an emotionalism fed by her involvement with Catholicism and the grief caused by her mother's illness and death. A vigorous creature, her emotions never stood still and by the summer of 1919 she appears to have transferred her affections to the newly arrived English teacher, Miss Florence Gibbons, who was persuaded by Molly to sponsor the Senior Dramatic Society. Another of the sponsors was Miss Isobel Monkhouse, the senior art mistress, a down-to-earth character, very proud of her well-lit art room with its shelves full of plaster casts of Greek sculpture. She ran her classes with tolerance and imagination; was stimulating, practical and blessedly uninterfering. When in the 1930s she was sent Stevie's first book of poems, she praised the illustrations as 'completely right and expressively excellent and in every way the right thing'.[41]

Miss Monkhouse (nicknamed 'Monkie' by her pupils) did not invite emotional tensions between herself and her pupils as Miss Gibbons did. The latter seems to have taken a particular interest in Molly who became her ardent disciple and was to read English under Ernest de Sélincourt at Birmingham University where Miss Gibbons had herself achieved an MA. Only five years older than Molly, Miss Gibbons offered an emotional sympathy. 'Went to Gib. after lunch,' Molly's diary records in June 1919, 'and had a long talk. I started weeping and she hugged me and was an angel. She is my friend I hope, and understands everything.' That Miss Gibbons did indeed regard Molly as a friend is proved by her willingness to meet her in town on a Saturday, for sundaes at Selfridges, to watch a march past in front of Buckingham Palace and to go to the Royal Academy. Though an inspiring teacher, she could be severe and did not lose her authority over Molly, whose diary records: 'Gib. wanted to speak to me . . . Did so for an hour and called me to book for my behaviour and selfishness.' By October their exchange was still affectionate: 'Had a talk with Gib. about my Roman difficulty. We loved each other hard, and she told me some things about her dear self.'

Florence Gibbons was an elegant, witty, charming woman but so pale, thin and fragile she seemed likely to disappear. After ten years service at North London Collegiate, ill health obliged her to leave and she died of tuberculosis in 1932 at the age of thirty-six. One of her pupils, Myfanwy Piper, recollects Miss Gibbons's unmistakable nervous giggle and her devout Anglo-Catholicism which attracted to her girls who shared this tendency, creating kind but slightly sentimental liaisons such as that with Molly. Outside school, she led a rather circumscribed life, owing to her poor health, and had a younger brother on whom she doted.

As a teacher she was impressive. Stella Gibbons recalls her 'weary and affected manner',[42] but Myfanwy Piper has described how this rather holy and elevated attitude was accompanied by a very lively approach which encouraged any positive reaction, whether it was academically respectable or not. She had an unusual feeling for words and gave the sixth form a lesson about writing and language that Myfanwy Piper describes as 'brilliant'.[43] She also had a wonderful ear and alerted her pupils to style by making them write in the manner of Sir Thomas Browne, or Dr Johnson, or Walter Savage Landor, at the same time encouraging them to write simply and truthfully. Although her appreciation of English literature was broad, she had a particular love for the seventeenth century and the Metaphysicals. Her taste in modern poetry was not entirely sound: she extolled Humbert Wolfe, but also admitted and admired Eliot. One of her pupils, who became a friend and admirer, was the Oxford scholar Helen Gardner.

Stevie showed Miss Gibbons the poem her aunt had declared 'unnecessary'.

> Spanky Wanky had a sister
> He said, I'm sure a black man kissed her
> For she's got a spot just here
> Twas a beauty spot my dear
> And it looks most awfully quaint
> Like a blob of jet black paint
> But when he told his sister that
> She threw at him her gorgeous hat
> And with airs that made her swanky
> Said, I hate you Spanky Wanky.[44]

Miss Gibbons saw that the doggerel contained originality, as a letter she sent Stevie in May 1920 reveals:

'Need I say how sorry I am about your having to lie up just now? Do write some dainty verse if you can possibly get up enough interest in life to do so. I enjoyed your "New" books, but I am convinced your forte ought to be quaint, well-made, clear-cut verse. Can you still do the "Spanky-Wanky" kind? "She threw at him her gorgeous hat" is a triumph.'

If Miss Gibbons furthered Stevie's desire to write poetry, her study of Latin filled her mind with tags that stirred her imagination. The Latin quotations that she incorporates into her prose and the passages she translates in her verse are the kind she would have encountered at school. The famous line which sums up the whole ethos of the *Aeneid* and Virgil himself, '*Sunt lacrimae rerum et mentem mortalia tangunt*', tolled in her mind. In one of her reviews it qualifies her remark that she would 'rather be a woman than a man (one does not have to protest so much and there is less vanity to be satisfied)' for she added, 'but it is the common human predicament that bites at all of us'.[45] Other instances of school Latin resurfacing in her mature work include a line from Horace's 'Roman Odes' – '*Post equitem sedet atra Cura*' – which began the quatrain:

> Behind the Knight sits hooded Care,
> And as he rides she speaks him fair,
> She lays her hand in his sable muff,
> Ride he never so fast he'll not cast her off.

Likewise Emperor Hadrian's address to his soul, 'Animula vagula blandula', supposed to have been written on his deathbed and translated by Byron ('Ah, gentle, fleeting, wav'ring sprite'), was a passage with which Stevie identified. Not only does Pompey in *Novel on Yellow Paper* refer to herself as 'an *animula, vagula, blandula* of the office',[46] but the poem in its entirety, which in literal translation might read

> Dear wandering gentle soul
> Guest and companion of the body
> In the places to which you are now going away
> Pale, numb with cold, naked,
> You won't make jokes as you used to,

becomes in Stevie's version a self-portrait, displaying striking technical assurance in its play of sound.

> Little soul so sleek and smiling
> Flesh's friend and guest also
> Where departing will you wander
> Growing paler now and languid
> And not joking as you used to?

Hadrian's poem opens chapter VIII of Pater's *Marius the Epicurean*, a book Stevie read in 1919, probably at school as she filled an exercise book with notes on it.[47] This, 'the golden book of English prose', as George Moore called it, with its rhythmic cadences and grave, intricate sentences, would have educated Stevie's ear. Her attention may also have been caught by a certain parallelism between her own interests and circumstances and those of Marius. He enjoys rambling over the marshes and along the coast to relieve the tension in his soul and wants to become a poet. We also learn that 'the death of his mother turned seriousness of feeling into a matter of intelligence: it made him a questioner; and by bringing into full evidence to him the force of his affections and the probable importance of their place in his future developed in him generally the more human and earthy elements of character.'

Marius moves towards a humanist philosophy of his own, 'with the individual for its standard of all things', as Stevie was also to do. Her notes pay detailed attention to chapters VIII and IX in which Marius's Cyrenaicism, his reflective, practical hedonism, is discussed at length. The programme Marius pursues invites comparison with the process of self-education that Stevie followed on leaving school. Marius experiences 'a novel curiosity as to what the various schools of ancient philosophy had had to say concerning that strange, fluttering creature [the soul]; and that curiosity impelled him to certain severe studies, in which his earlier religious conscience seemed still to survive, as a principle of hieratic scrupulousness of integrity of thought, regarding this new service to intellectual life.' Stevie's notes paraphrase what follows: 'He was kept from falling a prey to an enervating mysticism by the vigour of his intellect. Also he was beginning to realize the poetic beauty of clearness of thought, "the aesthetic charm of a cold austerity of mind".' This quality Stevie was to praise often in her reviews. Pater's book taught her that for completeness of life it was not pleasure but insight that mattered; 'insight through culture,' her notes read, 'into all that the present moment holds.'

Marius the Epicurean can be regarded as precursor of *Novel on Yellow Paper* in that the interior monologue technique which Stevie pursues is prefigured in Pater's concentration, not on character, action or plot, but on a series of meditations on sensations and ideas. It is also possible that Stevie's reading of *Marius* gave direction to her as yet inchoate ideas about poetry: when Marius's friend Flavian outlines a literary method he argues that colloquial idiom 'offered a thousand chance-tost gems of racy or picturesque expression', and that his aim was to combine the conservative and reactionary with the popular and revolutionary, a programme that Stevie was herself to achieve.

First and foremost, however, the book would have sharpened Stevie's ear, for Pater's sentences have a linked rhythm, as well as a very carefully selected vocabulary. At one point Pater himself remarks that Cyrenaicism is a philosophy of youth, 'ardent, but narrow in its survey': likewise Stevie later perceived an immaturity in her admiration for Pater. In *Over the Frontier* Pompey visits a young Professor Dryasdust who reads aloud Pater in order to demonstrate good prose. Pompey is instantly affronted:

'Now this is what I cannot bear to support for one moment longer. The too-ripeness, the concealed verse forms, the succulent young voice of the insufferably teaching young professor, the falling back of the ten years since I read Pater, the too familiar and infuriating intrinsic [sic] cadences, the dying fall at the end of each paragraph . . . Yes, at twenty one may read Pater – but not aloud to friends, not that, never that, at twenty it is even commendable to read Pater, it shows that at least one has an ear for the less subtle harmonies of English prose. At twenty I could, but I hope did not, quote just that passage, but without the book. Here I am getting a little superior.'[48]

Stevie was to replace Pater's stately rhythms with the more insinuating rhythms of the speaking voice that runs on. Nevertheless *Marius the Epicurean* may have been for her what Apuleius's *Metamorphoses* was for Marius: 'It occupied always a peculiar place in his remembrance, never quite losing its power in frequent return to it for the revival of that first glowing impression.'

Stevie once claimed in an interview that the only prize she won at North London Collegiate was for Scripture. Perhaps this was the 'Quotation' event awarded her at Sports Day in July 1920. It was Molly who in 1919 had collected the Senior Platt scholarship in English, passed her Higher Certificate in the summer of 1920 and went on to university. Stevie, having passed her matriculation, did not attempt the Higher Certificate and was not considered for university. She once said that the headmistress had advised against it. Certain of her contemporaries, however, recollect that she had no desire to go. She did not wish to follow Molly into the teaching profession and at that time there was little else available to women who read the humanities at university. In addition her health was poor and she was not eligible for a state scholarship, then only awarded to those who had been at state schools. Lack of funds may have been a crucial factor, for John Spear's legacy had been badly invested and had dwindled in value. But if Stevie's formal education now ended, her mental journeying had only just begun. Looking back on this period, in an interview with the poet John Horder, Stevie summed up her situation:

'I was rather *mal vue* at school, and I'm sure with reason, but when I left I suddenly became a real swot, *wanted it all*, you know, and really studied my Greek as I never had before. Of course, my school did not recommend I should go on to university. They suggested for me what they obviously considered the lowest form of gainful employment, a secretarial training course at the famous Mrs Hoster's.'[49]

CHAPTER 3

Bonded Liberty

Stevie and Molly left North London Collegiate in July 1920, to pursue different careers. Molly, after three years at Birmingham University, where she acted in many theatricals and came down in July 1923 with an honours degree, began to earn her living as a teacher of English. She was first employed by a small private school called Gardenhurst, at Burnham-on-Sea, where she excited one of her pupils, Cecily Mackworth (later to become a friend of Stevie's), with her reading of 'The Lady of Shalott'. Molly's talent for recitation, her sense of the dramatic and her profound love of her subject gave her natural authority, and she was never severe. But at Gardenhurst she stayed only one term and her sudden departure, Cecily Mackworth recalls, had about it something of a mystery. When many years later Cecily Mackworth met Molly in Stevie's company and excitedly identified her as her teacher at Gardenhurst, Molly gave the impression she did not want to talk about the school. Her next job was at Belstead House, in Suffolk, from whence she moved to Ipswich High School. Something of the unhappiness she endured at the second of these can be inferred from passages in *The Holiday* where Molly is called Pearl and her school situated in Wales. If Stevie's fictional account of the school is accurate, the children were beaten and harshly treated, one dying of meningitis. Not until 1943, when she moved to the highly respected public school, Westonbirt, did Molly enjoy her teaching career which in 1946 she was to exchange for the role of Drama Adviser to the county of Buckinghamshire.

She was, it seems, easily antagonized. By nature fussy and inclined, as her

Palmers Green friend Olive Pain says, 'to fly off the handle', she was to some extent a victim of her own temperament. Another Palmers Green acquaintance, Doreen Diamant, tells how they could not even go on a bicycle ride without Molly discovering some fault or inadequacy in the situation. Little is known about her private life except that at university, or soon after, she became engaged to be married. Once, when visiting her friends the Cockmans in Palmers Green, Molly began to complain about her job: Mrs Cockman, referring to Molly's engagement, remarked that she need not worry as all would soon change. Her daughter, Margaret Cockman, recalls that though Molly said nothing, it was evident from the expression on her face that the engagement had ended. Added to this disappointment was her constant regret that she had not taken up acting. We glimpse Molly through Stevie's eyes in *The Holiday* where the narrator recounts how 'when Pearl becomes miserable she also becomes cross'. This fighting spirit differentiates her from her sister.

'So instead of the rich death-feeling that is what I have, that is so richly anarchic and upon which one can rest, she has this furious feeling of earthly rage.'[1]

When in 1939 Molly applied for the headmistress's post at Kensington High School, she blamed her failure to get it on her 'despised' Birmingham degree. Hampered and possibly repressed, she developed markedly different characteristics to Stevie so that later in life friends of Stevie were sometimes surprised on seeing them together: whereas Stevie remained slight in build, Molly, by middle age, had grown thickset; and though equally strong in character, she could appear clumsy and coarse-grained. Almost certainly her domineering manner hid the hypersensitive nature of an unhappy and disappointed woman.

Stevie may also have experienced emotional turmoil soon after leaving school. One cancelled page relating to an early draft of *Novel on Yellow Paper* hints at this. Because the framework of Pompey's existence is grounded on autobiographical fact ('Please don't break your heart,' Stevie told Denis Johnston, 'everything in the novel is true.'[2]), there is good reason to believe that this rejected passage has more than novelistic origin. 'When I was eighteen years old just leaving school I imagined myself in love,' it begins, and goes on to describe a medical student whom she calls Norman Hicks and who returned her love. He proves an inadequate hero for romance. His habits are irritating (he talks a lot about literature but always praises the worst) and he comes laden with an unusually large share of disabilities, including Bradford origins, an invalid sister in a wheelchair, a slight cast in one of his eyes and a father with a small job in an engineering works, all of which deepen his sense of inferiority. 'This dreadful Norman Hicks affair,' Stevie writes, '. . . was put a stop to very soon by my Aunt but not before it had got to be something I could not forget.' Sweet but burdened, he hated, she adds, freedom and light and turned 'not to the darkness of night but to the dimness of the dead light'.[3]

If at this time some attachment did occur, it would have coincided with Stevie's training at Mrs Hoster's Secretarial Academy. Though she is said to have expressed interest in journalism while at school, she chose Mrs Hoster's as a safer route to a regular income. It must, however, have caused a temporary financial strain on her and her aunt, as the fees demanded by this institution placed it beyond the reach of most. Furthermore, to gain acceptance matriculation was essential. Finally, an interview contributed to the impression that only ladies were acceptable. Mrs Hoster's was situated in Grosvenor Place, in a Belgravian terraced house overlooking Buckingham Palace gardens. Training lasted six months and taught, among other things, the correct form of address for a bishop, the aristocracy or royalty. Mrs Hoster's was high on tact; trainee secretaries were advised to keep their eyes on their boss's shoes when taking dictation, so as not to induce self-consciousness or upset their train of thought.

The chief advantage of Mrs Hoster's for Stevie was its proximity to Hyde Park, as Phebe Snow's biographical outline records:

'Quite often she found the course tedious but fortunately there was a system whereby students could sign themselves OUT for the afternoon. It was mainly for the convenience of girls who were to be presented at Court and had to visit dressmakers. Stevie was not one of these but often she signed OUT and went for a walk in Hyde Park to wander round the Serpentine and feed the ducks.'[4]

Mrs Hoster also ran an employment agency which was highly regarded by employers. The mere fact of being 'Hoster trained' meant that all who wanted them got jobs. Stevie is said to have found her first job in an engineering firm where she remained for about a year. She then entered the magazine publishers, C. Arthur Pearson, becoming secretary to Sir Neville Pearson, son of the firm's founder. Though *Novel on Yellow Paper* suggests that Pompey, alias Stevie, entered this firm at the age of twenty-four, the age of twenty or twenty-one is more likely. No staff records dating this far back exist. It can, however, be assumed that by 1922 Stevie had found the mundane job that was to remain hers for the next thirty years.

*

The manner in which Arthur Pearson pursued his fortune was one which no son could imitate. He first entered the employment of George Newnes in 1884 as the result of a competition in *Tit-Bits* which offered a clerkship as a prize. Before the year was out he had risen to the position of manager and six years later he left to set up business himself with *Pearson's Weekly*. As a magazine proprietor, the *Dictionary of National Biography* records, his aim was 'to stampede rather than inform'. He soon began to publish other popular papers and in 1900 launched the *Daily Express* which he ran as a competitor to Alfred Harmsworth's four-year-old *Daily Mail*. Four years later, having in addition acquired several provincial newspapers, this man, described by Joseph Chamberlain as 'the greatest hustler I have ever known', bought the *Standard* and in 1907 began unsuccessful negotiations to purchase *The Times*. This marked the watershed of his career. In 1910 he sold the *Standard* and *Evening Standard* and in 1912 disposed of his interest in the *Daily Express*. His energies had not diminished: they had been redirected by the discovery that he was going blind. 'I am going to be *the* blind man,' he is on record as saying. He joined the council of the National Institute for the Blind and helped raise its annual income from some £8,000 in 1913 to over £350,000 by 1921. During the 1914–18 war he was instrumental in opening hospitals for the blind and in both public and personal ways did a great deal to improve their lot. In 1916 he was created a baronet.

When Stevie entered Pearson's, Sir Arthur Pearson had died the year before, having accidentally slipped in his bath, struck his head and fallen face forward in the water. His only son, Neville, then only twenty-three, had succeeded to the baronetcy. As a director of Pearson's he was to further his father's charitable work on behalf of the blind and continued to support the 'fresh air fund' which enabled children from poor areas of London to enjoy outings and holidays in the country. But in the running of the firm, Sir Neville had only limited control. The chairman was then Lord Riddell whose personal assistant, Herbert Tingay, had entered the firm in 1913 at the age of fourteen. Tingay, who modelled himself on his boss, had begun to arouse Neville Pearson's dislike, perhaps because of their closeness in age. He had been wounded in the 1914–18 war and rumour has it that while he was convalescing Neville Pearson tried to arrange matters to Tingay's disadvantage. Tingay never forgave Sir Neville and, as he rose steadily in importance, not only in Pearson's but also in Newnes after the two firms amalgamated in 1921, becoming vice-chairman and managing director and eventually chairman, he made certain that very little power ever fell into Sir Neville's hands.

Therefore when Stevie became secretary and personal assistant to Sir Neville Pearson, a director of a large publishing company, she found she did not have much to do. Many years later, after conversations with Phebe Snow, she approved this description of her position:

'She veered between feeling that the job was too good for her and that she was too good for the job, and often she was beset by a feeling of unreality. She learned many things about life, about finance and business, and about people, but the work was not excessive and she had time to write. She felt the contrasts and the conflicts of her existence very sharply and they inform a number of her poems especially "Childe Rolandine".'5

Foremost of these conflicts was perhaps the creative nurturing of hate that grew in these oppressed circumstances, and which Stevie evokes in the second stanza of 'Childe Rolandine', in a manner that echoes Blake's 'A Poison Tree'.

> It is the privilege of the rich
> To waste the time of the poor
> To water with tears in secret
> A tree that grows in secret
> That bears fruit in secret
> That ripened falls to the ground in secret
> And manures the parent tree
> Oh the wicked tree of hatred and the secret
> The sap rising and the tears falling.

This invisible process went on in the small antiquated rooms that composed Pearson's offices in Henrietta Street, in the Covent Garden area. The building stood on a corner opposite a hospital. Each room was heated by a portable electric stove which, when turned on its side, heated a kettle. Like other secretaries, Stevie would have inherited a huge Royal typewriter that took up most of the desk space. Not until 1936 or 1937 did Pearson's cohabit with Newnes in the office block around the corner in Southampton Street which, owing to the turret-like structure on its roof, is known as Tower House. For Pearson's employees the move brought a marked improvement in working conditions, also an element of prestige, for Tower House had a commissionaire at the door and girls working the lifts. Offices were split up according to their function (editorial, advertising, photography and so on), with a large art department at the top of the building and a staff canteen in the basement. Though it did not pay high salaries, Newnes was considered a good firm to work for, safe and paternalistic.

Tower House did not mark the limits of the Newnes empire. Situated on the corner of Southampton Street, it abuts the elegant *Country Life* building in Tavistock Street designed by Sir Edwin Lutyens. In Stevie's day there were ways through to this building on three floors. On the other side of Tower House, in Southampton Street, was an old building that had formerly been a post office. This too, was annexed, and access created, but as the floor levels of the two buildings did not coincide, the result was a rabbit warren of offices and a complicated system of mezzanine floors and connecting doors. Though for a short period Sir Neville Pearson had an office in the *Country Life* building, he was, after the merger, to be situated on the third floor of the old post office with a room at the back overlooking a well. Stevie had little more than a cupboard, a windowless room next door, which placed her between Sir Neville and the red-faced, kindly Sir Frank Newnes for whom from then on she also worked. Though very different in character to Sir Neville, he was in a similar position. His father George Newnes had founded his firm largely on the success of the magazine *Tit-Bits*. Having a canny understanding of how to appeal to popular instinct, he achieved success in part by launching competitions and insurance policies which enabled him to expand into a wide-ranging list of titles that included the *Strand Magazine*, the *Westminster Gazette* and *Country Life*. Like Sir Arthur Pearson, he too had philanthropic interests but was rewarded with a baronetcy for his ten years as a Liberal MP. In a less prominent fashion, Frank Newnes, who succeeded to the baronetcy in 1906, acted as chairman to his father's firm up until 1954, with Herbert Tingay the power behind the throne. Sir Frank's chief interest outside publishing was hospitals and he did much work on behalf of them and for charities.

When Stevie first entered Pearson's, Sir Neville, who was only four years older than herself, was in his mid twenties and an unusually handsome man. Stevie was inevitably much envied by office juniors, still more so when in 1928 Sir Neville extricated himself from his marriage to Mary Mond, daughter of the first Baron Melchett, and married the actress Gladys Cooper. Stevie, it would seem, was very loyal to Sir Neville and though she was in a position to do so did not gossip. Most people at this time were unaware that Stevie was anything other than a rather plain, dutiful secretary. One of the office juniors, Margaret Ralph, recollects her as 'a friendly, chirpy little person who had a smile for everyone including us juniors . . . She was always smiling and cheerful though somewhat eccentric. She always wore her hair straight with a fringe. A no-nonsense style that suited her way of life. She was a far too busy little person to fuss about her appearance.'[6]

Very quickly Stevie would have become familiar with the personality behind Sir Neville's good looks. The man she portrayed as Sir Phoebus Ullwater in *Novel on Yellow Paper* is a selectively composed, genial caricature of a person who in day-to-day life was very much less pleasant. At Eton he had not been popular. And though he cut a dashing figure, his dark brown eyes and dark skin giving him a slightly Spanish look, and had all the necessary accoutrements, the total apparatus of the English gentleman, he had a cold personality and to a discerning eye lacked breeding. His marriage to Gladys Cooper lasted just six years and his meanness of temperament is instanced by the fact that she only gained custody of their daughter by agreeing to let him divorce her, which he did. There is also evidence that he bore grudges remorselessly and was fundamentally ungenerous. When his son married, Sir Neville produced three presents: a battered cigarette case, formerly given him by Gladys Cooper; a set of cutlery, incomplete; and a pair of evening shoes, used. This, however, was the man who was Stevie's 'lodestar in a disordered existence, that lodestar of official duties',[7] and who, in the office, was always courteous to young women, if occasionally sharp. One administrative assistant, later to become Lady Strabolgi, never forgot his reprimand – that pearls should never be worn before six in the evening. It is, however, important to differentiate between the man with whom Stevie first became familiar and the person Sir Neville eventually became. 'What a sad dead man S.N. [Sir Neville] is becoming or rather has become,' Stevie wrote to a friend in 1939.[8] Descriptions of him in later life confirm her view. Despite an active social life at his home in Hyde Park Gardens, he was noticeably without friends. He arrived mid-morning at Newnes, sometimes with his poodle in tow, and for luncheon went across to the Garrick, taking his own wine about which he knew a great deal. Afterwards he could be seen reading the newspapers in the smoking room where he usually sat alone.

Even if the less attractive aspects of his character were visible from the start, Stevie, in her portrait of him as Sir Phoebus Ullwater, struck a teasingly jocular note.

'But yesterday Sir Phoebus was looking very fetching indeed in dark dark mourning clothes and a dark dark top hat. So when the funeral was over he came back and said: "Another good man buried" . . . So all the afternoon there was Sir Phoebus singing softly and happily in his own room . . . and what is he singing softly softly in his own room? Well then, he is singing "For all the Saints", very soft and winning.'[9]

The affection underlying this description was genuine. In some ways Sir

Neville delighted Stevie with his wholesome, if simple, reactions and grasp of right behaviour. When Pompey tells Sir Phoebus of a newspaper report announcing the existence of over three million illegitimate children in Britain, he exclaims: 'Hurrah! Who says England's going pansy?' Pompey recounts this to an assistant who asks: 'Can you understand people like that?'[10] Stevie could and did.

At the root of their working relationship lay the unspoken admission that both were misfits, beached in circumstances not entirely to their liking, with not enough to do. Sometimes news from the Stock Exchange came 'hissing and bubbling over the telephone' or there were messages 'from the suave and evasive elegants in Whitehall',[11] and occasionally there was an urgent task to fulfil, such as the finding of a dog for one of Gladys Cooper's plays or smoked cod's roe for Sir Neville's aunt. These small eruptions periodically broke but did not significantly alter the *longueurs* when

'the great link between us two is the happy way we both get quickly bored. And do I worry him with fool unnecessary queries? I do not. We indulge in the utmost limit of boredom, he in his room and I in mine, and stagger out when tea time comes, as it must, however it comes, whether rung for on the house phone, or trundled in by the hired girl, that's like an angel of grace breaking in on the orgy of boredom to which my soul is committed.'[12]

This tactful recognition of inactivity, together with her refusal to stall at any task (she even assisted Sir Neville's mother with a book she was writing), made up, as Stevie claims in *Novel on Yellow Paper*, for her typing, done with one finger on each hand. She accepted the limitations of her job and sought no change in her circumstances, partly because the focus of her life lay elsewhere and for the time being needed to be hidden. This left her able to take Sir Neville on his own terms. He was anyway good at dealing with people at a superficial level, knew how to exert charm and made the right gestures. Sir Phoebus, when on holiday, sends Pompey a double-sized tin of Harrogate toffee and receives the accolade: 'It is that sort of thing about Sir Phoebus that makes him stand out head and shoulders above the ordinary run of baronets. It is that something.'[13] So Stevie extolled this man in print, later privately admitting that Sir Phoebus was 'not entirely the loving chap one made out!!'[14]

One advantage of Stevie's job was that it brought her into contact with journalism, with the intense activity associated with the magazine world. This was especially true after the move into Tower House which was the home of prestige periodicals like *John O'London's Weekly* as well as unending weeklies such as *Peg's Paper*, *Tit-Bits*, *Woman's Own* and *Amateur*

Gardening. One division of Newnes, the Home Library Book Company, sold a great many volumes on the practical trades (plumbing, engineering, building and welding) direct to the public on a monthly repayment basis. In charge of this was Mr Harry Patchett who had the office next door to Sir Neville Pearson. He is said to have recognized Stevie's worth and to have acted as intermediary when, in trouble with one of her baronets, she momentarily came close to losing her job.

Both at Pearson's and Newnes Stevie had an easy job and much spare time. Travelling to and from work every day, her life during the twenties and early thirties was repetitious, with little outward change. But it was also a period of prodigious mental activity. Looking back on this period, Stevie recalled that, working in an office, she felt in disgrace for not having done better at school and that this made her ambitious for learning.[15] She also reflected that university education might have distracted rather than fed her. Left to her own devices, she read assiduously, creating inside herself that pool of knowledge and sensibility on which her own craft would sail. She read with a self-abandonment, a fanaticism which, as Pater remarks in *Marius the Epicurean*, 'occurs, quite naturally, at the onset of every really vigorous intellectual career'.

Insight into what she read is offered by two pocket notebooks which Stevie filled with annotations between 1924 and 1930.[16] In these she jotted down general observations, précis and quotations, creating commonplace books which she was to draw upon for many years to come. Reading about *Parsifal*, for instance, in Max Nordeau's book, *Degeneration*, in 1924, she found a description of Titurel which she re-evoked fourteen years later in *Over the Frontier* as an image of death in life.[17] Many of the quotations she transcribed later reappeared in her novels and reviews, for one characteristic of Stevie's creative life was her ability to make very good use of the material she assimilated.

The date at the start of the first notebook is January 1924. In November of that year Stevie was issued with a reader's ticket for the British Museum Library. It expired after six months and there is no record of her renewing it. She did, however, make use of other libraries, recording in her notebooks the date when a book was issued and when it was returned. In addition, she bought a great many secondhand books from circulating libraries such as Mudie's which, when a new title by a well-known author appeared, stocked several copies and sold the majority some months later, after the initial demand had diminished. Habitually, Stevie inscribed her name in these books (usually 'Margaret Smith' or 'F. M. Smith' during the 1920s) as well as the date of purchase. In this way we know that she acquired a copy of

Tristram Shandy in 1921 as well as a classical dictionary; that in 1924 she was reading Homer in Greek; and that throughout the 1920s and early 1930s she was reading in some depth Maurice Baring (a particular favourite, with his charm, humour and linguistic refinement), Hilaire Belloc, Joseph Conrad, Ford Madox Ford, Aldous Huxley, Henry James, Rudyard Kipling, D. H. Lawrence, George Moore, Edgar Allan Poe and Saki. She was also, in her purchasing of books, adding to those Shakespeare plays already in Molly's possession.

At first her reading notes offer nothing more than a brief comment, of approval or disapproval. Aldous Huxley's *Antic Hay* delighted her, but after completing his *Limbo* and *Crome Yellow* she observed that he was inclined to repeat himself, and his short stories in *Mortal Coils* she found 'ever so slightly nauseating'. Much of her reading in the 1920s was tied in with her interest in the Anglo-Catholic movement. After finishing the second volume of Compton Mackenzie's *Sinister Street* in March 1924 she observed how the search for understanding on the part of the character, Michael, paralleled Ronnie Knox's journey in *A Spiritual Aeneid*. 'Very interesting saga,' she concludes, 'and not a bit too long – a mere 1132 pp.' The following month she read Knox's *Sanctions, a Frivolity* and notes: 'Long discussions – not noticeably frivolous – on the religious question. Delightfully written. His argument is something like this: – The necessity of a decent conduct in life is only explicable logically by a belief in an objective duty. You must have "sanctions" for what you do and merely human sanctions are not enough . . . Of course if I could accept this hypothesis I should at once become a Catholic.' Instead she continued to enjoy the descriptions of Anglicanism which she encountered in Compton Mackenzie's *Parson's Progress* and *The Heavenly Ladder* as well as the portrait of Knox found in Arthur Waugh's *Recent Roman Converts*. She also found entertainment in the Roman Catholic novelists Belloc, Baring and Chesterton, but eventually came to feel that they were a little too much on the defensive, 'good fun when they leave the sword of religious controversy in the scabbard'.

She read relatively little criticism, and when she did looked in Peter Wright's *Portraits and Criticisms* for what she found lacking – 'the large mindedness and humanity which makes for fair criticism'. She did, however, enjoy André Chevrillon's *Three Studies in English Literature*, especially his essay on Kipling. She also made extensive notes on Virginia Woolf's *The Common Reader: First Series*, noting of the essays as a whole that they were 'full of meat'. Her growing confidence in her own opinion left her sometimes critical of that expressed in the *Sunday Times* or *Observer*, both of which praised Louis Golding's *Seacoast of Bohemia* which Stevie found 'tedious', a disparaging term she often used. Another critical book that aroused her admiration in the mid twenties was Osbert Burdett's *The Beardsley Period*. She termed it 'lovely', made extensive notes on it and copied out long passages. What she found lovely was probably Burdett's terse, disciplined, witty and epigrammatic style. Her notes on this book extract a pot-pourri of facts, ideas and quotations which provide no obvious insight into the book's importance for her. But it is worth noticing that Burdett would have provided Stevie with an understanding of what a poet in a post-romantic period could be. Burdett observes the romantic protest against synthesis: 'man's desires are more complex than any pattern he can invent to lend them form and dignity'. Stevie, in her notes, added the gloss: 'Manners, morals, religion – all patterns.' Describing the 'aesthetic type', Burdett, taking his cue from the postscript to Pater's *Appreciations*, dwells on the poet's incurable thirst for escape:

'They were disillusioned people without sympathy or understanding for the world in which they lived, who found hardly any living activities in that world to correspond with their susceptibilities to beauty. The curse from which all minorities suffer fell upon them. They experienced that extremity of solitude that can be felt most acutely in uncongenial company, or in a crowd, or in family life. They suffered from the egoism that has to be cherished because, in the circumstances, it can be escaped only at the price of self-treachery or surrender, since there is no healthy fellowship in which it can be merged or active tradition on which it can be grafted.'[18]

Burdett's conclusion is that the 1890s is a period more important for the attitude it revealed than for what it produced. This attitude, he argues, has become permanent. He stresses the disillusionment at the heart of the 1890s and, writing in the mid 1920s, observes: 'Disillusion is a little out of date, for this implies a conscience that is still sensitive. Disillusion has been replaced by indifference, and the change congratulates itself on the return of good taste, the recovery of sanity.'[19] The avoidance of disillusion, here described, invites comparison with Stevie's poem, 'The Frog Prince', where the frog, 'Habituated / To a quiet life', is content with his frog's doom, yet realizes that 'Only disenchanted people / Can be heavenly'.

Burdett is an instance of one of many, now largely forgotten voices that Stevie listened to at this time. She read without prejudice, absorbing books on witchcraft and demonology, memoirs, history books (including Ranke's *History of the Papacy*), the wit and epigrams of Oscar Wilde. As will be mentioned later, she had a liking for contemporary American novelists and noted of Anita Loos's *Gentlemen Prefer Blondes* that it was 'shrewd and most amusing, and excellently illustrated'.

At home much of her time must have been spent reading, books to some extent assuaging the intellectual loneliness of her life at Palmers Green. She was not without friends; among them were Dr Woodcock's daughters, Doreen and Nina, who recount how Stevie would turn up at their house and curl up like a waif in an armchair in order to enjoy a long chat with their mother. But the impression remains that none of her Palmers Green friends were ever soul mates. Nevertheless she was glad to return to the area after a working day in town. Here she enjoyed that quietness often praised in her writings, and which owed much to the stability of life at 1 Avondale Road, with its overfurnished sitting room, its ribbed chenille tablecloths with bobbles attached, its underfurnished and inconvenient kitchen and its small garden made gloomy by the enormous privet hedge which grew at the far end and where only ivy and earwigs flourished. The house, though comforting, was not comfortable. The overstuffed armchairs, ebonized furniture and cottage piano in the front room, its huge sideboard and clock supported by two musketeers, gave some visitors the sensation that it was prickly, slightly repellent. Nor was it free of the financial insecurity that was a characteristic of Palmers Green where many of the larger houses were now converted into flats. Financial strain contributed to those 'nerve storms' which Stevie describes in 'The Heriots',[20] a short story at the start of which Peg Lawless's situation closely parallels her own. Both have a great-aunt living in their home. It is probable therefore, given Stevie's habit of using autobiographical matter in her prose, that her great-aunt, Martha Hearn Clode, took issue with 'Aunt Maggie' over Stevie in the same way that old Mrs Boyle, in the story, argues with Miss Cator.

'Old Mrs Boyle felt every now and then that Peg should be taught how to keep house, but Miss Cator, who was affectionate and impatient, preferred to do it herself, and about this there was always disagreement between the two ladies.'

Peg is sent out to buy three bloaters and returns with three lobsters.

'Peg had a sort of absent-mindedness that worked in a queer way. Always between lobster and bloater there was this indecision. She said lobster and saw bloater. Her great aunt was exasperated, although in a way it was a support for her argument that Peg should have more housekeeping practice.'

If this was also the opinion of Martha Hearn Clode it was ignored. Madge

Spear continued to relieve Stevie of all domestic responsibility, an action no doubt partly determined by her awareness of how easily Stevie tired. In *Novel on Yellow Paper* Pompey is advised by one of her cousins to escape from the circumscribed, old-fashioned existence which her aunt creates around her: Stevie never doubted her need of it. Between aunt and niece existed an unspoken acknowledgement of their mutual needs. 'This lion', Stevie wrote of her aunt in *Novel on Yellow Paper*, 'has a very managing disposition, is strong, passionate, affectionate, has enormous moral strength, is a fine old Fielding creation.'[21] In this aunt's eyes, her niece was still ten years old, 'a tiresome difficult and delicate child' who was not allowed, even in her twenties and thirties, to spend a night alone in the house. Such dependency would have been intolerable if it had not been rooted in love and distanced by reserve. Bound, not in marriage to another, but to her aunt, Stevie enjoyed mental freedom:

'Though she loves me very much she does not say it, but she does, and I love her and respect and admire her. But of course my life runs on secretly all the time, as it must, and she has no idea that it does, and the way it does, and that I have been grown up in some ways since I was fifteen, in some ways since I was twenty-five.'[22]

If Steve Donaghue had provided Stevie with a nickname that others thought apt,[23] she still continued, even in her early thirties, to inscribe her books 'F. Margaret Smith' and at first acquaintance introduced herself as Margaret. Her aunt never ceased to call her Peggy, or 'Paggy', in her Yorkshire pronunciation, and this no doubt contributed to the slow transformation of Stevie into the different identity that seemed to accompany her change of name. She visibly matured. The slight plumpness in her face found in school photographs disappeared leaving her bone structure pronounced. For a period she let her fringe grow out and tucked her hair behind her ears. This made still more prominent the two front teeth which, when her mouth was open slightly, stuck out over her lower lip and may have caused her slightly hissing laugh. Her most distinguished feature was her eyes which were unusually dark. Neat in appearance, though always a little outside fashion, she managed 'office dress' with skill and there was little evidence at this date, apart from her liking for Peter Pan collars, of the slightly eccentric, little-girl look that began to characterize her appearance in the 1950s. On the contrary, her dark eyes, hair and dark skin gave her a hint of the gypsy and made her stand out. When she shook hands with people she left the impression that there was a nervousness there, some-thing immensely alive yet reserved. In conversation she already had a gift for the unexpected turn of phrase.

She had also begun to write. She had kept in touch with her English teacher at North London Collegiate, Florence Gibbons, with whom she exchanged occasional letters. Something of Miss Gibbons's liveliness and wit is caught in her description of Dadaist poetry:

'It's a very logical development really. Poets and artists generally have grown tired of asseverating again and again that there *is* a meaning in their perpetrations, if you know how to look for it. They now declare boldly that it is of the very essence of true art to have no meaning whatever ... But perhaps you have met Dada in *The Chapbook*, where I made its acquaint-ance. Did you see the gem of the whole collection? A Dada-iste poem entitled "Suicide":

a	b	c	d	e
f	g	h	i	j
k	l	m	n	o
p	q	r	s	t
u	v	w	x	
y	z			

I like that. It's good. It's just the whole jolly thing, isn't it? You see, it's exactly the elemental parts of *Hamlet*; the least common multiple of everything that any of us might say on the subject. Has just that splendid universality which we ought to demand in a work of art. Me for Dada!'[24]

The flippant tone is heavily ironic, for Miss Gibbons had fanatical convic-tions as to what art should be and do. After her death, the headmistress of North London Collegiate, Miss Drummond, wrote of Miss Gibbons in the school magazine: 'All great literature was for her the Divine Word spoken through the minds of men.' Her seriousness is reflected in a chance meeting with one of her former pupils on the London Underground. Stella Gibbons, who had begun a course on journalism at University College told Miss Gibbons she was 'having a whale of a time', and received in return a sad smile plus the observation that that was not what one went to college for.[25] Stevie was similarly admonished when she sent Florence Gibbons some of her early poems. In *Novel on Yellow Paper* Miss Gibbons becomes F. Caudle, 'the girl that taught me English at school', who tells Pompey her poems are offensive.

'She was real struck on church was this girl. And she said they [the poems] were just another nail in the cross that they put the Lord on, or maybe it was just another thorn in the crown that they put on Him, but the idea was, see, they was just swelling the mass of all the evil and cruelty in the world. But I thought then, well that's not how they are at all, she certainly has got them all wrong, yes, she's just got them all wrong from beginning to end.'[26]

But the rejection was not easily forgotten. Stevie returns to it, again through Pompey's voice:

'And I will say: What about swelling the mass of cruelty in the world by uncalled for remarks about people's poems, eh? What about that? You certainly want to think before you go making remarks about people's poems. There certainly was a lot of upstage work about F.C., she was very superior very eclectic was F.C., she had a way of saying: We who care for the finer things of life. Like meaning *I* who care etcetera, but letting you in for pure manner's sake . . . pure magnanimity and not a word of honest truth in it, just wicked superiority and eclecticism like I said . . .'[27]

After this, Stevie appears to have remained silent about her literary ambitions. In 1931 she began taking weekly German lessons with a woman called Gertrude Wirth who became a friend and had herself ambitions to write. Many years later, looking back on this friendship, Gertrude Wirth realized how reserved Stevie had been: 'After all, when we were roaming the thoroughfares of London together, I was infantile enough to rave about future writings. You safely nodded and wished me luck, and then – went ahead and – nonchalantly as it seemed to plodding me – poured yourself out into book after book.'[28]

One person in whom Stevie may have confided was Hester Raven-Hart, the childhood friend whom she had first met at the Broadstairs convalescent home. They had kept in touch, Stevie accepting invitations to visit her home, Fressingfield Vicarage at Harleston in Norfolk where Hester's father was vicar from 1906 to 1919, as well as Rural Dean of Hoxne and honorary Canon of St Edmundsbury. Stevie was evidently held in affectionate regard by the family as, after her mother's death in 1919, Hester's mother wrote a heartfelt letter, beginning 'My poor lonely little Peggy', and assuring her: 'They are *not* "taken from us", but closer, and more "understanding" than ever before and nothing can now come between us and their love for us.'[29] Whether or not Stevie could assimilate such sentiments, she accepted invitations to join the Raven-Harts in 1922 and 1923 on holiday, on one occasion at St Margaret's on the Kent coast. A photograph of Hester shows her lying on the beach wearing rimless spectacles and looking very much the bluestocking. She was evidently also something of an eccentric, fond, as one of her friends described, of 'steaming round her old haunts'. One of these was the Poetry Bookshop. Hester shared her love of books with Stevie whose copy of Conrad's *Victory* was bought by Hester in 1923 and given to Stevie in 1927. A similar transaction occurred with *The Poetical Works of William Blake* found in Stevie's library and which is inscribed: 'Hester Raven-Hart. Poetry Bookshop 1919. Margaret Smith (bought from Hester) 8 October 1924.'[30] A month previously Stevie had bought from Mudie's G. K. Chesterton's book on Blake, making annotations in the margin that reveal she had already familiarized herself with details of the poet's life.

Stevie's involvement with Blake coincides with her first sustained attempt to write poetry. Apart from a few items of juvenilia, her earliest extant poems are the handful in manuscript at the University of Tulsa dated, in Stevie's hand, '1924–27?'. It is probable she wrote many more than now exist, even if the mention in *Novel on Yellow Paper* of a poem about Russia written at the age of twenty-four and which 'is twenty-six pages long and more to come'[31] remains an unsubstantiated boast. The fact that Stevie kept these unpublished poems suggests that she acknowledged their importance in her development.

There are many echoes of Blake in her mature work. She titled one of her poems 'Little Boy Lost' and another, 'Little Boy Sick', begins: 'I am not God's little lamb / I am God's sick tiger.' Blake's interest in contraries may have encouraged Stevie's delight in reversal, for her poems often turn on an unexpected flouting of convention. Likewise, his distrust of an abstract moral code would have strengthened her own dissentient leanings. But there are many reasons why Blake would have appealed to Stevie: his use of parody and the rhythms of speech; his creation of many voices and his ability to unsettle meaning; his concentrated intensity, tautness and use of compressed syntax, all of which would have encouraged Stevie's own move in the direction of verbal thrift. Sometimes the echoes are quite specific: Blake's 'The Mental Traveller' ('She cuts his heart out at his side') lies behind Stevie's 'I'll have your heart, if not by gift my knife / Shall carve it out. I'll have your heart, your life.' This, despite her admission, made towards the end of her life, that 'one should be on one's guard' with this poet as his echoes are almost too easy to pick up.[32]

Blake was one of several mentors. Given her advice in old age to young poets to read Byron, in order to sharpen their sense of rhythm and rhyme, it is probable that she read much of his work. Molly Smith's edition of Byron, bought in 1915, has page numbers listed inside the cover in Stevie's hand, as was her habit. Another favourite was Richard Crashaw. Stevie acquired a volume of his poems at the Poetry Bookshop on 13 October 1920 and never lost her taste for a particular passage from 'The Office of the Holy Cross': this she incorporated into *Over the Frontier* and her short story 'The Story of a Story', quoted in a 'Poet's Choice' radio programme in 1965 and included in her poetry anthology for children published by Batsford in 1970. The passage she admired, with its powerful rhythm and insistent, almost monotonous rhyme, evokes the harshness and clangour of the crucifixion scene, then surprises the reader with its syllabic increase and sudden change of register in the last line.

> The third hour's deafen'd with the cry
> Of 'Crucify Him, crucify'.
> So goes the vote (not ask them, why?)
> 'Live Barabbas! and let God die'.
> But there is wit in wrath, and they will try
> A 'Hail' more cruel than their 'Crucify'.
> For while in sport He wears a spiteful crown,
> The serious showers along His decent Face run sadly down.

'He has such boldness in his play with rhyme and rhythm,' Stevie observed in the 'Poet's Choice' programme, 'and such pleasures [pleasure is] in it and lordliness; it could not be anybody but him writing.'[33]

Technically, she may have learnt much from Browning, whom she had first learnt to enjoy at school; his interjection of flat, cynical phrases prefigures the irony characteristic of much modern poetry. She would also have been aware of the vernacular speech and psychological realism that had entered poetry before the First World War, in the work of Hardy, Frost and Edward Thomas. At some point she must have encountered Edward Lear's concentration on the central loneliness of the individual self, as well as his emphasis on the fun, oddity and strangeness of life. Her taste in poetry was demonstrably vigorous and eclectic. It took in Edmund Clerihew Bentley's *Biography for Beginners*, a copy of which she owned, and the droll, whimsical, slapdash humour of Chesterton and Belloc as well as the controlled anxiety, the rhapsodic anxious questioning of Tennyson whose tension between religious doubt and affirmation had for her particular relevance. She was also haunted by ballads, the singing games of her youth and their eerie echoes and by advertising jingles such as 'The Pickwick, the Owl and the Waverley pen, / They came as a boon and a blessing to men'. These were added to her continuing fascination with Browning's 'Childe Roland'; 'this magnificent and sombre poem,' she once wrote, 'the only piece of writing I have ever read or heard that truly throws up – and in what hellish detail (". . . that harrow fit to reel / Men's bodies out like silk") the dark background of Edgar's song'.[34] Elsewhere she declared: 'that whole poem is so full of the feeling of courage without hope and resistance without belief'.[35] These poets and more contributed to the subterranean process which over the years created the complexity of Stevie's many voices.

The manuscript poems, dated in Stevie's hand '1924–27' and now in the University of Tulsa Special Collection, are various in style and content. Already she has a liking for bold, masculine rhymes, and would have appreciated Crashaw's simple and effective linking of 'loss' with 'Cross' in the antiphon response in 'The Office of the Holy Cross' ('Christ when He died / Deceived the Cross; / And on Death's side / Threw all the loss.'). In her early poem, with its Blakeian title, 'The Spectre of My Ancient Youth', the search for rhyme dominates:

> A cruel plaining youth
> Have you no truth
> Thus garishly to cry
> Nor heed my groans
> The time of youth is sped
> And you are dead

Elsewhere the desire to parody the poeticity in Caliban's speech, in Act III, Scene 2 of *The Tempest*, ending 'I cried to dream again', incites her love of repetition:

> This is my bed
> Heron I slept
> And wept
> and slept and wept
> and went and slept and woke to weep again

A similar use of compression later appears in the Sitwellian 'Croft', which Stevie once described as a self-portrait:

> Aloft,
> In the loft,
> Sits Croft;
> He is soft.

But this was not published until 1940, by which time her use of words had become more ingenious.

The humour in these early poems is also uncertain. One untitled poem which begins

> In captivity I dwell
> My jaoler is Necessity

investigates the paradox of bonded liberty and brings Blake's 'mind-forged manacles' to mind. But the philosophical tone is suddenly undercut by the ordinariness of the last line, the first instance of Stevie's taste for the incongruous and unexpected. The narrator, captive owing to his or her need to work, earns enough to give

> To those I greatly love, whose kith I am
> Bread and butter and sometimes a little jam.

Her liking for humorous verse led her in 1925 to type out in full a poem in *Punch* by one of Ronald Knox's brothers who wrote under the sobriquet 'Evoe'. Entitled 'The Everlasting Percy', it was a parody of Masefield's 'Everlasting Mercy', and confirms her delight in this genre. Similarly, the longest of Stevie's early, unpublished poems, beginning 'Morbid Maltravers / Lived in Jermyn Street', parodies the type of effete hero she had met in the novels of Belloc and Baring, the kind of upper-middle-class sensitive young man she later satirized in her poem 'Is it Happy?'. The diction in 'Morbid Maltravers' is at times deliberately laboured and unnatural ('A trove of verdity bestrewed the floor'). The momentum of the poem, however, is sustained, evidence of an interest in narrative that Stevie was to develop.

Much of the Maltravers poem, as it unfolds, is written in iambic pentameter, as is 'Lines addressed to the Fountain in Fuller's Restaurant, Regent Street, West Side'. This prosaic setting, fused with religious overtones, becomes an exercise in Miltonics

> Thou perfect form, graven felicity,
> Fountain of muted laughter, singing voice,
> Suckest all souls and on a little flight
> To thee with silent pinions open wide
> They flap, nor cares the guzzling host nor knows
> If its celestial visitor within
> Observes the process of assimilation
> And consumation [sic] of metabolism
> Or scaping on unspoken exeat
> Takes breath without. Flit Soul, and flesh thy pads
> On that cold fount whereon the water plays
> Like the captive in bonded liberty
> Like the loosed in a fenced space of time

She is a little obviously striving for what, in another early poem addressed to

Milton, she calls 'chords of upswelling sound and cadences / Of subtle, intricate imagining'. Though the mode is satirical, the central idea is serious: the poem broods on the various souls within the restaurant, attracted to the fountain but caged within flesh. That which shines out as a 'spiritual pearl' sadly belongs to a wasted body. The speaker fears that his or her own soul may outswell its host, and, with its unconditional desire for freedom, lead to the annihilation of the flesh. The poem ends:

> Yet flesh and soul I think must fret their course
> Till time have done with them and death divide.
>
> Come come, I have a lieu upon thee
> Thou shalt not puff nor fluff nor turn from me
> To heel, soul, long enough hast thou been free.

Again, this traditional subject recurs some thirty years later, by which time Stevie had acquired a deceptively simple, intimate and casual tone, and could condense her ideas into three lines.

> Man is a spirit. This the poor flesh knows,
> Yet serves him well for host when the wind blows,
> Why should this guest go wrinkling up his nose?

If these manuscript poems were the same as those shown to Miss Gibbons, it is not easy to see why she thought Stevie was 'swelling the mass of cruelty in the world'. Perhaps it was the heretical note that was already beginning to appear. In 'Ignes Fatui', a near Dadaist poem, the rejection of all philosophy, religion, logic and metaphysics is urged. But what is more likely to have caused offence is the poem 'Satan Speaks'.[36] Here it is argued that Milton, the sweet singer and Prince of Hell, is numbed and made silent by his exile in Heaven. The speaker urges him to leave but realizes the impossibility of him doing so:

> . . . full well I know
> Thou canst not help thyself by heresy,
> For once in Heaven no man may further sin,
> It is so writ. Farewell, Unfortunate.
> An Angel, still couldst thou rebellion raise
> To merit overthrow and swift exile,
> But thou art Man redeemed by Jesus' blood,
> And where thou sit'st for ever must abide.

As Pompey tells us in *Over the Frontier*, both Milton's and Crashaw's Lucifer had an attraction for her that changed her view of God: God is 'punk' compared with those noble failures. The magic of Milton's and Crashaw's poetic vision is wrong, she says, but irresistible and leads to an 'exceedingly delicious contrariness that is at the same time so dangerous',[37] drawing her towards darkness and doubt. Ironically, it would seem that it was these two great religious poets who began Stevie's disaffection with Christianity.

CHAPTER 4

Dear Karl

Stevie's zest for holidays and life outside the office was sharpened by her boredom at work. She was always very dependent on her friends and by the late 1920s had developed a motley range of acquaintance. Those who knew her at this time retained varying impressions. Gertrude Wirth, meeting Stevie in 1931, thought her unsophisticated and lonely. Others, even on first acquaintance, were struck by her originality and quick-wittedness, her humour always revealing an unexpected slant.

One friendship established at this time was with Rosemary Cooper, a young woman who worked on magazines and was to become editor-in-chief of the Commonwealth editions of *Vogue*. Living with her parents in Palmers Green, she first met Stevie at a dance organized by the social club 'Sixteen Plus' which flourished under the auspices of St Paul's, Winchmore Hill. At first sight Peggy Smith seemed 'a drab-looking little person who didn't appear to have much character and at a dance was almost invisible', a 'rather pathetic little creature' evidently not enjoying herself.[1] Partly because their homes lay in the same direction, Rosemary Cooper insisted, to the annoyance of her male escort, that they should walk back with Stevie. This began their friendship. No. 110 Woodberry Avenue, the Cooper family home, is in easy walking distance of Avondale Road, and Rosemary Cooper over the years became the kind of friend who would later look in on Aunt when she became severely invalided and Stevie was away, from whom Stevie would borrow a hat or demand a car ride into Hertfordshire.

Social club dances and other similar events, which Stevie, in her twenties, evidently felt compelled to attend, must have left her sharply aware of her mental and spiritual isolation. While seeking the company of others she also developed a craving for solitude, tasted and enjoyed in 'Suburb' where the world at night is found different, empty, haunting and close to death. The poem begins:

> How nice it is to slink the streets at night
> And taste the slight
> Flavour of acrity that comes
> From pavements throwing off the dross
> Of human tread.

This misanthropic vein did not diminish her friendships: one friend in particular she had no wish to throw off was Basil Scheckell, 'William' in *Novel on Yellow Paper*. 'Now William is always running through my life,' Pompey insists, 'something that is very quiet and strong.' Their relationship is 'quite *platonisch*, and quite steering clear and uncomplicated by sex'.[2] Scheckell gave the impression he was by nature celibate. He never married, enjoyed the company of young people, on whom he is said to have had a good influence, and had considerable taste. After the 1914–18 war he had gone to live in Aylesbury where, after working for a period in his brother-in-law's timber-merchant business, he took over the proprietorship of a pub. He was also for a period secretary to the Aylesbury Choral Society and, being a good mixer, attracted to its concerts the gentry as well as office boys. Stevie occasionally visited him at weekends and, owing to Scheckell's association with the Choral Society, in 1924 met its conductor, Maurice Jacobson, who was not long out of the Royal College of Music. Maurice Jacobson and his wife, Suzannah, were naturally sociable and befriended Stevie. They did not stay long in Aylesbury and after moving to London regularly invited Stevie to their parties.

At these music was always an ingredient. Maurice Jacobson had been a child prodigy and by the age of sixteen could play all Bach's 48 Preludes and Fugues and all Beethoven's sonatas from memory. His musicianship, combined with his extensive knowledge of instrumental, vocal and choral repertoire, made him a valued adjudicator at music festivals. Among those he discovered was Kathleen Ferrier whom he accompanied at her first London recital. He was also a composer – his finest work is said to be his setting of Francis Thompson's mystical poem, 'The Hound of Heaven' – and from 1923 for a period of almost fifty years he worked for the publishing house Curwen's, beginning as music adviser and taking over as chairman from Kenneth Curwen after his death. At one of the Jacobsons' parties, on 23 October 1929, Stevie heard Jean Stirling Mackinley ('Janet MacMurphy' in *Novel on Yellow Paper*) sing, and noted the titles of the songs in her reading notebook. Despite the interest this suggests, Stevie on another occasion irritated the Jacobsons by talking while Louis Kentner played the piano.

As a friend of the Jacobsons, Stevie attended parties given by Kenneth Curwen's mistress, Ursula Greville, in a studio flat at the top of Curwen's in Bernard Street. A description of one of these parties, at which Paul Robeson, Radclyffe Hall or Philip Heseltine might be among the guests, is given in *Novel on Yellow Paper* where Kenneth Curwen becomes 'Henry'. Ursula Greville, in the manuscript, was initially called 'Hesione', but last-minute alterations, probably to reduce the risk of libel, transformed her into 'Larry', a 'ladylike boy' who is Henry's elder brother. The portrait is also slightly muted: Hesione, in the manuscript, is 'a fair dishonest little liar and make-believer'; Larry, in the published version, merely 'full of clever ideas'. Nevertheless, 'backed as he was by Henry's money to cover his risks', Larry confidently hogs the limelight, as the novel describes. His duplicity emerges from Pompey's description of him 'running round and being oh so simple and full of fun, lots and lots of happy fun . . . just a brimful simple child of nature that never stooped to calculate. Oh no.'[3] The heavy irony turns to satire when 'Herman', based on Maurice Jacobson, accompanies the songs that Larry sings. 'and Herman, hastily putting his double Scotch out of reach behind the aquarium – pity the poor fish that never had a double Scotch – and remembering to smile the correct the obligatory Oh-isn't-Larry-Sweet smile would wipe his hands and place his fat little behind on the music stool and chase Larry through all the keys there are.'[4]

Through the Jacobsons Stevie also met Ionée Massada with whom she went riding. An image of them riding together is found at the start of *Novel on Yellow Paper* where Ionée is called Leonie. 'I look at Leonie, she has very good hands but her kneegrip is not so-o-o good. Leonie is a Jewess, but slim, and has a sense of *chic*. She is looking very elegant. She has a yellow pullover and fawn jodhpurs and a fawn felt hat. And who cares.'[5]

Both Ionée Massada and the Jacobsons cared very much about Stevie's use of the term 'Jew' or 'Jewess' in *Novel on Yellow Paper*. The night before the book was published Stevie attended a party at the Jacobsons and on leaving weaved her way tipsily down their steps. On reading the book Maurice and Suzannah Jacobson instantly recognized themselves as Herman and Rosa and were astonished by the vicious personal references. They also objected to Pompey's moment of elation at the start of the book when she recognizes she is the only non-Jew at a party. 'Hurrah to be a goy. A clever goy is cleverer than a clever Jew.'[6] The Jacobsons, themselves Jewish, neither saw nor spoke to Stevie again for more than thirty years. Ionée Massada also broke with Stevie. Not unadvisedly had she begun her book with a valediction: 'Good-bye to all my friends, my beautiful and lovely friends.'[7]

Stevie's anti-Semitic barbs are a part of her shock tactics at the start of the book. Not only does she undercut conventional expectations of the novel with her flippant, self-reflexive style, she also confronts the inadmissible: that Jews, despite her friendship with them, are somehow alien to Pompey. It is important always to distinguish between Stevie and her persona, and not to elide the two. Though Stevie may have felt in some part of herself a similar sense of alienation, and had in her possession a copy of Hilaire Belloc's anti-Semitic tract, *The Jews*, published in 1928, she never displayed anti-Semitic tendencies in her life. Hence her friends' surprise and shock at some of the remarks at the start of *Novel on Yellow Paper*. No truly anti-Semitic writer would have made Pompey the focus for anti-Semitic sentiments as Stevie does. She did so, perhaps because she wished to explore an aspect of her nature which, though she knew it to be discreditable, was a part of her life. Because this sense of difference was real to her she allows Pompey's thoughts to run on, even though, after her elation at being the only goy at the party, she has 'the feeling you must pipe down and apologize for being so superior and clever'. Through Pompey, Stevie mocks those who pretend racism does not exist. Pompey reflects:

'. . . you see I'm a goy. It just comes with the birth. It's a world of unequal chances, not the way B. Franklin saw things. But perhaps he was piping down in public, and apologizing he was a goy. And there were Jews then too. So he put equality on paper and hoped it would do, and hoped nobody would take it seriously. And nobody did.'[8]

Until Pompey emerged with the publication of *Novel on Yellow Paper* Stevie was often in the company of Jewish friends. Again through the Jacobsons she was introduced to the American singer Selma d'Arco who took the latter part of this pseudonym from the paint firm for which her husband worked. They had a car and once took Stevie and the Jacobsons on a tour of five country houses and a castle, all in one afternoon. Molly Smith was also sometimes one of the party, as a photograph of her, Selma d'Arco, her husband and Basil Scheckell attests. But Suzannah Jacobson recollects that Molly, whom she found 'hard and clumsy', only 'hung on' and was never really part of the crowd. Stevie, by comparison, seemed to the

Jacobsons mentally sophisticated, sociable and naturally gregarious. But though seemingly one of the gang, she was capable of extreme detachment, a person for whom friendship and sentiment never veiled human weakness. Her caricature of Selma d'Arco and her husband, and Selma's over-spoilt Pekinese, as Lottie, Horace and Fifi in *Novel on Yellow Paper*, is brief and biting.

'Lottie was mean and thrifty and Horace was too, and fat, and underneath greedy and cruel; but to Fifi and Lottie he was their papa, their little big boy that was clever, and had a great big office where he made money, so that Fifi need never toil but could sit up like a lady on a fine cushion and drink out of a Jacobean goblet.'[9]

One day Lottie decides that Pompey should be better dressed and, with Rosa's help, dresses her in some of her own clothes. Pompey, partly amused at Lottie's shop-assistant expression as she surveys the result, also feels, as she looks in the mirror, that she appears between Lottie and Rosa like Christ crucified between thieves. This martyr-like position, however, changes when Pompey takes hold of Fifi's drinking goblet, pours in stewed tea and holding it up to the light, so that the tea looks like wine, begins to tilt the glass.

'And my face was dark and brilliant and laughing, and Lottie's face was calculating, and then the calculations died, and the eyes were dead. And Rosa was frightened, and then the fright died and the eyes were dead. And I tiptilted the glass still further over, and I let the tea fall on to careful Lottie's carpet. I let the tea fall drop by drop till there was not any left in the glass at all, and I said: Blessed are they that shall not be offended.'[10]

A similar calculation lay behind *Novel on Yellow Paper* ('I should like then to say: Good-bye to all my friends . . .'). If Stevie in her twenties and early thirties observed her friends with unusual sharpness, with an integrity dashed with malice, it was her reading of Dorothy Parker, whose voice, blending with others, provided her with a vehicle of expression for all these thoughts and experiences. If her characters come close to caricatures in the savageness with which they are portrayed, Stevie's justification might be:

> 'Reader before you condemn, pause,
> It was a cynical babe. Not without cause.'[11]

Even those who perceived Stevie's originality were often not aware that she had any ambition to write. In the summer of 1927 she spent a holiday in

Cornwall with Molly and Aunt, and met a young woman called Joan Prideaux, as well as her parents and cousins. 'We were all much attracted to Peggy,' Joan Prideaux recounts, 'as an original and amusing person.' On discovering that they both worked in the same area of London, Joan and Stevie agreed to keep in touch and over the next ten years met fairly regularly for lunch, at the Samovar, a small restaurant in St Martin's Lane, or at Fuller's in the Strand, or sometimes, after the Newnes and Pearson amalgamation, in the canteen at Tower House. Occasionally they met in the evenings, for a meal or to go to the cinema or opera. According to Joan Prideaux, Stevie never talked about poetry. Nor did she give the impression that she was wrongly placed: 'Her job suited her well. She liked and got on quite well with Neville Pearson: it was not too demanding and left time for her to do her own work, and, for those days, was reasonably well paid and her means of support.'[12]

A more visible interest was her love of art. She jotted down in her reading notebooks what was on show in the British Museum print room, and advised herself to look out for Callot's engravings. She was familiar with the Leicester Galleries in Leicester Square, then one of the few London dealers promoting contemporary art. Her taste was unpredictable and literary. In 1925 she was delighted by a Leicester Galleries exhibition of work by Norman Lindsay, an artist she had first seen in a show of Australian artists at the Royal Academy in 1923. She made extensive notes on the 1925 show, compared Lindsay's 'ravishing line' with that of Beardsley, and of his lascivious imagery remarked: 'I don't know that I have ever seen the flesh and the devil so attractively portrayed.'[13] She seems to have been a regular at major exhibitions, catching the Academy's Winter Exhibition of Flemish art in 1927 and the Spanish exhibition sponsored by the *Daily Telegraph* and held at Olympia in 1928. This last she visited with Aunt. The paintings she listed in her notebook would have fed the poem 'Spanish School'.

> The painters of Spain
> Dipped their brushes in pain
> By grief on a gallipot
> Was Spanish tint begot.

Less stringent are her notes on the furniture and *objets d'art* in the exhibition. 'Everywhere lovely porcelain figures, lovely china lovely pewter and lovely furniture. Especially my pet walnut.'[14] Perhaps she was not as blind to the stale fashions and discomfort of 1 Avondale Road as she claimed.

This house remained Aunt's domain, her leonine quietness allowing 'no fuss up there, no fret and fume for guilt and delinquency, no mind sickness and a thought upon death'.[15] But Miss Spear was herself ruffled by Molly's conversion to Roman Catholicism. The friction this created was witnessed by Olive Cooper who felt the situation was not helped by Molly's fiery temperament and readiness to fly off the handle. To Olive, her childhood friend Stevie seemed more steadfast, kind and compassionate, if also highly strung.

What finally pushed Molly into the arms of the Roman Catholic Church was the debate surrounding the 'Deposited' prayer book during 1927 and 1928. Attempts to revise the Book of Common Prayer had begun some twenty years before, in the face of persistent controversies over ritual. The Church of England eventually decided to retain the 1662 prayer book but had incorporated a number of changes. The resultant book was, in 1927, 'deposited' with the Clerk of Parliaments for state approval. Though it had been approved by large majorities in the Convocations of Canterbury and York, it was rejected by parliament in 1927. One of its chief detractors was Joynson Hicks who argued that it leaned too much in the Catholic direction. Re-presented in 1928, with some revisions, it was again rejected, the biggest stumbling block being that it allowed for the Reserving of the Sacrament. Molly was outraged that matters of religious devotion should be subjected to the whims and opinions of secular powers. She became violently anti-Church of England and embraced the faith which looks to no earthly power for its spiritual authority.

Molly's conversion would have obliged Stevie to re-examine her own beliefs. It was at this time that she read *John Inglesant* which, as we have seen, left Pompey with the feeling that she was close to getting into the inside of religion. Stevie also looked at Roman Catholicism: she read Hilaire Belloc's *How the Reformation Happened* and made Molly take her to Farm Street where she talked with a priest. According to Molly, there were no points of rapport between them.[16] Stevie also dipped into Molly's Catholic literature and found those damagingly simplified theological statements which often introduce an element of caricature. Her growing dislike of Catholicism was fuelled by Catholic Truth Society pamphlets, particularly one which stated that unchristened babies would burn in hell. Such evidence of cruelty was not confined to contemporary pamphlets and their dogma but also horribly present in the history of the Catholic Church and its Inquisitions. The more she read, the more she approved Lord Acton's statement: 'If a man accepts the Papacy with confidence, admiration and unconditional obedience, he must have made terms with murder.'[17] Thus while Molly reviled Anglicanism, Stevie came more and more to feel that Christianity, and especially Roman Catholicism, was a mixture of sweetness and cruelty, sentimentality and love, sickliness and strength. This divergence of opinion inevitably created a rift between the sisters and left their relationship strained.

Stevie had lost more than sisterly affection. Looking back on this period when she gradually turned away from the gospels and from Christ, she remembered how her heart had leapt with joy in church when the passage beginning. 'Canst thou draw out Leviathan with an hook' was read. In her mind, it opened up 'spaciousness . . . an absence of dungeons and tortures, and the ghastly smell of the whole pattern of humanity'.[18] Even when she became a declared agnostic, she never lost a yearning for this omniscient power, a being who 'laugheth at the shaking of a spear', 'a king over all the children of pride'.[19] The loss of faith left her disarmed; sadly aware of 'the nerves and the thoughts, that keep such uneasy dance within the mind, the thoughts that go helter-pelter, shattering and scattering the peace of God that passeth all understanding, that never shall I come to know again'.[20]

Wide reading would have helped complicate matters of faith. The second of Stevie's two reading notebooks, which covers the years 1928 to 1930, shows her process of self-education still in operation. Her view of the Inquisition was partly shaped by Edward Gibbon whose prose she read with delight. She especially enjoyed his use of ironic understatement and jotted down page numbers inside the front covers of her 1925 edition of *Decline and Fall*, many of them referring to passages where this stylistic habit can be found. Stevie, herself, was to begin a poem

> Is it not interesting to see
> How the Christians continually
> Try to separate themselves in vain
> From the doctrine of eternal pain

and intended 'interesting', as she told her friend, the Swiss Professor Hans Häusermann, to contain a loud sneer. Interviewed by Peter Orr in 1961, she admitted:

'I think Gibbon's prose is absolutely wonderful and one clutches these wonderful sentences of his about the early Christians when he said: "For it was not in this world that they were desirous of being either useful or agreeable" . . . Indeed it was not an idea that would have occurred to the early Christians. One gets such pleasure out of that, you see.'[21]

Asked what influence this might have had on her own writing, she replied 'it sharpens it, perhaps'. To another interviewer, she openly confessed: 'an author who spurs me to a lot of poetry is Gibbon.'[22]

Another author whom she thought pre-eminent was Racine. In April 1929 she bought, in two volumes, *Théâtre Complet de Racine* and particularly admired his *Phèdre*. His subtle use of formality and reserve in the delineation of passion had for her a cathartic effect. 'Why this poet should have such a power of refreshment,' she wrote in the 1960s, in an *Observer* review, 'I do not know, but to any poor soul enduring melancholy I would recommend him above all others. Even the least loaded lines carry solace ... The mind lifts, the heart lightens. And when the lines are loaded what release is given.'[23] She preferred Racine to Shakespeare. In *Novel on Yellow Paper* she observes that with Shakespeare 'the verse is conventional and the feeling is so warm and so human and so disturbing ... But in Racine there is no feeling of antithesis, the verse and the emotion are perfectly at one, they fuse perfectly and effect the purgation which is the essence of tragedy.'[24]

She herself had learnt this from the Greeks. On leaving school she had taught herself enough Greek to be able to read Euripides in his own language. She also knew enough to criticize Gilbert Murray's translations for their 'too human soft imaginative rendering'.[25] She had, however, bought from Mudie's a copy of Murray's *The Classical Tradition in Poetry* and in her own poetry used not only fairy tales and myths but also various personae to expand and depersonalize her own thoughts and emotions. While admiring the romantic poets of the early nineteenth century, she also assimilated a classical mode of feeling. Racine and the Greeks were always linked in her mind:

'Look at Euripides' *Hippolytus*, and now look at Racine's *Phèdre*. It is the same story, the same story altogether, but Euripides is very profoundly unquiet and restless, so that it disturbs the tragedy, but Racine is very serene, very serene, very austere and simple, and the tragedy very strong and not broken up at all, but very strong and simple. And this tragedy is also very bracing ... very strong and very inevitable and impersonal. This is Greek. This is truly Greek, and what the Greek is.'[26]

She also admired Homer's sardonic handling of gods and mortals, the squabbles on Olympus and on the battlefield. She was later to protest at attempts to abridge the *Iliad* or *Odyssey* in order to make them more palatable for children. Her view: 'Why can't children just read Mr Rieu's glorious Penguin translation?'[27]

In the life around her, Stevie was adept at spotting the comic in everyday exchange, overheard in the office or on the bus. She jotted down examples in her notebooks and later used some of these in *Novel on Yellow Paper*, in the passage headed 'Favourite Quotations'. It fell to her at Newnes to deal with miscellaneous manuscripts sent in by authors who had failed to specify which of Newnes' publications they were intended for. Stevie dropped them all into a kind of jumbo-sized umbrella stand which she occasionally stirred with a shooting stick to see what would come to the top. 'From one of my MSS (office),' her notebook reads, ' – nobody could raise a cocktail like Valerie. At school she had always been top girl in chemistry.' Her attention might also be caught by a headline in an American newspaper – 'Oyster Bars Jam Probe' or by a line by Renan. All her life she was fond of quoting his 'Les natures profondement bonnes sont toujours indécises'. This and other quotations found stuffed into the small 1928–30 reading notebook served her well over the years. What she called 'that blast of objectivity' from Jean de Bruyère –

'Children are overbearing, supercilious, passionate, envious, inquisitive, idle, fickle, timid, intemperate, liars and dissemblers; they laugh and weep easily, are excessive in their joys and sorrows, and that about the most trifling objects; they bear no pain but like to inflict it on others: already they are men'

– thirty years later was incorporated into a review she wrote for *Time and Tide*.[28] As these notebooks confirm, she was stocking her mind with an unorthodox jumble of ideas and facts, jingles and limericks, poetry and prose.

Stevie's 1928–30 reading notebook also contains the refrain of the famous folk song, 'Ach du lieber Augustin', notes on a book of German short stories and others on Prince Max von Baden's memoirs which pay careful attention to von Baden's analysis of why Germany lost the 1914–18 war. These are perhaps the first indication of her friendship with Karl Eckinger whom she met in November 1928.

Eckinger was twenty-four years old, two years younger than Stevie, and still a student. His father was the director of a large electricity generating station at Basle, the town where Karl began as a student of electronics before changing to the humanities. In 1926 he moved to Munich where he continued his studies and met, at an embassy party given for Swiss students, Elfriede Thurner to whom he became informally engaged and whom, thirteen years later, he was to marry. When Eckinger moved on to Berlin to continue his studies, Elfriede remained in Munich, where she had trained at the art academy, and made a living doing a variety of jobs, designing clothes, sewing, teaching textile design and making wall hangings. In the winter of 1928–9, Karl, in order to further his research, entitled 'Lord Palmerston und der Schweizer Sondersbundskreig', and which he published in 1938, came to London and put up at 44 Chepstow Place, w2.

Among certain of Stevie's friends, who knew of Karl Eckinger only by hearsay, he wrongly became known as 'Stevie's Nazi boyfriend'. As a student, Eckinger did occasional pieces of journalism, some for the *Basler Nachrichten*, and, according to his family, was sent to Germany to report on the Munich Putsch in 1923, after which Hitler was imprisoned for a year. Eckinger always claimed that this experience had forewarned him of what was to happen and that he was among the first in Switzerland to recognize the danger of the Nazi threat. He himself felt an antipathy towards the Jews and during the 1920s took steps to eradicate this by living among Jews when he moved to Berlin. Nevertheless, his profound admiration for German culture left him not untouched by the Herren-Denken attitude. He was, therefore, anti-Fascist, but tinged with some of the instincts and beliefs that helped bring Fascism to power.

Culturally he was a child of the Enlightenment, an admirer of Lessing, particularly his *Nathan the Wise* and the respect for personal liberty and religious tolerance it taught. Though he professed a hatred for Wagner and Romanticism, he had a romantic aspect to his nature which he kept carefully hidden. An idealist, he found London sadly wanting, as his letters to Elfriede reveal:

'Oh my! These English are a strange people. There is no feeling of cosiness or comfort in their houses; they themselves are so wearyingly boring that after a bit one feels really unhappy when forced always to hear the same thing or everything viewed from the same limited standpoint. Nowhere that I have been up to now have money and possessions had such a social significance, nowhere else is art so little tied to seriousness, nowhere is it so insignificant in life . . . Everything here deadens joy and ideas.'[29]

English decency and reliability did, however, earn his recognition, partly because the Germans in the student club to which he belonged behaved badly. They caused Eckinger to conclude that Germany appeared to have learnt nothing from the 1914–18 war.

He had a great love of music and played the 'cello. In London he attended concerts given by the Prague String Quartet and by Pablo Casals. He was also unusually interested in art, partly because in Munich he had sat in on lectures given by Heinrich Wölfflin. His desire for culture applied not only to himself but also, by extension, to Elfriede to whom he enjoyed 'playing teacher', as his letters admit. He lost no opportunity to improve her knowledge of music, corrected her spelling of Count Waldstein and told her she used the word 'kontakt' too often: 'As a writer of German you shouldn't use such valueless foreign words.'[30]

His first mention of Stevie appears in a letter he wrote to Elfriede on Christmas Eve, 1928. The letter begins by reminding her how depressed he has been living in England, among businessmen and rationalists to whom art means so little. How fortunate it is, therefore, that he has met a young woman, one of two sisters, and who has a genuine feeling for art.

'She is called Margaret. I first got to know her on a Sunday excursion, about a month ago, through a friend. I've seen her frequently since and my friend and I were invited the day before yesterday and yesterday to spend two days with the two sisters at their aunt's house . . .

I found much that is likeable in her [Stevie]. Even if one discounts the fact that she has a really good knowledge of English literature, she's also a great advantage to me in that I'm learning a lot of English and have to speak it. She has an extraordinarily lively temperament, and if her imagination now and again leads her off the strict straight line of objective correctness, then that does have the advantage that one is never left sitting quietly. Her musical education has really been neglected but there never seems to have been an ideal opportunity for it. Otherwise, however, she is really a nice fellow.'[31]

Eckinger's letters to Elfriede, and Stevie's account of Karl in *Novel on Yellow Paper* are the two main sources of information we have on this friendship. Neither are wholly reliable: Eckinger's is inevitably circumspect, out of respect for his fiancée; Stevie's, for the sake of art, is selective. She once admitted to Olivia Manning and Reggie Smith that she could not invent characters but had to use people she knew, and could not alter the colour of the eyes or hair without losing hold of the character described.[32] The fictional 'Karl' acquires much from Eckinger who did indeed have a horse called Jupiter, as the novel describes, while teaching horse-riding to the cavalry during his period of military service. The two volumes of Goethe's *Faust*, in translation, which 'Karl' brings Pompey, when he arrives on his Christmas visit, bringing a friend called Pierre and a potted plant for Aunt, parallel those found, with Eckinger's card tucked inside, in Stevie's library. It seems likely therefore that the relationship between 'Karl' and Pompey, though fashioned according to fictional needs, contains in essence much of Stevie's relationship with Eckinger.

'Karl's' self-concern amuses Pompey; on visits to Hertfordshire she observes the care with which he, having only two suits, climbs through hedges. England and the English do not always meet with his approval: 'He had a bad way sometimes of getting cross and cantankerous as if he was on the defensive all the time. Do you know how it is with foreigners? They can't let alone but must for ever be telling you how they do things back home. Karl certainly was a sweet boy, bar this.'[33] In keeping with the light, rapid tone that predominates in *Novel on Yellow Paper*, Stevie kept her account of this relationship humorous and playful. Like two gamins, 'Karl' and Pompey break into a deserted house and, despite the cold, lie on some sacking in each other's arms. They are also found walking hand in hand down Bond Street, or in a tea shop discussing Luther:

'Karl and I were having tea at Gunter's when this conversation came up and he said that when Luther got those visions like St Anthony's he used to hop out of bed and stand there in the cold: "You can imagine with what part of his anatomy exposed," said Karl, beaming bright blue German eyes behind spectacles. And Luther was this and that, and strong and single-minded, and not ashamed of his human frailties, which he tried to overcome these ways. And not afraid of his enthusiasms like you English. And your reformation.'[34]

Vexed by his allusion to the Church of England, Pompey darkens with anger, then dissolves into tears and has to leave the restaurant. 'Karl put his arm round me and we walked up and down Bond Street and he said he didn't mind – didn't mind – and I wasn't so much not so much so English. Oh, were you ever so furious?'[35]

In *Novel on Yellow Paper* Pompey suggests that the quarrels which ensue cause the relationship to fail. In actual life the situation was more complex. Karl's account, despite its evasions and silences, reveals a more unhappy exchange.

Karl made it clear to his fiancée Elfriede that he had spoken of her to Stevie. He showed Stevie photographs of Elfriede's paintings and she observed the influence of Van Gogh and even said she would like to buy one. Her liking for these pictures, seen only in black and white photographs, reflected, Karl argued, 'an honest joy and enthusiasm which led her to ask me to write to you'. Perhaps he thought this the most tactful way to introduce Stevie to Elfriede. If so, he was subsequently plagued with doubt as to whether or not he had the right to discuss with another woman Elfriede's paintings and the possibility of a sale. His remorse seems out of all proportion to the issue in hand, and, as one suspects, has another cause which is revealed in the letter that follows. As before, Karl precedes his account of Stevie with a reminder of the difficulties he is experiencing in England.

'You do not know what it means to spend a whole winter in London when one is used to sun and air; what it means to see the sun only a few times during a whole winter and then also through a veil of cloud at a great, wide distance. There is no beautiful bright daylight. But often it is pitch dark in the middle of the day and damp, smelly fog permeates through all one's clothes into the skin. Almost every day it rains at least once. It is cold and damp; one drags oneself through the winter from one cold to another. For if one comes home soaked to the skin then there is nowhere to get warm. In the houses there is no heating but the open fire that is terribly warm close to but which one does not feel at all from a distance and which thus leaves the rooms cold.

He continues in this vein, reminding Elfriede how difficult it has been for him in London to meet interesting people, and how depressed he felt at the start of the new year. He then admits that what has happened between him and Stevie is all his fault. His confession begins:

'You know that I already liked Margaret a lot at that time I wrote to you. She was my only friend here in London; and if you knew how very much alone I felt, you know what that means. I had really got to like her very much and could not bear it any longer when I was so depressed; I had to tell her how much I had got to like her. I never guessed what the result would be, otherwise I would have chosen my words differently (if I had been capable of doing such a thing at all). I totally overwhelmed Margaret that time with my confession. At first she did not understand it at all and then she understood it wrongly and interpreted it as if I were thinking of a real liaison for life. When I then spoke of a friendship and also mentioned that I was leaving England possibly never to return again in the spring, she of course could not understand at all what was going on. She had all kinds of dark thoughts about my intentions and the separation which there is no point in repeating, and I set off in her a kind of terrible passion which often changes from love to great hate. Everything was so puzzling to me. I had known before that the face she shows the world is not the right one. I did not have any idea, however, how very sensitive and passionate she is.'

However biased this letter may be, and deliberately circumspect (at one point Eckinger admits that in making his confession he has deliberately avoided details), it reveals that Stevie's levity of tone, in the passages dealing with 'Karl' in *Novel on Yellow Paper*, is rooted in pain. The above quoted letter continues:

'O Elfriede, in the whole time that I have known Margaret I have seen so much that has touched me. I have got to know so completely the misery of city life where people are poor in the riches of nature and the soul and where they are all strangers to one another. I know how much she suffers because of this, and on that occasion I, still ignorant, fanned this flame with my clumsy hands. I completely lit her passion and totally made her feel the wretchedness of her life. Now you will understand me if I say that I cannot withdraw from her now at this moment. I promised to myself at the time when I made her so deeply unhappy . . . to do everything that I possibly can to give her something positive during the time I am in London. I cannot and do not wish to go back and if I have loaded guilt on myself, then I must now bear the burden of the atonement . . .

We have of course talked about everything in the meantime and she knows exactly how I feel. I have often and totally honestly told her about you, and I have been very pleased that she has always had only good and correct thoughts about you. I have also seen in this period that her pleasure in painting is genuine and natural and that she was always totally honest and objective when she liked your pictures. She spends most of her free time reading or on excursions; she has really read an amazing amount and we always have literature to talk about although I cannot of course keep pace with her in English literature. She also writes herself, every day, and her poems have given me a great deal of insight into her. We have been to the theatre and concerts together and, above all, to a lot of art exhibitions, and through her I have really for the first time gained real insight into the English character by being able to look fully for once into a person.'

The letter ends with an expression of faith in the nobility of Elfriede's soul. He begs her to tell him that he is doing the right thing, and ends 'fully and totally your Karl'.[36]

Despite Eckinger's attempt to exonerate himself, by reference to his unhappy circumstances and Stevie's wretchedness, he was given to 'affairs of the heart' and all his life took evident delight in the company of women. Even if his motive in continuing the relationship with Stevie was basically kind, the element of subterfuge soon came to the fore. Ten days after the above quoted letter he is writing again to Elfriede:

'It is strange; since I confessed to you in my letter the events surrounding Margaret, something seems to have been released within me. It is difficult for me to be with her, I can no longer pretend to be natural and I am so much aware of the great distance between us I almost see everything objectively, as a third person. I have within me the total conviction that she can hardly offer me much that is new any more and, although I owe her gratitude in so many things and I still like her, it would not matter to me to leave London now, at least as far as Margaret is concerned. It is a hard thing to say, I know, but from the beginning I had the feeling that it was this time so to speak "a mission of limited duration". And this time now seems to be over . . .

What Margaret and I had to give each other, we have given; I have seen and experienced very much, above all much, very much that is unhappy and sad. I have experienced a variety of things, so depressing I shall never be able to forget them, and if I have had my eyes opened here in many respects then the whole thing has left something positive behind.'[37]

The letter ends with a passionate restatement of love for Elfriede.

Stevie makes no mention of Elfriede in her account of Karl: it would have introduced complications out of key with the tone she adopts. This tone is distant, humorous and elegiac, capable of dealing with their 'winter campaign of love and strife'[38] without involving the reader too earnestly in its torment.

'And all up and down Hertfordshire from Hertford to Bayford through Monks Green woods over the estates of the Marquis of Salisbury, over Sir Lionel Faudel Phillips's fields, through the woods of Smith-Bosanquet, we fought and raged and also we laughed a lot and kissed and sang. But blacker and blacker grew the storms and the whole of our sky was overcast.[39]

In order to counteract 'Karl's' persistent denigration of England, Pompey instances its poets. How could a nation that has produced such poets be so 'base so materialistic so cynical savage and simian' as 'Karl' made out? 'I remember at this time writing a poem about Karl and me,' she continues, 'that certainly had the truth in it – "and an icy crackling wrath, lies in rimy ridges on us both".'[40] But even the venom in their exchange is treated lightly, humorously, and the pain extinguished.

'It was of course my peculiarly mixed feelings for Karl that drove me deutsch-wards,' Stevie later reflected.[41] This is true not only geographically, in that she was to make two visits to Germany, but also culturally. Association with Eckinger stirred her interest in German art and literature. Her awareness of Germany allowed her much later to look back on this period and condemn the widespread infatuation with France, largely begun by Bloomsbury, and which weakened confidence in native traditions: 'Then any book, any picture, any way of arranging the furniture, anything to eat or drink, if it was French was good. This was our fault, not theirs. The inferiority we wished upon ourselves bred resentment.'[42]

She made her first trip to Germany in the summer of 1929. Through a students' exchange bureau she had arranged to stay with a family called Studders in Halle, a university town, the birthplace of Handel, associated with the chemical industry and now in East Germany. Dr Herbert Studders, the head of the family, is described in a street directory of that period as a 'Referent' which suggests he was a civil servant at expert or consultant level. The Studders become the Eckhardts in *Novel on Yellow Paper* where the father has a government educational job. The house in which the Studders lived in the Saarlandstrasse (renamed in the mid 1930s, and again in 1963 after the Communist functionary, Ernest Grube) is near to the River Saale and situated in one of the top residential areas, in a road lined with chestnut trees. The large detached villa, split into two, where the Studders lived, occupies a corner site and has a large garden.

Stevie must have experienced difficulties with the language. Not until 1931 did she take weekly German lessons with Gertrude Wirth and in 1929 her German was self-taught, acquired from a teach-yourself book. As the Studders spoke no English, she was forced to put her self-education into practice. She spent much time in the company of Dr Studders' wife, called Ludmilla in *Novel on Yellow Paper*, and understood enough of what was said, and not said, to perceive a neurosis which Stevie thought particular not just to this woman but to the more general climate in Germany. The Studders had one child, Hannelore, called 'Trudi' in the novel and also described as neurotic. But this aspect of the family surfaced slowly ('that Eckhardt neurosis got more and more pronounced'[43]) and is not mentioned in the postcards Stevie sent home. 'The people here are ripping,' she told Molly, 'and ever so patient with my embryonic German!'[44] Frau Studders took her on pleasurable visits to Weimar, Dresden and Leipzig. Another card to Molly reads: 'I had a wonderful day in Weimar yesterday with Frau Studders. I really am becoming the complete tourist. Today I am "resting", tomorrow and Friday I shall be in Berlin.'[45] She posted the card on 13 September 1929, in Berlin.

In Berlin, according to *Novel on Yellow Paper*, she stayed with friends of her family called Reise who lived in Charlottenburg. It is not known who these were, nor is there any record that, whilst in Berlin, she saw Karl. It would seem unlikely. A card from Molly to Stevie, written that summer from Henley-on-Thames, tells Stevie of a young Swiss on the same outing who is 'a bit too reminiscent of Karl to be a choice companion'.[46] This suggests that both sisters had, by August 1929, written Karl off. However, among his papers after his death was found a photograph of Stevie inscribed on the back 'FMS Berlin 13 Aug. 1929'. Almost certainly the month given is incorrect. Both in *Novel on Yellow Paper*, and many years later in a letter to Hans Häusermann Stevie said that this first trip to Germany lasted only two weeks. The photograph makes it possible she saw Karl, though it is more likely she gave it to him when they met by chance two years later, on her second visit to Germany.

The brevity of these visits bears no relation to the importance they assumed in Stevie's life. She made pointed use of both visits in *Novel on Yellow Paper* and allowed her experience of Germany to feed the obsession with cruelty that imbues *Over the Frontier*. Even chance purchases, such as a paperback copy of Leo Nikolajewitsch's *Der Lebende Leichnam* (a translation of Tolstoy's play *The Living Corpse*), in Leipzig in 1929, proved useful, for a passage from it, reflecting on marriage and false attitudes, is tellingly incorporated into *Novel on Yellow Paper*. One visit by itself would have perhaps given the delight of strangeness without access to understanding. For her second visit Stevie was not only more mature, she was also better prepared, having advertised beforehand in the *Observer* her need for regular German conversation in exchange for advice on English. This began her weekly meetings with Gertrude Wirth and left Stevie more equipped to experience the complex forces affecting the climate in Germany in 1931.

Again she stayed with the Studders who had now moved to the Wilmers-dorf area of Berlin. Again Frau Studders, her daughter Hannelore and Stevie went sightseeing, this time visiting Neuesdorf on the Baltic coast and travelling by steamer to the spa town Neuhäuser near Pillau, ('Tilssen' in *Over the Frontier*). Before this she had unexpectedly encountered Eckinger in the National Gallery in Berlin. In *Novel on Yellow Paper*, where this is described, Pompey is with Ludmilla (Frau Studders) and 'Karl' is found standing in front of Franz Marc's famous painting, *Der Turm der Blauen Pferde*. 'I love this place [Berlin],' Stevie wrote to Molly, 'and always feel at home here. I went to tea with the Reises in Charlottenburg this afternoon and have spent several evenings in cafés, dancing and so forth. *I met Karl*! in the National Gallery this morning. Incredible but true. I am going with him to Potsdam tomorrow and to Wannsee Tuesday. Frau Studder likes him and has invited him to dinner.'[47] In *Novel on Yellow Paper* 'Karl' comes to dinner 'and Herr Doktor talked the feudal system at him. Certainly that Herr Doktor took ten for boredom every time.'[48]

Stevie spent the next three days in Karl's company. 'I've had a lovely three days in Berlin with Karl', a postcard to the Aunt reads.[49] In her novel she assures the reader that the situation between 'Karl' and Pompey is now *'ganz platonisch'* and they go dancing, swimming, sightseeing and laugh until they cry. 'We could stand up free of each other's exasperation and irritation and aggravation and sickness and love.'[50] This is corroborated by Stevie when many years later she mentioned Eckinger in a letter to Hans Häusermann: 'Feelings were all nicely worked out by then and we haven't written or seen each other since.'[51]

But was it so nicely worked out? Could Stevie have sat in a café with Eckinger for five hours, as Pompey did with 'Karl', without recollecting moments later re-evoked in *Novel on Yellow Paper*?

'But in England we must quarrel, the quarrels must come. Always we were at quarrelling over this and over that. At the foot of the Duke of York's steps Karl said: I love you Pompey. It was December. There was snow on the ground. Outside the door of the *deutsche Botschaft* we kissed: I love you Pompey.'[52]

Towards the end of this book, in a flashback, Pompey recollects being with 'Karl' in a Berlin café when a man carrying a great armful of dark red roses enters. 'Karl' buys some for Pompey and the sight of these roses against her black coat, her black, grey and white scarf and the silvered oak tables remained a vivid memory. Perhaps this incident reminded Stevie of Goethe's 'Heidenröslein' and the mutual wounding caused by the brash boy's plucking of a rose. In 1942 she published 'The Broken Heart' and once introduced it as 'a truly sad love poem, of desertion, I wrote it in Berlin between the wars. It has something German about it, I think.'[53]

> He told me he loved me,
> He gave me red roses,
> Twelve crimson roses
> As red as my blood
>
> The roses he gave me,
> The roses are withered,
> Twelve crimson roses
> As red as my blood.
>
> The roses are withered,
> But here on my breast, far
> Redder than they is
> The red of my heart's blood.
>
> He told me he loved me,
> He gave me red roses,
> Twelve crimson roses
> As red as my blood.

After her three days with 'Karl' in Berlin Pompey found her visit to Neuesdorf with the Studders unbearable and after four days left. She is given the run of her Jewish friends' house in Berlin: 'So there I stayed, with that sweet boy Karl to take me round. But the heart had gone out of it all and Karl said he understood and I just could not bear Germany but was panting to get out.'⁵⁴ They part on the railway station, 'Karl' calling out '*Komm' bald zurück*', as Pompey, leaning out of the window, waves goodbye.

Although this second visit to Germany was made before Hitler was in control, the economic crisis in the winter of 1929–30 had allowed the Nazi party a sudden increase in power; anti-Semitism was now evident. In *Novel on Yellow Paper* Pompey's Jewish friends living in Charlottenburg already have the black *Hakenkreuz* scrawled on their gateposts. If this was also the house where Stevie stayed on her return from Neuesdorf, it would explain why she felt 'awfully nervous' and, on leaving, felt as if she were taking the last train from Berlin.⁵⁵ On this second visit she became aware that Eckinger's idolization of German culture left her uncomfortable. By the time she came to write *Novel on Yellow Paper*, five years later, she realized that his ideal had become hideously perverted by National Socialism and the belief in racial superiority. 'Ah that beloved Germany', she then wrote, 'and my darling Karl. I too can see that idea of sleeping, dreaming, happily dreaming Germany, her music, her philosophy, her wide fields and broad rivers, her gentle women. But the dream changes, and how is it to-day, how is it to-day in this year of 1936, how is it to-day?'⁵⁶ In 1938 she published the poem 'Dear Karl' which acts as an envoi to her relationship with Eckinger. In it, she sends Karl a sixpenny anthology of Walt Whitman's verse. The cheap edition allows her to imagine Karl's scorn and voice his high-mindedness. 'Taste's, blend's, multum-in-parvo's Walt Whitman' is offered as a counterblast to élitism and cultural superiority. Her choice of Whitman, with his all-embracing, tragi-exultant, proud anarchistic attitude to all authority, combined with his love of the demotic, was surely intended to challenge Karl's orthodoxy, his love of high German culture. The farewell – four lines in Whitmanesque style – wishes Karl well in his journey through the book's terrain.

Inevitably, Karl Eckinger himself realized that a sickening parody of German culture was in the making. In Munich and Berlin, as a student, he experienced the collapse of the Weimar Republic at close quarters. When he became a full-time journalist around 1934, working first for *Der Basle Nachtrichten*, then for the *Zürich Oberlander*, of which he became editor-in-chief, his hatred of totalitarianism was always to the fore. He joined the Freisinnige-Demokratische party, then liberal, and fought against German influence in Switzerland and to preserve Swiss neutrality. He continued to serve the Freisinnige with great loyalty, acting for ten years as President of the Wetzikon district group, for fifteen years at the head of the Hinwil regional party and for as many as twenty-seven years as a member of the canton party leadership. As editor-in-chief of the *Zürich Oberlander* he revealed an astonishing range of knowledge, impressing the sports editor with his awareness of the latest athletic records and discussing both Beethoven and the current hit parade with the music critic. He had two daughters by his marriage to Elfriede in 1939 and at home remained always the pedant, becoming, in one daughter's opinion, a bit of a tyrant. But in company, he was admired and respected as a well-known public figure, a man of high political principle, a *bon viveur* and excellent conversationalist. He had a lifelong interest in China which focused more and more on its food, and he sat for hours reading Chinese cookery books. He also had a great love of cats, kept a dozen and on Sunday mornings rose, collected as many as could be found, and returned with them to his bed.

CHAPTER 5

As tiger on padded paw

'She also writes herself, every day, and her poems have given me a great deal of insight into herself.' Karl's discovery was soon to be shared by another. In 1934 Stevie submitted some of her poems to the literary agency, Curtis Brown, and received in return a reader's report initialled 'E.B.'. 'There is more verse here', the reader commented, 'than is put out by most poets in half a life time.'[1] Much of this early verse, some of it quoted in the reader's report, no longer exists. When in 1937 and 1938 Stevie was approached by the University of New York at Buffalo for specimen manuscripts of her poems, to become part of a Poetry and Rare Book Collection, she sent pages torn from two different size notebooks. This suggests that, alongside her reading notebooks, Stevie kept others in which she inscribed her own verse. All her life she continued to use the cheapest of exercise books for early drafts of her poems. But once she achieved recognition, her final drafts would be typed, ready to send off to literary editors. The sheets at Buffalo, however, take us back to the period when she had no outlet for her poetry: written in minuscule script, it remained hidden in the privacy of these books, and the few extant pages torn from these remind one of Pompey's claim: 'I think of my poems as my kiddo.'[2]

Up until the late 1920s her knowledge of English poetry was probably uneven, fed by instinct and personal taste. What may have broadened her grasp was her discovery of Walter de la Mare's packed anthology *Come Hither*, with its rambling, idiosyncratic notes. Stevie's enjoyment of this anthology is made evident in her 1928–30 reading notebook where several of its poems are transcribed in full. This notebook, as a whole, contains more evidence of her interest in poetry than her earlier reading notes. Apart from the pages dealing with *Come Hither*, we find her copying out Byron's 'On this Day I complete my Thirty-Sixth Year' as well as short passages by Chaucer, Marlowe, Donne, Shelley, Victor Hugo, Wilfred Owen, Edith Sitwell and Tennyson which she had encountered in Humbert Wolfe's *Dialogues and Monologues*. (Her notes on this book include advice to herself: 'Do hurry up and get out Joyce's *Portrait of the Artist as a Young Man* and *The Dubliners* and Eliot's *Waste Land*.') Similarly, the poems she transcribed from *Come Hither* affirm her eclectic taste. We can also find in them allusions, echoes and in some cases sources for her own poems, for her assimilation of this anthology was crucial to her poetic development.

She inherited a tradition which, even before the Romantics, associated the bird with the soul, its song with lyric flight. Trapped by earthly love or riches, as in Keats's 'I Had a Dove', the bird dies; or pines, as in Ruth Manning-Sanders's 'Come Wary One' which Stevie copied into her notebook. Here an elf's magic opens the cage and brings the bird release. Stevie, in 'Anger's Freeing Power', was to give this theme a new twist by encasing her bird (a raven) in a three-walled prison where it lives, blind to the ease with which it can escape, until mockery from two other birds arouses its anger. Another poem Stevie transcribed was Sydney Dobell's 'The Orphan's Song', in which a cherished bird repines. This again suggested a theme for Stevie to develop. In Dobell's poem the orphan sees his own helplessness reflected in the bird's famished condition and voices a description of himself with which Stevie may have identified:

> I never look sad,
> I hear what people say,
> I laugh when they are gay
> And they think I am glad.
>
> . . .
>
> With my mouth I read
> With my hands I play
> My shut heart is shut,
> Coax it how you may.

In Stevie's poem 'The Orphan Reformed' a similar famished desire for affection is resolved by the adoption of social deceit: the plangency of Dobell's poem is replaced with a more complex guile:

Now when she cries, Father, Mother, it is only to please
Now the people do not mind, now they say she is a mild tease.

Thomas Hood's 'The Two Swans' was another poem in *Come Hither* that held Stevie's attention. 'This is very beautiful,' her notes read, 'and is also included in Alfred Noyes's collection of fairy poetry.' Again, as in many of the poems she admired, it deals with enchantment and escape: a youth imprisoned in a tower built on a lake and guarded by a monstrous snake, is freed by Love in the form of a swan and, similarly transformed, makes his escape. So great was Stevie's admiration for Hood, both his 'deathly addiction to punning' as well as his straight, non-punning verse, such as his famous 'Song of the Shirt' which she praised for its 'admirable simplicity' and 'careful observation', that she later wrote a radio programme on him.[3] It is possible that the reflected image in Hood's 'The Two Swans' –

> A solitary Swan her breast of snow
> Launches against the wave that seems to freeze
> Into a chaste reflection, still below,
> Twin-shadow of herself wherever she may go

– inspired the verbal reflections in Stevie's 'The Bereaved Swan'

> Wan
> Swan
> On the lake
> Like a cake
> Of soap
> Why is the swan
> Wan
> On the lake?
> He has abandoned hope.

Technically, however, the poem is very obviously indebted to Edith Sitwell, particularly to her delight in the sliding of meaning as one word, owing to slight changes of consonants, slips into another. This and other of Stevie's poems ('Spanish School', 'Bag-Snatching in Dublin' and 'The Man Saul') suggest that in Edith Sitwell, with her cunning use of assonance and dissonance and her control of sound to create subtle changes of speed, she found a technician from whom much could be learnt, one who gave her the confidence to play with words, abuse conventions and be as childlike as she wished.

'E.B.', the Curtis Brown reader of her poems in 1934, was bewildered, not only by the extent of Stevie's output but also by her stylistic experiments.

Internal evidence reveals that the author of the report was female and most probably Eleanor Brockett, one of Curtis Brown's regular readers. Trying to make sense of this 'bewildering conglomeration', she noted 'imitations of Milton: imitations of hymns (example 'Gentle Jesus meek and mild'): ecstatic praise of Lawrence and Huxley and several valiant attempts to out-Sitwell the Sitwells'. She also observed a fixation about sexual perversion and that these, for the most part, apparently formless poems seemed the outpourings of a neurotic mind. 'Ugliness of everything under the sun is dragged out and commented on – particularly sexual ugliness.' At one point, she admits her own taste in poetry may be too old-fashioned to appreciate poems 'so "bitty", so very ultra-1934 and', she added wearily, 'so many'. In her opinion there were too many poor items in the collection to justify submitting them to a publisher. But she had a slight hesitation: 'The reader very much doubts the literary quality of most of the poems but feels there may be some power in them which she has failed to find.'[4]

With the advantage of hindsight, much of Stevie's power seems to lie in her ducking or subverting of traditional expectations. Often she refuses to play the game, preferring an allusive, apparent simplicity to verbal richness and density. If the Romantics formed the central core of her poetic inheritance, it was to be contradicted by her impatience with solemn romantic postures. In her dread of rhythmical flaccidity and verbal deadness, she uses frequent shifts of tone, diction and style. Her mature poetry sometimes slides between varying registers, between grandiose rhetoric and everyday colloquialisms. It is, therefore, not surprising that she admired both Milton and Donne, and herself experimented in high and low styles. She had an eclectic taste and admired great as well as minor poets. Among the poems she copied out from *Come Hither* are many old favourites – Shelley's 'Ozymandias of Egypt', George Herbert's 'Love', Christina Rossetti's 'Up-hill', Hardy's 'Midnight on the Great Western' and Byron's 'So we'll go no more a-roving', as well as less familiar items such as John Fletcher's brief meditation on death, 'I died true', and Walter J. Turner's 'Romance' in which 'Chimborazo, Cotopaxi' magic the speaker away in much the same way that the dark wood transforms the narrator in Stevie's 'I rode with my darling . . .'.

Slowly Stevie was moving towards the stance she outlined in note form in 1952: 'Poetry must be based on religion and philosophy. But only too aware of the ticklish comic element in human suffering. Sense of exile. Human creature "finding its own way home" will have last laugh for all the god's cynical laughter and Nature's equivocal smile.'[5] When she read Stephen Potter's *The Muse in Chains: A Study in Education*, published in 1937, she noted in the book's margins that the question 'Will it live?' must be asked of poetry, and added: 'If so it must have some universal appeal.' She also marked the passage where Potter discusses what qualities a first-class writer must have. For him, these include 'an ethic of vaguely Christian type and knowledge-of-the-heart'.[6]

Crucial in the formation of her own poetic voice was her love of ballads and fairy tales. From *Come Hither* she transcribed the ballads 'Thomas the Rhymer' and 'Fair Annie'. Ballads not only stirred echoes of childhood singing games, they promoted virtues she admired: faithfulness, wiliness and courage. When reviewing *The Faber Book of Ballads* in 1965,[7] she regretted the omission of Kipling's

> What's that that hirples at my side?
> The foe that you must fight, my lord.
> That rides as fast as I can ride?
> The shadow of your might, my lord,

a poem from which Stevie's 'Behind the Knight' is descended. Ballads, like the best, classic fairy stories, are unfudged by sentimentality. 'That is what one wants in fantasy,' Stevie once observed, 'hardness and boldness and fancy riding them.'[8] With modern fairy stories she frequently found, and abhorred, a self-conscious quaintness. The Grimm brothers, by comparison, as she once remarked, were straightforward: 'It is for their reasonableness the stories frighten and hold, for their matter-of-fact, almost gay exploration of hazards, the easy cruelties being no more than is to be expected, if you do not behave yourself.'[9] In Stevie's poems fairy stories offer existential dilemmas in simplified form; they use fantasy materials to reflect on inner experiences, for she knew that fairy tales, though unreal, are not untrue. The Brothers Grimm are noticeably free from moralizing. The role of their stories, like that of religion, as Stevie once said, is to 'carry our hopes and fears and be exciting'.[10] Whether one considers the passage in *Novel on Yellow Paper* where the reader is taken inside a lonely house in a wild landscape, up a stone staircase and into a dining room where food is waiting, after which descriptions of a large stone bath and high bed follow, the whole evoking an enchanted castle, rugged, grand and timeless; or the many occasions in her poems when we are transported into a world of enchanted woods and frozen lakes, and where the Frog Prince, Rapunzel, dragons and knights appear; all bear witness to the legacy of fairy tales in her work. 'There's such a play of imagination in their simplicity,' Stevie remarked of the Brothers Grimm in a radio interview.[11] And elsewhere: 'I love Grimm's Fairy Stories, they are so simple and pure – pure as art – yet

cruel too, as life is cruel. And I like to read them in German . . . The words –
'Es war einmal ein König's Sohn (Once upon a time there was a king's son)
– open up for me the world of dark forests and strange enchantments.'[12]

Of the many forces goading her to write, one was indubitably Newnes,
and the way it both patterned and restricted her life. Often tired, Stevie
wrote poems, in snatched moments during and after office hours, for
pleasure and relief. Exposed to interruptions and the intrusion of others'
personalities and demands, she wrote in conditions that were not advantageous. 'But to a writer,' she averred in print, '. . . the spur of irritation,
storming upon occasion the heights of supreme anger, is of the most
valuable.'[13]

When *Novel on Yellow Paper* appeared in 1936 Stevie became, overnight, a
celebrity. But even before this date she already enjoyed a constantly
expanding network of friends. She made weekend visits to friends at
Ipswich; spent others in Oxford with Mary Alden ('Margaret of Bedford' in
Novel on Yellow Paper and 'Mary of Oxford' in *Over the Frontier*), wife of the
physician and surgeon, John Wenham Alden and who lived on the Wood-
stock Road. In Palmers Green she had been introduced to a family called
Mitchell and was on friendly terms with the two sons, Charles and David.
The Mitchells had moved to Palmers Green in 1918 and even before an
introduction had taken place, had been aware of Stevie's slight, nun-like
figure kneeling in one of the front left-hand pews in St John's Church. Both
the Mitchell brothers had won scholarships to Oxford and went on to enjoy
academic careers, Charles as an art historian, and David as a philosophy
don and specialist on Locke. Charles Mitchell recollects that on their visits
to 1 Avondale Road, where they sat in the dingy sitting room talking to
Stevie, Miss Spear watched over them with a beady, protective eye.

Through the Mitchell family Stevie was to gain introduction to the
Flower family who moved from Croydon to 100 Ullswater Road, Southgate
in the summer of 1936. The Mitchells knew the Flowers before they moved
to this area, owing to their acquaintance with Sir Idris Bell, Keeper of
Manuscripts at the British Museum. His deputy was Dr Robin Flower, a
Celtic scholar who dedicated a large part of his life to an important
collection of manuscripts written in Middle and Old Irish. Every year he
had taken his family on holiday to Blasket Island where the stories told by
the Irish natives were, as he discovered, versions descended from medieval
originals. The whole family could, when they wished, chatter in Gaelic, but
of Robin Flower's four children the most brilliant linguist was Barbara. She
entered Lady Margaret Hall, Oxford, in 1931 and became the first woman

to be awarded the Craven prize for classical scholarship. Her work as an undergraduate, however, was interrupted by a nervous breakdown and as a result she left with only a pass degree. Though from then on dogged by ill health, she remained a gifted philologist and was associated with various scholarly projects, including the translation of Apicius's *De Re Quoquinaria* as *The Roman Cookery Book*. She also taught, at University College and at Glasgow, worked for a short period in the Foreign Office and from 1949 until her death found a congenial home in the Warburg Institute where she assisted with P.S. and H.M. Allen's great edition of Erasmus's letters. Despite an active career, she never fulfilled her initial promise and died from a brain tumour in 1955 at the age of forty-three.

Stevie became a regular visitor to the Flower family home in Ullswater Road. One daughter, Sila, recalls that at one period Stevie seemed to appear every weekend, often quite early in the morning, to join in free-wheeling conversation with the family in the breakfast room which over-looked the garden with its enormous peach tree. In this bookish, relaxed company, Stevie's conversational talent was unleashed. Though she always kept an especial fondness for Mrs Flower (giving her a copy of *Tender Only to One* on her seventieth birthday in 1961), it was in her daughter Barbara that Stevie found a witty, abrasive, malicious humour that matched her own. When alone together, as Sila Flower attests, the two women would crack away without restraint.

Barbara Flower did not share Stevie's love of the countryside. 'I'm just a plain Palmers Green girl,' she would often say, as Stevie reminded a mutual friend after her death, adding, 'She was as obstinately (perversely?) hostile to the countryside as she was to her own scholarship.'[14] Friendship with Barbara Flower extended Stevie's knowledge ('Barbara told me to read this,' another mutual friend, Sally Chilver, recollects her saying) as well as her acquaintanceship. She came to know the poet, novelist and eccentric E. H. W. Meyerstein who often spent Christmas with the Flowers. In addition, intimacy with Barbara helped give Stevie an insight into some of the tensions within the Flower and Mitchell families that were not to be found in her own.

In 1935 Charles Mitchell married Prue Yalden-Thompson who had been at Lady Margaret Hall with Barbara Flower and who obtained a job, first with the Nonesuch Press, then with Chatto and Windus. By 1936 or 1937 the couple were living just around the corner from the Nonesuch Press (in Great James Street) at 4 Great Ormond Street. It was there that the dinner took place which Stevie incorporated into *Over the Frontier*. Though present in the fictional account, Aunt was not there in actuality, nor was the evening quite as uncomfortable as Stevie recounts. In the fictional account, Charles Mitchell is cruelly characterized as 'young professor Dryasdust', a 'clever baby' whose knowledge is wholly confined to books ('the rime of the pedant is upon his young bones'[15]) and who insists on reading aloud from Pater. If Charles Mitchell annoyed Stevie on this occasion, he and his wife were in turn irritated by Stevie's literary name-dropping. Mitchell admits he did read a passage from Pater, and thinks it was, not *Marius the Epicurean*, but Pater's essay on Leonardo. Stevie did threaten to put his topic of research (not Paracelsus, as in the book, but Grünewald, on whom he was working under Fritz Saxl at the Warburg) into one of her books. In *Over the Frontier* the dinner takes place in Edinburgh. Stevie may have at some point visited Edinburgh for she had, on at least one occasion, met H. J. C. Grierson, the professor of rhetoric and English literature at Edinburgh University and the man who did much to advance the study of Donne and the Metaphysical poets: her 1928–30 reading notebook observes the American use of the word 'plant' for 'bury', in relation to the dead, and she adds: 'Prof. Grierson tells me that in the States you can "major" i.e. graduate in embalming.' Grierson's name is also associated with Walter Scott, whose letters he co-edited and whose biography he wrote. Stevie's choice of name, 'Dryasdust', for her host is almost certainly an allusion to 'Dr James Dryasdust', the fictitious character who appears in the prefaces of several of Scott's novels.

Stevie's Dryasdust is harshly drawn. Closely based on fact, the portrait seems cruel and ungenerous. Time and again Stevie used her friends in this way, something that can only be explained by reference to the intensity of her feelings and need to realize them in prose and poetry. What makes the Dryasdust incident still more cutting is the description of the tension, attributed in the novel to financial difficulties, between Dryasdust and his wife whose irritation with her husband eventually embroils her, too, in the angry row. 'Oh return to the vegetable reverie dear Mrs Dryasdust,' sighs Pompey to herself, 'no alas never can the vegetable reverie if returned to be quite what it was before, so happy, so quiet, so inconspicuous, leaving to the professor and myself the onus of the quarrel.'[16]

Surprisingly, Stevie's use of her friends in this instance did not cause a rift. Charles Mitchell, at the time of publication, apparently felt no bitterness. During the war he was sent to Oxford with Naval Intelligence and while he was there, his wife, still in London, was killed by a bomb while dining in a friend's flat in 1940. Stevie received news of this from Barbara Flower, and to her friend Sally Chilver, admitted that uninvited death was a dreadful thing. The tragedy changed Charles Mitchell's attitude to *Over the Frontier* and he now bitterly resented Stevie's use of Prue for Dryasdust's wife. Barbara, informing Stevie of this, admitted that she, too, had for a period shared Stevie's anti-Prue complex.[17] Nevertheless she intervened on Stevie's behalf and evidently healed the situation: when in 1944 Charles Mitchell married Barbara's sister, Jean Flower, and for the next four years lived with her parents in Ullswater Road, Stevie regularly visited.

Perhaps the cruel and slightly patronizing sketch of Dryasdust's wife in *Over the Frontier* was influenced by Barbara Flower's dislike of Prue Yalden-Thompson. Certainly Barbara's view of the Mitchell family shaped 'Over-Dew', the short story incorporated into *The Holiday* and later transformed into a poem. The facts that lie behind it are as follows: around 1938 Barbara Flower and David Mitchell became engaged; at the same time David Mitchell's father retired from accountancy, let his house in Palmers Green and moved with his wife to Oakenrough, a large house in Furnham Lane, Haslemere, founded by the Gurney family as a base for missionaries on furlough. He had previously been a trustee of this house: now he took on full responsibility for its management. In Stevie's story the house, called 'Over-Dew', involves the parents, 'Mr and Mrs Minnim' in difficulty and hardship. Her tale details frozen pipes, money spent on chasubles for visiting priests, financial tightness. Nothing was invented: the chasubles *were* bought and the financial strain made still worse by the fact that the Mitchell's Palmers Green house was now let to the wife of a prisoner-of-war who paid a minimum rent. Stevie's knowledge of these circumstances came through Barbara Flower. Her fiancé, David, on leaving Oxford had experienced difficulty in obtaining a job and had gone to assist his parents at Oakenrough. In a letter to Stevie she described the situation at Oakenrough where there was only one servant to 'do' for as many as thirty people and where Mrs Mitchell was exhausted by overwork and beginning to see through her husband's ambitions.[18] Soon after this Barbara's engagement to David Mitchell was broken off. In 'Over-Dew' Barbara becomes 'Cynthia', the name by which Propertius in his poems alludes to his mistress, and David becomes 'Georgie', the nursery-rhyme character who kisses the girls and makes them cry. Cynthia blames 'Over-Dew' for destroying their relationship, and, in a moment of despair, utters the prayer, 'I devote to Hades and Destruction', an inversion of the Christian principles upon which the parents' endeavour was founded. This vignette of misdirected piety and its effect on others would have shored up Stevie's view that sweetness and cruelty characterize Christian belief.

Stevie herself was to experience a broken engagement, to which the Mitchells, before they moved to Haslemere, were puzzled witnesses. By her late twenties and early thirties Stevie had reached a critical age from the point of view of marriage, on which the suburbs placed much emphasis. She would have been exposed to this pressure which occasional invitations underlined. 'Would you maybe be thinking of a walk at all?' reads one postcard she received from an H. G. Hilton who lived at New Barnet, 'and sup here? or on a Sunday or Saturday (Sunday preferred) earlier in the day?'[19] If she had admirers, only one came sufficiently close to merit fictional afterlife as the character 'Freddy'. Born Frederick Hyde Armitage, but always known as Eric, he was the son of a solicitor who lived in Palmers Green. His family was not uncultured: his father published *A History of Collects* and *Old Guilds of England* and was regarded as an authority on Masonic history, and his grandfather had been a comic writer, one of the earliest contributors to *Punch*. His mother was an imposing, intimidating lady with Victorian standards who doted on her elder son, Arthur, and tended to ignore Eric and his sister Dora. Eric was a nervous child and, though left-handed, was made to write with his right hand. In adulthood he retained a stammer and an excitable, slightly eccentric disposition. As his family was associated with St John's, Palmers Green, it may have been through the church that he and Stevie first met.

Part of the attraction between them may have been a similarity in their circumstances: both were in jobs that left their intellectual powers unchallenged. Eric Armitage spent his working life in insurance, with the Guardian Royal Exchange. In his spare time he enjoyed classical music, as well as Gilbert and Sullivan, and had a particular interest in church history, later in his life giving Workers' Educational Association lectures on church architecture, based on his travels and illustrated with his own slides. He could engage Stevie in theological argument and had a good knowledge of English literature. He was also tall and good-looking, with aquiline features and a neat, if conservative, appearance. He did not, however, impress her friends: David Mitchell found him 'not a very efficient sort of a chap'; Olive Cooper thought Stevie tolerated him out of pity and that he was 'not in her class at all'; Doreen Diamant never forgot her surprise when, in a St Martin's Lane café, Stevie said: 'What do you think – I'm engaged!'; and Joan Prideaux considered him 'the last kind of person (very ordinary) that you would have thought she would want to marry'.[20] While the engagement lasted Molly Smith let it be known that she disapproved.

The scene of their courtship was suburbia. Though geographically Stevie felt an affinity with this landscape of Avenues, Rises and Crescents, spiritually she on occasion viewed it was intense dislike, regarding 'the suburban classes', in her poem of that name, a menace to England's greatness, asses who lie 'Propagating their kind in an eightroomed stye'.

Mentally, but not physically, she wanted to escape. What finally separated Stevie and Eric Armitage was their differing attitudes to suburbia: for Armitage it was a setting in which he was content to find a niche: Stevie, on the other hand, never surrendered her own mental landscape and remained always an alien. But before these differences became insurmountable, both were prepared to step momentarily into the other's territory, even though this caused some discomfort, as the poem 'Freddy' describes.

> Nobody knows what I feel about Freddy
> I cannot make anyone understand
> I love him sub specie aeternitatis
> I love him out of hand.
> I don't love him so much in the restaurants that's a fact
> To get him hobnob with my old pub chums needs too much tact
> He don't love them and they don't love him
> In the pub lub lights they say Freddy very dim.
> But get him alone on the open saltings
> Where the sea licks up to the fen
> He is his and my own heart's best
> World without end ahem.
> People who say we ought to get married ought to get smacked:
> Why should we do it when we can't afford it and have
>   ourselves whacked?
> Thank you kind friends and relations thank *you*,
> We do very well as we do.
> Oh what do I care for the pub lub lights
> And the friends I love so well –
> There's more in the way I feel about Freddy
> Than a friend can tell.
> But all the same I don't care much for his meelyoo I mean
> I don't anheimate mich in the ha-ha well-off suburban scene
> When men are few and hearts go tumptytum
> In the tennis club lub lights poet very dumb.
> But there never was a boy like Freddy
> For a haystack's ivory tower of bliss
> Where speaking sub specie humanitatis
> Freddy and me can kiss.
> Exiled from his meelyoo
> Exiled from mine
> There's all Tom Tiddler's time pocket
> For his love and mine.

These moments of exile, of haystack bliss, occurred unexpectedly after a long walk, in her fictional portrait of their relationship, or when Pompey sits on Freddy's knee in the churchyard in the rain: 'in these moments of close approach and touch and unanimity, how easy it is to think no differences of mere thought can come between us.'[21] Pompey feels very differently when she visits Freddy's home ('I cannot always be in that atmosphere, it is warm . . . too warm and too close.'[22]) and gently mocks the familiar snobbishness with which the family distinguishes itself from their more commonly behaved Bottle Green (Palmers Green) neighbours. But what outraged Eric Armitage's mother when *Novel on Yellow Paper* was published was a reference to their dog whom Pompey is not allowed to smack, even when it damaged her stockings with its claws.

It was not, however, the family that alienated Stevie so much as Eric Armitage's retreat into a suburban mentality. At the start of their relationship, if the fictional account can be trusted, Freddy gives Pompey the impression that he cares little for the suburban scene and more for the things that interest her. A different attitude is, however, revealed when he starts calling Pompey 'high-brow' and begins using the language of popular journalism with which Pompey is all too familiar. Pompey has to offset her irritation against her affection for Freddy; the words of the office messenger – 'Oh Miss Casmilus, I do not know whether I am coming or going' – seem to her all too apt, and she compares her restless drift with that of Paolo and Francesca, her Inferno, 'the gaslit haunts of the waifs of Euston and St Pancras'.[23]

This anguished relationship on which Stevie drew in her novels was also useful to her. As Seamus Heaney so accurately observes: it is essential to bring to her poems 'an ear aware of the longueurs and acerbities, the nuanced understatements and tactical intonations of educated middle-class English speech'.[24] Through her friendship with Eric Armitage, Stevie gained greater familiarity with the social mores of Palmers Green. Likewise, in *Novel on Yellow Paper*, Freddy becomes Pompey's guide, her Virgil to Bottle Green. 'He is a very keen observer is Freddy, and tells me a lot that is so vivid, that I might have known it myself.'[25] She learns that a Tennis Club is, in Bottle Green, a means to an end. For as the magazine agony aunts advise:

'Arrange to play the last set with him, and then linger hopefully and perhaps he will see you home.'

This invites Stevie's irresistible gloss:

'Oh how that is a lovely phrase. Oh how I could not have thought of that phrase it is so rich and full and so pictorial in quality. Well see, can you not see up and down the suburbs, up and down the provincial towns, up and down the country house parties, up and down India, up and down Singapore and Shanghai, how there are girls who have arranged to play the last set and who are lingering hopefully?'[26]

Marriage, she observes, is the *leitmotif* in the lives of suburban girls who believe 'that if only they were married it would be all right'.[27] The lack of self-esteem in this situation arouses Pompey's scorn.

'They ought to be drowned, they are so silly and make so much lamentation, and are wet, and are a burden. And are the public on whom we rely to buy and read our two-penny weeklies . . .

God loves a cheerful buyer of two-penny weeklies, and so do we. These are the girls who believe anything our contributors tell them. They put a spot of scent behind the ear, they encourage their young men to talk about football, they are Good Listeners, they are Good Pals, they are Feminine, they Let him Know they Sew their own Frocks, they sometimes even go so far as to Pay Attention To Personal Hygiene.

It is awfully funny I think the way their allowance of fiction is doled out to these little sweeties. Because they are allowed fiction as well as instructive articles on erotics, oh yes, as well as hard hard lessons in sex appeal, they are allowed to fill their little permanently waved heads with lovely lovely dreams of the never was. That I fear is where they get their funny thoughts on matrimony.'[28]

If here she is attacking an ideology foisted on women, her sarcasm is no less bitter when she proceeds to describe a marriage, soured by domestic drudgery, in which children and hire-purchase instalments create a 'bright little tight little hell-box'. The wife is visited by a former friend from the office who, assessing the situation, suggests that the wife might leave husband, children and home and return to her job. The wife is momentarily tempted, but then reasserts her superiority and reflects pityingly on her friend, unmarried, with no man to wash up for, no children, and empty arms. By now, as Stevie makes her narrator admit, she has sickened of her subject. 'No, I should not have said all this. It is the ugliest thing that could ever have been conceived, because it is also so trivial, so full of the negation of human intelligence, that should be so quick and so swift and so glancing, and so proud.'[29] The mention of pride returns the narrator to the thought of death: 'that rich and spacious thought where human pride is paramount,'[30] and where the self-esteem, so lacking in the lives of suburban girls, is regained.

Inevitably Stevie's distrust of marriage came between her and Eric Armitage. In *Novel on Yellow Paper* Freddy remains Pompey's friend and playmate for two years. They consider marriage and Pompey agrees to wear her mother's engagement ring. But marriage, she realizes, is impossible, and Freddy breaks off the relationship. This announcement is led up to in the novel by a passage in which many of the images and allusions that appear earlier in the book are drawn together. Short staccato sentences beginning with the exclamation 'Oh' create a sense of mounting frenzy. 'Oh night of Pompey,' the narrator cries, and then – 'My sweet boy Freddy has left me' – which, in its suddenness, severs the preceding lament from the recollections that follow:

'No longer prancing forth light and malicious as tiger on padded paw, to play, scratch, pat, prod, prink; to hug, kiss, lick, bite; to lie in the firelight; to be happy; a hearth-rug's ivory tower of bliss, a little space, a time-pocket for love and play and friendship; long days in the summer, playing, tearing, laughing. Long happy hours sped. O'er toppled towers of several ivories. Oh blessed tense that was not was.'[31]

In the analysis that follows, woven into a conversation with William and a digression about a character called Fanto, the narrator reproaches Freddy for losing his sweetness and 'lusting after the habits and thoughts of the insignificant, the timid, the mediocre'.[32] Like Karl in *Novel on Yellow Paper*, Freddy remains something of a caricature, the substance of his character diminished by Stevie's light, mocking style. We are told that he insists on long cross-examinations of their relationship during which he revives in detail past conversations and inveighs against Pompey with constant recrimination. His moods of frustration are contrasted with William's equanimity. Pompey's chief complaint against Freddy is his mediocrity and the cruelty inherent in it. This aspect of their relationship is also the theme of Stevie's poem 'The Devil-my-Wife' which she once introduced: 'It is mediocrity (though people cannot help being mediocre) that makes things so suffering for other people.'[33] In the manuscript of *Novel on Yellow Paper* a fuller analysis of disharmony is given, for this includes passages on Freddy (originally called Ricky) which were omitted from the final book, and which, like the rest of the manuscript in its early stage, as will be discussed later, has the very minimum of punctuation.

'. . . in our hearts we know never never can we marry always when I am with Ricky I know we can never be married it is partly because we have no money but that could be overcome but I work I have my money I live on it it is a little more than his money together ah but there it is we could not really be together at all always he is resenting this and he is very jealous of that and he is saying When will you do my mending, but surely that should not be said because it has to be done certainly but in this sort of a marriage the sort of marriage ours must be if it comes to it the mending must be done but it is not to be stipulated the thoughts run through his mind I must possess you in every way he says I long to possess you altogether when you are married to me you will not want to see so much of Harriet we shall be in our own little home just a home for two for me and you where skies are blue but no human being should wish so selfishly so cruelly and so ungenerously to possess another human being and in Blake's poems I have read these very ominous lines 'Love seeketh only self to please, And builds a hell in heaven's despite' [sic]. Oh now I remember these lines while I am talking to Baz and laughing and so happy to be in his free generous and unexacting company where there is so much happiness for us both and no demands or formulations or stipulations.'[34]

In the published text Stevie corrects her quotation from Blake, omits the comparison with William (called 'Baz' in the above) and deletes the more particularized and personal objections to Freddy (Ricky). Likewise her trenchant analysis of his character is modified in the printed version, here given with the original words and phrases included in parenthesis.

'Oh *männlicher protesting* mereness [Ricky choosing always the inferior], oh inferiority lusting for power and by its [your] own neglect of its [your] own true happiness forced to live at what low level of intellect [intelligence] and spirit [and yet before and at times so loving and so kind could you not have torn that Other out of yourself], taking pleasure in imagined insults and affronts [no never always he must have his own dear pet grievance his injuries and his affronts], to brood upon them in the darkness and operating upon them to beget such knock-kneed down-at-heels wispish, waifish progeny.'[35]

In the published version William warns Pompey against marrying Freddy. In a cancelled passage Pompey reflects. 'I shall find I shall find that little warped and crippled mind nagging worrying turning inevitably for safety to the mediocre and insignificant. I would rather be a king among mice. He has said to me ... oh how very very dim are the friends of Ricky.' In the published account Freddy's friends are also held up for criticism, for it was the suburb that brought them together that keeps them apart.

'"I like simple minds and kind hearts." Ah now wait now just wait one moment, for I know these kind hearts and simple minds, they are not being so very kind and simple at all, they are often very narrow little minds that these people have, and they are not kind at all but very cruel very bitterly cruel, they are not growing at all but very entirely stunted. They turn away from the sunshine, they are strong to come together and in a mass of littleness to oppose every great idea that is at all difficult to understand . . .

Oh my darling Freddy do not be so deeply dippy. You have nothing to do with these people, nothing at all, they are not your people. Leave them to fume and brood and turn ever upon themselves, in what sad place of egotism and imagined injury, growing ever less, contracting, diminishing, becoming more apart and separate, dwindling, diminishing to death.

But in his extreme moods of exasperation he has said to me: Bring your ideas down to earth. You want sense knocked into you. Keep your feet on the ground. You want sense knocked into you.'[36]

This Stevie resisted. The wife Eric Armitage married around 1935 and took to live in a semi-detached house in Potters Bar, a place that had only recently submitted to the march of suburbia, was quiet and supportive. She shared his love of music and reading, knitted dresses and made toy animals for other people's children and outrageously spoiled their own large ginger cat. She had a gentle wit but, as Eric Armitage's niece recalls, never upstaged her husband's humour and always let him be the 'star'. He continued working for the Guardian Royal Exchange until his retirement. He then suffered a kind of nervous breakdown and voluntarily committed himself to hospital, one side effect of which was that his stammer improved. He again went to pieces after the death of his wife in 1975, was at one point hospitalized for dehydration, and a year later died in the street from a heart attack.

Stevie never entirely lost contact with Eric Armitage. All her life she remained on friendly terms with his sister, Dora, who married a Winchmore Hill solicitor, Frank Vanderpump, and would occasionally call round on Sunday mornings for a sherry. She was regarded with affection. When in 1953 the Vanderpumps' daughter and her husband, domiciled in the United States, returned home on a visit, two parties were held, one for the daughter's friends and one for the 'elders': Stevie was the only person invited to both. At the second of these she again met Eric Armitage and was introduced to his wife Katherine. The Vanderpumps enjoyed Stevie's personality but never took her poetry seriously. Nor did it appeal to Eric Armitage, as he once admitted to his niece. 'If only Freddy were not quite so emphatically Freddy but perhaps a little of the chimera I fell in love with,' Pompey at one point exclaims, 'that sweet shape that has vanished from my eyes.'[37] But with it vanished also any possibility of 'the matrimonial swamp'.[38]

Breaking with Eric Armitage left Stevie disinclined to involve herself further with the life of Palmers Green. By the mid 1930s, as *Novel on Yellow Paper* suggests, she and her aunt, and Molly when on vacation, had formed 'a duo-trio of non-communication',[39] a lop-sided family unit, self-sufficient and reserved. Pompey admits to an occasional sadness that the people she sees in the streets of Bottle Green she knows nothing about. Stevie's life was now focused elsewhere, on her friends in town and in the country. There is only slight exaggeration in Pompey's claim: 'at home where I live there is no one I know except the lion my aunt. In town it is almost too exhausting, at home almost too quiet and isolated.'[40] This was to remain the pattern for the rest of Stevie's life.

As her friends increased, the likelihood of marriage diminished. Through Pompey Stevie observes that the rhythm of friendship is antipathetic to the rhythm of marriage: the former has the advantage in that it allows one to come and go. When William tells Pompey, ' "You ride your friendships lightly . . . it is amazing how adaptable you are, how you can get on with everybody" ', Pompey replies, ' "Yes certainly I can get on with everybody, but I am never wanting to get on with them for very long".'[41] What is interesting is the way certain of Stevie's friends inhabited her imagination more than others. She was attracted by independence. The model for Josephine in *Novel on Yellow Paper* and *Over the Frontier* has never been identified, though we know her name was Angela and that she lived in Folkestone. Pompey admires her integrity, her clear-mindedness and her relentless pursuit of the matter in hand. Stevie visited this woman frequently but inevitably saw more of the friend she worked with at Newnes, Narcisse Crowe-Wood, nicknamed 'Bim', and who was often seen hurrying from one office to the next hugging armfuls of paper. Beneath bobbed hair, she had slightly blunt features and a crumpled but attractive face. Partly Greek, with a very individual voice, she was affable and warm-hearted to Stevie who was the subject of occasional unkind stories at Newnes. Grateful for Bim's friendship, Stevie used her as the basis for Harriet in *Novel on Yellow Paper*. 'What I admire most in my women friends', Stevie there avers, 'is what I get in Harriet. She makes me laugh. Second, she has a great sense of *chic*. Third, she is lovely to stay with.'[42] As Pompey recounts, she stays with Harriet when Aunt goes away and they sit up much of the night, smoking and drinking and talking shop: 'That is magazine publishing and colour pages, and the craft, guile and moral turpitude and essential timidity of directors.'[43] As described in the novel, Harriet's flat comes very close to Bim Crowe-Wood's in St John's Wood which reflected the influence of Art Deco. With Harriet, Pompey enjoys gossiping about office life and men, in bars, brasseries and restaurants. Like her fictional counterpart, Bim Crowe-Wood wrote poetry, some of it published in the short-lived Newnes periodical, *Eve's Journal*. Like the fictional Harriet, who has 'a quick bright flashing and illuminating mind', she may also have been planning the composition of two books. If so, her literary interests would have deepened the bond which the novel glancingly evokes:

'And sometimes when we are laughing together, and thinking that together it is easier and we have so very much more fun together than ever we do with our exacerbating, sulky messiah-maniacal, or cross-patchy young men, suddenly the talk will touch lightly on some subject and then up it flares, and out. And sweeping up and out, it is an exultation and an agony, but so sweet it should not be missed.'[44]

When Pompey announces her break with Freddy, Harriet is pleased. One of Freddy's demands on Pompey, in a cancelled passage in the novel's manuscript, is that she should not see so much of Harriet. Loss of Freddy causes Pompey to reflect on her exchange with Harriet. 'How very pleasant and easy and unexacting this friendship is, and how very unconsciously it goes very deep indeed.'[45]

After her misalliances with Karl Eckinger and Eric Armitage, Stevie depended more on female friends; two of those closest to her during the second half of the 1930s were Inez Holden and Olivia Manning. In 1958 Stevie told Professor Hans Hausermann that she had known Inez 'since 1930 or thereabouts'[46] but there is no evidence of this (the earliest letter from Inez to Stevie is dated 1937) and Stevie's dates were not always reliable. It is more likely that they met around 1936, for Inez does not appear in *Novel on Yellow Paper*. Not until Stevie's third novel, *The Holiday*, did Lopez, as the figure based on Inez is called, emerge as crucial to the life of the narrator.

Inez Holden had published her first novel, *Sweet Charlatan*, in 1929. Another, *Born Old; Died Young*, uses as its heroine an adventuress who, like Inez herself, is the daughter of an Edwardian beauty and has begun to live on her wits. Inez also lived precariously. She retained as her earliest memory the sight of her father aiming a gun at her mother and firing. He missed, but even before this relations between Inez's parents had not been perfect. Her mother was said to be the second best horsewoman in Britain; she kept fifteen hunters and refused to spend any money on her daughter; if her visits to London brought her to the Ritz they brought nothing to Inez. Able to get by with the small allowance which her uncle, Jack Paget, gave her, Inez had to supplement this, first by working for the *Daily Express*, then by writing short stories which she placed with the *Evening Standard*, the *Manchester Guardian* and various magazines. She had a sharp ear for dialogue, though this was marred at times by a sardonic irony related to her growing hatred of money, power and privilege. During the Second World War she became a skilled documentary journalist; *Night Shift*, based on her experience of working in an aircraft factory, was praised by J. B. Priestley as 'the most truthful and most exciting account of war-time industrial Britain'; a subsequent book, *There's No Story There*, was based on her experience of a Royal Ordnance factory. She was also sent to report on the Nuremberg trials, journalism, and film scripts for J. Arthur Rank gradually taking over her literary career. Though she had early on won a *succès d'estime* as a novelist, she never reached a wide public, and awareness of this sometimes made her friendship with Stevie tense.

There was also a tragic aspect to Inez. Having been a society beauty, one of Evelyn Waugh's circle and at one time, briefly, mistress to Augustus John, she altered greatly in appearance after an operation, followed by glandular trouble, and put on a great deal of weight. She also suffered from an unhappy love affair with Hugh (Humphrey) Slater, the painter, journalist and editor of the magazine *Polemic*, after which she became slightly misanthropic, disinclined to leave her flat and her cats. Her humour and imagination, however, remained unimpaired. According to Anthony Powell, she was 'a torrential talker, an accomplished mimic, her gossip of a high and fantastical category; excellent company when not . . . obsessed by some "story" being run by the papers, of which she was a compulsive reader.'[47] Another friend, Cecily Mackworth, tells how she and Inez indulged in long conversations in which they adopted the roles of Shakespeare's characters. Cecily Mackworth was not surprised that Inez and Stevie got on: they shared tremendous hypochondria, a readiness to giggle and a love of fantasy. What did surprise was that though Inez was for a period Stevie's closest friend she seemed to know very little about her. According to Sally Chilver, Inez was 'a very brave and remarkable person' with whom Stevie enjoyed an 'easy and humorously argumentative friendship'.[48] Inez encouraged Stevie and like Aunt could be trenchantly dismissive; 'flaming bugger' was her description of one very unlikely candidate. She and Stevie amused each other, discussed plots, people, behaviour; both were sharp, entirely free of sentimentality. Inez once remarked that her friend's fascination with death was the only thing that kept Stevie alive. In 1943 Inez published *It Was Different at the Time*, ostensibly a diary of the period 1938 to 1941. In this, Felicity, 'an average girl of chaos', is based on Stevie.

'Two days ago Felicity came to see me here. She wore a straight black dress and some sandal-shaped shoes; she has a forehead fringe and when she talks her eyes move restlessly from side to side. It was as if I had a girl-Eddie Cantor galloping round my room.'[49]

Felicity, like Stevie, has an inability to be one of a gang, yet a great desire to belong.

'She needed to belong to a group, but could never get a group to suit her. At the time of Munich she felt that she wanted to come out violently for some group – but which one? That was the difficulty. There she was, instinctively against certain sets of people, and these, like the objects of unhappy passion, attracted her most. She attended political meetings. Apparently she did not go to these meetings because she liked them, but because she hated them. But being in the company of only two or three individuals was for her like having to sit through a long and tiresome recitation. She became dull, dumb and deaf with distrust.'[50]

When Stevie retaliated with her creation of the character Lopez in *The Holiday*, her portrait of Inez is warmly affectionate. Lopez is 'this admirable girl . . . who has this admirable courage and this admirable high heart'.[51] She is also 'vigorous' and 'buccaneering', again the kind of brisk, positive, no-nonsense person Stevie enjoyed. But in her account of Lopez's writing Stevie speaks of Inez's work with undeviating accuracy:

'Lopez has this method, she has a quick ear and a wonderful gift for mimicry . . . But in writing, though it is very good in Lopez's writing, it is not always so good, because it is so often something that gets an effect of significance, that is without significance. It is often indeed being an offence against the people, because it is without understanding. So it does not, oh it does not show what people are like.'[52]

For Inez, who had during the 1930s swung from High Bohemia to the extreme left, such a criticism must have been hard to take. This passage may have caused one of the rows that punctuated their friendship and which, after a breakdown in communication, was never entirely repaired.

It was Inez who coined for Olivia Manning the sobriquet 'Whiney' Manning. This was, however, not until the 1950s when, as an established novelist, Olivia felt she was not getting the reviews she deserved and others were getting reviews well beyond their merits. In an unpublished autobiographical fragment written towards the end of her life, Olivia recollected dining with the publisher, Hamish Miles, in Soho in the 1930s when Stevie came over to speak to Miles and was introduced: 'The meeting was momentous. Although she was older than I was and inclined to be patronizing, we saw a great deal of each other.'[53]

Olivia was six years younger than Stevie and, like her, the daughter of a naval officer. She had an Anglo-Irish mother and had grown up in Northern Ireland and in Portsmouth where she took art classes at the Technical College. When she began working in London she had even less background and money than Stevie. She at first lived in a Chelsea bed-sit and typed van lists in the delivery department at Peter Jones. Whilst doing previous temporary jobs, she had used her nights to write two novels and had begun to publish romantic fiction under the pseudonym Jacob Morrow in women's magazines. At Peter Jones she moved on to the studio, to the painting and 'antiqueing' of furniture, and from there moved on again to the book production department at the Medici Society. All this time she continued to write at nights. She also had in Hamish Miles, who had read some of her writing, a mentor, friend and, eventually, lover.

In 1955 Olivia Manning, drawing upon her early experiences in London, published *The Doves of Venus* in which the two friends, Ellie Parsons and Nancy Claypole, bear certain resemblances to Olivia and Stevie at this time. Nancy Claypole, though tall and bespectacled, has many of Stevie's characteristics. It is tempting to conclude that the meeting with Stevie which Olivia found 'momentous' bore a resemblance to Ellie Parsons's meeting with Nancy Claypole.

'Ellie's eyes widened in admiration at Miss Claypole's wit, and Miss Claypole, conscious of having made an impression started to giggle. Her small, ginger-brown eyes, pinpointed behind spectacles, jigged about, giving her so mischievous a look that Ellie giggled, too. Ellie did not know why Miss Claypole was laughing so much, but the extraordinary naughtiness of Miss Claypole's expression, compared with the propriety of her staid body, her severe features, seemed to Ellie unbearably funny. She almost wept as she laughed. Suddenly the two girls were caught up in a madness of giggling. Each time each caught the other's eye, their giggles were renewed: they became convulsive, wild, almost sick with laughter . . .

"What *is* the joke?" Bertie asked with patient impatience.

Neither could answer, but, looking affectionately at each other, they felt the alliance of their femininity, their girlhood and their understanding of each other. They had fallen into friendship, immediate and complete. Their friendship started fully grown; later it was confirmed by the similarity of their circumstances.'[54]

When Stevie and Olivia first became friends both were earning small salaries in untaxing jobs, both had literary ambitions and both were unusually quick-witted. Like Ellie Parsons and Nancy Claypole, they took to roaming London together at weekends and in the evenings. ' "The truth is," said Nancy, "we are natural Londoners." '[55] Many years later Olivia, when walking with her husband Reggie Smith in Covent Garden, broke into giggles as she remembered how she and Stevie had in that area discovered the sign, 'Bananas ripe and turning in the basement'.

As with Inez Holden, Stevie's friendship with Olivia seems to have been marred by professional jealousy. The success of *Novel on Yellow Paper* did not trouble it because soon after, in April 1937, Jonathan Cape published Olivia's first novel, *The Wind Changes*. That same year Walter Allen, novelist, critic and, like Olivia, script reader for Edward O'Brien of Metro Goldwyn Mayer, met Olivia for the first time. Invited to her flat, 466 Russell Court, Woburn Place, he was there introduced to Stevie. Allen, who has attested that Olivia 'had a wit that was devastating and was as formidable a young woman as any in London',[56] observed that both women could be snobbish and malicious and, in their shared views, seemed to present a combined front: 'You could count yourself a friend of Olivia Manning the moment you were introduced to Stevie Smith.'[57]

This bond survived despite a small incident which Olivia describes in her autobiographical fragment, 'Let me tell you, before I forget . . .' When Hamish Miles suddenly died from a brain tumour, Olivia was desolate. Stevie silently observed her grief, but then, in a chatty conversation, let drop that Hamish Miles had regularly visited a certain woman's flat. Seeing Olivia's expression change, she clapped a hand to her mouth and pretended guilt at telling her. As recounted by Olivia Manning, it is another instance of Stevie's capacity for calculated cruelty.

That their friendship survived is proved by what followed. Not long after Hamish Miles's death Olivia was introduced by Walter Allen to two of his friends from Birmingham University, the poet Louis MacNeice and Reggie Smith, then working for the British Council in Bucharest and on leave in London. When Reggie Smith proposed, Olivia discussed the matter with Stevie:

'I am still undecided as ever about getting married. Marriage is so permanent nowadays when one has to wait three years for a divorce. What a barbarous law! Reggie is now staying with Louis MacNeice and I have been seeing a lot of him. He is a nice person. He has asked Reggie and me to go and stay with him in Ireland. His father is Bishop of Belfast and has a place in Cushendael. I know the district well and like it and the weather could not be worse than here. Ernst Stahl is also going. My difficulty is the fact that the very time we should be away is the time when Anthony Gibbs wants me to do film work. I need the money badly, too, what should one choose – experience or money? Money doesn't last long, does it? Louis has also offered us his house on Primrose Hill for a reception should we marry. Such inducements, dearie, make the problem harder.'[58]

Despite her cool indecisiveness, Olivia married Reggie on the day MacNeice and Stahl left, as planned, for Ireland. Stevie acted as witness-come-bridesmaid at the ceremony that took place in a Bloomsbury registry office. Beforehand, as Louis MacNeice recalled, they drank at the Ritz.[59] Walter Allen, who was also present and put this event into his memoirs, does not mention the Ritz but describes the lunch party held afterwards in an upper room at Chez Victor in Wardour Street.[60] Afterwards Olivia and Reggie toured their parents and were about to join MacNeice and Stahl in Ireland, when news arrived that Reggie was needed back in Bucharest. Within a matter of hours they left for Romania. From there Olivia wrote to Stevie explaining her sudden disappearance and asking if books in her London flat could be moved for safety to Stevie's home at Palmers Green. 'Stevie darling, do write soon and tell me lots . . . Take care of yourself. You know how much I want to see you again.'[61]

Stevie did what she could for Olivia while she was abroad during the war. She sent news of mutual friends and London life, and tried to place Olivia's short stories. Meanwhile Olivia moved from Bucharest to Cairo and then Palestine where Reggie became Controller of English and Hebrew Broadcasting. Here, as with his later work as producer for the BBC, Reggie Smith benefited from a disarming directness of manner. 'Amiable as a Newfoundland puppy,' Elisabeth Lutyens has remarked of his BBC years, 'with a generosity as big as his huge frame . . . he befriended the world, giving jobs, money and cheer to all and sundry, almost indiscriminately.'[62] Stevie, however, resisted his charm. Three years after she left London Olivia still felt obliged to commend him to her friend. 'Reggie works terribly hard,' she wrote to Stevie from Palestine, 'he has developed tremendously since you knew him and now the responsibilities of this job are making him much maturer.'[63] He provided Olivia with the original for her character Guy Pringle in the Balkan trilogy and she allows his wife Harriet, to observe: 'In the past she had been irritated by the amount of mental and physical vitality he expended on others. As he flung out his charm, like radium, dissipating its own brilliance, it had seemed to her indiscriminate giving for giving's sake. Now she saw his vitality functioning to some purpose. Only someone capable of giving much could demand and receive so much. She felt proud of him.' It was, however, Guy Pringle's original who had taken Olivia away from London and caused Stevie to lose one of her closest friends. Whatever her personal feelings this was their base. She took imaginary revenge in her poem, 'Murder', published in *Mother, What is Man?* in 1942. In this the man standing beside the grave, taking his farewell of the dead man, admits:

> My hand brought *Reggie Smith* to this strait bed –
> Well, fare his soul well, fear not I the dead.

In subsequent reprintings of this poem tact prevailed: 'Filmer Smith' replaced 'Reggie Smith' and the personal allusion was veiled.

CHAPTER 6

Novel on Yellow Paper

You are not looking at all well, my dear,
In fact you are looking most awfully queer.
Do you find that the pain is more than you can bear?

During the period preceding the appearance of *Novel on Yellow Paper* there are suggestions that Stevie was often subject to nervous strain. She hints at this in *Over the Frontier* where Pompey, having broken with Freddy, takes tablets containing luminal, chloroform and valerian in Josephine's presence. Stevie, on holiday in Cornwall in July 1935, wrote home: 'Doctor's present safely to hand but don't think I shall need it.'[1]

Yes, I find that it is more than I can bear, so
    give me some bromide
And then I will go away for a long time and hide
Somewhere on the seashore where the tide

Coming upon me when I am asleep shall cover
Me, go over entirely,
Carry beyond recovery.

The sudden lift with the word 'carry', in this final verse of the poem 'The Doctor', is lost again with the flat repetition of 'cover' in 'recovery', the poem as a whole, with its to-and-fro movement between colloquialism and lyricism, rising and falling like the sea. The sea, though often linked in her poems with the concept of death, was for her an unfixed symbol. It was also a place to recuperate when on holiday either at Bandol (the subject of her poem 'Bandol (Var)') in 1933, at Port Yerrock in Wigtown Bay, Scotland in 1938, or on the Brittany coast in 1939. Still more strengthening was the unfailing presence in her life of Aunt ('lucky indeed those in close immediate touch with an older calmer undriven generation . . . to draw from them at need upon their strength'[2]) and who, with her sister Molly, represented those familial ties to which Stevie always returned: 'I shall come back to them, my one secure hold, my anchorage in this world of stormy seas, how could I not indeed come back to them, tried a hundred times, faithful and excusing in the most desperate of my sadness.'[3]

Novel on Yellow Paper originated from Stevie's desire to have some of her poems published. Not discouraged by the adverse reader's report she had received from Curtis Brown in 1934, she sent a bundle of her poems to Ian Parsons at Chatto and Windus in June 1935. She may have been acting on the suggestion of her friend Alice Ritchie, whose sister Trekkie was Parsons's wife. Alice Ritchie herself published two novels with the Hogarth Press and was at this time editing *International Women's News*, the journal of the International Alliance for Suffrage and Equal Citizenship, and living in St George's Square, Pimlico, where Stevie occasionally stayed the night. Trekkie Parsons recollects meeting her there around 1932–3 when she came for dinner and throughout most of the evening talked nothing but office gossip. Alice Ritchie was to play a significant part in the making of *Novel on Yellow Paper* where she appears as the character 'Topaz'. She greatly encouraged Stevie, who read to her passages while the book was in progress; she also lent her the Dorothy Parker short stories which influenced the book's tone.

According to Stevie, Parsons told her: 'Go away and write a novel and we will then think about the poems.'[4] In mid August he wrote to her: 'Have you succeeded in placing any [poems] in the quarters we discussed together? I do hope so. Also that you are well away on a best-selling novel which is going to make both our fortunes.'[5] Stevie's reply to the remark about the novel was evidently negative. Parsons wrote again: 'How sad about the novel – but of course I quite see your point and there's no earthly use in your sitting down, scratching your head and sucking your pen, if you don't really feel that you've got it in you. I think Liz's [Alice Ritchie's] suggestion that you should try your hand at some humorous stuff is a very good one, and I very much hope you will be happier being funny than being a novelist.'[6]

If she had initially experienced dejection at Parsons's advice, she now found her direction. In the autumn of 1935 the *New Statesman and Nation* accepted six of her poems, three of which were published on 30 November, two more appearing a week later. David Garnett is credited with their acceptance, though in March 1935 he had ceded the literary editorship of this paper to Raymond Mortimer. Garnett did, however, continue to write the Books in General page and may have supported the acceptance of these poems when he was standing in, as he did on occasion, on Mortimer's behalf. However, in a letter to John Lehmann, Stevie claimed that another *Statesman* employee, G. W. Stonier, had been responsible for the acceptance of her poems.[7] Meanwhile, she had begun *Novel on Yellow Paper*, not with any scratching of the head or sucking of the pen, but writing six thousand words in one night 'in a dream state', as she told a journalist, adding that she had completed it within ten weeks,[8] if not six, as Molly Smith afterwards claimed.[9] Almost certainly it was finished before Christmas 1935 because by 9 January 1936 she had returned a 'revised' typescript to Ian Parsons. At that stage the novel was called *Pompey Casmilus*, a name Parsons thought brilliant but unsuitable as a title for a book.[10]

Like Laurence Sterne, who composed his first volumes of *Tristram Shandy* at fever heat, Stevie had swiftly released an intoxicating stream of observations which, though fresh and surprising, grew out of a body of thought that had matured over a long period of time. Sterne acknowledges in *Tristram Shandy* his debt to Locke's *Essay concerning Human Understanding* – 'a history book . . . of what passes in man's own mind'. Stevie, who had acquired a copy of *Tristram Shandy* in 1921, may have had this in mind when, near the start of *Novel on Yellow Paper*, she alludes to Johnson's *The Vanity of Human Wishes*: 'For this book is the talking voice that runs on, and the thoughts come, the way I said, and the people come too, and come and go, to illustrate the thoughts, to point the moral, to adorn the tale.'[11] This talking voice leads us through incidents, descriptions and states of mind which create a chain of opposites: elation and despair; the cruelty and neurosis of 1930s Germany and the Aunt's soundness and integrity; a vision of hell and the bliss of a haystack – Pompey's ivory tower. The narrator's throw-away and often malicious humour belies an underlying seriousness; gradually Pompey's chatter discloses her 'tiger-clawing' response to cruelty, vulgarity and stupidity as well as the underlying theme of death, not death as an end in itself but as an ever-present possibility that can strengthen our ability to cope with the appallingness of life: 'Always the buoyant, ethereal and noble thought is in my mind: Death is my servant.'[12]

At Ian Parsons's suggestion Stevie revised her original manuscript. In its original state, as certain manuscript pages reveal, she made only minimal use of punctuation, the words flowing unhindered until a natural pause invites the use of a period. Almost certainly her model was the final chapter of *Ulysses* which captures the flux of thought and feeling left in the mind after a day crowded with impressions. After revisions had been made, Stevie's text was divided into paragraphs and treated to orthodox punctuation. In doing this she experienced some regret, and inserted into her text a passage that warns the reader about the kind of book she has written and records her dislike of punctuation: 'Oh talking voice that is so sweet, how hold you alive in captivity, how point you with commas, semi-colons, dashes, pauses and paragraphs?'[13] Yet, following another's advice, she compromised her talking voice, thereby radically altering the nature of her text. Once punctuated the book became more ordered and polite. There is a loss of flow, a stifling of the voice. Whereas before the unravelling thought created its own pauses and rhythms, the introduction of correct punctuation artificially divides it up; and this segmentation of the veil of conversation, from behind and through which interesting things emerge, damages the relationship between this flow of chatter and what lies beyond it.

The revised typescript pleased Parsons who passed it on to Chatto's readers, meanwhile telling Stevie he hoped soon to be able to make her a formal offer. He was unprepared for the resistance he was to encounter in his seniors at Chatto's, Harold Raymond and Charles Prentice, who were influenced by a reader's report that complained of a lack of backbone. This reader concluded: 'I think the lady is brilliant, no less. But I think her vein, her most profitable vein, would be as a regular contributor to the *New Yorker*. She has that humour which, delicious even the length of a long article, simply does not do in a book.' A second reader added to this report his opinion that the book was 'clever and impossible'.[14] Parsons, to his infinite regret, was instructed to reject the book. He was perhaps the first to perceive that, far from wanting a backbone, the book has 'a continuously developing theme, a kind of spiritual Quixote's Progress with a very definite unity and shape', but in the same letter he was obliged to state: 'I find myself in the hateful position of having to hand back to you a book which I encouraged you to write, praised you for when you had written, and even insisted on making you attune to my suggestions.'[15]

This letter would not, however, have caused Stevie despair. When in November and December 1935 the *New Statesman and Nation* had published five of her six accepted poems they caught the attention of Hamish Miles, who, as a reader for Jonathan Cape, asked Stevie if she had written anything else: 'I feel sure that we should read any manuscript of yours with unusual interest.'[16] Stevie told him of her novel, promised to Chatto and Windus, and Hamish Miles replied: 'As for the novel, I quite understand that in the circumstances Chatto and Windus have first claim, but if they should not wish to publish it I should be very glad to read the manuscript.'[17] Miles would also have read Stevie's poem 'Freddy', the last of the original batch accepted by the *New Statesman* and which they published on 11 January 1936. This, for many readers, was the poem that signalled the appearance of a new voice, and its originality and charm helped create the readership for *Novel on Yellow Paper*. Hamish Miles received the manuscript on 14 February and wrote to Stevie on 2 March telling her of his delight in it. This, he added, was his 'personal reaction', and she will understand 'it would not be an easy book to publish'.[18] Nevertheless when the book appeared in September of that year it won instant acclaim.

Many who read the book at the time felt it was quite unlike anything they had read before. 'Its personal, button-holing narrative brought one vividly and intimately into her world,' the novelist Helen Fowler has written.[19] But despite its singular appeal, the book (accurately described in the blurb, not as a novel, but as a soliloquy) is rooted in the stream-of-consciousness technique and is indebted to Stevie's assimilation of Proust, Joyce, Dorothy Richardson and Virginia Woolf, all of whom find mention in her reading notebooks. She had, for instance, read the first of Virginia Woolf's collections entitled *The Common Reader* which contains her famous essay 'Modern Fiction'. In this Woolf demolishes traditional conceptions of plot and character and promotes instead a roving, glancing consciousness receptive to the 'myriad impressions' that the mind receives in the course of a day. One passage, in particular, could stand as a manifesto for *Novel on Yellow Paper*:

'Examine for a moment an ordinary mind on an ordinary day ... the moment of importance came not here but there; so that, if a writer were a free man and not a slave, if he could write what he chose, not what he must, if he could base his work upon his own feeling and not upon convention, there would be no plot, no comedy, no tragedy, no love interest or catastrophe in the accepted style ... Is it not the task of the novelist to convey this varying, this unknown and uncircumscribed spirit. . . ?'[20]

Stevie's admiration for this book has earlier been mentioned. The notes she made on it include a passage copied out from the essay 'The Russian Point of View' in which the novels of Dostoevsky are compared to 'seething whirlpools . . . composed purely and wholly of the stuff of the soul'. Woolf's concern to reinstate human nature at the centre of the novel, and to rid them of circumstantial clutter, enfranchised Stevie from the need for plot, chronological development and the more traditional play of character. In her well-known essay 'Mr Bennett and Mrs Brown' Woolf argued that in order to reflect the soul accurately we must 'tolerate the spasmodic, the obscure, the fragmentary, the failure'. *Novel on Yellow Paper*, with its abrupt changes of mood, its apparently random use of quotations, tags, homilies and invocations, and its confrontations with human imperfection, fits within this vein. After reading this book, the poet Robert Nichols assumed the author's name to be pseudonymous and wrote to Virginia Woolf: 'You are Stevie Smith. No doubt of it. And *Yellow Paper* is far and away your best book.'[21]

What makes the book so very unlike Virginia Woolf is its inspired and distinctive chatter. It darts and swoops from incident to incident, from the lyrical and poignant to the comic, colloquial and sometimes cruel. Pompey's interior monologue has an effervescent naturalness; she flirts with her readers, takes them into her confidence, rebuffs them, the book having an openness and immediacy that Virginia Woolf's prose does not allow. Stevie was much influenced by her reading of American novelists. Not only does her informal humour relate to an American tradition that goes back to Mark Twain, but her vocabulary signals her delight in the conversational American voice, its energy and vulgarity. This was still something fairly new in English novels. When Sinclair Lewis's *Babbitt* appeared in 1922, the English edition had appended a glossary of American slang. Reading Lewis's *Martin Arrowsmith* Stevie had jotted down in her 1924–27 notebook: 'Good . . . the Americanese is beautiful.' And in a cancelled passage in the manuscript of her third novel, *The Holiday*, she remarks of the American language: 'why look how sappy it is, full of juice isn't it, real live growing stuff.'[22] Nowadays terms like 'kiddo' and 'bratto' which appear in *Novel on Yellow Paper*, may seem dated and irritating, but in 1936 they presented an effective and delightful challenge to mandarin prose.

Certain American novelists would also have extended her awareness of the monologue's potential. After reading Sinclair Lewis's *The Man Who Knew Coolidge* she remarked: 'It's amazing that you can read this book at all, it's just one long monologue. But you can, easily. Did ever anyone so completely reveal himself?'[23] The monologue is delivered by Lowell Schmalz who claims friendship with President Coolidge with whom he was at college. He tells, among many other things, of his visit to the White House to see Coolidge and how he was respectfully turned away by the staff. The story is later retold and embroidered, with Schmalz actually meeting Coolidge and discussing with him taxation and foreign affairs. Schmalz is a garrulous, very average business man whose speech is full of colloquialisms, euphemisms and contemporary slang. Sinclair Lewis obliges the reader to

assume the role of Lowell Schmalz's audience. Stevie's handling of monologue is more self-reflexive, more subtle and more completely representa-
tive of the play of thought.

American influence can also be felt in the rhythms of Stevie's prose. The
model for those passages where there is an insistent repetition of word or
phrase ('So he put equality on paper and hoped it would do, and hoped
nobody would take it seriously. And nobody did') is Gertrude Stein. There
is no mention of Stein in Stevie's reading notebooks, which cover the years
1924 to 1930, but almost certainly she had read the best-selling *Autobiography of Alice B. Toklas* which appeared in 1933. Both authors energize their
prose through self-conscious rhythmic effects, but Stevie's rhythms are
noticeably lighter and less ponderous. The debt to Stein is important, even
though Stevie chose to acknowledge only the influence of Dorothy Parker
whose concentrated hatred of stupidity fired some of Stevie's more satirical
passages. It is, however, the American accent in *Novel on Yellow Paper* that
Stevie later recognized as 'brassy', 'pseudo' and unnatural to her. It quickly
dated and, in later years, aroused her dislike.

Stevie's discursive, gossipy voice descends from a long tradition of
talkative writers which inspires a tone of voice that is gay, mocking, at times
good-natured, at others reproachful, intimate and often teasing. One
precedent for this that Stevie clearly had in mind was De Quincey's
Confessions of an English Opium Eater in which the author's avowed aim was
'to think aloud, and follow my own humours'. Pompey, in *Novel on Yellow
Paper*, admits to having learnt 'purple passages' from De Quincey by heart,
and she draws a parallel between the anchorage provided by De Quincey's
sister and that which she has in her aunt.[24] In addition both authors conceal
distinct intentions beneath an engagingly idiosyncratic manner, leave their
readers in doubt as to how seriously we are to take the narrator, and
combine autobiography with visionary fantasy, gaiety with sadness. De
Quincey's observation – 'So blended and intertwisted in this life are
occasions of laughter and of tears' – perfectly describes Pompey's condition.

Like De Quincey, Stevie cleverly weaves quotations from others into her
prose, snatching, for example, a well-known passage from Tennyson's
'Tithonus' to evoke the 'loamishly sad' days of her childhood. Her handling
of narrative and its tempo is extremely skilful. Drawing upon quotations
from others, perception, memory and speculation, she keeps up a brisk pace
('Brace up, chaps, there's a 60,000 word limit') which distracts, at first
reading, from the melancholy which, as the book proceeds, increasingly
pervades it. Looking back on this period, in an essay on Eliot's *Murder in the*

Cathedral, published a year before *Novel on Yellow Paper*, Stevie suggested that a prevalent frivolity masked guilt and uncertainty.[25] A similar dichotomy characterizes her novel.

The title 'Pompey Casmilus' was presumably abandoned by Stevie after Ian Parsons objected to it. Story has it that the manuscript circulated Cape's untitled and was referred to as 'the novel on yellow paper', owing to the cheap yellow paper, used at Newnes for copies of letters, on which it was typed, and in this way it acquired its name. The name of its persona was less arbitrarily chosen. 'Pompey' is taken from Pompey the Great whom Stevie would have encountered in her *Selected Letters of Cicero* and which she read in Latin. Cicero describes Pompey as a man of integrity and high moral character, but this was after his death and masks earlier criticisms; nowadays he is regarded as a highly complex character. One aspect of his make-up that may have appealed to Stevie was his capacity for deep and lasting friendships. Perhaps, too, she noticed in her Lemprière's *Classical Dictionary* that Pompey the Great, despite his wealth, 'lived with great temperance and moderation, and his house was small, and unostentatiously furnished'. In *Novel on Yellow Paper* Pompey observes in passing that there is something meretricious and decayed and elegant about her name. Stevie's characterization of her persona may in part have been influenced by Sacheverell Sitwell's poem, 'Doctor Donne and Gargantua', for she had copied out the following passage into one of her reading notebooks and quotes the first two lines in her novel.

> Pompey is an arrogant high hollow fateful rider
> In noisy triumph to the trumpet's mouth,
> Doomed to a clown's death, laughing into old age,
> Never pricked by Brutus in the statue's shade.[26]

Casmilus also carries diverse allusions. In this case Stevie admitted that she resorted to Lemprière's *Classical Dictionary*, and having the 1832 edition, found under the entry dealing with the god Hermes or Mercury, the phrase 'known also to the Phoenicians as Casmilus', which is a misprint for Camilus. One of this god's attributes is his ability to come and go freely in hell. Writing to the playwright, Denis Johnston, after a fan letter on *Novel on Yellow Paper* had begun their friendship, Stevie argued:

'Casmilus is a dark name to fight under and he was a most awful twister he is the Phoenician Mercury-Hermes but the fact that he had the right of entrance to (and ahem exit from) hell has always fascinated me what a bore for instance he must have been for Pluto, Minos and Rhadamanthus, pursuing his frightful trivial quarrels into their country and doing a good deal of self-advantageous business on the side I make no bones to say.'[27]

In subsequent editions of *Novel on Yellow Paper* Stevie underlined the relevance of 'Casmilus' by adding a brief introductory verse begging indulgence for stealing his name. She also wrote the poem, 'The Ambassador', which, in her friend Polly Hill's copy of *Harold's Leap*, she subtitled 'the god Hermes, known as Casmilus'. It begins, 'Underneath the broad hat is the face of the Ambassador', which refers to Lemprière's argument that Hermes's 'petasus' imitates the broad hat worn by the Phoenicians on their way to places of exercise. Significantly, in the publicity photograph taken by Howard Coster for *Novel on Yellow Paper* Stevie also wears a broad-brimmed hat.

By the time Stevie wrote *Over the Frontier*, where she again makes use of the name Pompey Casmilus, she had begun to tire of the joke: 'But enough of the Casmilus motif, shiftiest of namesakes, most treacherous lecherous and delinquent of Olympians, enough.'[28] But in *Novel on Yellow Paper* it is a crucial strategy. By placing her persona under this conductor of souls, this tutelary deity, described in the book as 'double-facing, looking two ways, lord of the underworld, riding on the white horse, riding through hell, opener of doors; Hermes',[29] she is able to allude, through Pompey Casmilus, to her own ambivalent feelings towards the Jews, to her manipulation of her past for future advancement, to her love of horse-riding and, most of all, to her fascination with death. She makes the reader confront the modern hell of German cruelty and neuroticism and in several vignettes opens doors on to others' lives. Pompey Casmilus's free-ranging thought parallels Hermes's uncircumscribed journeyings; her ability to look at discomforting truths and intolerable despair parallels his familiarity with the underworld. As guides into another world, both are by nature well equipped to attack dullness and folly.

Pompey Casmilus is related to, but by no means a copy, of Stevie's personality. Pompey's hale and hearty manner ('I am a forward-looking girl and don't stay where I am. "Left right, Be bright," as I said in my poem. That's on the days when I am one big bounce, and have to go careful then not to be a nuisance'[30]) exaggerates Stevie's liveliness. When Pompey insists, 'I certainly have a flippant and frivolous mind,'[31] the persona presented imitates only one aspect of Stevie's character. Pompey's bravado – 'But oh how I have enjoyed sex I do enjoy myself so much I cannot pass it over'[32] – contradicts the absence of sensualism in Stevie's life. In *Gentlemen Prefer Blondes*, which Stevie had read and admired, Anita Loos, for ironic purposes, gives to her scheming adventuress, Lorelei Lee, a naïve tone of voice. Similarly, Stevie imposes on Pompey a certain brashness, at times even a silliness, that helps sustain her easy, conversational monologue but which now and then edges dangerously close to the facetious and creates a tone of voice that lacks the complexities found in Stevie's own character. Pompey, the gossipy, office-girl persona, can irritate: she deplores 'smarties' who write high-faluting books on social problems; she passes a large amount of her time in 'enjoyable frivolity', in savouring the lives of others for, like her author, she spends much time visiting friends and is *'toute entière* visitor'.

Some of Pompey's mannerisms can be traced to Geoffrey Dennis's novel, *Harvest in Poland.* Stevie read this in 1926 and made extensive notes on it. Like Pompey, Dennis's hero Emmanuel Lee frequently addresses the reader; he dilates on his reading and knowledge in a tone of voice that is rapid and inconsequential. He quotes a poem written on the back of a programme after watching the Russian ballet, and adds: 'How dare the fool reproduce such sorry stuff? – Search your own programme-backs, Camerado; fossick and rummage among your own sweet-and-twenty bits of paper: are there no sorry verses there?'[33] Elsewhere he ends an argument over the translation of a temperature from Fahrenheit into centigrade with, 'Work it out for yourself', the advice Stevie repeatedly gives her readers. When Pompey calls herself 'the cleverest living Pompey' she echoes Dennis's character who claims, 'I am the cleverest living Pole'. Elsewhere, the play on good and evil and religious questions in general, as Neville Braybrooke has shown,[34] makes *Harvest in Poland* a book of especial importance for Stevie. His Gothic fantasy has an absurd, at times almost surreal quality, and its wackiness may have given Stevie the encouragement to make her own imaginative leap, to treat emotions and ideas with a certain fling. Dennis's racy flippancy showed Stevie how to hurry past certain things without allowing the reader to ask too many questions. This glancing lightness also enables her to deal swiftly, but piercingly, with that 'vision of cruelty' presented by 1930s Germany. The neurosis Stevie experienced in 1931 she never forgot.

'And now look how it runs with the uniforms and the swastikas. And how many uniforms, how many swastikas, how many deaths and maimings, and hateful dark cellars and lavatories. Ah how decadent, how evil is Germany today.'[35]

Pompey, recollecting her previous thoughts about the Jews, now realizes the full danger inherent in her pride at being a goy, for it is 'as if that thought alone might swell the mass of cruelty working up against them [the Jews]'.[36]

Stevie merely nudges her readers on the issue of Jews. No mood stays with her for long. Travelling back from Germany engulfed in sadness, she filches a fellow traveller's copy of *Lady Chatterley's Lover* which instantly cheers her. *Novel on Yellow Paper*, we have been reminded in an early self-explanatory section, is a 'foot-off-the ground novel': 'And the thoughts come and go and sometimes they do not quite come and I do not pursue them to embarrass them with formality to pursue them into a harsh captivity.'[37] Instead, like Kismet, the horse Pompey is riding when the book opens and who crops at everything in sight, her mind darts from one thing to another. The horse, prancing and strong, must be held in check but, like Pompey's spirit, is only partially tamed; though Pompey asserts 'I can pull up when I want to,'[38] her spirit, like the horse as its name implies, has a will of its own. Kismet is, perhaps, a personification of the tremendous mental energy animating Stevie's life. 'Crop, spirit, crop thy stony pasture!' is the injunction with which her poem 'The Failed Spirit' ends, and Kismet's omnivorous cropping can be compared with Stevie's ruthless use of her friends in this novel: all experience is food for her. As a writer, she is an adventurer in human understanding, her motivation a cropping beast which she must ride, for it is through the consumption of pain and experience that immortality is reached. This idea ('All the writer can do . . . is to offer his life, which seems to him so shadowy and inconsiderable, to some god or other for him to chew upon and make the best of'[39]) recurs in Stevie's writing, in her poems 'So to fatness come', 'God the Eater' and 'Childe Rolandine' ('This cropping One is our immortality'). The notion, that spiritual power can be achieved through the assimilation of suffering, is eloquently stated in the passage from *John Inglesant* which Stevie quotes in *Novel on Yellow Paper*. Stevie's interpretation, however, is less Christian than Platonic, placing the form of the good, the potentially god-like, in us.

Kismet is no stately horse and Pompey sometimes finds herself 'full of wicked bounce'.[40] It was always unlikely that Pompey, the adventurer, would have been trapped in domestic and suburban circumstances through marriage with Freddy. Freddy's departure represents a climax, not only because it is a moment of high grief but because it returns Pompey to her own spirit, her own energy, her Kismet.

Novel on Yellow Paper is essentially a poet's book. Not only does Stevie at intervals incorporate her own poems, as Lewis Carroll and the Grimm brothers also do, but she tells the reader 'you get the first look in' at verse she intends to publish. Writing this novel must have given her enormous release. It was, as Paul Bailey has remarked, 'a clearing-ground for later simplicities; the necessary letting-off steam of a poet in embryo'.[41] She had appeared in print as a poet before the appearance of *Novel on Yellow Paper* in the pages of the *New Statesman and Nation* and, as has been mentioned, the last of her six poems, 'Freddy', drew considerable attention. Its use of plain statement ('Nobody knows what I feel about Freddy') and deliberate lack of emphasis; its unexpected half-rhymes and abrupt changes of mood and rhythm; its daring use of syllabic variation in each line; and its seeming casualness and rhythmic cunning gave it a striking originality and charm. Eager to see more of her poems in print, Stevie wrote in May 1936 to John Lehmann, who had just produced the first issue of *New Writing*: she had around 180 unpublished poems – would he like to see some or all?[42] Lehmann took none. Not until after the appearance of *Novel on Yellow Paper* were Stevie's poems in demand.

Stevie perhaps had an intimation of the book's success when William Morrow and Co. of New York bought up the American rights in August 1936. The English edition appeared in early September. One of the first reviews was David Garnett's in the *New Statesman*. He found 'the slapdash pseudo-American slang acquires . . . a strangely poetical quality',[43] and gave it a laudatory reception. Richard Church, writing in *John O'London's Weekly*, was struck by Stevie's 'wild poetic sensuousness', her 'gift for just the right phrase to create a scene, or present a mood', noting also that 'she does it always by this trick of slight derision and understatement'.[44] Edwin Muir, on the other hand, found the book 'compellingly exasperating', only 'probably worth reading' as a 'well-sustained picture of a disillusioned flapper's mind'.[45] The delight and disgust voiced by the critics found an echo in the letters Stevie received. On the one hand there were fan letters from eminent people: Kenneth Clark, then Director of the National Gallery, praised her invention of a style 'with the rhythms of speech made poetry, and the rhythms of poetry disguised in slang';[46] the literary critic Raymond Mortimer admired the book's poetry and humour, predicted it would have wide appeal and invited Stevie to lunch; and Clive Bell, the art critic, declared it one of the best books he had read for some time. But why, he asked, did she call herself a 'foot-off-the-ground person'?[47] Stevie replied:

'I think when I say I am an off-the-ground person I am thinking of my own mind, that is perhaps not very perfectly balanced, at least it seems to fly off at a tangent rather easily . . .

I take it when you say you are a two-feet-on-the-ground person you mean that you have this balance and quietness? I think and hope I have it too in some ways, for instance when I am talking impersonally in this book. But the Freddy-situation seems to have got well away on the wings of Casmilus, and the Thanatos-Hades bit might appear a final off-the-ground gesture and flight into darkness?

But thank you again very much for your letter. It cheered me up enormously, because you know a lot of people do not like my book at all. However these people are mostly my friends who are cross because they are in it, or because they are not in it.'[48]

Those angered included her Jewish friends, as she told her editor at Cape, Rupert Hart-Davis: 'I am getting rather isolated now because a great many of my not-so-dear friends will no longer speak to me – Rosa, Herman, all the Larry-party crowd and Leonie more in sorrow than anger has withdrawn because she thinks I am an anti-Semite.'[49] She had also enraged her uncle, Alf Hook, with her portrait of 'Uncle James' and he told mutual relations that 'Peggy' needed her bottom smacked. Even Madge Spear at first disliked the book but regarded it more favourably after she read some of the reviews.

Novel on Yellow Paper turned its author overnight into a celebrity. Pompey's conversational tone had left many of Stevie's readers as her fan letters reveal, with a sense that they had direct access to her mind and could therefore assume intimacy, many addressing her as Pompey and disclosing the unhappiness caused by their own Freddies. Success inspired confidence and encouraged Stevie to hope afresh that a volume of poems could now be published. Since May, when she had sent John Lehmann 180 poems, she had written many more. Some she posted to Frances Phillips, an editor at William Morrow and Co., who were bringing out *Novel on Yellow Paper* in the States. She also sent 186 poems to Rupert Hart-Davis at Cape. Simultaneously she was at work on a sequel to her first novel – *Over the Frontier*. In this Pompey refers in passing to 'these three hundred poems that must be retyped selected and discarded', a number that does not seem exaggerated for there were by now so many Stevie had begun to lose track of them.

'No I am not surprised that you have not had time yet to read the poems [she wrote to Hart-Davis] because there are so many of them. Today I have a letter from Frances Phillips to say that Morrow cannot do them in book form but you know I really did not know they had them and I cannot now remember which ones they have but I think they did not have so many as you have so it is getting rather confused . . . this poem situation.'[50]

A further complication was that, though she wanted her poems published, they caused her discomfort. Many years later, in conversation with Jonathan Williams, she admitted that these early poems had 'not much recollection in tranquillity – there's fear and pain and disgust and dislike and all those rather negative things'.[51] Similar feelings are expressed in *Over the Frontier*, written whilst this first collection of verse was being made.

'Do you see, dear Reader, the cold feet I am getting, and the feeling as I read through these rather disturbing rather unquiet rather hateful poems that I had better quit writer quit or prove the bane of all that on earth I love? It is a neurosis and to be resisted, of course . . .'[52]

Perhaps, too, she was fearful of the distress that adverse criticism can cause. She referred in her prose not only to the excoriating remarks of F. Caudle (Florence Gibbons) but the damning observation of another, probably a literary editor, who remains anonymous.

'There is nothing worse than the not perhaps quite funny enough. For this, Reader, is what the young man said to me when I sent him a poem. And then I felt, There is certainly nothing worse than to be not funny enough. Indeed it is better to be serious. And I thought, in future I will just write little delicate and sad pieces that are full of unshed tears, and at the same time *noble* . . .'[53]

With help from Rupert Hart-Davis and Hamish Miles, she eventually selected seventy-six items for her first book of poems, *A Good Time Was Had by All*, a title that she took from parish magazines where the phrase frequently concluded descriptions of social events or church picnics.[54] Though Rupert Hart-Davis is said to have suggested illustrations which Stevie then offered to do herself, this seems unlikely. In the course of making the selection Stevie told Hart-Davis that the *New Statesman* had copies of some of the poems as well as 'a lot more drawings'.[55] From the remarks that follow it is clear the magazine had had these drawings for some time. Moreover, the poignancy and precision of the illustrations to *A Good Time Was Had by All* suggest that Stevie was a practised draughtswoman. She had an eye for good illustrations, admiring, for instance, Chesterton's understated art in his drawings for Belloc's novels, and never forgetting her delight when at the age of eighteen she discovered Colette's *Claudine à l'Ecole*: 'I particularly liked the pictures, beautiful line drawings, as lively and

malicious as the story.'[56] The claim that Hart-Davis originated the illustrations is further thrown into doubt by the fact that when the poems first
reached him they already had 'the beastlies', as Stevie referred to her
drawings, attached.[57]

When the book appeared in the spring of 1937 the *London Mercury*
thought the illustrations 'delicious', some of the poems 'too private and
personal to be satisfactory' but that all had 'an agreeable bite'.[58] Almost no
poem in *A Good Time Was Had by All* is without its surprise. Not only do they
span a variety of genres – lyrics, satires, epigrams and variations upon
nursery rhymes – but within a single poem are often to be found abrupt
changes of tone and mood. 'Alfred the Great', for instance, begins with the
rhetoric of the *Te Deum* ('Honour and magnify this man of men') only to
deflate it in the next line with its reference to crude financial facts ('Who
keeps a wife and seven children on £2.10'). Still more prosaic is the third
line ('Paid weekly in an envelope') which is rhymed, mock-heroically, with
'hope' ('And yet he never has abandoned hope'). Elsewhere it is the skilful
distribution of emphasis that keeps the reader alert. 'Up and Down' begins
with a tripping rhythm –

> Up and down the streets they go
> Tapping tapping to and fro
> What they see I do not know

– which is broken in the last verse by the sudden introduction of two
spondaic feet and the increase in gravity this brings.

> I shall be glad when there's an end
> Of all the noise that doth offend
> My soul. Still Night, don cloak, descend.

If this diverse collection has a unifying characteristic it is this deft handling
of quicksilver changes of tone. In 'Papa Love Baby' the voice teeters
between the formal and colloquial, recounting tragedy in what at times
sounds like drawing-room comedy. Disturbed by its ambiguous sentiment,
one critic has remarked of this poem: 'We feel like mourners at a funeral
where the coffin is dropped and the corpse rolls out. We are torn between
horror and mad giggles.'[59] This awareness of the comic or absurd element
inherent in human life and human relations punctures portentousness and
is one of Stevie's strengths.

Another recurrent feature is the frequent use of echoes from and
allusions to the poetry of others. This is most noticeable in 'Maximilian
Esterhazy' and 'Death of Mr Mounsel'. In the second of these the poem

opens with a phrase from *Antony and Cleopatra* and then continues, line by line, with quotations and misquotations. The obvious paradigm for this use of fragments is *The Waste Land* which Stevie advised herself to get after reading Humbert Wolfe's *Dialogues and Monologues*. Wolfe's comment on this poem could apply to 'Death of Mr Mounsel':

'*Waste-Land* may be regarded as the chapter headings in a library on ethnology. It is, in fact, an encyclopaedia on the origins and decay of life. Eliot realized that each line must be the headline for a volume, and, by so constituting it, would become poetry.'[60]

She did not repeat the experiment represented by these two poems which, if not her most memorable, contribute to the diversity of *A Good Time Was Had by All*. As a first collection, the book has a range and flexibility that are impressive. Moreover it delivers its messages in a cunningly deceptive manner: with an openness and ease that contain unexpected, unsettling complexities, as her most perceptive reviewer observed:

'These poems are triumphs of tone: and the tone is doubly controlled. For the tone of each individual poem – whether gay, ironic, witty or reflective –is subject to the further control of a reserve tone which forms the unifying background of reference of this book. This is Miss Smith's habitually detached and critical frame of mind. This system of double reference, and the use of a characteristic thought-structure which expresses only prominent ideas clearly and the rest implicitly, enables Miss Smith to deliver her intensities – however slight – without change of voice, and in the manner of public utterance. The result is a seemingly careless verse whose impact is both immediate and personal.'[61]

To the novelist, Naomi Mitchison, Stevie admitted that *A Good Time* represented 'the scouring of about ten years of illicit office scribbling, generally as you will see in a rather unsatisfactory and futile round or is it square peggishness'.[62] *Novel on Yellow Paper* had introduced her to Naomi who had written a fan letter which began a friendship: over the next three years, up until the outbreak of war when Naomi left London for Carradale in Scotland, they were in frequent contact, Stevie attending parties at River Court, Hammersmith where Naomi and her husband entertained artists, writers, politicians, Fabians, pacifists and supporters of the Labour Party. At one of these Stevie met the critic, Philip Toynbee. 'Dearest Stevie,' Naomi afterwards wrote, 'Here is your Little Cross; I suppose it came off when tempted; or something. I know absolutely ALL because I nearly sat on you by mistake and so did several others . . . Seriously, if you can cope with Philip at all, I do wish you would.'[63]

Occasional asides in their correspondence suggest that both women, whilst enjoying literary success, felt outsiders in the literary world owing to their sex. Stevie's affection for Rupert Hart-Davis did not blind her to Cape's slightly underhand behaviour with regard to payment for legal advice on the dangers of libel in *Novel on Yellow Paper*. She told Naomi: 'I had the most awful fight with Cape over the nauseating sum of £2. 14s. 1d. I repeat *and a penny*, won my point (I'd already fought and won it last September but that is ganz gleich the pets nicht?)'[64] Rupert Hart-Davis had grudgingly to admit: 'You write like an angel, but you argue like a fiend.'[65] But immediately prior to this it had been Stevie who had erred; she sent in further addenda and proof corrections when *A Good Time Was Had by All* was already half printed. Informed of this, she telegrammed Hart-Davis:

'Deeply shocked sad news letter eleventh instant stop please advise Alden [printers] future limit themselves errors manuscript not invent own beast-lies avoid apostrophes idiotic interpolation of stop query acknowledgement [omitted] New Statesman poems previously published stop God make me better girl Love and XXXXXXXXXXX Stevie[66]

The success of *Novel on Yellow Paper* drew Stevie firmly into the literary world: editors, now familiar with her name, either accepted or asked for her poems or offered her reviewing. Overnight this anonymous secretary had become a personality with so distinctive a voice that for a long while afterwards she was to be hampered by association of her name with the 1930s.

A New York agent suggested she should write short sketches for magazines. Lydia Lopokova, the ballerina, actress and wife of the economist Maynard Keynes, asked for monologues that could be performed on the radio. Stevie wrote two, one based on a society woman watching a cricket match whose thoughts 'run backwards and forwards like the long shadows across your beautiful green grass', the other voicing the thoughts of a young wife, alone in an apartment in Shanghai, as she writes a letter to her husband who would be offended by emotional display. The trivialities that she permits herself to write bear no relation to the 'very ferocious and secret' personality that she keeps hidden.[67] Lydia Lopokova rejected both monologues on the grounds that they needed visual contact and dramatic action to make them work. But she was grateful for Stevie's quick response to her request and thought both pieces had 'beauty, imagination and a sort of silliness with inteligence [sic]'.[68]

The writing of *Novel on Yellow Paper* seems to have unleashed Stevie's creative energies. She straightway began work on a sequel, as John Hayward the critic and bibliographer discovered, when he struck up a friendship with her in the autumn of 1936. Not only had he puffed *Novel on Yellow Paper* in his weekly London letter for the *New York Sun* but he had written to thank her for the 'intense and continuous pleasure' the book had given him.[69] He also wrote to the novelist Rosamond Lehmann:

'I'm quite mad about Pompey's book. I had to write to her about it and she wrote such a charming letter in reply. It's all true – I mean her story! And I'm going to meet her next week at Jonathan Cape's.'[70]

What had charmed him was perhaps her suggestion that his letter had helped her. She told him:

'Already there is half of a new Pompey written, but then it suddenly seemed to me impossible that anyone would at all care for Miss Casmilus, so I stopped. Your letter encourages me to go on . . .'[71]

The sequel, *Over the Frontier*, was completed by November 1936 and would have appeared late 1937, in time for the Christmas market, if fear of libel had not delayed publication until January 1938. In the meantime Stevie's name had begun to appear with a certain prominence in a variety of magazines.

Not only did she begin reviewing for *John O'London's Weekly*, *Life and Letters* and the *London Mercury*, but her poems seemed to proliferate in print. The witty and elegant *Night and Day*, modelled on the *New Yorker* and edited by Graham Greene and John Marks, published a clutch of her poems in 1937. Though the magazine ran for a mere six months, Stevie found herself among a glittering array of talent for the contributors included V. S. Pritchett, John Betjeman, Cyril Connolly, William Empson, and Alistair Cooke, among others. Nevertheless, as a letter from John Marks to Stevie reveals, the magazine had a fear of the highbrow and at first rejected the poems she submitted. When she sent another batch, Marks accepted ten outright and was prepared to print two more – 'Portrait' and 'Via Media Via Dolorosa' – if Stevie would allow them to use, in each case, only the first verse. With the second of these two poems, Stevie agreed, which suggests a lack of confidence in her own judgement. A fear of seeming highbrow may explain why the poems that appeared in *Night and Day* do not show her at her best and were never collected in book form. In the case of 'Sterilization' (posthumously reprinted in *Me Again*) the reason must be that the poem is too nakedly declamatory, lacking in resonance, whereas Stevie's poetry, at its most characteristic, works subterraneously, obliquely; instead of being sensibly pedagogic, it acts insidiously, its words allusive but its meaning often ambiguous and unfixed.

During the course of 1937 she was also approached for verse by the *Bystander*, for their Christmas edition, by the *Fortnightly*, who also held out the possibility of reviewing, and by *Granta* who incorporated into their May Week Number (9 June 1937) eight of Stevie's poems, some of which were never reprinted. This was also to be the case with other poems published this year, in *Lilliput* and the *London Mercury*. The latter was a distinguished magazine, founded in 1919 as the first monthly review to devote itself exclusively to literature and the arts. It had praised *Novel on Yellow Paper* and in its November 1937 issue featured four of Stevie's poems as well as a drawing of her by the South African artist, Geoffrey Wylde. The following month eighteen short poems appeared in the *London Mercury*, fourteen of which were never republished. Stevie's leaning towards minimal presentation could result in slightness, both of form and idea. Even the humour is sometimes weak: 'This Baronet is very funny / And I do so hope he makes some money / He deserves to for not being a pompous ass / Like the Bishop of Bye and Mrs Grumpus'. But even in this group of mostly short poems grief, loneliness and desolation emerge as prominent themes. Both *Granta* and *London Mercury* used Stevie's illustrations, and were unusual in doing so. All her life Stevie had to battle with editors and publishers to get her drawings accepted. They look particularly good in the *London Mercury* December 1937 issue, contributing a festive note and alleviating the monotony of the previous pages where long lines of print are punctuated only by the occasional gloomy woodcut.

In the offices of these magazines Stevie sometimes made new friends. At *London Mercury*, situated over the *New Statesman* in Great Turnstile, she met Armide Oppé who had taken over from Dilys Powell as reader of manuscripts. Armide had read classics at Somerville College, Oxford and had worked for a period in Rome, as secretary to the famous classical scholar, Mrs S. A. Strong. With her knowledge of classics Armide quickly saw that, though Stevie's grasp of this subject was very limited, it was well used: 'She made great play with the little she knew, but knew it in a consuming way so that it really did become a part of herself. And her analysis of it was very perceptive from a human point of view.'[72]

Another person in the literary world who became a friend and ally was G. W. Stonier at the *New Statesman*. An Australian, educated at Winchester and Christchurch, he had spent all his working life with the magazine, having joined it on leaving Oxford, and had been groomed to succeed its first editor, Clifford Sharp, but never did. For a period after the departure of Desmond MacCarthy, he had stood in as literary editor until David Garnett was officially appointed to this position. Garnett, being something of a 'sleepy' editor, left much of the work to Stonier who continued to act as right-hand man to his successor, Raymond Mortimer. Though he did once propose to Sonia Brownell, Stonier was shy and misanthropic, quiet and elusive, with a wispy moustache and a bald tonsure-like head. He was, in his own estimation, a poet who never wrote a line of poetry and who was afraid of nearly everything. This and other perceptions about himself, writers and writing he put into his book of aphorisms, *The Shadow Across the Page*. But the gentle image that he created did not prevent him writing scathing reviews, if he so wished. After the 1939–45 war he became the *New Statesman*'s film critic, writing under the pseudonym, William Whitebait. He also set weekend competitions under the name Willy Tadpole. Elsewhere a fishy name could usually be ascribed to him. His editor, Kingsley Martin, observed: 'He never seemed to belong to the world in which the rest of us lived.'[73] After a late marriage, in which tropical fish took the place of children, he turned his back on civilization and acted as navigator to his wife as she drove across Africa in a land rover, a journey that began at Cairo and would have ended at the Cape had not misfortune, either illness or accident, stalled them permanently in Rhodesia.

Stonier was certain that it was either he or Garnett, and not Mortimer, who first accepted Stevie's poems. When *A Good Time Was Had by All* appeared he reviewed it perceptively and favourably. 'Soon,' as he recalled,

'she took to dropping in at the office with a folder bulging with poems typed on little pink or pale green slips, each with a drawing attached. These we'd go through, or she would leave them for me to mull over. (After Garnett left . . . I had charge of the miscellany section – poems, stories, etc.) In general I preferred the short bright pieces to the long and weeping, not only because they fitted in better, but I thought she strayed too easily down sad corridors with Death's door at the end. In this way I may have tended to overlook or push back something essential to her; certainly it preponderated later.'[74]

When Cape turned down her third novel, *The Holiday*, in which tears play a significant part, Stevie asked that it be sent to Stonier for a second opinion. He panned it and for some time afterwards they did not meet. Thereafter the book was never mentioned, though the friendship continued, lasting in all some fifteen years, as Stonier describes:

'We enjoyed a light, occasional lunchtime sort of relationship. I'd ring up and we'd go to Soho or St Martin's Lane. Her spontaneity was infectious.

"I'm glad it's you," she might say as we threaded our way on the sunshiny pavements, "and not the other George – we'd probably be going to the Express Dairy." This was George Orwell, who like many saints had his comic side. So, over scallops and white wine, we'd exchange gossip and fun, she with her two baronets, I with droppers-in at the N.S. [*New Statesman*], including some mild monsters such as Joad, Laski, Herbert Palmer, Claude Cockburn and others. She'd tell me about the parties she'd gone to, and I'd enjoy the telling more than going myself. There was much then, it seemed, to giggle about – even through the war years – and our mice-in-the-wainscot relationship might have gone on and on if I hadn't got married (in '52) and drifted away.'[75]

Stonier was himself a source of gossip in relation to Stevie. It was said she invited him to Palmers Green once while the Aunt was away and was obliged to ring up a friend and ask what one 'did' to a tin of sardines. Stonier, in fact, made more than one visit to Avondale Road, the Aunt was always present and they never ate sardines. 'Between me and Stevie,' he recalled, 'there never existed more than a possibility which may have grown stronger at the time of my visits to Avondale Road, but nothing more.'[76] His own story regarding Stevie's cooking was that once when Auntie broke a leg Stevie rang him at eight in the morning to inquire how one boiled an egg.

If helpless in the kitchen, Stevie in the office played nanny to her baronets. Once when Stonier dropped in at Newnes Stevie had gone out to buy a christening mug because one of the baronets had to perform as godfather and had made no preparations. At Newnes, in an age when office discipline was strict, dress and behaviour very much more formal than today, Stevie appeared trim and efficient. 'Back in the thirties when I knew her best,' Stonier has remarked, 'there was always refreshment in that little odd neat world with her at the centre. One stepped in and out of *Novel on Yellow Paper*. It was all so self-sufficient . . . and of course those little poems on pink and green slips, the nub of it . . . She had her crystal world, clear, indestructible, while I flitted through overlapping worlds, belonging to none. So her talent shone bright, till it and she were used up. Lacking certainty, I never extended myself enough . . .'[77]

If self-sufficient, her world was not always secure. Within the firm's higher echelons there was a certain distrust owing to her recent success. In October 1937 Stevie told Denis Johnston: 'I have been warned that here they do not look with favour upon my writing; that I am immoral, and subversive . . . I think it is an amusing situation, rather a little bit dangerous too, for instance they made me alter lavatory to washplace, that shows you how refined we are in Southampton Street; but in many ways they are also very kind people and have perhaps been after all very longsuffering, so I shall hope I shall go quietly if I must go.'[78] If the threat was real, it soon passed. 'Storms at the office seem to have drifted overhead,' she reported to Johnston in November, adding that things might change in January when *Over the Frontier* appeared.[79]

Stevie had much to distract her from friction at the office. She led a party-going existence which was counterbalanced by life at Avondale Road, Aunt's soundness creating an unchanging horizon that threw into perspective the frenzy of Stevie's social and literary world. She, who enjoyed the catty, malicious wit of a literary pundit like Malcolm Muggeridge, returned home late at night to savour the sight of Lion Aunt feasting on cold game pie, a bottle of beer and crusts of bread. This same aunt was one to whom the writing of a letter to her relative at Somerset House on the problem of tax caused much difficulty.

'First she has to make a rough draft, which she reads over to me. It is very funny, and very indignant, and very indistinct, like someone is choking they are so cross. And always the word position comes in, because my aunt never knows how that there is only one "s" in this exasperating word. But somehow all the same the letter gets written, with all its i's dotted and its t's crossed. And then there is some more fuss up, and another roaring and lashing because the stamp she put under the bronze statuette of Van Dyck is no longer there. But finally and at last the letter is posted, and then there is a moment when you are almost deafened it is suddenly so quiet.'[80]

Simplicity and ordinariness were two of Aunt's virtues: she did not have clever ideas about painting and literature, Stevie gladly observed. After a hilarious description of her Aunt, dressed as a fan for a church bazaar, she quickly adds an apology:

'Darling Auntie Lion, I do so hope you will forgive what is written here. You are yourself like shining gold.'[81]

When *A Good Time Was Had by All* finally appeared, Stevie's friend Naomi Mitchison wrote a review that began by discerning a fundamental difference between the poet and reviewer. Stevie had talked with Naomi about Blake and this provided a central idea. 'Because I myself,' Naomi Mitchison begins,

'. . . care passionately about politics, because I am part of that "we" which I am willing to break my heart over, and can no longer properly feel myself an

"I", because that seems to me to be the right thing for me to do and be, I see no reason why everyone has got to. Stevie Smith can still be an "I". And that's good.'

She describes Stevie as one of those 'who are aware of their epoch but don't let themselves get done in by it'. She concludes: 'Such people don't have to be "we"; they can be "I", proudly and bouncingly as Blake was . . . Stevie Smith bounces with Blake.'[82]

If Stevie was attracted by Naomi Mitchison's independent thought, she was sometimes irritated by her trenchant views. Looking back on this period, Naomi Mitchison has herself admitted: 'I was a lot too fond of making strict judgements, especially political ones and sticking by them irrationally in the way politicians tend to do.'[83] Stevie evidently thought the same, for after dining with her she told Denis Johnston, 'more talkie from Naomi Mitchison, and she's got world problems on the brain too'.[84] She reproached Naomi: 'Yes, our times are difficult but our weapon is not argument I think but silence & a sort of self-interest, observation & documentation (I was going to say "not for publication" but I am hardly in a position to say that!).'[85] Nor indeed was she, for when *Over the Frontier* appeared in January 1938 much in it reflected on the threat of war. But all her life Stevie objected to a pessimistic indictment of current affairs, suspecting that it contained a self-gratifying element, and herself preferred a more stoical outlook. 'There is a sort of hubris in this world-worrying,' she told Naomi Mitchison. 'For if you have achieved peace in your own mind, when the worst happens (if it does) you will have reserves of strength to meet it.'[86]

CHAPTER 7

The Power of Cruelty

A year before she died Stevie sent Lord Moyne a copy of *Novel on Yellow Paper*: 'I don't really like this, you know. But I am delighted to send it to you, though now you may agree with me. Perhaps it was all right in 1936.'[1] That same year she autographed Roger Senhouse's copy of *Over the Frontier*, adding, 'I do not *very* much like this one.'[2] *Over the Frontier* opens in a similar conversational style to its predecessor whose brassy tone, as has been mentioned, Stevie came to dislike. Freddy also reappears, owing to a temporary reconciliation between him and Pompey who is still subject to oscillating moods: 'How arbitrary is the rhythm of existence, with mood succeeding mood and power shifting from hand to hand.'[3] Even in *Novel on Yellow Paper* the 'talking voice that runs on' could not contain the full range of expression which rises at one point to prayer and invocation. In *Over the Frontier* the conversational style, though it effervesces at the start, is soon exchanged for another mode which contributes to the sensation that this is, as one critic has observed, 'an inconclusive and uncomfortable book'.[4] Accompanying this change of style is the introduction of allegory: Pompey's removal from Bottle Green to the Baltic coast and an ambience suggestive of espionage creates a narrative through which Stevie is able to explore the contemporary political and moral climate in the face of forthcoming war. To an extent the book is tinged with neo-romantic tendencies: psychological states are explored through the use of symbol; there is an obsession with death in life and a language which, though never overwrought or apocalyptic, now and then attains a heightened lyricism.

In its use of symbol it shares with other novels of this period, such as Rex Warner's *The Wild Goose Chase*, Edward Upward's *Journey to the Border* and Ruthven Todd's *Over the Mountain*, a debt to Kafka. Pompey's mysterious commission recalls K's relationship with authority in *The Castle*, a book Stevie had read in the late 1920s. 'A bureaucratic nightmare – brilliant,' her reading notes record.[5] And when *Over the Frontier* appeared, critics drew attention to its Kafkaesque quality.

As with her previous book, Stevie's interest in Germany fed her imagination. She owned a copy of George Grosz's *A Post-War Museum*,[6] which Faber's had published as a *Criterion* Miscellany in 1931, and admired the delicate precision and bitter contempt with which he unmasked the Weimar Republic. She may also have seen an exhibition of Grosz's watercolours at the Mayor Gallery, London, in June 1934, because in May 1936, at a time when John Lehmann was preparing another volume of *New Writing*, she offered him an article on this artist. The article was rejected but Stevie, not one to waste work, put her thoughts on Grosz into the opening section of *Over the Frontier*. Pompey visits an exhibition of his work and muses on his cynical, malicious humour. In passing she salutes his *A Post-War Museum* and reflects that in England there is scant willingness to understand 'the tearing seering suffering of Germany after the war, the disintegration and diminution the backward journeying the fear the cringing corroding terror of poverty and hopelessness'.[7]

Here, as in *Novel on Yellow Paper*, Stevie uses the visual arts to provide analogies for her thought. Pompey's reflection on a Grosz painting of a horse and rider not only offers a reminiscence of the Kismet motif, but it also prefigures the night riding that is to follow. In front of this image Pompey finds herself haunted by the image of the rider:

'He is perhaps rather a nigger in the woodpile . . . he is forgetting to remember the shame and dishonour the power of the cruelty the high soaring flight of that earlier éclaircissement . . . he is very actively forgetting and instead he will think of the easy generous light-running laughter of the English and Americans, and he is thinking of that American nationality that shall come dropping down dropping like a curtain to shut off from him for ever that sad sad situation, that already perhaps he is a little ashamed to have seen once and for all time . . . to the very last outposts of the black heart of despair of the situation.'[8]

Pompey is here alluding to Grosz's political reaffiliation which followed his move to the United States in 1932 and eventual adoption of American citizenship. She vows herself not to forget cruelty, shame and dishonour, will allow no curtain to fall between her and what she sees and knows. In *Over the Frontier* Pompey bears witness to Stevie's belief that our nature is rooted in pain and cruelty.[9] The book is imbued with awareness of, in Auden's words, 'The expanding fear, the savaging disaster'. And though the second half of the book takes on the quality of a dream or nightmare, it is directed towards understanding not escape.

'Oh war war is all my thought.'[10] Pompey's soliloquy repeatedly reminds us 'this book is set to anger and disturbance',[11] and is written in a period that carries 'a great burden of stress and strain'.[12] Much of it had been produced in the autumn of 1936: in October Stevie had told Rupert Hart-Davis, 'I am getting on and getting on with the new novel which I want to call *Over the Frontier.*'[13] She was therefore writing it in the aftermath of Mussolini's invasion of Abyssinia, the reoccupation by German troops of the Rhineland, and the onset of the Spanish Civil War. No mention of the last is made in this book but Mussolini's position in Abyssinia is viewed from two stand-points: with anger by Josephine and equivocation by Pompey, aware of the advantages with regard to Egypt and its coastline that this has brought Britain. Pompey's reflections, as they run on, seem to parody British double-thinking and complacency. The question raised in the reader's mind is soon put to Pompey herself: 'And on whose side are you?'[14]

Stevie's own politics are hard to pin down. Opposed to Fascism, she attended a rally in June 1938 at which writers united in the cause of freedom. Held in the Queen's Hall, which had a seating capacity of almost two thousand, it was an emotive occasion. Cecil Day Lewis's speech on the warping of children's minds in Germany and Italy received lengthy applause. Stevie was intensely irritated by the whole proceedings, as she told Osbert Sitwell:

'. . . of course Kingsley Martin [editor of the *New Statesman*] was on the platform. Though of course actually he only dislikes *other* dictators. However, Day Lewis brought the frightfully emotional house down by quoting for *Horror* – Goering. Goering said: When I hear the word culture, I reach for my gun. And I thought: When I hear the word Kingsleymartin, I reach for my gun. And when I hear the word Daylewis I reach for my gun. (Not that I know anything about his poetry, but as a thinker. Why does he have to think such a lot – or rather to think he thinks, because really he *feels*. "We do feel, don't we? . . ." The absolute curate!) And what do you think the *mouse* of those *mountains* of oratory was? You will never guess, so I must take yet another page – A telegram to Freud, groupily wishing him a happy stay in England.'[15]

Stevie, with her dissentient mind, disliked national hysteria. Reviewing Osbert Sitwell's *Those Were the Days* in the spring of 1938 she wrote: 'We are very much what we were; the eve of Sarajevo may prove too much a shadow of 1938.' And she concluded: 'How vile we were, and are. Is the human race then never to be trusted round the corner where the hobby-horses of ideology neigh?'[16]

Like Aunt, she scorned the peace-at-any-price attitude. But despite her awareness of the German threat, she felt uncomfortable in any group alliance. In *Over the Frontier* Pompey protests: 'I am not interested to concentrate upon politics, fascism or communism, or upon any groupismus whatever; I am not interested to centre my thoughts in anything so frivolous as these variations upon a theme that is so banal, so boring, so bed-bottom false, so suspect in its origin. *C'est la vie entière que c'est mon métier.*'[17] The buck ends with our own humanity, Stevie told Naomi Mitchison who had referred in a letter to 'the forces of evil'. Stevie replied: 'If there are these forces of evil . . . you are siding with them, in allowing your thoughts to panic. Your mind is your own province – the only thing that is.'[18] In *Over the Frontier*, in the imaginary war being fought at the end of the book, the arrogance, weakness and cruelty of Germany has infected the enemy, never specified, never directly confronted and which at times seems to lie within Pompey and ourselves, for power and cruelty corrupt those who fight against them. This recognition of the power of cruelty, together with Pompey's realization that her hatred is mingled with guilt and, though it pretends to be hatred of others' cruelty, is also an expression of the cruelty in herself, results in a book that offers no simple solution. While abhorring the will to power, it does not promote a non-militant pacificism and is too complex to be labelled an anti-Fascist fairy tale. Its acceptance of paradox and deceit as aspects of the truth reflect Stevie's own thinking which resisted the patterns imposed by religion, ideology and conventional morality. Thought, itself, she argues in *Over the Frontier*, is partial, not reflective of the mind's entirety but merely 'a torchlight flame upon a part of it'.[19]

Awareness of contradiction extends to Pompey's self-estimation. Near the start of the book she warns the reader that one of the components in her character is 'the raffish black and hateful demon that runs alongside',[20] alongside her gaiety and sadness. It is perhaps the demon in her that now and then charges her soliloquy with contempt: for pedantic professors; critics who sully art with their dreary commentaries; lesbian women who grossly imitate men in dress and behaviour; mishandled personal relationships; the politically self-righteous; her own work ('these rather disturbing rather unquiet rather hateful poems'[21]); for radios, electric drills and the underground railway, all of which help create the 'nervous irritability that has in it the pulse of our time'.[22] Her contempt also focuses on cruelty: the young Professor Dryasdust is accused of producing commentary on the work of poets that is 'cruel in its stupidity';[23] a fellow traveller's book, *The Pleasures of the Torture Chamber*, has, for Pompey, a 'very desperate and bitter cruelty' because it affronts our immortality, darkens the mind, sets up the flesh in domination of the spirit and leads to death.[24] This kind of cruelty, she reflects, 'is very much in the air now'.[25] She goes on to distinguish between two kinds of cruelty, as she had done in *Novel on Yellow Paper* where the cruelty of the Olympian gods and goddesses ('cynical and always laughing . . . cruel in a cold callous and divine way'[26]) is contrasted with human cruelty. In *Over the Frontier* Pompey distinguishes between a cruelty that whips up the nerves and senses, creates fear and leads to death, and a cruelty which leaves the 'artist's soul creating and brooding upon the darkness of pain'.[27] Great artists such as Goya, she concludes, can portray cruelty without negating the spirit, can embrace and transcend it.

The narrative reaches a climax towards the end of the book when Pompey, crossing a stockade, confronts cruelty, hostility and obstruction hideously personified by a fiend who grabs her leg. Her obsession with cruelty was something she shared with Geoffrey Dennis whose demonic tale, *Harvest in Poland*, as has been mentioned, she so much admired. Many years later, reviewing Dennis's autobiography, *Till Seven*, she saw that, like herself, he had gained much from his childhood love of hymns: 'There was a demon in these old hymns a child might feed on; Geoffrey chewed him and grew fat, and chewed on the demons of hilarity, fear and cruelty – the mean school bullying, the fear of eternity . . . the cruelty of the world.' In the same review she praised Dennis's novel *Mary Lee* for touching 'the nerve of sadism at plain life's root'.[28]

When published, *Over the Frontier* baffled many of its readers who were surprised by the change of direction half way through when the book takes on the tone of a bizarre Agatha Christie, an air of menace, suspicion and innuendo. Few recognized it as a parable at once timeless and pertinent to the issues of the day. Writing to Denis Johnston in September 1936 Stevie had expressed a wish for a play 'that transcends space and time and is classically-modern without being teaching . . . or facetious'.[29] This was surely her aim in *Over the Frontier* which never slips into propaganda for any particular political viewpoint, is of the moment yet not tied down by period detail. Hans Häusermann has argued that Pompey's discovery of the dead bird on the balcony of the room in which she is proof-reading symbolizes the moment when her former self is no longer able freely to take to the air.[30]

It is soon after this that she leaves for Tilssen on the Baltic coast and the book's investigation of the power of cruelty really begins. At Schloss Tilssen, for instance, Pompey dreams that she puts on a uniform which represents 'something that is not perfectly assimilated'.[31] Later, Major Tom Satterthwaite, with whom she sets out on a war-like mission, brings her a uniform to wear which she now recognizes as 'an outward and visible sign of my inward and spiritual sensation . . . what there is in my secret heart of pride and ambition, of tears and anger'.[32] Having become some kind of mercenary, Pompey eventually supersedes Satterthwaite in drive and strength. 'Is then power and the lust for power the very stuff of our existence,' Pompey asks her reader, 'the prop of our survival, our hope of the future, our despair of the past?'[33] The book closes with the assertion: 'Power and cruelty are the strength of our life, and in its weakness only is there the sweetness of love.'[34]

The book's title invites question as to which frontier has been traversed. There is an actual frontier which Pompey crosses in the course of her night riding and which separates her from her former life. But her soliloquy constantly strains against other frontiers, giving the reader the sensation that in her actions and behaviour she is about to step beyond the bounds of reason, logic and honour into a world where conventional goals and values have no meaning. One instance of this is when she dances with Josephine in the enormous drawing room in the Schloss with its hard cruel electric lights. The two friends dance 'with such a mad increasing pace'[35] that they exceed conformity and Pompey momentarily experiences sensations of elation and triumph. In this and other ways the book suggests a world on the edge of dissolution, of frontiers under threat.

Over the Frontier is an impressive, haunting, difficult book. The writing enchants and surprises with its verbal richness and rhythmic felicity, its grammatical liberties and syntactical quirks. As in *Novel on Yellow Paper* the sudden digressions disrupt traditional expectations of the novel; the mobile viewpoint creates fissures and dislocations that unsettle the reader. We move from the comic to the tragic, from the ironic to the plangent and heartfelt, these different levels of experience allowing for no single, univocal meaning. The question 'And on whose side are you?' is asked not only of Pompey but also the reader.

Of all those who reviewed the book, Edwin Muir was the most perceptive. For him *Over the Frontier* was infected with contrariety, the serious and the trivial, 'the sense that experience is an improbable mixture of the petty and the enormous'.[36] The chief lesson of the book is that truth is equivocal and that political and ideological formations caricature humanity. When asked which side she is on Pompey replies that she is on the side of her friends, that 'friendship is a more final truth than policy or the argument of history'.[37] Not for her Auden's 'conscious acceptance of guilt in the necessary murder' but a determination to resist ideological terrorism with the help of the anarchic freedom that laughter creates.

'Oh how much of the splendour of torment and dismay is wrecked and splintered upon the seas of our ideas, not held to be discussed in a reasonable quietude, to be measured in a proud humility against a common thought, but thrust, thrust to the hilt of its destroying fury and dyed deep with the insensate blood of a too willing martyrarchy. Scatter the salt before the Roman gods, acquiesce in the uttermost fantastic formularies of the inquisition, ratify the amendments, sign the protocols, scatter, acquiesce, ratify and sign, but keep your heart to yourself for a space to laugh in, for not the most searching pang can strip naked that inmost core of laughter within a secret heart, that holds fierce and close within itself the power to dispel the dream, the dream that persecutes and is persecuted, *the dream that slew the slayer and shall be slain*. Slain? By no avowed slayer, bringing death upon himself, but slain, slain and finally slain by the laughter behind an acquiescence that mocks and kills.'[38]

With two novels and a volume of poetry to her name, Stevie was enjoying considerable recognition. Fan letters poured in, many of them convincing her that she was living in famished times. 'My God – the hungry generations,' she wrote to Naomi Mitchison, '. . . If you knew the letters I still get. The ones from the women – all so hungry & worrying. Hungry for a nostrum, a Saviour, a Leader, anything but to face up to themselves & a suspension of belief.'[39] Some of her fans, however, occupied influential positions. Malcolm Muggeridge, for instance, was then working on the Londoner's Diary page for the *Evening Standard* and promised to try and get her next volume of poems noticed. He himself reviewed *Over the Frontier* in the *Daily Telegraph* and invited Stevie to lunch. His nimble mind and love of malicious gossip delighted her. When she was invited by the journalist Nina Condron to accompany her on a visit to Austria to stay with Kay Boyle, the American novelist, Stevie thought she would enjoy the trip (never made) if Malcolm Muggeridge and Inez Holden were also of the party.

In Cambridge she acquired a coterie of admirers. The economists Joan Robinson and Richard Kahn threw a tea party in her honour. Before this she had made friends with Lyn Newman, wife of a St John's College mathematician, Professor Maxwell Newman. They may have met through the *New Statesman* to which Lyn contributed, having established her reputation under the pseudonym Lyn Irvine with *Ten Letter Writers* which the Hogarth Press had published in 1932. Stevie had stayed at least twice with the Newmans by the summer of 1937 and it may have been on one of these occasions that she attended a Cambridge garden party and met Rachel Marshall, David Garnett's sister-in-law, and her husband Horace. They too took a shine to Stevie who became one of their weekend guests. Despite great divergences of character all these Cambridge friends lived a vigorous mental life and enjoyed books. Rachel Marshall's love of poetry was affirmed by her extensive library and the loyalty with which she followed certain poets' careers. She herself had trained as a singer and violinist and had returned to her career after her third child had reached school age. She taught music at Homerton College, also concentrating on the spoken word, and was to give Stevie valuable advice when she began broadcasting. Stevie became very fond of this woman, who was some twenty years her elder, and was in turn regarded with affection by the family. She gave additional spice to the Sunday breakfasts given for the Marshall's undergraduate son, Nat, and his friends. With the Marshalls she also made her only visit to Hilton Hall, the home of David Garnett, and so enthusiastically entered into a game of chase with his two sons that she ended in a bed of nettles.

If her conversation entertained, it could also be exhausting. 'One of my more erudite friends said to me, after enduring a weekend of my conversation,' she admitted to Rupert Hart-Davis, ' "Stevie, you must have a very clear unconscious".' In the same letter we find her complaining about the reviewer's lot: 'It's an awful job. And I suspect, if paid for at staff rates [Stevie was reviewing for Cape's house magazine *Now and Then*], not worth the *awfully* hard work.'[40] Despite th's and other complaints about the task of reviewing it became a major outlet for her intellectual energies, perhaps using more than was wise: as she became increasingly eminent as a reviewer, her novel writing slackened and eventually ceased. In September 1937, however, as she told the editor of the *London Mercury*, she was contemplating a third novel. It is mentioned again in a letter to Denis Johnston written in December of that year.

'It is funny the lady turns out to be Death, I mean here was I thinking of my next, and going to call it Married to Death . . . please keep this idea of my next very secret because I have already told them I am never going to write again, and I expect perhaps it will come to nothing. But there it is, death death death lovely death – so far 40pp.'

She adds that her writing is becoming disjointed because of the difficulty she has in finding time to do it. She admits also feeling guilty towards Aunt: 'I am hardly ever at home and when I am I do not feel I should not talk to her but get out the typewriter and give her no attention at all, she gets lonely, does the Lion, but never grumbles, which makes me feel worse.'[41] However, she continued with *Married to Death* and a year and a half later sent David Garnett a completed manuscript. The manuscript no longer exists, but from Garnett's reply it appears that she was experimenting with a greater degree of indeterminacy than is found in either of her two earlier novels.

'This is a painful letter to write and probably to receive.

I have done my best with *Married to Death*, but I can't read it, and what I have read leaves a confused impression in my mind. I cannot describe it better than I could describe the landscape of what I see when I have been swimming under water.

One does not know who is who or what is what as you say yourself in one place.

I think it is absolutely fatal for you to write about yourself any more. A book must have shape, bones, foundations. It ought to be built like a house. This is liquid, a flowing stream of words. And while you still write in this pouring way: it is like talking to oneself . . . of what one could do if . . . It is in fact day-dreaming . . .

It is terrible – because *you are a writer*. Every page shows what a fine writer you are: and the pages add up into an impenetrable dossier of private day-dreams . . . you've been writing for yourself and not for us.'[42]

His negative response killed the book. When in 1949 she sent him a copy of her third published novel, she added the following note:

'You were so kind to me when I first began to write and I know how very disappointed you were in the manuscript novel I sent you after *Over the Frontier* was published and it was certainly very bad. I do hope you will not be disappointed in this one.'[43]

What prose remains from the year 1939 consists solely of reviews, the short story, 'Surrounded by Children', which the *New Statesman* published on 14 January, and a series of diary-like sketches which appeared under the title 'Mosaic' in the monthly, *Eve's Journal*. This short-lived magazine was Newnes's attempt to imitate the highly popular *Lilliput*. Its sub-editor, Jane Stockwood, had read *Novel on Yellow Paper* and approached Stevie on behalf of the editor, Christine Jope-Slade. In these 'Mosaic' pieces the tesserae are the snippets of conversation that Stevie, in the course of a day or an outing, picks up. One of them catches the drift of opinion with regard to the

Munich settlement and makes use of some wise aphorisms of her own. Another describes a visit with her friend Clem, based on Campbell Mitchell Cotts, a director of the *London Mercury*, to the home of Lord Bubble (Lord Berners). All betray irritation, with money ('the burden of our times and not to be laid down, I guess, this side of the grave'), with those left-wingers and rich Communists who refused to believe in the likelihood of war, with complacency and special pleading. The conversational style is characteristically Stevie, as is the manifesto with which one piece opens: 'Friendship and the revolt from friendship is the stuff of life.'[44]

Through *Eve's Journal* Stevie made a friend of Jane Stockwood, who was then living in digs in St John's Wood and pleased to accept invitations to spend the weekend at 1 Avondale Road, to go on walks in Hertfordshire or to accompany Stevie to see John Clements perform at Palmers Green's Intimate Theatre. 'Propinquity threw us together,' Jane Stockwood has said, '. . . the literal closeness of that kind of easy-going friendship depends a good deal . . . on geography.'[45] Stevie, considered difficult by some office staff, never quarrelled with Jane who found Stevie's occasionally fractious remarks never harsh enough to provoke. Jane also noticed that a tonic trace of Stevie's astringency was also to be found in Aunt. In both, she admired a naturalness, an absence of any self-consciousness. Having joined Stevie on many occasions for appetizing lunches at Fuller's, or at the Strand Palace among the palms, or at the Coalhole on the opposite side of the Strand, Jane left Newnes in 1939 and saw less of her friend, despite Stevie's frequent rejoinder, 'Dial a Pal', a reference to the telephone exchange for Palmers Green, when letters instead of numbers were in use.

Stevie's fractiousness, however, could make for difficulty, as Rosamond Lehmann discovered. After John Hayward had recommended *Novel on Yellow Paper* to her, she had shared his delight in Pompey. Rosamond Lehmann had been an established novelist since the success of *Dusty Answer* in 1927 and Stevie, who respected literary talent, was probably gratified when an introduction was effected and the two women met. After the appearance of *A Good Time Was Had by All* Rosamond wrote to Stevie: 'Reading your poems has given me a nostalgia to see you again. Could you be persuaded to come for a (quiet) week-end?'[46] Stevie accepted the invitation, visited Ipsden House, near Oxford, where Rosamond was living, and charmed both her and her sister Beatrix with her constant chatter. When *Over the Frontier* appeared in January 1938 Stevie asked Cape to send Rosamond a copy. She received a frank, critical response:

'I revelled in the first part and found it as moving, as funny, as fascinating, as

1. Stevie Smith. Publicity photograph taken by Howard Coster for *Novel on Yellow Paper*.

2. John Spear, Stevie's maternal grandfather

3. Charles Ward Smith, Stevie's father

4. Madge Spear, Stevie's aunt

5. Ethel Smith, Stevie's mother

6. 'Peggy' Smith, aged three

7. Stevie as Ali Baba

8. Sydney (Basil) Scheckell

9. Ethel Smith, summer 1918

11. Hester Raven-Hart

10. Stevie

12. Molly Smith

13. Karl Eckinger (*Kaethe Augenstein*)

14. Eric and Katherine Armitage on their
wedding day

15. Aunt and Molly

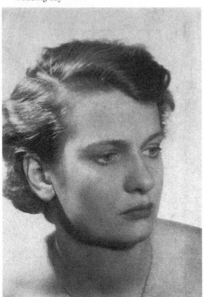

16. Inez Holden

17. Stevie at the home of Horace and Rachel
Marshall in Cambridge

18. Kay Dick

19. Kathleen Farrell

20. Mulk Raj Anand (*Howard Coster, National Portrait Gallery*)

21. Olivia Manning (*Michael Dyer Associates Ltd*)

22. Stevie Smith, 1965 (*Jorge Lewinski*)

intelligent as ever . . . It is just the last bit that worries me . . . I felt it had worried *you* and you hadn't been able quite to bring it off. I feel so uncertain about the clues – as if they were too private; and I lose the sense of Pompey offering up her incandescence for all to profit by . . . Pompey is one of the most adult and enlightened women I've ever known. But sometimes I feel she lets herself be caught in her illness and weakness and little-girlness – then I am disappointed.'[47]

Angered by this failure to recognize the deliberate use of ambiguity in the novel's second half, Stevie wrote a reply that no longer exists. Rosamond Lehmann can recall only the words, 'Sniff, sniff', alluding to what Stevie took to be Rosamond's upper-class snobbishness. She sent a sharp rejoinder: 'Oh don't be so cross and snappish . . . By sophistication and being adult I meant the opposite of being childish, sentimental and prejudiced, as most writers are. Sorry if the terms annoyed you. I always told you what I liked best was your seriousness, and you didn't mind before.'[48] Sadly, Stevie's reply to this is also lost or destroyed. It must, however, have contained views similar to those later expressed in her poem 'To Carry the Child'. Rosamond commented in response to it: 'I don't quite understand about the child being the direct heir to the Kingdom, the power and the glory. You seem to be saying that to be a child is the best thing and *I* think to be grown up (in the way I mean it) is the best thing . . . To remain at the kind of anarchistic or disintegrated stage which (I think) you describe – being both child and the other thing in shifting moods – seems to me to be destructive, and as if it *must* end in fantasy and daydreaming about life.'[49] If, as in the poem Stevie wrote about Eve and Mary, the difference between them was radical, a semblance of friendship was recuperated. But in the course of their exchange, others had become involved. Almost certainly Stevie had this dispute in mind, when she wrote to Denis Johnston in July 1938: 'I've been getting rather involved lately with the literary boys and girls, you know how bunchy they are, phew, words fly round and lose nothing in the telling, I now have to keep on asking people out to dinner to Explain I didn't say what I was reported to say, and so on, this is very tedious and expensive.'[50]

Literary squabbles failed to distract from what was happening elsewhere. Stevie began attending first-aid lectures, telling Rosamond Lehmann, 'every now and then things get so frightful in Germany I think one ought to make sacrifices'.[51] When invited to set a *New Statesman* weekend competition in July 1938, she did so with black humour.

'You are invited to compose, for the friendly use of the German Government in England, an *Appeal* to the people of Great Britain and the Empire seriously to consider the voluntary absorption of themselves – a regrettably separate aryan-blood brotherhood – by the Third Reich. Passing reference, in the lightest of German diplomatic language, may be made to possible difficulties, but these should be recognized only to be disposed of. The tone of the appeal should be friendly, persuasive, plausible, and where emphasis is required, sorrow rather than anger should be the note.'

Since the appearance of *A Good Time Was Had by All* Stevie's reputation as a poet had continued to grow. On 18 September 1937 the *New Statesman* had published 'The Abominable Lake', one of her most haunting and melodious poems, and probably reflective of G. W. Stonier's taste. ('Yes, I agree about Stonier,' Rosamond Lehmann once wrote to Stevie, 'when it comes to poetry. He does know.'[52]) She constantly looked to literary editors for advice on her poems and was grateful when R. A. Scott-James, editor of the *London Mercury*, wrote a ten-page letter on the subject. 'I sometimes think I write too much and use too little of the blue pencil and the waste-paper-basket,' she admitted in reply.[53]

A similar uncertainty characterized her preparations for a second volume of poems during the summer of 1938. Five poems, rejected in the final stage, were posthumously published by *Poetry Review* in September 1984. As her letters to Rupert Hart-Davis reveal, still more were cut out at the last moment. She discarded

> Henry Wilberforce as a child
> Was much addicted to the pleasures of the wild;
> He observed Nature, saw, remembered,
> And was by a natural lion dismembered

as being 'too like a cautionary tale',[54] as well as 'Lulu', 'Salon d'Automne', 'I Forgive You', 'My Earliest Love' and 'When I Awake', all posthumously published in *Me Again*. One substitute she suggested, with some uncertainty, was 'Souvenir de Monsieur Poop', her rebellious satire on a literary critic. She regretted it, perhaps because it is too easy and unambiguous, if also very funny. 'You will have got the awful poems about which I feel pretty desperate,' Stevie wrote to Rosamond Lehmann after the book appeared. 'I cannot sleep for thinking of "Poop", how I let it get in I can't imagine, I get so sick of my poems I cannot really bother to read them in proof and am always chopping and changing, it is desperate for Rupert he has whole new batches set up for me and still I cannot make up my mind.'[55] Further proof of her indecisiveness is found in her suggestion that the haunting lyric,

'Tender Only to One', should be dropped. The reason may have been that it reorchestrated an idea found in 'My Earliest Love' –

> This is my earliest love, sweet Death,
> That was my love from my first breath

– which, on the typescript manuscript in Rupert Hart-Davis's possession, bears the suggestion 'Title page?' in Stevie's hand. Hart-Davis cannot now recall whether it was at his or Stevie's suggestion that it was rejected and 'Tender Only to One' used as the title poem.

Tender Only to One, characterized by Stevie's insidious wit and guileful craft, brings to the fore her obsession with death. There is death on the road, in dreams, an accidental murder; a parrot waits for death, a patient yearns for it; one poem begins 'Proud death with swelling port comes ruffling by' which conflates 'Death, be not proud' with 'why swell'st thou then' from Donne's *Holy Sonnets X*; twice the invocation, 'Come death', occurs. Closely associated with her thinking on death and the cessation of consciousness it brings is Stevie's use of the image of the sea or water: in 'Death's Ostracism' the waves swing apart, denying the dreamer death; in 'The Doctor' the patient longs for a tide that will carry him or her beyond recovery; in 'Noble and Ethereal' a bishop pauses before a river before turning aside from the idea of suicide. Two poems – 'The Abominable Lake' and 'Will Ever?' – envisage a silent, 'precreation' world, in one, frozen beneath a lake, 'beyond the soft sensual touch of the seasonal flow', in the other, timeless beneath the sea where are found 'The lightless dead in the grave of a world new drowned'. Here, as the first poem describes, is 'A freedom unthought, manumission unhoped, undesired'. Often there is an uncertainty as to whether Stevie is referring to death, or death in life, or a transfigured state in which all contact with the everyday world is strangely suspended. Pompey reaches such a state in *Over the Frontier* when she dances alone:

'I am borne upright, suspended in the fathomless deep waters of a sombre and phosphorescent sea, swinging in silence and desolation between the poles of the world. How silent and sombre the deep swinging sea, swinging in malevolent intent upon its own storm basis of volcanic fury, what depths above me and below, how hellishly cold it is, how bitter and how solitary.'[56]

Stevie regarded her poetry and prose as a single vehicle, the one performing in tandem with the other. Because they inhabit a similar mental landscape she was able to incorporate several of her poems into *Over the Frontier*, as well as a digression on her admiration for the seventeenth-century and the Metaphysical poets. Their love of paradox and dialectic informs 'The Friend' in *Tender Only to One*: after opening with Browning's 'We needs must love the highest when we see it', Stevie jolts us to attention by adding the contradiction 'And having seen it knowing lower flee it'. She proceeds to argue that because we know high *and* low, bliss *and* smart, we are ranged higher than the angels: 'But thou of present depth and former height / Has highest height attained and needs no flight.'

A still more important link between her prose and poetry is found in the theme of night riding. For Stevie the image of the horse and rider, though variously allusive, was associated with the compulsive and inescapable. In 'The Fugitive's Ride' she describes

> . . . my poor horse so lost so wan
> That cannot understand
> Why we must ride and ride and ride
> And never yet come home . . .

which recalls of Browning. In his 'How They Brought the Good News from Ghent to Aix' the emphasis is all on the ride and we never learn what the good news is. In 'Childe Roland' the hero's quest is as indeterminate as Pompey's in *Over the Frontier*, though the psychological urgency of their journeying is never in doubt. Though Stevie's interpretation of the dark tower in 'Childe Roland' – 'symbol of loss in a lost land'[57] – may seem clever but restricting, she responded fully to the rich potency of this image and that of the ride. The horse and rider became for her a symbol of that which, as Yeats wrote, there is for everyone – 'some one scene, some one adventure, some one picture that is the image of his secret life'.[58] This may be why Pompey's night riding through a bare wintry landscape gives to *Over the Frontier* such haunting effect.

CHAPTER 8

Wartime Friendships

In spite of her dislike of groups, Stevie's awareness of impending war aligned her with those who denounced Neville Chamberlain. 'Though we don't much like all the demonstrations,' she said of herself and another in relation to For Intellectual Liberty which she had joined in the winter of 1938–9, 'we hope they hamper horrible Chamberlain.'[1] She was writing to Storm Jameson, the novelist, one of the few to discern in *Over the Frontier*, at the time of its publication, its relevance to the historical moment. 'This has the poetry,' Jameson told Cape's editor, Ruth Atkinson, 'the malice, the sadness, of a mind peculiarly sensitive to something which is happening in the world, which perhaps only a poet can deeply feel.'[2] As President of the English Centre of PEN, the society founded to promote international relations between intellectuals, Storm Jameson invited Stevie to join. When Stevie objected that subscription rates were too high, Jameson replied sympathetically. PEN was then making a stand against Fascism and giving help to refugees. 'Writers of your quality are desperately needed,' Jameson told Stevie, urging her to join if not that year, at a later date.[3] Two years later Stevie still had not officially joined, though she had attended occasional PEN events as Inez Holden's guest. She enjoyed 'literary gaddings' and felt a need for contact with other writers, but lack of affluence kept her out. 'It is really only for rich and middling well-to-do people,' she complained to Hermon Ould, PEN's secretary.[4]

In the period leading up to the outbreak of war Stevie began to rethink what her contribution might be. She had now realized that first-aid lectures were a waste of time as she never got the hang of what was taught her. She feared a loss of freedom of thought and realized that in wartime the BBC would assume increased importance, in part because the inevitable paper shortage would curtail journalism. 'I have a fine port winey voice,' she told Denis Johnston, 'and when the poor BBC young men are called up I am just wondering if I could not Announce.'[5] Sir Neville Pearson removed this hope: her voice, he told her, was awful, unclear and marred by a lisp. Her job throughout the war years did not change. It continued to arouse in her a mixture of gratitude, boredom and hate. Whilst recuperating from German measles in February 1939, she wrote to Joan Robinson: 'I must go back to the office on Monday but I feel a tired old horse, I sometimes wish I *was* sixty (and pensionable) and could be turned out to grass. Why on earth I should be pensioned I don't know, as I have never really done any work . . .'[6]

Whilst ill she read a great deal. 'It's a case of voyage au tour de mon bookshelf,' she told Joan. Among battered French novels, dictionaries and relics of school days she found C. Linklater Thompson's seven-volume *A First History of England* and romped gleefully through the first four volumes, reaching the reign of Elizabeth I.

'How frightfully *vigorous* people were in those days . . . in a way it is admirable and healthy. None of that sickly king-worship. It says: the Londoners disliked the queen so much that they used to stand on the bridge and pelt her with mud as her barge went by. (No 'little Princess Elizabeth' neurosis there!) . . . It's amazing how they fought and suffered and raged and roared and spat, it's grand. Now it all happens inside, and how ugly that is when it works outwards don't we know.'[7]

It was at this time that Stevie abandoned *Married to Death*, the novel Garnett had abhorred. 'It's awful,' her letter to Joan continues. 'No good at all. Displaying (as I beautifully said about somebody else once) the very dregs of feminine talent.' She asked Joan to send her a fresh idea for a plot: 'Just something simple . . . With no loophole for fancies that are so baneful.'

Living as she still did with Aunt, it was always unlikely that Stevie would lose her astringency. Inevitably the older woman imposed a narrowness on the other's life that would not otherwise have been there: Aunt disliked 'the noise', as she termed the wireless, and for a long while would not have one in the house. But this is the woman who is described admiringly in Stevie's third novel, *The Holiday*, as 'strong, happy, simple, shrewd, staunch, loving, upright and bossy',[8] the epithets pinned like medals on her chest. This is also the woman who is described as having no patience with men or with

Hitler, and who would remark, 'He is a very soppy man, a most soppy individual'.[9] To Joan Robinson Stevie declared her aunt to be 'my true prop and support', but she also admitted the realization that by now their roles ought to be reversed. This awareness of unfulfilled debt, mixed with very great love, left Stevie less easy in her relationship with Aunt than her novels suggest. 'It is all very full of guilt-gefühl!' she admitted to Joan.[10]

Whether or not Stevie shared in the mixture of apprehension and elation that accompanied the onset of war, she would, like everyone else once the Blitz began, have been exposed to the discomforts caused by blackout, rationing and shortages. Yet when Naomi Mitchison, who spent the war in Carradale in Kintyre, visited her in February 1941, Stevie served sausage rolls, burgundy and gossip in her office with perfect equanimity. Naomi recorded in her diary: 'She hasn't been out of London except for four days since the beginning of the war, is quite unshaken. "Never had such quiet nights – no dogs, no motor cars, no babies crying." She really doesn't seem to worry at all.'[11]

In these changed circumstances she had lost certain friends whom previously she had seen regularly, among them Olivia Manning, now with her husband in Bucharest, and Barbara Flower, now working in Oxford. The person she probably saw most during the war years was Inez Holden, then living in a mews flat situated over a garage at the end of H. G. Wells's garden. 'I often have tea with Inez at weekends,' Stevie told Rachel Marshall, 'and H. G. Wells comes across from the big house for twenty minutes or so for a nice bit of toast.'[12] The flat was quiet and restful and looked out on to trees, giving Inez the illusion that she was living in the country. Stevie's visits occasionally find a mention in Inez's diaries. 'Supper at H.G.'s,' reads one entry:

'He came here to tea and asked Stevie over there to supper . . . we listened to the news afterwards . . . heard of the Japanese attack on America. H. G. was very optimistic, to him it seemed the grand long run grand slam clarifying of the big situation – out with the isolationists and in with the F.D.R. Certainly we do hope that the Americans will come in and do something in a dynamic way.'[13]

On occasions like these Stevie extracted what she needed for her sketch of Wells in *The Holiday* where, though unnamed, he is easily recognizable as the famous writer who arrives for tea at Lopez's house. This 'old pink man, looking like a baby, in a hooded cloak' demands kisses from Lopez (Inez) and Celia (Stevie). And then begins to talk. Despite his contentment

'this famous writer's books are still hitting the note of self-pity for the days when he served shop – "my bankrupt boyhood". Self-pity is the devil. But the old chap is in good form this evening and instructs us – misinstructs us I rather think – upon the political situation. We sit at his feet, making toast for him, gazing up at him with bright eyes and fire-flushed cheeks . . . We beam generously upon the old frail one – oh sir, oh sir, oh I say, Sir – it is rather that note. We are his young ones, his instructed. He thinks that we are children and believe every word that he says.'[14]

Elsewhere Stevie affirms her fondness for Inez in her descriptions of Lopez as 'this admirable girl . . . who has this admirable courage and this admirable high heart'. In the description that follows the circumstantial details troubling Inez's life are forgotten. Lopez 'writes and entertains the Government and the Section people, and the editors, and all the time it is nothing but a wonderful adventure for her to have, it is in the spirit of the Scarlet Pimpernel, or Sideways Through Patagonia, it is like that'.[15] Stevie enjoyed sparring with Inez, and both respected each other's wit. Much of the chatter between these two friends concerned the elaborate dramas they encountered on public transport. Together they visited the BBC unit at Evesham in April 1941 and quickly discovered the mercenary motives behind the family atmosphere that their landlady tried to create. Afterwards Inez noted in her diary: ' "If she were a woman in a Russian story," Stevie remarked, "she would say *My love of money imprisons me I am in chains*".'[16]

Through Inez in 1939 Stevie met the twenty-two-year-old Antoinette Pratt-Barlow who, having trained at the London Theatre Studio under Michel St Denis, was working at the Old Vic. Despite her difference in age she fitted in easily with Stevie and Inez when all three began making occasional weekend visits to Pill Heath, a cottage Inez had rented near Andover. According to Antoinette, Inez cooked a stew nicknamed Bubbling Beaujolais, they drank copiously, talked endlessly, returning often to the subject of how appalling men could be, laughed a great deal and returned to London a great deal better in spirit.

A mutual friend of both Inez and Stevie was Sally Chilver, the niece of Robert Graves, author of *A History of Socialism*, published by the Hogarth Press, and wife of the civil servant, Richard Chilver. During the war she worked in the Cabinet Office in the Strand, in close proximity to Stevie in Southampton Street which enabled them to meet frequently for lunch. Of all Stevie's friends, it was probably Sally Chilver who had the most formidable intelligence, as well as tremendous vitality and striking good looks. This sophisticated, erudite woman once howled hymns with Stevie in a restaurant, collapsed with laughter and was asked to leave.

Sally Chilver observed that Stevie and Inez had repeated disagreements. These suggest that Inez's outlook was much less confident than that of her fictional likeness, Lopez. The trouble was chiefly economic. Stevie did what she could to help place Inez's stories and in December 1942 guaranteed one of Inez's overdrafts. But her greater professional security may have aggravated Inez's jealousy of Stevie's success. Nothing Inez did could bring her earnings into line with her living expenses. Just how close to penury she was is revealed by her diary; it records her many debts, to Stevie, Betty Miller and others, and the fact that she had on occasion to pawn both her typewriter and briefcase.[17] By the early 1950s Inez was so desperately poor that Sally Chilver, by then working for the Institute of Commonwealth Studies, with others concocted a plot to give her money which involved engaging her in research into the archives of the Baptist Mission to West Africa, a task with which Inez became fascinated. Meanwhile her friendship with Stevie deteriorated. In 1959 Stevie was delighted to learn from a Swiss-German professor that one of Inez's stories was to be translated into German, but she added, sadly, apropos of their former friendship: 'the old thing has been very odd indeed for years now and will hardly address a word to me.'[18]

It was probably through Inez that Stevie first met George Orwell. In 1940 Fredric Warburg had suggested that Inez and Orwell should collaborate on the publication of a joint diary, an idea that never reached fruition because the approach of each was so different. Inez's half of the project, however, was published under the title *It Was Different At the Time* in 1945. In September 1941 she recorded in her diary how she and Stevie, at a PEN luncheon, had sat at a table with Arthur Koestler, Cyril Connolly and others, and Koestler had bet five bottles of burgundy that in five years' time George Orwell would be a best seller. Two months later her diary records that she and Stevie dined with the Orwells.

Orwell had recently been made Empire Talks Assistant in the Indian Section of the BBC's Eastern Service, a post that he held until November 1943. Before the war he and his wife, Eileen Blair, had run a smallholding and village shop in Hertfordshire, but in May 1940 they had moved into a small flat in Dorset Chambers, Chagford Street, NW1. Whilst there Orwell wrote weekly theatre and film reviews for *Time and Tide*, his book *The Lion and the Unicorn* (1941) as well as occasional pieces for the *New Statesman*. None of this added up to the prestige that in wartime attached itself to broadcasting, and his job in the BBC enabled him and his wife to move again, to Langford Court, St John's Wood. In his new role Orwell conceived the idea of a poetry magazine to be broadcast with the poets themselves reading extracts from their work. The series was called 'Voice' and it prefigured the kind of poetry programmes later to be transmitted by the Third Programme. Orwell relied for assistance on his close friend Mulk Raj Anand, a graduate of Punjab University whom he had met in Spain during the struggle against Franco. According to W. J. West, the authority on Orwell's wartime broadcasts, it was Anand's job to contact likely contributors whom Orwell then chased up. This division of labour may have caused a misunderstanding between Orwell and Stevie.

Invited to make a contribution, Stevie was angered to discover that her work in one of these 'Voice' programmes had been read by Herbert Read. 'I did not hear one word about that last broadcast until 20 minutes before it went on the air. Jolly good show, BBC! And if you want to know what I feel about you at this moment,' she told Orwell, 'take a look at the drawings on p. 54.' This referred to the proofs of her new book of poems, *Mother, What is Man?*, to drawings of a hungry wolf and a man's head illustrating a poem that begins, 'I was consumed by so much hate'. Cross but still friendly, her letter ends 'love and fond messages'. What turned annoyance into fury was Orwell's reply. He claimed that he had told her orally the date of the programme, had arranged with her what poems she was to read and had sent written confirmation to the only address that Stevie had given him – Inez's. Stevie replied:

'Dear George,

Lies are the most irritating thing in the world and would make an angel grisel and you are the most persistent liar and these fibs are always coming back to me from other people. You never gave me the date for the bloody broadcast or breathed one word about my reading my own poem. I sent the poems to you from this address and also the three short stories you've had since last March. I never gave you Inez's address, why the hell should I, specially as she was on the point of leaving? I'm sorry about it, but not very, as I'm sure [Herbert] Read read better than I should as I've never broadcast before or had a rehearsal. I'm bored to death by the lies.

Steve.'[19]

Having vented her scorn, Stevie was soon back on good terms with Orwell. Only a month later she was sending him a lively, catholic list of items for possible inclusion in a 'mid-highbrow' Christmas number of 'Voice'. If broadcast, her selection would have included extracts from Saki, Lawrence, T. S. Eliot, Dickens, children's singing games, sea-shanties, from her own work, and from that of Inez and Elizabeth Bowen. She was not optimistic about her proposal. 'If we know anything about the Bay Bay Say,' she wrote to John Hayward, 'they'll turn it down and put in a bit about saving jam jars. Or Eastern poetry in Eng. translation – that I fear is really what may happen, some of those mingy little verses by C. Bax I suppose, or a Waley Waley up the Banks.'[20] She was not mistaken: Orwell thanked Stevie for her 'excellent idea' but doubted if there was time to produce it. His Special Christmas Number of 'Voice' merely made use of carols.

Much rumour and speculation has been expended on the relationship between Stevie and Orwell. Her liking for Orwell is not difficult to explain. The incisiveness of his thought would have satisfied her sharp mind. She had read, at least, his *The Lion and the Unicorn* which she mentions in her programme for the proposed Christmas edition of 'Voice'. She would also have admired his sceptical agnosticism and his refusal to accept received opinion without subjecting it to independent scrutiny. But she was also amused by the confidence with which he propounded his prejudices and satirized this tendency in *The Holiday* where Orwell's character is split between Basil and Tom.

'Basil said that eventually England would have to choose between money and kids, because under capitalism people would not have kids, it was too much to ask, and he began to inveigh against our ex-Ally which put me for once in a good humour with them. He said that America would be the ruin of the moral order, he said that the more gadgets women had and the more they thought about their faces and their figures, the less they wanted to have children, he said that he happened to see an article in an American woman's magazine about scanty panties, he said women who thought about scanty panties never had a comfortable fire burning in the fire-place, or a baby in the house, or a dog or cat or a parrot . . .

Or a canary, I said.

Or a canary, went on Basil, and he said that this was the end of the moral order.'[21]

If Stevie let her mixed feelings towards Orwell influence her writing of *The Holiday*, it is perhaps telling that at one point the narrator can barely stifle a snigger at the look of satisfaction that appears on Basil's face. The manuscript of *The Holiday* mentions 'this icy feeling between Basil and me, come by the drawings and the income tax', a line omitted in the published book and which may also spring from small disagreements between Stevie and Orwell. Her fascination with him, however, cannot be doubted. Lettice Cooper during 1941 was working in the Ministry of Food with Eileen Blair, with whom she often lunched in a restaurant in George Street that had large glass windows. Not infrequently they looked up to see Stevie and Inez peering in at the window. Lettice Cooper had the impression that they were looking for Eileen and in conversation with her would, with transparent lack of disguise, lead the conversation round to George. Bernard Crick, Orwell's biographer, reports that Stevie and Inez sobbed on Eileen's 'not entirely sympathetic shoulder about their unrequited loves for George'.[22] Not only is this out of character with both women, but Lettice Cooper, to whom this observation is attributed, recollects that Eileen was sympathetic to Inez and Stevie and did not regard either as a threat. Of the two women, Inez was always the more expansive, more willing to talk about herself.

Stevie never regarded Orwell uncritically. With George Stonier she would joke about Orwell's need for a hair shirt, the fact that after the war he *had* to be hard up and lived in Islington behind a cracked frosted-pane door. Her most severe statement on Orwell appeared after his death. Reviewing Sean O'Casey's *Sunset and Evening Star* she declared him 'dead right' on Orwell 'and his sick-man fancy of a pool of self-abasement for all the world to dip in, and his sick man's lust for extreme future cruelty. And will he not be a disappointed ghost if 1984 when it comes, comes with the Bank Rate at four per cent and Mr Priestley's successors still whining cheerfully about nothing worse than currency restrictions and passports? Was it contempt based on ignorance of what makes people tick, and the British people especially, with their long tragi-comic history of being tyrants on the right hand while blasting tyranny with the left, that put such a gloom of Pétainismus into his books?'[23] These strictures are partly explained by the intensity of her regard. 'And what most I love I bite,' is a line from her poem 'Little Boy Sick'.

As in the case of Karl Eckinger and Eric Armitage, no letters from Orwell were found among Stevie's papers after her death. Only those concerning the 'Voice' programmes in the BBC Written Archives now exist. Both Stevie and Orwell were by nature discreet, not given to flaunting their emotional affairs before friends. Orwell did, however, boast to Anthony Powell that he had once made love to a woman in a park as they had nowhere else to go, and male literary gossip has associated Stevie with this tale. Stevie herself encouraged surmise. She told Jane Stockwood that Orwell had made a pass at her in her office. To her friends, the publisher Norah Smallwood and the civil servant Ronald Orr-Ewing she dropped allusions to an affair between herself and Orwell. She told Orr-Ewing, in addition, that *The Holiday* drew on her difficult relationship with Orwell; the love between the fictional Celia and Caz cannot be consummated owing to a suspicion of consanguinity; similarly whatever the relationship that existed between Stevie and Orwell, it would have been constrained by his marriage to, and love for, Eileen. Norah Smallwood was convinced that this affair was a reality: Orr-Ewing was left wondering if it could possibly be true.

Stevie put contradictory remarks about sex into her work, perhaps to disguise her own inadequacy. The phobia aroused in her by snakes (she would change carriage if a person boarded a train with snakeskin bag or shoes) invites an obvious conclusion. And once at a Norfolk dinner party she startled her fellow guests by saying that any husband she might have married would have had to have been undersexed. However, her fictional counterpart, Nancy Claypole, in Olivia Manning's *The Doves of Venus*, is knowing about sexual experience, alert to the possibilities that exist. Her liberated stance, however, is more boast than actuality, and when questioned about her boyfriend of the moment, Nancy replies: 'I'm bored with men. I was thinking only tonight how much nicer it is to have a woman friend. Don't you think we have much more fun together, enjoying things, saying what we think, being free, instead of each trailing around pandering to the vanity of some stupid man who expects you to be grateful because he buys you sardines on toast?'[24] At some point in her life Stevie also substituted friendship for love, while making a lack of love or genuine companionship a dominant theme in her work. In 1959 she cut out and kept a *Daily Mail* interview with Dame Edith Sitwell whose remark – 'My mental life is so violent that I have no physical life to speak of'[25] – is a view Stevie may to some extent have shared.

Her capacity to love is not in doubt. 'To be in love is awful,' she once said to her friend Kay Dick, who has remarked: 'the impression was it would tear you apart; she couldn't take the risk.'[26] Kay also felt that *nervosité* was an inherent part of Stevie's make-up and that there were certain things she would not discuss. 'It was like a child – you couldn't touch, not so much her innocence, but her fear.' One mannerism she had was a grimace, a gesture that was almost a nervous tic. With this facial shrug she would bring to a close any conversation she did not wish to pursue.

'Do you ever feel so cold,' asks the character Tiny in *The Holiday*, 'so frozen cold, so far away, and that love is a desperate chance clutch upon a hen-coop in mid-Atlantic?' The character Celia replies: 'listen, Tiny, love is everything, it is the only thing, one looks for it. Yes, everybody is hankering after it and whining. This hunger we have is a good thing, it is the long shin bone that shows the child will grow tall.'[27] Tiny remarks that the growing is very painful. It is possible that Stevie's recurrent exhaustion was partly the result of frustration in love, the suppression of love creating a weight on her spirit. She herself was to describe how 'when the elation of love passes to fruitless melancholy of loneliness, a dreadful restlessness oppresses the mind, a restlessness and a fatigue. Every employment then seems pointless, friends are too much absent, or, if present, they seem like phantoms.'[28]

On Orwell's side, a liaison with Stevie is not impossible. During the early 1940s he was to some extent estranged from his wife by the intense depression she experienced after her brother's death at Dunkirk. In London she did not take the same enjoyment as her husband in the literary life associated with certain pubs but sat loyally by his side. If she kept herself in the background, remaining, even to his closest friends, an elusive character, she was also central to Orwell's life. After her sudden death while undergoing an operation in 1945, Orwell seemed 'desolate without Eileen and grieved deeply'.[29] With Eileen he had discussed *Animal Farm* as the book progressed. He himself was not a good judge of literary ability in others, as Tosco Fyvel discovered when he took over from Orwell as a literary editor of the socialist weekly, *Tribune*: 'Only contributions by personal friends like Julian Symons and Stevie Smith stood out.'[30]

Orwell is reputed to have been unfailingly courteous and quietly spoken. It seems likely, therefore, that the outspoken row between him and Stevie over the 'Voice' programme provided outlet for emotional tension elsewhere. His gentle manner, however, did not always mean that he treated women well. Part of his desolation after Eileen's death was caused by his guilt at having been unfaithful to her. An affair between him and Stevie cannot be dismissed. This 'very private and very concealing'[31] man went out of his way to entertain her when she visited his flat in Canonbury Square soon after the war ended. Susan Watson, then acting as housekeeper and nanny to Orwell's son, Richard, recollects Orwell behaving with unusual charm, rushing out for beer and making the BBC's 'canteen special' – Welsh Rarebit, Stevie making cracks as he stood over the stove. Equally memorable was the sight of Stevie bouncing Richard around the square in his pram, to the evident satisfaction of both. But no further visits were made and after Orwell disappeared to Jura in the late spring of 1947, it was Inez, not Stevie, who journeyed to see him, a fact that may have contributed to the friction between the two friends.

In *The Holiday* the mocking, and at times openly critical, treatment of Basil and Tom contrasts with the unqualified affection shown to Raji. This character is based on Mulk Raj Anand, whose father, a clerk in the British Indian army, had mostly been stationed on the North-West Frontier, where the aim had been to keep the Pathan tribesmen under control. As a child, obliged to accommodate English ways, Mulk Raj Anand had also assimilated, chiefly through his mother, the songs, tales, myths and epics of village communities. The tension this created is evidenced in his novels and short stories which deal with various perspectives on Indian life, its traditions as well as its response to modern pressures. An admirer of Tagore and of his attempt to harmonize Western and Eastern traditions, Anand himself sought to adapt Indian folk elements to his understanding of the European novel. His radical conscience had always been to the fore. As a student at Khalsa College, Amritsar, he had been caned by the police for breaking curfew the day after General Dyer opened fire on an unarmed crowd in Jallianwala Bagh. Raji, in *The Holiday*, tells how he 'was beaten for his opinions when he was agitating in India; he was slung from side to side of the prison yard by the Indian policemen.'[32]

On the advice of the poet Iqbal, Anand had come to England to complete his studies in the late 1920s and read for a doctorate on Hume at University College, London. He was also active in politics, joining the Communist Party and the Indian League, the student branch of the Congress Party in England. High-spirited (he once poured the contents of an ashtray into Tambimuttu's beer), he displayed a directness, humour and mental agility that found a response among the sophisticated intelligentsia. Once, while visiting the Hogarth Press, Anand overheard Edward Sackville-West remark that no writer could deal with the working class without making a joke of them. This, Anand says, began his first novel which describes the day in a life of an outcast, and which, after being several times rejected, was published in England under the title, *Untouchable*, with an introduction by E. M. Forster. Stevie refers not to this book, but to another, Anand's *Letters on India*, in *The Holiday*.

'In Raji's own book that he wrote, that is so true about India, and so much the book that English people ought to read, and is so much the book that so many of them do not want to read, why in this book Raji says that the English are practically invisible in India, by reason of the anger and the pride, and that all the cruelty there is, and the beastliness, is done by avaricious middlemen and Indian paid subordinates, and by the rich Muslim trading families, like the great mill-owning rich families of Bombay. And he says that one of the most oppressive things the English have brought to India is that sense of secret opulence in a land of poverty, and this opulence shows itself in close-curtained bungalows with plain outsides, and the luxury going on within in a secret way, not sin, mind you, which anyone could understand, but just plain comfort, unindictable, untouchable, invisible and foreign.'[33]

It may have been her admiration for Kipling's *Just So Stories* that led

Stevie in *The Holiday* to give the narrator, Celia, an Indian childhood. But it may also reflect her sympathy with Anand whose experiences clearly fascinated her. Contact with him appears to have changed her views on India. In *Over the Frontier* she had represented Aunt as swayed neither 'to the sentimentalism of the pseudo-Kipling tea planter,' nor to those who cry 'Abdicate, evacuate, India for the Indians', and adds 'a something perhaps that must not come to pass yet for a long time'.[34] But in *The Holiday* the narrator asserts: 'We are right to quit India.'[35] In this book Raji gives a lecture on English novelists who write about India. Again this is based on actual experience, for Stevie accompanied Anand to a lecture he delivered at the Royal India Society. According to Anand, Stevie's satire on the Anglo-Indian audience ('. . . first of all our Raji had to be introduced by the lady that was in the Chair. So this lady spoke at great length about all the people she had known and loved in India, and about the children she had reared, and their lovely Ayah, their dog and their washerman . . .'[36]) is spot on. Moreover the 'young violent English person' who supports Raji and declares 'that no easy feeling of equality between intellectual Indians and English people was possible in India so long as this evil thing (the British Raj) was still in existence',[37] was, in actuality, George Orwell.

Anand recollects that he had first met Stevie at the home of Margaret Gardiner and went on meeting her in Orwell's St John's Wood flat and at Inez Holden's, as well as in pubs and cafés around the British Museum. This friendship developed during the early years of the war. 'An extremely charming fellow,' Inez's diary records, in November 1941:

'It is surprising to find a foreigner also coloured belonging to a dominated race so free, well at ease and without any kind of neurosis as Mulk, he is very good company, affectionate and witty – Orwell is anxious to get him to broadcast . . . Six months ago Mulk says he would not have been able to do so because so many of his friends were imprisoned by the British that the arm-chair broadcast from the Indian poet would have done a lot of harm, now it is better he himself fully supports the Anglo-Soviet war and the only thing that prevents him broadcasting is lack of time as he has to finish a novel to give several lectures a week for the LCC in the East End. He said he would put Orwell in touch with the right kind of Indians for his broadcasts. Mulk is going to ask us all to dinner with him and cook.'[38]

Stevie affirms Inez's views in her portrait of Raji ('it is wonderful that Raji can be so generous and so free, for his upbringing was in an oppressed atmosphere'[39]). She also offered hospitality and on three or four occasions Anand visited 1 Avondale Road. Here this young radical met Miss Spear with her formidable knowledge of India culled mostly from pro-Raj publications. According to Anand, Miss Spear and he talked at some length, and the admirer of Francis Younghusband's *The Relief of Chitral* was shocked to learn about the indiscriminate killings of tribesmen by the British Generals in their fear of the rebels and she began to see Lord Roberts of Kandahar, whose book *Forty-One Years in India* sat on the bookshelves at Avondale Road, in a somewhat less heroic light. Anand thinks Miss Spear did not believe all he said and they argued over the behaviour of the tribesmen. Anand's experience of seeing cartloads of corpses of Pathan tribesmen transported across the Lunda river in Now-shera after a platoon of soldiers had opened fire on a peaceful Jirgha, along with other memories, had haunted his childhood. He told Miss Spear how ghosts of the dead were said to haunt the cantonment, and how he never got over his fear that ghosts of these tribesmen would take their revenge on his family, because his father was on the side of the British. This fear had placed him as a youth under permanent stress and made him neurasthenic.

Anand believes that his friendship with Stevie made her more able to understand why Orwell had resigned from the Imperial Police Service in Burma. He thinks also that she began to sympathize with Orwell's politics, though she was never as forward as Inez in her attitude towards socialism. He recollects discussions in which both Inez and Stevie accepted Orwell's anarchistic opinions, because they too were against Imperialism, Fascism and Communism of the Russian kind. Anand, however, thought anarchism an idealistic hypothesis and continued to put his faith in the social revolution represented by the USSR. Stevie did not share his views but respected his integrity and made her character Raji 'an honest person upon a centre fixed'.[40]

Belonging to no literary clique and associated with no single magazine or influential review, Stevie found herself isolated as a writer during the war years. As a poet she was not part of the neo-romantic movement which gave rise to the Apocalypse group and its anthology, *The White Horseman* (1941). Nor did she belong to 'Soho' which comprised a major aspect of wartime London's literary life and which met in pubs. The poet David Wright avers that Stevie was respected in 'Soho' but never part of it. The idiosyncratic humour in her poetry and the rawness of her short stories, resulting partly from her distrust of literariness, made her work difficult to place. John Lehmann, editor of *Penguin New Writing*, rejected some of her short stories in 1939. Reginald Moore accepted one for *Modern Reading*, then never used it. Robert Herring, for whose *Life and Letters Today* Stevie did book reviews, asked to see some of her poems after he learnt that literary editors were rejecting them for not having the right 'tone' or 'voice'. He at first agreed to publish seven, unillustrated. Stevie must have rejected his offer as the poems never appeared.

In January 1940 Joe Ackerley of the *Listener* had rejected one of Stevie's poems on the grounds that his editor would not accept it and 'it would upset far too many of the old ladies who read us'.[41] This probably referred to 'Goodnight', published posthumously in *Me Again* and which Stevie was considering for inclusion in her new collection of poems in the spring of 1942. Centred around a husband's remark to his wife, on a dog's behaviour, it starkly evokes a strained relationship. 'Do you think this is too obscene, Rupert?' Stevie asked, on an attached note, when she sent the poem to Hart-Davis. 'About You-Know-Who, and *quite true.*'[42] In a letter to John Hayward, Stevie again affirmed that it was the product of a very vivid incident 'and shows how awful marriage can get and yet go on'.[43] On Hayward's advice, she omitted it from *Mother, What is Man?*

The possibility of a new collection had first been mooted by Stevie in the spring of 1940. Hart-Davis agreed to look at new poems but was not optimistic: only four hundred copies of *Tender Only to One* had sold, almost half the total sold of her first collection. Aware of Cape's hesitancy, Stevie asked if she might take her work elsewhere. This caused Jonathan Cape to reconsider the situation early in 1941 and by September the book was under way. As Hart-Davis was by then in the army, his place at Cape's had been filled by the historian C. V. Wedgwood. Stevie, meanwhile, had sent a bundle of her poetry and prose to Naomi Mitchison for advice. Naomi found the prose good but formless and the poems 'a very queer mixture'. She was not entirely sure that they all said what they were meant to, and wondered if one or two of the longer ones had come off.[44] Her views perhaps helped shape the selection of *Mother, What is Man?* as her doubts about certain poems on death may explain why it is a less prominent theme than in the previous collection.

Stevie's doubt about her work had not lessened. In January 1942 she wrote to John Hayward:

'I am really in an awful state about my poems and I have a strong temptation to send the whole lot and a separate envelope full of drawings to you for your help. I have to select about 80 out of 200 for Cape to make a book of, but which to keep and which to discard and which drawings to attach to which poems I cannot decide. I wish I wasn't cursed with indecision or that I had not got this love for my drawings and hatred for my poems. There is a very nice girl at Cape now who has taken Rupert's place – Veronica Wedgwood – do you know her? She made a sort of provisional selection, but then she gave them back to me for my final choice, and you know I was so inspired by her appreciation that I wrote six more poems and did 24 new drawings, and now I am terribly tied up and my room at the office looks like a paper chase.'[45]

She evidently felt her drawings had sufficient eloquence to stand alone with captions because she asked Hayward's opinion on the following one-liners: '18 months Old and Already Odious'; 'my left arm turned blue'; 'I dreamed I was dressed in cellophane; was I to blame?'; 'Think it Over' and 'From the maniac life of Blessed Mary Agatha'. In the final book none was used. All the drawings serve as illustrations to poems. They are reproduced smaller than their actual size and suffer a loss of quality owing to a slight thickening of the lines.

Several of these new poems pursue the mother–child relationship, making one or other the speaker. The gift of life cannot be returned and is often undesired: 'Ah! Will the Saviour never come / To unlock one from the tomb, / To requite the tears that falter / For a birth I could not alter.'[46] A similar protest is voiced by Francis Thompson in 'An Anthem of Earth' where a former child addresses his or her mother –

> Being once bound thine almsman for that gift,
> We are bound to beggary, nor our own can call
> The journal dole of customary life,

– and which ends with the speaker breaking free from 'the tomb of life'. Stevie owned a copy of *Selected Poems of Francis Thompson*[47] and used the 'ceremonial manumission' brought by Death in 'one hid dark lake', in 'An Anthem of Earth', as a source for her poem 'The Abominable Lake'. Thompson's poem also gave her the title for her 1942 collection, *Mother, What Is Man?* It is drawn from a passage Stevie quoted more fully in *The Holiday* –

> Ay, Mother! Mother!
> What is this Man, thy darling kissed and cuffed,
> Thou lustingly engender'st
> To sweat, and make his brag, and rot,
> Crowned with all honour and all shamefulness?[48]

which summarizes the teasingly ambivalent nature of the human condition, for Stevie at once so painful and so humorous.

Through the adoption of various masks or personae Stevie explores the more desperate reaches of human life. Her characters suffer loneliness ('The Sad Heart', 'Dirge', 'In the Night') or unrequited love:

> For still I hope
> He may return
> And while I hope,
> Still must I burn
>
> All with desire
> That waits on hope
> As doth the hangman
> On the rope.
>
> Hope and desire,
> All unfulfilled,
> Have more than rope
> And hangman killed.[49]

Others endure wretchedness and isolation, wish for change, consider suicide or sigh for a more heavenly existence. A few look their misfortune in the face. When reading her poem 'The Recluse', Stevie provided the following gloss: 'Here is a lady who really enjoys her fears and loneliness; she doesn't turn them into fairy-stories or heavenly dreams, she just enjoys them.'[50] Others, either doleful or slightly crazed, sustain the melancholy outlook, one poem even taking the form of an epitaph ('La Speakerine de Putney'). A lion is used to sustain this theme of ḥuman misfortune and imprisonment. Captured in the zoo of the poem's title, he personifies displacement.

> His claws are blunt, his teeth fall out,
> No victim's flesh consoles his snout,
> And that is why his eyes are red
> Considering his talents are misusèd.

What prevents this view of human nature from becoming too bleak, mournful and depressing is the exuberance and wit with which Stevie handles words, rhyme and metre. Each poem is cleverly and tautly written. 'Murder', for instance, opens with a chiasmus ('Farewell for ever, well for ever fare'), then employs deliberately awkward syntax in order to introduce an element of doubt: ''Tis easy said by one who had a care / Soul should doff flesh.' The exact meaning of that sentence is not made clear until the fifth and penultimate line, when the speaker admits to murder, before gaily taking his leave: 'Well, fare his soul well, fear not I the dead.' Equally cunning is Stevie's use of quotations and echoes: in 'Old Ghosts', she blends dialogue from *Henry IV Part I* –

> *Glendower:* 'I can call spirits from the vasty deep;'
> *Hotspur:* 'Why, so can I, or so can any man;
> But will they come when you do call for them?'

– with a passage from De Quincey's *Confessions of an English Opium Eater* in which he reports a child's admission that phantoms come when he calls for them and sometimes, too, when he does not call. Stevie compresses the two passages and introduces blame:

> I can call up old ghosts, and they will come,
> But my art limps, – I cannot send them home.

Likewise two lines from Tennyson's *The Princess* –

> Deep as first love, and wild with all regret;
> O Death in Life, the days that are no more.

– become, in Stevie's hands, especially when combined with the illustration of an ill-matched couple, a witty evocation of frustration:

> Cold as no Love, and wild with all negation –
> Oh Death in Life, the lack of animation.

Similarly the fierce exultancy in Blake's 'Gnomic Verses' which produced

> The Angel that presided o'er my birth
> Said, 'Little creature, form'd of joy and mirth,
> Go, Love without the help of anything on earth.

is transformed by Stevie into something querulous, colloquial and tragi-comic:

> She said as she tumbled the baby in:
> There, little baby, go sink or swim,
> I brought you into the world, what more should I do?
> Do you expect me always to be responsible for you?

One recurrent technical ploy is the adoption of familiar metre at the start of a poem followed by a sudden rejection of it. The introduction of prose lines may give the impression of a formal freedom that borders on carelessness. But this is not correct. Precisely because 'Lady "Rogue" Singleton' begins

> Come, wed me, Lady Singleton,
> And we will have a baby soon
> And we will live in Edmonton
> Where all the friendly people run.

with its ditty-like, four-stress lines, is she able to play fast and loose with the second verse and truncate its last line with such shattering effect.

> I could never make you happy, darling,
> Or give you the baby you want,
> I would always very much rather, dear,
> Live in a tent.

Our expectations, both of form and subject, are teased still more by the balmy serendipity of the concluding verse:

> I am not a cold woman, Henry,
> But I do not feel for you,
> What I feel for the elephants and the miasmas
> And the general view.

It is laughter that directs these poems, disavows any leaning towards portentousness and which gives the collection an enduring gaiety. This, despite the melancholy insistence on pain and isolation, a theme so constant that it gathers personal significance. Ironically, these poems express with consummate skill a failure in communication. Those that deal with this inability to relate to others, among them 'Dirge', 'Love Me!', 'In the Night', 'Lot's Wife' and 'The Failed Spirit', are among the most memorable, none more so than 'The Face'.

> There is a face I know too well,
> A face I dread to see,
> So vain it is, so eloquent
> Of all futility.
>
> It is a human face that hides
> A monkey soul within,
> That beats about, that beats a gong,
> That makes a horrid din.
>
> Sometimes the monkey soul will sprawl
> Athwart the human eyes,
> And peering forth, will flesh its pads,
> And utter social lies.

So wretched is this face, so vain,
So empty and forlorn,
You well may say that better far
This face had not been born.

Mother, What Is Man? was favourably but not extensively reviewed, one critic, E. C. Bentley, comparing her 'subtly clever' drawings with those of Edward Lear.[51] John Hayward felt the reviews had not been equal to the poems. 'Yes, there is a lot that hasn't been said about them,' Stevie replied by letter, 'but pretty sad stuff, I'm afraid, not sophisticated at all really, but sad, because most of them – on a quick glance – seem to be suffering either from not being loved enough, in the warm cosy affectionate way that we all like rather, or from being loved in this way by the wrong people. I am sure people read a lot of sophistication into my stuff that isn't really there. I mean they think it *couldn't be like that* just straight. Oh couldn't it. Example:

Dear female heart, I am sorry for you,
You may suffer, that is all that you can do,
Or else, if you like, with the rest of the human race,
You may also look most absurd with a miserable face.'[52]

If Stevie enjoyed epistolary friendship with men, at parties, as Mulk Raj Anand observed, she talked more to women. She enjoyed the company of intellectual women such as Sally Chilver or the art historian Phoebe Pool; her Cape editor, Veronica Wedgwood, became a friend, a useful friend in that, being also the literary editor of *Time and Tide*, she gave Stevie books to review, and they lunched together in cafés and restaurants down Museum Street and Charlotte Street. With other friends, Stevie would insist on going to her local, the Strand Palace Hotel whose Palm Court seemed to others vulgar and all too obviously a place for illicit lovers. Polly Hill, author of a book on unemployment, then working in the Civil Service, later to become economics correspondent for the magazine *West Africa* before finally leaving England in 1953 for Ghana and a career as a distinguished anthropologist, was one who lunched fairly regularly with Stevie during the war and who was taken by her to a reading given by Edith Sitwell. For Polly Hill, Stevie's ability to effervesce did not disguise a depressing sadness. She also had the impression that Stevie's obsession with herself clouded her judgement of others. 'I don't think she had the faintest idea of who I was,' Polly Hill now reflects. 'She giggled and that made the wheels of her internal world go round.'[53]

It is chiefly through her women friends that we gain glimpses of Stevie during the war years. Cecily Mackworth, who was to establish her reputation in 1947 with *A Mirror for French Poetry 1840–1940* as well as a study of Villon, first met Stevie in the offices of Mass-Observation in 1942.

'She stood in the doorway, waiting for someone, I suppose, a small, dark, skinny person, gazing sharply around her, taking everything in, yet remaining curiously apart. At first sight, I took her for a schoolgirl, because of the pre-adolescent figure and the navy-blue coat-and-skirt and the sailor hat perched on the back of the head. Then I saw the old-maidish lines marking an unfulfilled face and thought she must be full of sorrow and non-experience.

Later, we became friends. She was touchy and aggressive, a mixture of *naïveté* and wry wit. I understood that under the jaunty exterior, she was out of step with the world, or like a scale with one note played sharp instead of flat. She was always exhausted, forcing herself to stay erect when she would have liked to lie down.'[54]

Invited to Palmers Green, Cecily Mackworth was surprised by the gauche discomfort of Stevie's bedroom which contained only bare necessities. Her suggestion that Stevie should install a bedside lamp met with no positive response.

Stevie was not so occluded by her egocentricity as to be unable to act on another's behalf. She helped place a book of Polly Hill's poems with Chatto and Windus; and when Rachel Marshall lost a close friend in an air raid, Stevie wrote with direct sympathy and practicality, offering to cancel a visit to Cambridge: 'Visitors whoever they are are always something extra and when one is tired one simply cannot cope emotionally and all that I mean; my word I do understand that.'[55] Visits to the Marshalls enabled her to keep in touch with her Cambridge friends, the Newmans, Joan Robinson and also John Hayward who was temporarily living in Lord Rothschild's house. On one occasion Naomi Mitchison was also present. Her diary for 15 February 1942 records: 'To tea with the Marshalls, Stevie Smith there, much as ever: am not so good at talking to intellectuals.'[56]

At one of the Marshalls' parties Stevie met Helen Fowler, then working in Cambridge for the Ministry of Information. She was taken along by John Lowe, a colleague, who knew she was an admirer of Stevie Smith. Rachel Marshall seemed to her a handsome, grave woman, and Horace, silent and shy. 'At some point in the evening,' Helen Fowler has written, 'I must have been introduced to Stevie; we never seemed to stop talking after that, though I hope perhaps politely we did at times, for others to come up and make their mark or take their fill or whatever. By the time John took me away, it was arranged that she should come up to stay with me for the following weekend.' This was the first of many wartime weekends which Stevie spent with Helen in Botolph Lane. 'All I can remember of these,' she recounts, 'is crouching over a gas fire, endless talk, various friends to coffee and meals and Stevie's habit, even then in her late thirties/forty?, of returning to bed for rests, plus eiderdown and hot-water bottle. She was easily tired and easily bored: bed and solitude were necessary retreats. I was fourteen or fifteen years younger and geared to uneasy sympathy with geniuses.'[57]

They talked about books, poetry, plays and films, Stevie often making her visits coincide with a Cambridge Film Society showing. Helen, whose fiancé Laurence, was in the Indian army, fighting in Burma, was herself an Intelligence Officer for the Eastern Region and her work often took her to London where she would meet Stevie in the Arts Theatre Club for a drink or a sandwich, usually before a film. For Helen, the choice of activity scarcely mattered. 'Whatever one did with Stevie was spiked with flavour. Her flat rather drawling voice with its South Cockney vowels, was a perfect instrument, not only as she proved later, for the reading of her poems, but for the delivery of dry caustic or curious remarks. It was a voice for pungent criticism, for ribald relation, for ironic comment. It was also the voice of authority and learning, slightly nasal . . . It was a voice which echoed, not disguised, thought . . . To have Stevie's commentary on any commonplace activity one was engaged in with her, was to have a new view on life; situations tilted upside down, people assumed new dimensions, trivial episodes became as polished and important as New Yorker short stories.'[58]

Like most humorists, Stevie had a knack for seizing on the essential in any situation. But in conversation it was not so much what she said that mattered as the way she said it, in a voice at once naïve and sophisticated, and inclined to drawl. When she laughed she sometimes threw back her head in a sudden, unexpected movement. Likewise her humour was sudden and knife-like. It could disconcert, making people aware of her penetrating intelligence, her ever-vigilant curiosity. Sometimes it was used at others' expense: before visiting friends, of whom she was genuinely fond, she could be mordantly witty about the food she would be given. Her humour not only contributed to the comic achievement of her work but brought out its philosophic content. For the anarchy of her humour runs deep, making comparisons with James Thurber or Ogden Nash wholly unsatisfactory. Thurber's humour, for Stevie, had merely 'the blunt fun of the comic picture postcard, slightly upgraded'.[59] Her own use of irony and satire made her receptive to these qualities in the work of others. She greatly admired Evelyn Waugh's *Scoop* and was provoked by it, in a review, to declare satire to be a weapon proper to angels; 'or at least to the more angelic of our sort; a heart in the right place (and well in hand), a burning indignation, refined to the temper of a steel blade; a reformer's zeal; these are some of its attributes; I think of Voltaire and Swift'.[60]

CHAPTER 9

Fits and Splinters

Much of Stevie's mental energy during the war went into journalism. In 1940 and 1941 her book reviews appeared on average twice a month in *John O'London's Weekly*, and between 1943 and 1949, at more irregular intervals, in *Tribune*. For *Modern Woman*, she ploughed through as many as fourteen books each month, her book page first appearing in February 1941 and continuing for just over a decade. Shortage of space meant that each book had to be dealt with in a paragraph or less. 'These ladies' papers are a bit terrific you know,' she explained.[1] What distinguishes Stevie's *Modern Woman* contributions from the work of a hack is the combination of light tone with the unexpected remark. 'Drawn from the life, we suspect, with quite deadly precision' was her comment on Mary Westmacott's *Absent in the Spring*.[2] Such work fed her knowledge of contemporary fiction and left her very well practised, able, at a later date, to emerge as a distinctive, authoritative voice in the pages of the *Spectator*, the *New Statesman*, the *Observer* and the *Listener*.

Newnes remained her substructure: it paid her a salary and provided that spur of irritation necessary to creativity. It also left her familiar with the industry of journalism and taught her professionalism; she could be relied on to produce copy on time. Through Newnes she acquired useful friends and acquaintances. She was on good terms with those in the *Country Life* office and, though no contributions have been traced, agreed to review for them. She became friendly with Oliver Stewart, the editor of *Aeronautics*, a magazine that began in August 1939. It aimed to provide, its first editorial announced, 'an authoritative review of aeronautical information and opinion'. Story has it that Stevie, who knew little or nothing about aeroplanes, contributed to the humorous column, 'Candid Comments', which drew attention to ironies or absurdities connected with the Air Ministry, aircraft production or the RAF. The articles were simply signed 'Quax'. The person initially responsible for the column was called up in the autumn of 1939 and replaced by Quax II. In July 1940 a third person took over and under Quax III the articles took on a livelier note. None, however, are inaccurate in the information they use, and it seems probable that Stevie merely contributed suggestions, the odd phrase or joke. She may have volunteered illustrations to replace those by Bruce Angrave: Oliver Stewart's daughter, Madeau, recalls that Angrave once took Stevie out to lunch and a terrible row ensued.

She did, however, do four book reviews for *Aeronautics* and revealed her impatience, when writing on Vera Brittain's *England's Hour*, with wartime sentimentality, self-pity or whipped-up patriotism. She deplored Vera Brittain's shrillness: 'never once does she catch the authentic voice of England, as little hysterical as the growl of her guns.'[3] Also irritated by the condescending American attitude to England-at-War, she wrote for *Modern Woman* a short humorous piece entitled 'Helen Comes to Town' which pretends to report a conversation with a visitor from New York, Helen Vassar. It takes a positive view of the effect of rationing on the English diet and of utility clothes, and finds the general outlook phlegmatic but optimistic. Reflecting on the war in her novel *The Holiday*, Stevie again insisted on realism: 'People say people were heroic in the raids. They were certainly good humoured and plucky and uncomplaining, but is it heroism to endure the unavoidable? Is not heroism rather to seek an end through danger? There was no end thought of or sought.'[4]

On her walks in Grovelands Park Stevie watched the Home Guard practise bringing in the wounded. At night she, like everyone else, had to make her way through dark streets. In the mornings the air was sometimes filled with dust from bomb-damaged buildings. The nearest that the Blitz came to Palmers Green was when a V1 fell on Carpenter Gardens on 7 July 1944, about half a mile from Avondale Road. 'Everything in this world is in fits and splinters,' Stevie wrote in *The Holiday*, 'like after an air raid when the glass is on the pavements; one picks one's way and is happy in parts.'[5]

During this precarious but surprisingly carefree period Stevie continued to make new friends. One of these was Kay Dick who arrived at Newnes in 1943 to take up the assistant editorship of *John O'London's Weekly*. Though thirteen years younger than Stevie, Kay had a considerable reputation; she had previously managed the old publishing house, P. S. King and Son, having become, at the age of twenty-six, the first woman director in English publishing. She had also published poems and short stories in little magazines and was set on a career as novelist. In addition, she had great personal charm: her androgynous appeal was heightened by her sense of style and used to proclaim her sexual ambivalence. Her appearance at this time has been described by Wrey Gardiner:

'Kay is tall and wears a shirt open at the neck like a man in summer. She bends forwards slightly towards you as if she would dominate you with her blue eyes like the small flowers you find on the very cold heights of mountains, but which soften and deepen in certain eerie lights. Her beloved period is the nineties and she lives on her nerves and books.'[6]

Soon after she had started at Newnes Kay became aware that Stevie seemed to be making an unnecessary number of visits to the *John O' London's* office, as if wishing to assess this newcomer. As Kay was anxious to meet the author of *Novel on Yellow Paper* a friendship was soon established. Kay's sharpness and wit enabled Stevie to share with her in-jokes about Newnes employees, especially Wilson Midgeley, the editor of *John O'London's*, whom both women regarded as a Philistine. They frequently lunched together at nearby restaurants. Stevie was drawn to Kay's cheerfulness and 'go', her capacity to inject any social occasion with energy and humour. Related to this flair was a generosity that meant if she had to borrow £10 from a friend, £5 might disappear in a taxi driver's tip. On several occasions Kay felt that Stevie was attracted to her. She was occasionally excessively high-spirited in Kay's company and once, when dining with Kay and Barbara Vise at the Café Royal, Stevie behaved like a bad-tempered child because, Kay thought, she suspected a relationship between Kay and Barbara.

Kay's flamboyance may have drawn to the surface Stevie's own sexual ambivalence. Whilst working at Newnes, Kay was living with the novelist Kathleen Farrell in a flat in Belsize Park. Here, and later in a house in Heath Street, Hampstead, the two women enjoyed a well-established domestic arrangement which owed much to Kathleen. 'Small with large eyes,' Wrey Gardiner wrote of her, remarking also that she ran about the flat 'to a great deal of purpose exactly like a squirrel, a nice homely squirrel intent on the efficient harvesting of the moment.'[7] She also became a friend of Stevie's and offered her the use of the spare bedroom. On one occasion when it was agreed that Stevie would spend the night she arrived for a meal and the evening passed ordinarily. However, when bedtime arrived, Kathleen went into the spare room and found Stevie, as if affected by a sudden fever, in an hysterical state, banging her head against the wall. Kathleen persuaded her to go to bed and in the morning no explanation of this display of nerves, tension or frustration was asked for or given. But both Kathleen and Kay recollect that on this or another occasion Stevie left behind three poems,[8] one of which begins 'I love you darling / The moment before it is absolutely certain that you love me / Is flying', and which they presumed was addressed to Kay. Again no remark was made and neither incident prevented Stevie from enjoying an unproblematic relationship with both writers for several years.

In Kathleen Farrell, Stevie found a feminine, practical intelligence often lacking in her more intellectual friends. When Stevie gave a party during the war with two other women, one of them Inez Holden, she dragged Kathleen upstairs on her arrival to do what 'these academic gairls' couldn't do: pin up her skirt. In Kathleen's company Stevie once spent an afternoon in a Hampstead hat shop, acquiring two or three rather delicate items which Aunt declared 'unsuitable' and had to be returned.

Kay and Kathleen witnessed Stevie's evident pleasure in her wartime friendship with a Viennese refugee, Friedl Benedikt who lodged with her couins Margaret Gardiner in Downshire Hill. The daughter of Moritz Benedikt, the editor of the unrivalled, high-principled newspaper, *Neue Freie Presse*, Friedl had grown up in a home visited by many artists and writers, including Stefan Zweig, Thomas Mann and Elias Canetti. Friedl, who has been compared in appearance with the young Simone Signoret, married young and was swiftly divorced. She then trained as an actress and, under Canetti's influence, began to write. Their master pupil relationship continued in London during the war years and Friedl's first book, *Let Thy Moon Arise* (1944) was dedicated: 'To Elias Canetti, in gratitude and admiration.' Two subsequent books were also dedicated to Canetti whom Stevie met, in Friedl's company, at Downshire Hill.

It may have been through Stevie that Friedl was introduced to her publishers, Jonathan Cape, and to the reader-in-chief, Daniel George, who became a close friend. Kay Dick, who on leaving Newnes published excerpts from Friedl's journal in *The Windmill*, noticed an unusual rapport between Stevie and Friedl; often found giggling together, they were united by their sharp sense of the absurd. Stevie took Friedl to dinner with Kay and Kathleen in May 1943 and afterwards stayed the night at Downshire Hill. 'I feel a bit raddled as we didn't get to bed till 5 am,' she told Kay. 'We found old Des [J. D. Bernal] already in bed and had more pots of tea with him and infinite talk.'⁹ Friendship with Friedl may have encouraged Stevie to introduce into *The Holiday* an element of non-naturalistic farce, as when Captain Maulay, announced by a loud crash, bounds into the room with a paper bag full of cream buns, or when a German officer, his plane shot down, is fished out of the lake. In *Let Thy Moon Arise*, in which the main character is, as Friedl admitted to Susan Watson, in part based on Stevie (most noticeably when she grins and her red gums show), the humour is frequently grotesque and bizarre, the characters simplified or distorted for satiric effect as in an Edward Burra painting. Friedl delighted in the strange and unexpected and pushed things to an extreme, partly in reaction against her upper-crust Viennese background. Her moods swung violently between a lively gaiety, which brought her many friends, and a morbid depression which left her on some days unable to get out of bed. When low she vented the belief that she would die young, a prophecy that proved correct: she died of Hodgkin's disease in Paris in 1953 while still in her thirties.

While living at Downshire Hill she was not the easiest of house guests. Nevertheless, when Margaret Gardiner left London for Fingest to give birth to her son by J. D. Bernal, she left Friedl in charge of the house. For a while Susan Watson stayed there, and on Christmas Day she, Friedl and Stevie attended a party in West Hampstead. Stevie, making use of Desmond Bernal's sola topi and Margaret Gardiner's emerald-green leather slippers and emerald-green beads, went dressed in khaki shorts and shirt, as Pompey does in *Over the Frontier*. Afterwards she again spent the night at Downshire Hill where, on another occasion, Margaret Gardiner had returned home late to find Stevie sitting disconsolate in the kitchen, wanting her usual late-night drink of warm milk but unable to make it for herself.

Under the name Anna Sebastian, Friedl continued to publish novels and short stories much influenced by the example of Canetti, and, though herself heterosexual, left unpublished at the time of her death a homosexual novella. Stevie, mixing with writers and intellectuals, was very aware of various types of sexuality. If, as her novels suggest, butch lesbianism and 'masculine agape' irritated her, she was too sophisticated and urbane to demand of others sexual orthodoxy. When another of her friends, Jane de Gras, who was head of Soviet Studies at Chatham House, introduced Stevie to the political journalist T. E. Utley, he felt, his aural intelligence sharpened by his blindness, that the *possibility* of sexual ambiguity was evident in her voice. What he heard was a more than usual detachment from conventional pressures. It explained for him her political scepticism, her freedom from radical enthusiasms.

During the second half of the war Stevie continued to spend occasional nights at Inez Holden's flat, going to PEN events with her and in June 1944 attending a lecture given by Arthur Koestler and afterwards dining with him, Inez and Herman Ould at the Étoile in Charlotte Street. Fire-watching also obliged her to pass some of her nights in central London. In this way she met Norah Smallwood, who worked at the publishers Chatto and Windus and was to become its chairman. Together they discovered one night that a door into the Coliseum was open. Going inside to look round they found themselves in a dressing room with a box full of false noses and other such props. Stevie fell on it with delight and twirled and mimed.

Another friend who willingly put Stevie up for the night, at her house in Maida Vale, was Sally Chilver. Her husband, Richard, discussed biblical texts with Stevie, egged her on in her agnostic beliefs and suggested books she should read. In turn, Sally Chilver was invited to Avondale Road where her deep resonant voice made her attractive to Aunt for it was at a pitch that she could hear. Whereas most of Stevie's friends recall how, after making them welcome, Aunt remained noticeably silent or slipped away, in Sally Chilver's company she joined in the conversation, revealing a remarkable memory for domestic detail, the price of oysters in 1910 or the way people used to trim their hats. Her reminiscences were vivid: the subject might be slight but her manner was engaging. Sally Chilver had the impression that Stevie and her aunt enjoyed many conversations of this kind.

The first mention of Stevie's third novel occurs in a letter to John Hayward, dated 19 August 1942: 'John another reason I haven't written to you is that I am writing another novel. I have got to 25,000 words already. I am not particularly happy about it but I suppose one never is meanwhile it pours out with never a point virgule or whatever it is. Everybody is in it and everybody's conversations. I do hope I see you again soon so that I can put some of yours in, heigh ho . . .'[10] Some of her originals are recognizable: the character Tengal is based on Desmond Bernal, and, as has been mentioned, Lopez on Inez Holden, Raji on Mulk Raj Anand and Tom Fox and Basil Tait both to some extent on Orwell, a division that helped avoid libel, always a risk where Stevie was concerned. In addition, the poet Blind may allude to W. H. Auden who was a friend of Margaret Gardiner. But despite recognizable characteristics, Stevie's characters do not come weighed down with realistic detail but exist more as disembodied voices. As Stevie herself warned: 'My characters start off by being themselves but are soon unrecognizable as real people.'[11]

By August 1943 she began to wonder if what she had so far written had any value. 'It is this terrible personal stuff,' she admitted to John Hayward, '. . . written in a jig of private feelings and secretarial odd jobs.'[2] She had been reading the more conventional author, Somerset Maugham, whose cool, controlled manner, she thought, showed that he had learnt what to do with private feelings. Meanwhile *The Holiday*, with its swift changes of mood, incidents and ideas, reflected the conditions under which Stevie wrote, in the intervals of office life where she was always a prey to interruption. We glimpse her state of mind in another letter to John Hayward:

'How much my so interrupting baronets give me the fidgets, dear, you cannot imagine. But then on the other side – damn the other side – They do pay me, and they are fairly merciful employers, an opinion I have always held, in print or otherwise! "What is the matter, Pompey?" "Nothing only I SO MUCH WANT YOU TO GO AWAY." . . . it does get one into the habit of interruptions, so that even if there actually aren't any, one makes them for oneself.'[3]

As with her previous two novels, *The Holiday* is something of a portmanteau into which Stevie threw whatever concerned her at that time. It not only draws upon themes and ideas that had already surfaced in her poems, but provides a blueprint for much that was to come. Again, it demonstrates her commingling of voices for not only are quotations from others, including a long passage from Dostoevsky's *White Nights* or *Notes from the Underground*, found here, but it also incorporates her own verse, a condensed version of her short story, 'In the Beginning of the War' as well as a review she had written for *John O'London's* on Helen Barrett's *Boethius*.

In *The Holiday* Stevie abandons the name Pompey Casmilus for Celia Phoze who works not in a publisher's office but in a government ministry. This alteration in her narrator's employment made possible the many references to the war, all of which had to be altered or cut when the book was updated to the post-war period, a change that was thought desirable when it was published in 1949. Despite this concern with external matters the narrative is again selectively autobiographical. Celia lives with her aunt in a suburb in circumstances not unlike Stevie's. In the manuscript of *The Holiday* Celia complains that unlike an army moving victoriously across a desert, she is 'stuck in the corruption of a literary mash, the trivial, the boring, the inescapable'. This self-reflexive allusion is, however, lost in the published version where 'literary mash' is replaced with the less specific 'post-war consequence'. Also cut is another passage that referred perhaps too obviously to the author rather than the narrator: 'But to sit indoors, I said, and see the friends come and go, and write a little, and review the books that you do not want to read – la guerre est triste et j'ai lu tous les blurbs – that is not pleasure.'[14]

The characters who ornament the book are few in number and close links unite the central core. Tiny, who works in the same Ministry as Celia, has a brother called Clem and a sister, Lopez, who is Celia's friend. Celia, herself, has two cousins, Caz, who is about to depart for India, and the mentally unbalanced Tom. The pairing of characters suggests that in each case one is the complement of the other, Tom's madness a negative counterpart to Caz's maturity and good sense, Clem's viciousness, the opposite to Tiny's meekness. It could be argued that Caz is the male counterpart to Celia and that in the same way that she divides Orwell's opinions between Basil and Tom, so she was able to share her split feelings over India between Caz and Celia. The love that unites Celia and Caz is prevented from finding full expression owing to the aforementioned suspicion of consanguinity. Their forbidden happiness, as Richard Church noted, 'colours the whole book and gives a tinge of desperation to all the other relationships, touching them with that light of catastrophe and finality which we all experience during moments of disaster'.[15]

Despite a greater use of dialogue, Celia's voice dominates the book. She satirizes pretension and hypocrisy, admits to a patriotism that makes her think of England 'with pride, aggression and complacency',[16] is caustic about office life and the social importance of writers, and talks with humorous affection about her aunt. Near the start Celia remarks that the post-war situation has left England 'stretched out and thin'. She adds: 'I feel that I am frozen. It is cold *inside* too.'[17] The book throughout conveys a sense that private life has become inseparable from the general climate. Celia's melancholy or 'sadness deficiency feeling' makes her ask:

'What is the dog within us that howls against it [happiness], the dog that tears and howls, that is no creature of ours, that lies within, kennelled and howling, that is an alien animal, an enemy? It is the desire to tear out this animal, to have our heart free of him, to have our heart for ourselves and for the innocent happiness, that makes us cry out against life, and cry for death. For this animal is kennelled close within, and tearing out this animal we tear out also the life with it.

> I'll have thy heart, if not by gift my knife
> Shall carve it out, I'll have thy heart, thy life.'[18]

After the passage on Boethius, which tells how, unjustly imprisoned and sentenced to death, he overcame despair and wrote *The Consolation of*

Philosophy, Celia observes that 'he operated with integrity in situations of horror and depression and from a full heart of black experience he wrote his book'.[19] She, too, wishes to write a noble book but feels that the times are wrong. What we are given in *The Holiday* is, in Hermione Lee's words, 'a spiritual autobiography, a political essay, and an idiosyncratic exercise in poetic prose',[20] written in a style that is abrupt, playful, free-wheeling, comic and poetic. Its fast-changing mood is unsettling; it not only makes the book difficult to pigeon-hole but also conveys the impression that the final text, despite its revisions, remains close to the moment of creation. Political views are often challenged by another speaker and no single view is given decisive authority. As Celia remarks: 'Always there are these under-tugs and cross currents, nothing is simple, nothing to be settled.'[21] And when her Uncle Heber remarks that there is no answer in politics she feels immensely lightened.

Celia's 'pick-rag mind . . . full of tags of the church, and the classics'[22] is reminiscent of Pompey's mental agility. It helps give to *The Holiday* a fragmented narrative, rapid and light, sustained more by mood than by plot, and which hints at depths on the surface of which the tale skims. If *Novel on Yellow Paper*, as Stevie once admitted, 'just happened to come off, it had a sort of lightheartedness that scraped it through',[23] *The Holiday* underwent considerable revision. It is a light but not light-hearted book. The drawing on the dust-jacket was also used by Stevie for her 1948 Christmas card. It shows a female figure, naked and alone, in a wood beside a stream, communing with her own thoughts and with nature. In 1950 she again used this drawing to illustrate the poem 'Voices about the Princess Anemone' in which the Princess is married to fear ('fear is a band of gold on the King's daughter'). Likewise, *The Holiday* is a book committed to pain and fear. Not only does Celia feel she is suffering from 'a black split heart' that disavows any possibility of innocence, but Uncle Heber reinforces her despair by declaring 'the times are the times of a black split heart'.[24] When reading J. C. Powys's *The Pleasures of Literature* in 1940, Stevie had admired his chapter on St Paul, as she told Naomi Mitchison,[25] perhaps because for Powys St Paul's greatness lay in his constant awareness of world-pain: 'he alone of the New Testament writers is conscious of this dark and terrible background to the tenderness and sweetness of the new dispensation.'[26] Stevie's own response to the dark side of the Scriptures led her to quote in *The Holiday* from Psalm 137 which tells of the captivity of Israel and ends with the bitter words: 'Blessed shall he be that taketh thy children; and throweth them against the stones.'[27]

One ambiguity at the heart of the narrative is Celia's desire for God and her impatience with Christianity. She finds Christian philosophy inadequate, its system of belief too much bearing the mark of our humanity: 'In its extreme tidy logic it is a diminution and a lie.'[28] Yet while Uncle Heber tends his church Celia kneels in the aisle and asks: 'How can we come back to God, to be taken into Him, when we are so hard and so separate and do not grow . . . if we are to be taken back, oh why were we sent out, why were we sent away, why were we sent away from God?'[29] This desolation is not momentary but closely related to the melancholy that suffuses the entire book. At one point Celia recollects a foreign graveyard where she prayed: 'Thou art all that we know of good and very much more, Thou art all wisdom, truth and beauty, Thou art love, Thou art the source of our being and the desire of our hearts, grant that we may return again to Thee.'[30] While resisting Christian orthodoxy, her thoughts return to one recurrent idea: that, as with Christ, it is through suffering that we attain glory, immortality, reconciliation with the divine. The philosophical framework upon which this idea is built is given near the start of the book through the metaphor of a man playing cards watched by another:

'And the cards are the fate, and the player is the life, and the watcher is the spirit. Yes, this Watcher is a bit of an enigma. Perhaps he is the *Weltgeist*. So then it is like a dream, it shifts, and the player and the cards vanish, but in their place there is now a stream that is made of two parts, that mix together, that make a food mixture. But the spirit is there, and he is hungry. So he stoops and drinks of that food mixture. And now he is no longer hungry.'[31]

This idea returns towards the close of the book:

'But close within there sits the soul that is a crystal carapace that no claw can scratch, that has no mark upon it for all mind's storms, that feeds upon the tears and the blood. And why should it not so feed? Is it not of God? sent out to be lost for a time? to return? So let it feed and grow fat, and return to God in admirable plight, yes, let it feed.'[32]

In spite of this yearning for a divinity, Celia returns us to the here and now with her final comment to Uncle Heber: Confucius is right: 'human beings are our concern, and not heaven or hell or the life to come, and indeed, with human beings, yes, just with this and no more, it is already enough.'[33]

The Holiday reflects no diminution in Stevie's obsession with death. 'Death is the scope of our immediacy,' she began her short story, 'In the Beginning of the War'. And in another, the Lewis Carroll-like 'Is There a Life Beyond the Gravy?', her characters progress from adults into children before realizing that they have been dead for ages. 'The dead, then survive, but only fragmentarily, feebly, as mere wisps of floating memories,' wrote Aldous Huxley in *Music at Night* (1930),[34] where the Romans' belief that the dead squeak and gibber is affirmed for him by the findings of modern psychic researchers and compared with what he calls the 'harp and scream' view of immortality associated with Platonic and Christian theory. Stevie, in her copy of this book, marked, 'The living sometimes have dreams or waking visions of the dead'. It is tempting to regard *The Holiday* in these terms. At one point Celia, surprised to discover that Caz's skin is cool and firm, remarks that he is very much flesh and blood. Caz laughs: 'I am the most flesh and blood of all your dream.'[35]

While discussing his 'squeak and gibber' theory, that the dead survive, faintly, as mere shadows, Huxley quotes *Ecclesiastes* 10:9: 'There is no work, no device, nor knowledge, nor wisdom in Sheol, whither thou goest.' This passage, familiar to Stevie, merged in her mind with what she once referred to as Emperor Hadrian's 'poignant, pagan and unserious question': 'In what places, my soul, separated from the body, will you now wander, naked and exposed, where there is little familiar laughter and no warmth.'[36] Both passages find an echo near the end of the book in the sermon Celia writes and which begins: 'There is little laughter where you are going and no warmth . . .'[37] It proceeds to evoke a desolate landscape where the soul 'frivolous and vulnerable' and 'racked by useless grief' attains a 'slow death'. There is no suggestion here of what is promised elsewhere in *Ecclesiastes* (12:7), that 'the spirit shall return unto God who gave it', a desire Celia had earlier expressed, but instead an account of death that brings to a climax the black melancholy which suffuses the book as a whole.

Helen Fowler's response to the book was one that others shared: more used to Pompey's easier, conversational tone, she was initially disappointed in *The Holiday*. Its heightened reality can seem raw and artificial. It affronts our expectations of the novel and operates on a level that is closer to poetry than prose. When Celia writes a letter home, Caz asks why she signs it 'Sailor': 'Because I left them, I say, I left them, I sailed away. Oh, Death,'[38] she replies, in terms that are metaphoric and elegiac. In its almost unbearable intensity, *The Holiday* invites comparison with Sylvia Plath's *The Bell Jar*. In both the main character experiences a nervous breakdown and attempts suicide. But whereas the mental torture described by Plath is located in a world of asylums, doctors and electric shock treatment, Celia's suffering is, as the reference to Persephone suggests, more mythical and symbolic. Stevie, who in 1940 had complained of Wells that he had 'no conception of spiritual strife or of the importance of spiritual things',[39] insists on this terrain, which, like the effect of the Lincolnshire park on

Celia, leaves impressed 'a sense of melancholy sweet sadness, of a tragedy of huge dimension but uncertain outline, of wrongs forgotten whose pain alone remains . . .'⁴⁰

The Holiday never enjoyed the success of *Novel on Yellow Paper*, though it sold well and became a Book Society recommendation. The critics admired it but their praise was often heavily qualified. Inez Holden praised its 'dancing prose', its understanding and lightness of touch but felt it marred by too many tears.⁴¹ R. A. Scott-James observed that Stevie's light-heartedness carried 'a terrifying burden of serious import . . . the tragic problem of the individual and the corresponding problem of the human race in its present perplexities'.⁴² P. H. Newby thought that the book caught 'much of the post-war confusion of mind'.⁴³ He wrote again on *The Holiday* in *The Novel 1945–50*:

'*The Holiday* . . . strikes me as an act of courage rather than a work of art, but courage of an order few contemporary writers of integrity would be capable of. She [Stevie Smith] is a poet of quality and there are moments in her prose when she rises to a strange unanalysable beauty . . . she can be very funny indeed; but the undercurrent is, it seems to me, dark, cold and frightening.'⁴⁴

In spite of the appreciation *The Holiday* received, Stevie never attempted another novel. When Professor Hans Häusermann wrote an article on her novels in 1957, she revealed her distaste for them in her reply. Some 'ghastly human confusion and chill' underlay all three books, she admitted, adding: 'How right you are about the nervousness of the writing, there is some dreadful fear that pursues always, and that has no form or substance . . . It *is* like the sea, sunny and bright (sometimes) on the surface and black and so cold seven miles down, and with such pressure the water lies . . . So now you know why I don't want to write another novel.'⁴⁵ To Jonathan Williams six years later she admitted being afraid of novels and of what she said in them: 'In a poem you can turn the emotions and feelings onto someone else, onto different characters. You can invent stories. You'd think you could do that in a novel. Other people can, and have. *But I can't.*'⁴⁶

The return of peace brought little outward change in Stevie's life. She was still in full-time employment at Newnes which on its book publishing side had enjoyed increased sales during the war, and once the paper shortage ended, again flourished as a magazine empire. Credit for its success is usually given to Herbert Tingay who ruled the firm with a gimlet eye. One Newnes employee, James Drawbell, has described him as 'a business man first' with 'a remarkable understanding of the editorial mentality and temperament and a real flair for knowing how to ally it to his needs'.[47] Tingay's control may explain why Sir Neville Pearson's attempts to introduce his son Nigel into the firm failed. The problem of management succession, combined with the need to adapt to changing conditions, were to trouble the firm in future years and led to amalgamations and takeovers. But during Stevie's time Newnes remained in competition with Odhams and Amalgamated Press, one of the three leading magazine houses.

If Stevie had become a fixture at Newnes, the staff around her changed rapidly. Kay Dick left to go free-lance; Barbara Vise was soon to enter public relations. Stevie was never averse to making new friends, but a middle-aged spinster of increasingly eccentric appearance can seem rebarbative to a young person of limited experience. Not always, however. Bill Shrimpton entered the firm in 1945 at the age of fifteen, read a Penguin edition of *Novel on Yellow Paper* and took every opportunity he could to carry messages to Stevie's office where a bay wreath on the inside of her door rustled as it opened. He saw that Stevie was not well treated by the firm, was often sent on errands that an office junior should have done and was the butt of office jokes. The slightest eccentricity, even a glimpse of her greying pink bloomers, became a subject for mirth. Odd views were expected of her, for she was all too obviously now a person who did not fit in. She still had friends within the firm, among the researchers at work on a reprint of *Chambers' Encyclopaedia* and also Miss Wilkinson, the librarian, but in the canteen she often sat alone. To the young Bill Shrimpton, there was no one to touch her in Newnes, by way of intellect, and he delighted in the wholeheartedness with which she entered into conversation with him. He saw too, however, that to Stevie, always on the outside, most Newnes employees had only a shadowy existence.

Privately, in the spring of 1945, she feared she had cancer. Two doctors were consulted and an X-ray taken. Though her fears were unjustified, some physical disorder was discovered as she was advised to drink two pints of milk a day and eat small meals at frequent intervals. Meanwhile, in 1946, Molly resigned from Westonbirt School and became Drama Adviser to Buckinghamshire County. She bought a flat in Aylesbury where the Aunt stayed when Stevie went away. The flat had 'gadgets of every description',[48] Aunt said, herself accustomed to the domestic arrangements at Avondale Road that had prevailed since the Edwardian era. When staying with Molly, Aunt waited as anxiously for news of Stevie's health and travel arrangements as if her niece were still in her teens.

In *The Holiday* Celia remarks of one of her aunt's floral dresses that it looks like an advertisement for Carter's seeds. 'My Aunt thinks it was pretty awful of me to write about her dress ("unnecessary" is the word) but I think she is pleased all the same.'[49] So she told Anthony Powell, then in charge of novel reviewing for the *Times Literary Supplement* and who had steered *The Holiday* into sympathetic hands. Something of Stevie's relationship with Aunt is caught in *The Holiday* where Celia says: 'I love my Aunt, I love her, I love the life in the family, my familiar life, but I like also to go out and to see how the other people get along.'[50] In her manuscript this passage originally read: 'I love my aunt I love her, as I do not love men, as I do not love parties, but I can get by with men and I can get by with parties. I love my aunt, but I like to go out . . .'[51]

Compared with her love for her aunt, all other intimate relationships in Stevie's life were abortive. After reading one of Helen Fowler's novels, Stevie admitted that she could have only an inadequate response to it as love for her was foreign territory. She confessed the same to Sally Chilver in 1956, after reading some of her friend's poems:

'There's a stir in most of them that seems to be about *love* that I do not always quite catch successfully (to be infected by, I mean) that troubled stirring world of Two's is always strange to me, people *generally* are a stir & a trouble, & a pleasure, too, of course, but I cannot ever get the *à deux* fix.'[52]

Her profound distrust of the *à deux* situation inspired her translation of Mallarmé:

> 'We shall never be one mummy only
> Beneath the antique deserts and the happy palms.'

And led her elsewhere to say of the biblical tag, 'they twain shall be one flesh', that it was: 'Not true. Separateness is our nature, never can two be one, nobody would wish it.'[53]

Her apparent failure to sustain an intimate relationship may be related to her love for her aunt. Fascinated by the aunt–niece relationship, she discussed with Kathleen Farrell the 1890s poets, Katherine Bradley and Edith Cooper who adopted the pseudonym, Michael Field. She was as intrigued by the partnership of Edith Somerville and Martin Ross, again aunt and niece, who together wrote some thirty books. Her own aunt demonstrated that one could live quite happily independent of the male sex. Stevie's remark, in the manuscript of *The Holiday*, 'I do not love men', may have been a playful extension on Aunt's habit of exclaiming, 'Men!', in such a way as to imply that they were a grubby, unfortunate species. Stevie may, however, have excised her remark because its opposite could be inferred.

Not long after the war, at a time when she was revising the manuscript of *The Holiday*, Stevie had a brief affair with a woman introduced to her by Inez Holden. Scottish by birth but brought up in Canada, she had worked in Prague and Berlin before war broke out, had been involved in underground activities assisting Jewish emigration and had narrowly escaped capture by the Gestapo. After the war she began work as a psychiatric social worker and underwent analysis, eventually herself becoming a psychotherapist. Married to a barrister, she found she could neither adjust to nor alleviate his alcoholism and their relationship soon ended. She remained living in their maisonette in Fitzroy Street, next door to the composer, Elisabeth Lutyens, who became curious as to her neighbour's relationship with Stevie.

Whereas Stevie was nervous and diffident, this woman, who shall here be called Mary, was unhesitatingly direct. Similar in height to Stevie, she too enjoyed swimming in Hertfordshire rivers and chanting gloomy hymns. Her knowledge of hagiology allowed Stevie to indulge her interest in the more lurid lives of the saints. She also shared Stevie's belief that, in certain conditions, suicide was acceptable. Stevie was intrigued by her friend's work and expected her to have an exceptional understanding of others' motives. Psychology amused, fascinated and frightened Stevie. Nevertheless, she probably talked more freely to this woman than to anyone else about her own sexuality. She once expressed the wish that someone should write the equivalent, in sexual terms, to William James's *Varieties of Religious Experience*. When Mary suggested that Havelock Ellis had done so, Stevie admitted having read him but thought he used too many words. From the paperbacks, acquired secondhand, that were added to her collection of books, right up until the end of her life, it would appear that Stevie remained inquisitive about the psychology of sex, perhaps never attaining that 'tent of quietness'[54] she so much desired.

Before a year was out Stevie had brought the affair to a close. The conflicts it created in her, particularly in relation to Aunt and her own creativity, must have been considerable. Though she would spend nights at Fitzroy Street, she never seriously considered Mary's suggestion that they should share a flat in St John's Wood. Mary had, however, already met the woman who was to replace Stevie in her affections and with whom she was to establish a lasting relationship. Stevie remained on terms of friendship with both and was a frequent visitor to the home they established. 'We gave her a certain stability,' Mary avers. They also shared her love of rice pudding.

'Nothing is more secret than a woman's existence,' Marguerite Yourcenar has written. 'Life . . . is far more complex than any of its possible definitions; every simplified vision of life always risks being crude.'⁵⁵ Likewise any attempt to pin down Stevie's attitude to homosexuality runs the risk of caricature. In the 1920s, when reading *Harvest in Poland*, she responded with conventional piety to Geoffrey Dennis's description of a homosexual nightclub. 'The sins of Sodom and Lesbos', her notes read, 'are graphically portrayed. The poor Lesbians – so unhappy in their vice.'⁵⁶ A few years later she read Radclyffe Hall's *The Well of Loneliness*: 'with reversed covers and a delicious sense of guilt – since Joynson Hicks' heavy feet went down with such reverberations. I don't think RH makes her case, although she jettisons humour and taste in her efforts. Taste, in those tiresome lapses into near-biblical language, *humour* notably in the description of Mary and Barbara discussing in their best Home Notesy tradition the idiosyncracies of their "men" folk. There is a preface or note of recommendation by Havelock Ellis. But he writes without discernment, deliberately perhaps, in an effort not to spoil his own market.'⁵⁷ Reading and experience continued to broaden her view, though she remained critical of certain behavioural patterns and stereotypes associated with homosexuality. In 1953, when reviewing Mary Renault's novel, *The Charioteer*, which dealt with homosexuality, she quoted the schoolmistress's plea in the film *Mädchen in Uniform* – 'Die Liebe ist tausendformig', and added, 'love of any sort being held preferable to an absence of love, and this without prejudice to the sad commonplace that among the lower denizens of the world of inversion love so often takes a shape indistinguishable to the normal eye from plain malice'.⁵⁸

To Mary, Stevie admitted that she could give love but found it difficult to accept that she could be the object of love. Adopting Chesterton's title, she felt, she said, the Wrong Shape.

> It was as though a fiend had swung
> Him by the toe when he was young
> And swung him so
> And to and fro
> And swore and said he should be most oppressed
> When most against a loving friend he pressed.⁵⁹

She often repeated a line from *The Holiday*, that 'love is a desperate chance clutch upon a hen-coop in mid-Atlantic'.⁶⁰ She makes Celia observe that sadness 'stops anything but the most sketchy of the love-sex idea'.⁶¹ Her own sadness went hand in hand with a fear of life which, as she wrote in the blurb for *Mother, What Is Man?*, is more common than fear of death. After reading a biography of Dame Ethel Smyth, she remarked of the affair with

Virginia Woolf that it was 'helped by those letters the two ladies exchanged, those wild, peculiar, sensitive letters that make one wonder how any mere human soul, let alone the nervous human soul of an artist, can survive such intimacies'.[62] If Stevie herself briefly survived such intimacy, she did so in privacy. She herself retained no letter that reflected any great intimacy or passion. Unlike present-day radical feminists, she did not regard personal relationships as an arena for political change. If 'love of any sort' is preferable to an absence of love, it had to be managed with tact: 'once out of bed, pursue your own way, but do not make such a fuss up, it is for a dirge and disturbance of all peace.'[63] Her own gift was not for feminism, nor, as Paul Zweig remarks of Walt Whitman, 'for love but for poetry, and for the obscure moral courage that keeps the deep source of emotions fully alive, even when the familiar sentimental satisfactions are lacking'.[64]

Of the eleven existing short stories by Stevie,[65] most were written during the 1940s when she still considered fiction a possible vehicle for her thought. She admired skill ('This beautiful writing,' she said of Carson McCullers's *The Heart is a Lonely Hunter*, 'is most careful and the persons and scenes are picked with the highest skill and played upon for shifting emphasis and for the thing as a whole'[66]) but her own short stories resist fine writing or any technique that might interfere with accuracy, that precision of statement, dialogue and feeling which makes them so sharp and vivid. Primarily attempts at catching experience, they lack the formal rigour which rhyme and rhythm gives her poetry. They are also often very spare. Reginald Moore, editor of *Modern Reading*, turned down 'Over-Dew' because it seemed to him merely a synopsis, containing only the bare outline of the story.

Her short stories demonstrate her enjoyment in the inconsequent and absurd. In 'A Very Pleasant Evening', which Cecil Day Lewis published in *Orion*, the conversation lurches from kangaroos and their young to the limitations of modern poetry, knocking against other topics en route. The idiosyncracies in human character and thought are also vividly used in 'Sunday at Home' which was originally titled 'Enemy Action'. Based on her friends, Francis and Margery Hemming, it is a tragi-comic portrait of marital discord. This was one instance where the story's closeness to actuality (the couple soon after split up) caused offence. Francis Hemming, a brilliant, erratic civil servant saw his own paranoia and sense of doom in the portrait of Ivor. He objected to the publication of the story and in the row which followed Stevie's friend, the art historian Phoebe Pool, who was devoted to Francis Hemming, was caught up. This tug of war became another tale, 'The Story of a Story', in which Ba is based on Phoebe Pool. In this Helen (alias Stevie) dreams she is being cross-examined by Roland (alias Francis Hemming) who says: 'You go into houses under cover of friendship and steal away the words that are spoken.' This seems an accurate description of what Stevie did. Helen's defence is that her story is beautiful and truthful: 'It is a spiritual truth.' 'You want it both ways,' replies Bella (alias Margery Hemming).[67]

These two short stories temporarily lost Stevie Francis Hemming's and Phoebe Pool's friendship. The same thing happened in 1949 when she published 'Beside the Seaside'. In this case Stevie lost the friendship of a woman of great charm and originality. Irish by birth and the cousin of Henri Bergson, Betty Miller was in 1946 the author of eight novels, having published her first at the age of twenty-two. In 1933 she had married the psychiatrist Emmanuel Miller, eighteen years her senior, and was to draw on his professional knowledge, allowing a strong Freudian bias to infiltrate her biography of Robert Browning (1952). More intellectual than Stevie, Betty Miller delighted Isaiah Berlin, among others, with her rambling talk and collected at her home in St John's Wood a circle of literary friends which included Stevie, Olivia Manning, Naomi Lewis, Kay Dick and Inez Holden. Emmanuel Miller did not like his wife's sly, mocking literary friends and the coven they created. His son, Jonathan Miller, recollects that, together, these women were snobbish, fastidious and easily grated by vulgar suburbanisms, and that in addition, Stevie and Inez represented Fitzrovia, the more bohemian end of London's literary world with which Emmanuel felt ill at ease. Aware of his dislike, Betty Miller never vaunted her work: typewriter and papers were swept off the dining-room table the moment she heard her husband's key in the door. She also adopted a rueful, self-derogatory sense of humour.

Sally Chilver once accompanied Stevie to the Millers's and remembers how Jonathan, then a schoolboy, later to become renowned as a theatre and opera director with a flair for original interpretations, behaved outrageously. He himself as a child thought Stevie extraordinarily funny, 'an exotic visitor from another world, altogether ethereal, not unlike Mary Poppins'. But when he saw Laurence Olivier play Richard III he was also struck by a likeness to Stevie. When she was present there was much talk about Palmers Green which, to the young boy, seemed 'a mysterious place of infinitely extended greenery where Stevie was at play'. She was 'never a disapproving or silencing figure', but someone who, with his mother, generated 'a great deal of funny, subtle, spare amusement'. The brief letters the two women exchanged also struck him as 'tiny fairy notes'.[68]

Stevie's view of the young boy was less kind. Francis Wyndham has told how at a small gathering at Inez Holden's flat Stevie read her poem 'A Mother's Hearse' shortly after Betty Miller left.

> Oh why is that child so spoilt and horrible
> His mother has never neglected the trouble
> Of giving him his will at every turn
> And that is why his eyes do burn.
>
> His eyes do burn with a hungry fire
> His fingers clutch at the air and do not tire
> He is a persecuting force
> And as he grows older he grows worse.

Francis Wyndham had no idea that the mother and child related to Betty and Jonathan Miller. The day after the party he was rung up by Olivia Manning who wanted to know what Stevie had read. Francis Wyndham told her and later heard from Inez that Olivia had immediately rung Betty and described the incident in a most hurtful way. Betty was not 'furious', as has been stated,[69] but understandably upset. It was, however, not this poem but the short story, 'Beside the Seaside: A Holiday with Children', published in 1949, which caused Betty Miller to sever relations with Stevie.

It is the best of her short stories, capturing the tempo of a summer holiday as well as slight incidents and altercations that disturb it. Helen is staying with her friends Henry and Margaret Levison, and their two children, Hughie and Anna, in the same way that Stevie stayed with the Millers and their children, Jonathan and Sarah, at the Marine Guest House, Marine Parade, Hythe in August 1947, and again at Swanage, in August 1948. On the second of these occasions Elisabeth Lutyens was staying at a clinic near by, and visited Stevie and the Millers one day when Reggie Smith and Olivia Manning were also present. They all ate in the very ordinary guest house (Seaways, The Parade) where Elisabeth Lutyens, in a loud and very upper-class tone of voice digressed on the sexual limitations of her first husband. To Reggie Smith, Betty Miller seemed gentle and quiet, the somewhat crushed Jewish wife, as Stevie portrays 'Margaret' in her story. Much else in the story is lifted direct from life. Helen's observation, that the child Anna is like a seal, echoes Stevie's habit of referring to Sarah Miller as 'my little seal'. The portraits of Henry and Margaret are recognizably Emmanuel and Betty Miller, and the abominable Hughie, with his driving need for an audience, all too obviously the young Jonathan Miller who excelled at, among other things, take-offs of Danny Kaye.

Betty Miller initially responded to the story on the telephone. She then sent a short letter.

'As a story, I enjoyed it enormously – I think it is charming – full of nostalgic quality – and I could not help but admire it. What distresses me however is that you have described in it an episode which upset me considerably at the time, and which I myself, as you may remember, told you about – in confidence – next morning.

I did not think that under the circumstance you would choose to make use of that.'⁷⁰

It is difficult to ascertain which incident she is referring to. It may have been Hughie's fury over his exclusion from a car ride to Dungeness and the tirade of abuse he hurls at his mother, a scene interrupted by the return of the father, too absorbed in his thoughts about the Clinic (Emmanuel Miller founded the East End Child Guidance Clinic) to notice anything amiss. But more offensive is perhaps Stevie's observation of the parents' anxiety over their Jewishness. Emmanuel and Betty Miller had relaxed in their observation of the strict Jewish rites with which they had both been brought up, but as second generation English Jews they were conscious of being outsiders. Stevie makes her character Margaret say: 'But, Helen, you cannot know quite what it is like; it is a feeling of profound uncertainty, especially if you have children. There is a strong growing anti-Jewish feeling in England . . .'⁷¹ Earlier she remarks that her husband 'is more locked up in being a Jew than it seems possible'.⁷² Using this insight, Stevie exposed Betty Miller's perception of her husband and therefore also her loyalty. 'Beside the Seaside' stripped away the privacy surrounding the Millers' marital relationship. Stevie, unable as she claimed to understand the '*à deux* fix', probably did not perceive the harm she had done.

CHAPTER 10

Madness and Correctitude

The late 1940s and early 1950s were an exasperating time for Stevie. It was flattering to be asked by Desmond Fitzgerald to review novels for the prestigious monthly, *World Review*, but mortifying to discover that the *New Statesman* now would not take her poems. It accepted one about the Führer but did not print it. 'I can't help wondering whether that poor beastly poem of mine . . . can possibly have gone in yet,' Stevie wrote to Kingsley Martin in March 1945, 'as alas I don't seem to have had a cheque not that one cares about the money ahem but the honour and glory et cetera would be immensely gratifying, like coming successfully through an assault course, assault and battery I am afraid you will think.' She mentions also that in her proofs 'the printer wrote: "The squirrel brings nits", possibly true, but I wrote (and prefer) nuts.'[1] This letter brought her three guineas and the message that her poem was in the queue. But when in July 1945 it still had not appeared and Hitler was dead, Stevie wrote again suggesting that she might try and peddle it 'in some mossy Monthly where they are less topical'.[2] Kingsley Martin admitted her 'excellent and amusing poem' had lost its relevance and agreed she could take it elsewhere. It finally appeared in her collection, *Harold's Leap*, in 1950, under the title 'The Leader'.

Changes in literary editorship at the *New Statesman* brought Stevie no better luck. When Janet Adam Smith took over in the early 1950s Stevie felt barred from this periodical. In fact Janet Adam Smith only ever saw two or three of her poems, the rejection of which so offended Stevie she never tried again.

As a poet, Stevie could not at this time succeed. The 'anti-women pressure' which Naomi Mitchison had noticed in literary circles during the war,[3] had done nothing to rectify the scant space given to the work of women in anthologies and magazines. Stevie was not only a woman poet but also a most unorthodox one. Derek Verschoyle, literary editor of the *Spectator*, rejected one of her poems for being 'theologically unsound'. Others balked at the drawings which Stevie insisted should accompany her verse. Cecil Day Lewis published 'Touch and Go' in *Orion* in 1944 but, on the advice of his fellow editors, rejected its illustrations. Many doubted that Stevie's poems could be taken at face value, for their directness suggested a *fausse-naïveté* that threw doubt on their seriousness. 'Touch and Go' begins:

> Man is coming out of the mountains
> But his tail is caught in the pass.
> Why does he not free himself
> Is he not an ass?

Aside from the lines,

> The enemies of man are like trees
> They stand with the sun in their branches

the poem's diction is flat and laconic:

> No, there is no one to help him
> Let him get on with it

It is left to the reader to decide whether the abruptness and awkwardness deal straightforwardly with an absence of illusion or whether the poem, in its verbal slightness, provides only a mocking gloss on a major theme, its *naïveté* disguising a sophisticated teasing. Stevie thought her literary contemporaries suspected her of double-bluffing. She was aware, too, that to some extent she was the victim of fashions and counter-fashions and of the old-boy network that operates within literary circles.

> Oh why does England cherish her arts in this wise
> Picking inferiority with grafted eyes?
> It is because it is like the school they never forgot . . .
> So-and-so must be driven out, this is the pet.[4]

She was further dismayed by the rejection of *The Holiday* on the part of Cape and Duckworth, and somewhat bitterly amused when a letter arrived from Oswell Blakeston inviting her to contribute to the anthology, *Holidays and Happy Days*. She sent the short story 'Beside the Seaside' to Blakeston, together with much gratitude. 'She was badly neglected at this time,' he later recollected. 'She said there should be lots more people like me around stinging her into doing something. All her instincts were to retire from the literary scramble and go to sleep.'[5]

Out of the tribulation caused by *The Holiday* emerged the poem 'The Crown of Gold', in which the author's search for an established publisher is imaged in the mother's search for a crown of gold for her child. The poem remains obscure unless the reader has access to biographical information, for the German-Jewish man who offers the child a crown of affection is a reference to Leo Kahn, an amateur who at one point offered to publish *The Holiday*. Leo Kahn had himself published in 1946, *Obliging Fellow*, a novel which Stevie reviewed for *Modern Woman*, admiring its 'good sense, very sly humour and true humanity'.[6] She told the fiction editor, Barbara Vise, that she would like to meet Kahn and this proved easy enough as Kahn was then doing editorial work at Newnes on a part-time basis. He and Stevie established an immediate rapport and met regularly, mostly for lunchtime meals with Stevie occasionally visiting Wembley where Kahn and his wife lived. It sometimes surprised Kahn that, though his conversation with Stevie was uninhibited, there was never any awareness, as there often is when a man and a woman talk freely, of their sexual differences. He also saw that Stevie's easy sociability hid shyness, and that her critical sharpness was, not a contradiction of her former shyness, but a balancing mechanism.

When Kahn admitted that he had difficulty in understanding her poems there was an awkward moment. On another occasion they had a slanging match in the Strand when the British withdrew from Palestine. Stevie did not support Zionism, perhaps because she shared Orwell's conviction that it would lead to Israeli militarism. Despite these disagreements Kahn never lost interest in *The Holiday* which he first heard of when Stevie expressed anxiety that she would never achieve a shape that the novel reader would accept. He also witnessed her distress when the book was rejected. Then he unexpectedly benefited financially from the death of an American uncle and decided to try his hand at publishing. With Nicholson and Watson he published a book of Daumier lithographs which Stevie praised in the pages of *Modern Woman*. Confident of further success, he embarked on other ventures, took over *The Holiday* and had it typeset. Unaware of the pitfalls that awaited him, he suffered a setback with a biography of Catherine the Great when W. H. Smith reneged on their agreement over the distribution rights, Kahn's Dutch printers having failed to keep to schedule. Finding himself in severe financial plight, Kahn was obliged to look for salaried employment and told Stevie he could not continue with *The Holiday*. Over the telephone she rebuked him in acid terms for making promises to authors with insufficient knowledge of the publishing business.

Their friendship, however, survived. A little while afterwards Stevie rang and apologized and Kahn did what he could to save the book. At one point the firm John Nevill considered taking over the galley proofs, but when they cavilled Stevie sent the typescript to James MacGibbon, then managing director at Putnam's. He wanted to publish it but the firm's chairman, Constant Huntington, hated it and exercised his power of veto. With Stevie's agreement, MacGibbon then sent the typescript to Jack McDougall at Chapman and Hall and the book was promptly accepted. Loss of *The Holiday* was for MacGibbon a factor in his decision to leave Putnam's and set up MacGibbon and Kee. It also cemented his friendship with Stevie. Kahn, meanwhile, agreed Stevie was right to accept Chapman and Hall's offer and expressed relief that his failure had done the book no permanent harm.

When *The Holiday* finally appeared Stevie sent Kahn a copy inscribed with an allusion to a passage in Maurice Baring's *Friday's Business*: a young man, asked by a countess what his novels are about, replies 'People'. 'Ah people,' the countess remarks, 'they are very difficult.' Baring's light, nimble humour, his sense of the past and evocation of a romantic sadness delighted Stevie who once declared his novels 'as refreshing as clear water in a wilderness'.[7] In the spring of 1946, she had agreed to write a book on Baring for Home and van Thal's 'English Novelists' series. But though she signed a contract, and gave the project a great deal of thought, it came to nothing.

People may be difficult but they are also essential. Stevie continued to look to her friends for remission from loneliness. She attended many parties and at one of these, given by Elsa Barker Mill, found herself sitting on a sofa, which had artificial eyes in place of buttons, next to Ronald Orr-Ewing, a civil servant in the Home Office but soon to exchange his high-up position for the junk trade. Stevie gossiped freely to Orr-Ewing, whose *métier* was talk, each recognizing in the other an iconoclast. He occasionally visited her at Palmers Green and in turn offered hospitality when she needed to spend a night in town, for he had moved out of marriage, to the novelist Isobel English, into a house in Kensington Square where others lived not exactly with but around him.

Her meeting with Elisabeth Lutyens probably took place at the BBC's local, the George. Some thought there was an element of snobbery in Stevie's enjoyment of this friend, an acclaimed composer and daughter of the famous architect, Sir Edwin Lutyens. But not only did Elisabeth

Lutyens, at her own request, set nine of Stevie's poems to music, she also suggested that *Novel on Yellow Paper* offered material for a musical and wrote letters which reflect sincere admiration. 'Your book has affected me as have your books of yore,' she once wrote from Seaford where she made up for the lack of decadence in her surroundings with the help of mild and bitter. 'You stimulate more than M and B,' she added, urging Stevie to telephone and come for the weekend. 'It's awfully bracing. I've walked miles to-day and looked in seapools and watched the sea gulls, found a new local and postponed death.'[8]

'The pleasures of friendship are exquisite,' begins one of Stevie's poems. Her friends variously recount how in order to obtain these pleasures she could be ruthlessly selfish. Elisabeth Lutyens was one of several friends with a car whom Stevie would ring in order to announce her need for a walk in the countryside. She also liked her friends who lived in the country to invite her for weekends and expected a style of entertainment more typical of the 1920s and 1930s. She was a not infrequent guest of Barbara and Alan Clutton-Brock who had put Stevie up in their Essex farmhouse before the war and now lived at Chastleton House in Oxfordshire. 'They are old friends of mine,' she wrote after one visit, 'and have inherited a Jacobean Old Treasure, built in 1603, mixed up with Catesby and the Gunpowder Plot and with Charles I and his Bible – but alas, not much money to run it, so we have the tramp tramp of many feet at 2/6[d] a head . . . and a wonderful haphazard sort of life in between. Alas, also no electric light at night, and over the 2nd merry bottle of gin and the paraffin lamps, the old place does rather creak.'[9] She enjoyed talk, not only with the Clutton-Brocks and their other guests but also the local parson and the near-illiterate undergardener with whom she had long discussions in the kitchen. In time, as her loneliness increased with age, the contrast between the easy, sociable existence at Chastleton and her life at Palmers Green left her empty and depressed on her return home.

She valued still more her association with two families with houses near the Norfolk coast. Soon after the war ended Armide Oppé, then working at the Treasury in the Overseas Finance Department, had given a party at which Stevie had met the barrister Michael Browne and his wife, Anna. Anna Browne became someone of special importance for Stevie, offering generous hospitality and conversation that brought into play Anna's love of English literature and a well-stocked mind. At their first meeting Anna, who was familiar with the character Pompey, remarked on their shared love of the East Anglian coast. 'There are parts round the Norfolk coast,' Stevie once wrote, 'that look like nobody had ever been there before just dunes and

sand and sea and nobody at all.'¹⁰ The Brownes divided their time between
London and Norfolk, and staying with them at Wiveton Stevie could swim
in the sea or go walking on Cley beach or across the salt marshes at
Blakeney. But even here, the place she loved best and in company that she
came greatly to depend on, she carried her isolation with her.

> Life bustles in the country, you know; it should be easy.
> But I was outside of it, looking, finding no place,
> No excuse at all for my distant wandering face.¹¹

Part of the bustle in Norfolk arose from its social life. Through the
Brownes Stevie met Mungo and Racy Buxton who lived nearby at Wiveton.
They also opened their home to Stevie and deepened her involvement with
the area and its Norfolk gentry. 'We pay and receive innumerable visits and
everybody is of the Very Nice sort, you know, almost royal, if often poor.'¹²
The pace of life suited Stevie. Staying with the Buxtons meant, as another of
their guests remarked, that 'one's whole tempo was halved'. Mungo
Buxton, in particular, was renowned for his charm. An aeronautical
engineer and an expert on gliding, he became fascinated by the world of
finance on retiring from the Air Force, invested cleverly and, like Stevie,
had a respect for the stockbroker mind. Though Stevie often felt children
presented unfair competition, she got on well with the Buxton and Browne
offspring. The only alteration that her presence demanded was that meals
had to be punctual and old-fashioned. Aside from this she caused little
effort and as a guest had, according to Racy Buxton, a revivifying effect.

'People do bother,' Celia insists in *The Holiday*, '. . . in friendship as in
love, they do bother. Nothing that produces suffering can be nothing, and
friendship does produce suffering, so it cannot be absolutely nothing.'¹³
Now that Olivia Manning and Reggie Smith had returned to London,
Stevie could resume an old friendship. If she occasionally fell out with
Reggie, this did not prevent her from trying her poems on him. She sang 'Le
Singe Qui Swing' and broke off with the aside – 'They *do* swing you know,'
accompanying this with a schoolboy wink.¹⁴ She did this, seeking not advice
but confirmation: Sally Chilver tells how suggestions were firmly rejected.
Sometimes she delivered her poems in a bluff chant, with apparent
nervousness, but capped them with exclamations such as 'Oh, that's awfully
good, isn't it?' or 'Oooh, that's terrific!'. Like Stevie, Olivia Manning also
required confirmation as a writer, a need that in her case amounted to a
neurotic degree of self-doubt. Once Kathleen Farrell reported Ivy Compton-Burnett's remark that Olivia Manning was 'remarkable'. Olivia at first
looked pleased, then suggested that Kathleen had made it up, or misheard

and finally concluded that Ivy had not meant what she said. Stevie may have had Olivia in mind when, in a review, she quoted George Sand with approval: 'She says to Flaubert: "I write to influence my own times; tomorrow you will be read as much as you are today; tomorrow nobody will read me." She says it frankly, affectionately, without bitterness. This is not quite the picture we are often given of the female novelist with her tiresome airs and self-absorption.'[15]

Added to her perfectionism as a writer which made her touchy and difficult, Olivia was greatly inquisitive about others and fond of interfering, traits that are found in the character she inspired, Sophia, in Kay Dick's novel, *The Shelf*. But even in a negative frame of mind she was oddly fascinating. Stevie caricatures her conversation in a letter to Kay Dick:

'I have just lunched with Olivia who gives such a gloomy reading to the *News* that I feel I must sell all my investments and retire to the most outer of the Hebrides clad in pure wool combinations ("wool will be practically impossible to get") and *diamonds*, where I shall spend the long northern twilights seeing how many words I can get out of INFLATION. Not so good as CONSTANTINOPLE for the purpose, but apparently there will be *simply no* choice.'[16]

Predictably, what soured relations between Stevie and Olivia were their opinions of each other's books. Olivia is known to have been very cutting about the book on cats that Stevie produced in 1959, and Stevie, when told that Olivia had produced another novel, would ask, 'Is it all about Reggie again?' This teasing did not prevent her from having a very high regard for Olivia's novels. She admired, in particular, *The School for Love*, which she reviewed percipiently.

'Miss Manning is a scrupulous and gifted writer who will admit no compromise. For her the novel is a work of art or it is nothing. There is a ferocity and exclusiveness in this attitude . . . In her last novel *Artist among the Missing* there was also at times a hint of bad temper. No pettishness mars this book . . . All through this imaginative book run the fresh colours and contrasts of the Palestine of winter and early spring. Miss Manning is getting into her stride; this book is a great advance; she is a professional writer in the highest sense, a conscious artist.'[17]

Olivia, who would pounce on the only line of criticism in a review full of praise, may have been irritated by Stevie's even-handed account. Two years later Stevie reviewed Olivia's *A Different Face*, praising 'a use of words most elegant and strict' but confessing an inability to feel much sympathy with the book's hero.[18] Again this may have contributed to the animosity that now veined their friendship. In Hampstead literary circles the rumour went round that Stevie and Olivia had fallen out. To everyone's surprise, when they met again at a small Hampstead party, they rushed towards each other, kissed and spent the rest of the evening engrossed in conversation on the sofa. This uneasy relationship continued until the mid 1950s, after which the two women had only infrequent contact. After Stevie's death, Olivia expressed regret in a letter to Anthony Powell that she had not acted on Stevie's repeated invitations to Palmers Green: she had been unable to face the journey.

That which is thought to have more or less terminated their friendship was Stevie's review of *The Doves of Venus* in 1955. Perhaps annoyed by allusions to her younger self in the character, Nancy Claypole, Stevie allowed a note of irritation to enter her review:

'Nobody in this novel seems a tolerable human being except Ellie . . . there's a lack of balance here. Miss Manning writes always with a poet's care for words and it is her usual distinction of style and construction that sets this novel, for all its faults of moral naïvèty, far, far above the average run. It is balance of thought one misses.'

Where she perhaps overstepped the mark, from Olivia's point of view, was her observation that the tendency to give a hero or heroine too bad a time of it is a trap that sensitive women writers often fall into.

'Perhaps it really is something feminine, like little girls playing with their dear dolls and giving them fits. Like my little god-daughter who said to me the other day, "My dolly's got measles. *And* complications."'[19]

It may have been after this that Stevie showed Anna Browne a letter from Olivia, complaining about one of Stevie's reviews and ending, 'What else can I expect of an inveterate bitch'. Stevie laughed at this but was also bitterly hurt. According to Maurice Cranston the biographer and critic, Stevie, by this time, had very little affection for Olivia and saw clearly how tiresome she could be. She told Cranston that she felt Olivia, who was very aware that a younger generation of novelists were superseding her, was full of bitterness and the conviction that her efforts had gone unrewarded. Stevie's own view was that the more a person yearned for fame the less it was given them.

Stevie was a regular at Maurice Cranston's parties, to which came a literary crowd. He found her easy and relaxed, not shrill and self-conscious like other literary women he knew. But she did not always inspire respect.

Anna Browne, attending a tea-party at Ivy Compton-Burnett's in Stevie's company, had the distinct impression that Ivy did not approve of Stevie. Stevie herself claimed she was straightforward but not simple. Her awareness of the complexity of human motives denied her the carapace of innocence. This may have been why she accepted the opportunity to write on L. P. Hartley's trilogy, *Eustace and Hilda*, for Kay Dick's *The Windmill*: 'I will try not to think about it too much, or like the poor Baring "Life", it will never get done.'[20] L. P. Hartley was so delighted with what she wrote that he began a lively correspondence with her. She had accurately concluded that behind the light, agreeable surface of Hartley's tale lay murderous intent: 'the subtlety is veiled, the claws sheathed, the smile only is visible. But the theme is tragic in the grand manner, and the thoughts of the writer support it. The smile only is visible? It was a tiger that vanished, not a cat.'[21]

In conversation with Stevie, Maurice Cranston observed her familiarity with nineteenth-century poets, Arnold, Tennyson and Browning in particular, but was surprised how little she knew about French literature. She could, however, read French and often preferred Agatha Christie in translation. Sometimes when on holiday with Aunt, they read the same Agatha Christie, Aunt, in English and Stevie, in French, and over breakfast went through the amusing translations that English colloquialisms invited. 'Her murders are so polite,' Stevie once told a reporter,[22] but there are many reasons why these saturatedly English tales appealed. Chiefly she admired them for their 'tremendous power of taking weight off the mind . . . You might say that any "light" reading has that, but it simply isn't true.'[23]

Writing poetry offered further release from pressure. Stevie shared Eliot's view, that poetry is not a turning loose of emotion but an escape from it, not an expression of personality but a continual extinction of personality. His claim, that 'it is not the "greatness", the intensity, of the emotions, the components, but the intensity of the artistic process, the pressure, so to speak, under which the fusion takes place, that counts',[24] upholds much that she said about her own creative process. She used her poems as a means through which to control, delimit and objectify what she found burdensome. As a post-romantic, she illustrates Eliot's argument that poetry springs out of suffering, an effort to metamorphose private failures and disappointments. In a radio talk for schools she talked freely about how her poems were composed.

'They were written from the experiences of my own life, its pressures and fancies. And they are written to give ease and relief to me. While they are being written, nobody else comes into it at all. I want to get something out that is working away at me inside. I think pressure is the operative word here. The pressure of daily life, the pressure of having to earn one's living – possibly at work that is not very congenial; the pressure of one's relations with other people, the pressure of all the things one hears about or reads about – in philosophy, history and religion for instance – and agrees with, or does not agree with; the pressure of despair, and the pressure, too, of pleasures that take one's breath away – colours, animals tearing about, birds fighting each other to get the best bit of bacon rind. And the funniness of things too . . . Then of course there is the great pleasure of simply walking around and looking at things. It is by no means easy to get all this into a poem – and often one doesn't want to. It spoils the fun. So often I am afraid my poems get written from the struggles and melancholy rather than from happiness. Like I said in this poem:

> Happiness is silent or speaks equivocally for friends
> Grief is explicit and her song never ends.

I draw a lot and often a drawing will suggest a poem. It is often that way about. Or perhaps I may read something in a newspaper that disturbs me rather and makes me want to write about what I feel . . . You will say: But your poems are all story poems, you keep yourself hidden. Yes. But all the same, my whole life is in these poems . . . everything I have lived through, and done, and seen, and read and imagined and thought and argued. Then why do I turn them all upon other people, imaginary people, the people I create? It is because . . . it gives proportion and eases the pressure, puts the feelings at one remove, brings the temperature down, and – again – eases the pressure . . . Pressure is the forcing ground of talent, the stern master that drives us on. And we had better obey this master, or we shall be very unhappy. My favourite motto, a Roman motto, sums this up: *Fata nolentem trahunt, voluntem ducunt.* The fates drag the unwilling, the willing they lead.'[25]

Unwilling publishers also needed an occasional push. Having persuaded Chapman and Hall to follow up *The Holiday* in 1950 with a collection of her poems, Stevie admitted to Daniel George that her publisher had 'fallen a prey to morbid fancies, one of which runs to the tune of. Never again'.[26] *Harold's Leap* nevertheless reflects an increase in confidence in the elaboration of her themes. Its title poem confronts the issue of suicide and her admiration for Harold is announced in the opening lines:

> Harold, are you asleep?

> Harold, I remember your leap,
> It may have killed you
> But it was a brave thing to do.

Stevie had in mind Seneca's remark to the slave, 'Dost thou see the precipice?', and the freedom it implied, as well as a line from Browning: 'A man's reach should exceed his grasp, or what's heaven for?' The poem may also have been nudged into existence by a visit Stevie made to see Molly at Westonbirt School, when it was evacuated to Corsham Court, near Bath. This visit is re-evoked in *The Holiday* where Celia, after being taken over the school, is shown the 'great limestone cliff, where Clem's great grandfather threw himself down, and so died'.[27]

Aside from the line, 'And fell to the sea's smother', 'Harold's Leap' characteristically resists poeticization. The diction is stark, the poem pungent and offhand. Though the collection as a whole reveals her rhythmic cunning and technical adroitness, her poems refuse to promote presentation over meaning. Terry Eagleton, observing 'a comic disparity between simple recalcitrant facts and the poetic shapes which try vainly to subdue them to precise, sophisticated uniformity', finds in Stevie's work an 'ironic determination to be honest to the facts at the cost of the form – to show how formal predictability is devastated by sheer truth'.[28] Formal predictability *is* devastated, but only now and then at the cost of form.

Introducing her poems on the radio in 1951 Stevie admitted that the people in them do not feel at home in this world: 'Always the problem that presses most is Man's loneliness and his inability to get on with his fellow creatures.' After reading 'I rode with my darling . . .', in which the narrator chooses to be lonely, she added: 'This feeling of wanting to get away to the woods, paths, ponds, lakes and seas of an earlier noumenous world is very dominant in the poems in spite of the love of friendship, and in my novels too, and often it may be understood as a soft sighing after shadowy death.'[29] Muriel's isolation in 'Do Take Muriel Out' is only resolved by the arrival of death. In 'From the Coptic', a poem which plays upon rabbinical speculation on Genesis 2:7 ('And the Lord formed man of the dust of the ground, and breathed into his nostrils the breath of life; and man became a living soul') and presupposes that the angels, not God, made the clay human, it is the third angel's promise that persuades the clay to become Man.

> Then the third angel rose up and said,
> Listen thou clay, raise thy downy head,
> When thou hast heard what I have to say
> Thou shalt rise Man and go man's way.

What have you to promise? the red clay moans,
What have you in store for my future bones?
I am Death, said the angel, and death is the end,
I am Man, cries clay rising, and you are my friend.

When death is not immediately confronted the characters in *Harold's Leap* are often beyond reach: Mary, in 'Cool as Cucumber' is bewitched; Joan in 'Deeply Morbid' is transported into another existence by a Turner painting. 'Is this escape-into-the-frame a fine game for a hot afternoon,' asked Stevie in an essay on art, 'or is it rather something that conceals itself beneath a frivolity? To be isolated for ever in some romantic and forlorn landscape, enchanted oneself and imprisoned "out of time", beyond the necessities of human life, their humilities and importunities, without hope, without hope of return, without the aggravating possibility of some knight-errantry, how delicious, when one is in the mood, the contemplation of such a fate.'[30]

Despite this obsession with death, suicide and other-worldliness, *Harold's Leap* is broader in theme than her previous volumes. The comic and tragi-comic poems, such as 'Our Bog is Dood' and 'Pad, pad', seem more assured. *World Review* (March 1951) rightly observed that only the truly sophisticated could achieve such simplicity, for behind this simplicity lies a concentration that is mature, deft and precise. Her moral stance is more pronounced. 'With compassion see life,' is urged in 'Do Not!'. Elsewhere a writer is damned for having a flinty heart: 'Then also as a writer she must fail / Since art without compassion don't avail?'[31] A sense of spiritual import attaches itself even to those poems built on legends or fairy tales. In another radio programme Stevie insisted that though her characters are unhappy in this world 'they do not mind because they think they are not meant to be. They see themselves as Pilgrims – royal princes in disguise – travelling in temporally embarrassed circumstances to a rich inheritance. Hazards and temptations lend excitement to the journey; arguments, witchcraft, pride, nobility, despair and religion are their solace and affliction.'[32]

She herself took solace in Fred Hoyle, the astrophysicist whose blunt, plain-speaking Northern manner added to the appeal of his radio talks. Hoyle made the controversial astronomical discovery that all the chemical elements are made in stars. This contravened the big-bang theory that all the elements were produced in the first moments of the universe and replaced it, temporarily, with the steady-state theory. This inspired Stevie's poem 'Protocreation' which, like 'The New Age' later published in *Not Waving But Drowning*, is subheaded, in manuscript form, 'Homage to Fred

Hoyle'. 'I am much indebted to Mr Fred Hoyle,' Stevie admitted in a lecture, 'for he gave me this sense of freedom, of liberation, in those talks he gave on the expanding universe, and the years going on a million million times, and the flatness, he gave me that, and the large space to lie out in.'[33] She was referring to radio programmes, transmitted January–March 1950, which were subsequently published in the *Listener* and in a small book, *The Nature of the Universe*, a copy of which Stevie owned. The reference in 'Thought is Superior' in *Harold's Leap* –

> And what is the greatest thought since the world begun?
> Galileo's discovery that the earth goes round the sun.

– draws on Hoyle's argument: 'The case for the Copernican theory is not that it is right or true in some absolute sense, but that it was the only point of view from which progress could have been made at the time. In short, that it had the virtue of simplicity, and this was demonstrated with great cogency and skill by Galileo.'[34] Realizing that she had mistakenly credited Galileo with the discovery, Stevie altered 'Galileo' to 'Copernicus' in Kay Dick's and Polly Hill's copies of *Harold's Leap*.

This volume also pays homage to John Cowper Powys.

> This old man is sly and wise,
> He knows the truth, he tells no lies,
> He is as deep as a British pool,
> And Monsieur Poop may think him a fool.

Monsieur Poop (the prefix suggesting the Francophile leanings associated with Bloomsbury) is the kind of literary critic, satirized elsewhere by Stevie, whose comfortable opinions leave him unable to assimilate outsiders like Powys, here portrayed, jauntily, as a bearded man playing a harp. Stevie's admiration for this writer dated back at least a decade. Reviewing his brother, Llewellyn Powys's *A Baker's Dozen* in 1941, she had referred in passing to John Cowper as he who 'wraps thoughts of sulphurous and volcanic power in language eminently suited to such matter'.[35] *The Pleasures of Literature*, which she first read and recommended to Naomi Mitchison in 1940, entered her library when a second edition appeared in 1946, and was extolled by her for its wisdom and cunning in *Modern Woman* in December of that year. But her most accurate description of his qualities is found in *The Holiday*: 'It is the writer John Cowper Powys who has this fullest free feeling of the pleasures of *instinctuality*, the fleering humble cold fish that he is, the wily old pard of the rocks and the stones, the Welsh carp fish in his British pool.'[36] In September 1951 Stevie sent him a copy of this book, together with *Harold's Leap*. 'Jesus Holy!' was Powys's reply, 'but you've got my numbers to a T. lady – no mistake about it, "fleering humble" is almost just perfect.'[37] The poems also pleased him 'hugely and microscopically'. This first reaction to her gift was sent to her, probably, via her publisher He wrote again after Miss Playter, Powys's companion, had read aloud to him *The Holiday* entire. After this, Stevie arrived at Newnes one morning in November 1951 to find the following:

'My dear Stevie Smith,

And now I must say to you yourself what a lot of pleasure I've got from your books *Harold's Leap* and *The Holiday* – especially the former because of your pictures. Aye but your attitude to life and your power of expressing it – both suit me so particularly well and I can tell you I am monstrous proud of so suddenly and unexpectedly appearing – *exactly as I am*, save that I've not even that curious kind of beard . . .

One poem after another I really am thrilled by; and I turn the pages to read them aloud to my American girl-friend over and over always with new discoveries. And those characters in *The Holiday* – the excellent uncle and poor Tom and – the whole lot of them – in and out of my brain they crowd – one after another beckoning to each other and making subtle signs and mystic signals like the ghosts did last night (All Hallows) through the corridors of my mind . . .'[38]

Stevie replied:

'Your wonderful letter came this morning this murky wet London November morning, I opened it at the office of Messrs. George Newnes Limited – publishers among other magazines – of Country Life at one end of the golden chain and Glamour Incorporating Peg's Paper at the other, and I need not tell you how golden indeed the chain is – and it was after paddling through Covent Garden Market over the sodden cabbage leaves and in and out of the charging lorries, and you can imagine how truly wonderful your letter was to have at the end of this journey and on a Monday morning. (I am still permitted to work at this office for the Harley and St John of *The Holiday*, which shows you what benignant gentle loving creatures magnates may be.) Thank you for this wonderful letter and the beautiful drawings you have done, the portrait of yourself with the harp is better than mine, it is more like you and the expression is less vegetable, and I think he is right to be turning his head to see what on earth is coming along now. I am so full of your *Porius* by this time that I can think of nothing else it is the leaping lively landscape I love (leaping like a tiger, lively like an elephant) and the nervous people with the wily minds making such a figure of cunning and glory beneath that particular smile of the Natural World with its mists and thunders, how I love it. I love scenery as much as the next cockney, I would think (if it wasn't for you) that one must be in a London office to love scenery with this feverish preposterous love of the imagination. I nose it out in your books and wuff it down like any antique pig in the old forest of Middlesex, where the place names (near my home) still stand to remind us – Turnpike Lane, Wood Green . . . and Southgate . . . And added to it all now are the rocks and black mountains of Wales and the landscape and iron spiked ball of *The Glastonbury Romance* . . .'[39]

Porius and *The Glastonbury Romance* remained her favourites of Powys's books. By comparison with *Porius*, the Arthurian tales of T. H. White and Tolkien, for Stevie, rang false. *Porius* also inspired her to write 'The Blue from Heaven', her own Arthurian legend. She sent a copy of this poem to Powys, with her own gloss: 'I was thinking *that* governing warmth', she wrote, with reference to King Arthur, 'might be saved in the end by growing tired. I always think fatigue is a great Saver from Ambition and worldly values, when all else fails!'[40] In the same letter she apologizes for what may seem to him a 'cheekily incomplete' review of his book, *The Inmates*: she had been obliged to produce copy before she had finished the book, but was pleased to find herself again in 'that world of volcanic landscape and violence'. She acclaimed *The Inmates*, in her review, as 'a book that has the madness and correctitude of poetry'.[41] Powys not only thanked her profusely but told his publisher, apropos of her remark: 'I couldn't beat or equal and I can't think of any *living* writer who could equal or beat her *last sentence* of this review and I am proud to think how many will read it.'[42] There were still other occasions when Stevie extolled J. C. Powys's erudite mind, for his strange and demonic books, with their cragginess, beauty and sensuousness had for her exceptional merit.

In February 1944, at Rachel Marshall's invitation, Stevie had attended a concert at Homerton, the Cambridge teacher-training college, at which some of her poems were read. This gave her the opportunity, not only to hear her poems performed, but also to experience audience reaction. 'That was an occasion I shan't forget,' she afterwards wrote to Rachel Marshall. 'It was a revelation and a very encouraging one too.'[43] Five years later she listened to Hedli Anderson perform Elisabeth Lutyens's song-settings for some of her poems: 'My tunes, some of them, I firmly state,' she told Jack McDougall of Chapman and Hall, adding: 'the audience reacted in a way that made me think perhaps they had better not be looked upon as pure poems but rather as intimate revue stuff, you know, they laughed quite a lot and clapped really like anything. Does this suggest that there might be a wider public for them than the highbrow sort? Two of them were quite melancholy, so it isn't only the funny ones.'[44]

As her notion of an audience expanded, her involvement with the BBC increased. She wrote a script on Thomas Hood, in which commentary and poems are equally mixed, which the Eastern Service transmitted in their *Book of Verse* series in March 1946. Next she produced 'Syler's Green', an evocation of the Palmers Green of her childhood, for Reggie Smith's *Return Journey* series which also drew from Dylan Thomas 'Under Milkwood'. The programme, transmitted 5 August 1947 (and repeated 26 December 1959), brought Stevie fifty guineas and much praise. One friend, however, complained that the reader, Stevie's former schoolmate, Flora Robson, had been too robust: 'Not at all foot-off-the-ground. For me, at least, one of the charms of your writing is the sudden lack of stamina, the abrupt dropping of a subject or an emotion.'[45]

Encouraged by its success, Stevie aimed more work at the BBC. She sent two stories, 'The Story of a Story' and 'Enemy Action', to Roy Campbell who regretted he could not use them. Undeterred, Stevie sent the same stories plus another to H. N. Bentinck who was organizing a Third Programme short story competition. As one condition was that the story had to be unpublished, he kept only 'Enemy Action', by then retitled 'Sunday at Home'. Five months later she was invited to attend an audition which was preceded by a rehearsal. The producer, D. F. Boyd, reported to Bentinck:

'I did my best with Stevie Smith and her story "Sunday at Home" and came to the conclusion it was hopeless. I told her so. I told her the story was impossibly difficult for her voice and that I should not recommend its inclusion. It was not in fact written for telling as her "Return Journey" was.

I am asking Miss Kallin to record all or part of the story to play back to Stevie Smith. She would like to hear her voice and how she tackles the script.'[46]

Three weeks later Miss Kallin sent a memorandum to Boyd:

'You may remember that before you left for leave you asked me to record bits of Stevie Smith and play it back to her. I found her when she arrived at the studio even more nervous and shy than I remembered her from former days. I rehearsed her for about an hour, thought that she was rather good, recorded the whole story, and it was then played back to Henry Bentinck and I think a few others. To me she sounded not at all bad . . . I thought that with more time for rehearsal and particularly with more time for putting her at ease one could do something very good with her.'[47]

An hour with Miss Kallin had had its effect. Stevie's story was among the runners up and was broadcast on 20 March 1949, after further rehearsal. 'First of all,' Bentinck wrote, 'allow me to say how *enormously* your reading had improved over the first time, and how much we enjoyed hearing it.'[48] 'Thank you very much for your letter,' Stevie replied, 'and I am so glad you thought the story was getting better, all of which I am sure is due to Miss Kallin who I must say was wonderful . . .'[49]

The aim behind this short story competition had been the discovery of an author–broadcaster able to put over his or her personality through the medium of a short story and its particular atmosphere. This Stevie did, in a subsequent series of programmes, but through her poems, not short stories. In the creation of these programmes, Anna Kallin played a crucial role.

Anna Kallin was four years older than Stevie and a White Russian. Her family had left Russia for Germany in 1912, and, after a brief period of internment as a civilian prisoner of war, she studied at Leipzig University, afterwards moving to Dresden to study music. There she met Oskar Kokoschka whose mistress she became. In 1921 she followed her father to London. This did not terminate her relationship with Kokoschka, for they saw each other when he visited England and she, Dresden, and they also met from time to time on the Continent. For nineteen years she free-lanced, as a reviewer, translator and publisher's reader, also spending long periods abroad. In 1940 she first joined the BBC as a German monitor at Evesham, soon becoming a Russian assistant in the BBC's wartime European Intelligence department and ending her time there as senior assistant in the Bulgarian section. In January 1946 she was made producer in Home Talks, an appointment that settled her career. Associated with the Third Programme from its inception, she produced, most years, well over a hundred talks annually and was closely associated with the Reith lectures. She was the first to produce A. J. P. Taylor and Isaiah Berlin and other intellectuals who, largely through radio, became household names. Highly regarded by other professionals, this exceptionally intelligent woman was an astute editor of scripts and had uncompromising standards with regard to thought and expression. Becky Cocking, a guest producer in the Talks Department, found her 'impatient of and scathing about anything intellectually or aesthetically second rate'.[50] Her criticisms occasionally infuriated scholars and intellectuals whose scripts she produced, but she made no concessions and usually got her way; Maurice Cranston thought her 'impatient and bossy'. This vein of arrogance was not unjustified, for in the period when she had associated with Kokoschka her formidable mind had made her a part of a European intelligentsia.

As a child she had once heard her mother discussing with a visitor what a tragedy it was that her daughter was so plain. From then on determined to make the most of what she had, she managed always to look impressive even though her office dress – sweater, skirt and rope of pearls – never varied. Stylish and composed, she kept a tin of Earl Grey in her office and never offered her visitors canteen tea; and though not openly affectionate, she emitted warmth and was widely admired.

Stevie asked her publishers to send Anna Kallin a copy of *The Holiday*: 'because you were so awfully nice over the broadcast and because you asked me to send you "something else". So now you see what happens to people who ask for something else!'[51] Miss Kallin's response was gratifying: she was fascinated, compelled, charmed: 'It is quite unique in its genre, and the genre is the fresh, of one-piece, strong and fragile thing which we need to-day . . . I would so very much like you to "do" something for us, for the Third . . . cannot we have a meal together someday and speak about it all?'[52]

Out of this came a series of three programmes, all entitled 'Poems and Drawings', in which Stevie read a selection of her poems and provided linking commentary on them and their illustrations. The commentaries are slight but say just enough to allow for an alteration of mood between poems. They also established the method by which Stevie was later to introduce her poems at readings. The success of the first programme made possible the other two, and all three were produced by Anna Kallin who responded to and understood Stevie's work. Partly because she was at this time receiving little encouragement from literary editors, Stevie became to some extent emotionally dependent on this woman, as her letters reveal. 'I did listen last night,' she told Miss Kallin, after the second programme was broadcast, 'and I thought it was beautiful and I have you to thank, and do and do.'[53] After the last in the series was recorded, Stevie wrote again: 'It is wonderfully happy for me to have you as my mentor because you always know exactly and at once what the poems are up to.'[54] Their professional relationship grew into friendship in which Anna Kallin remained affectionate but firm; Sally Chilver remembers her admonishing Stevie with 'Now don't go on' and 'You've said that before'. But if Anna Kallin got quickly to the heart of Stevie's poems, talking intelligently and animatedly about them to Veronica Wedgwood, she may have begun to lose interest once she thought she had cracked the code. Stevie was disappointed that Anna

Kallin, pleading ill health, was not present at the recording of the last of these three programmes. If this was the first sign of Miss Kallin's withdrawal, Stevie ignored it and importuned her with requests to be allowed to do another programme, this time with some of her poems set to music.

Stevie's letter, now filed in the BBC's Written Archives, bears annotations in Miss Kallin's hand. These reveal that she had lied to Stevie about her health at the time of the last recording, that she now refused to meet her on purely social terms in the evenings and that she scorned Stevie's desire to record tunes for her poems. Alongside Stevie's comment, 'All this is a long rigmarole and you may already have had enough of the poems,' Miss Kallin simply wrote 'Yes'.

Stevie was not easily deterred. Three months later she approached Miss Kallin again with an idea for another programme of her poetry to be entitled 'The Weather in the Soul'. Miss Kallin passed her letter to the Third Programme organizer, Christopher Holmes, with her own remarks attached:

'No hurry: I put her off, saying "Perhaps in late spring". But do you think we should at all? She was good of course, in her un-compromising brittle way. I like the new title "Weather in the Soul". She takes *months* to do these programmes, so if we want them we have to give warning now for spring.'[55]

The programme was never made. Though poems by Stevie were occasionally included in radio magazines, such as G S Fraser's 'New Poetry', Stevie was not again involved in a programme of her own until 1956. In 1953 the producer Robert Gladwell proposed using her in a conversation with another literary woman. Stevie suggested the topic 'The Illusion of Modern Life', 'her point being', Gladwell's memorandum records, 'that plus ça change plus c'est la même chose. That although the exterior trappings of life change, the essential and fundamental human condition has always been the same. One of generosity, envy, jealousy, love and loathing.'[56] Rose Macaulay's name was put forward as the other participant, and Gladwell was told to ask what she thought of Stevie and the idea. Her response is not recorded and the programme was never made.

While *Harold's Leap* was in preparation with Chapman and Hall, Stevie asked Cape to republish her previous collections. Her aim was to regain the rights on her early poems, which revert to the author if the publisher will not re-issue within six months of being asked. 'I understand I am off your list,' she wrote to Jonathan Cape in July 1950. 'After all these years I cannot say goodbye without thanking you [for] all your past kindness and especially, if I may say so, for the really beautiful production of my books. *Tender Only to One* looks as fresh as a daisy, really beautiful.'[57]

She was approaching fifty and had been at Newnes some thirty years. Around 1950 she once again had her hair cut in a fringe and this made more pronounced the childlike aspect of her nature. Her friend from the 1920s, Joan Prideaux, meeting her in the 1950s, was surprised to see 'that she had become a little girl – no hint of that before'.[58] At Newnes she seemed to other employees a lone wolf, but outside the office she continued to strike up new friendships. After hearing a radio programme on governesses by Naomi Lewis, Stevie asked to meet her. Though Naomi Lewis was then at the start of her career, as writer, anthologist and critic, she and Stevie had much in common, not least a love of poetry and an uncommon insight into the details of things. They lunched together, Stevie sometimes giving Naomi an impression of meanness by pretending she had very little money on her.

What is surprising is how few of her friends, even those she saw regularly, knew her intimately. Protected by a carapace of wit and easy conversation, and by an appearance that increasingly helped sustain the myth of a slightly eccentric, childlike personality, she created a sharply etched impression that obscured much. Around 1952 Sally Chilver visited Stevie at Avondale Road in the company of an American anthropologist, Ruth Landes, who recollects 'Stevie's wildly gentle comedy, her intense, rapid, bright, clever talk – all addressed to Sal but not isolating me'. Stevie's face seemed to her like an Egyptian orphan's; it added to the enigma. 'Sal had mentioned Stevie's involvement with Orwell, but no more . . . and I wondered because there was no hint of personal responsiveness in Stevie's chatter or expression . . . A further obscuring factor was the contrast between Stevie's tiny person (withdrawn behind her chatter) and Sal's handsome, big, successful womanhood, very extroverted. Sal was very protective of Stevie, who glowed in Sal's then magical warmth . . .'[59]

With Sally Chilver Stevie gave a party in January 1950, inviting among others the publisher James MacGibbon whom she was to make her literary executor. A year or two later she gave another with Polly Hill in a large Hampstead studio flat, and on another occasion made use of the Brownes' London house for this same purpose. Her friends, their children and houses, often featured in Stevie's conversation, but it was only at these parties, that the various names and faces, jigsaw-like, fell into place. 'We seized each other,' Helen Fowler has written. ' "You must be . . ." "I've heard such a lot . . ." "And your house is the one . . ." '[60] Stevie's sociability was pronounced; she even attended North London Collegiate's centenary dinner in 1950 and sat, gossiped and laughed with Peggy Angus and Ishbel Macdonald, daughter of Ramsay. But the obverse side of this was a recurrent desire to escape human contact, human pressure.

> I longed for companionship rather,
> But my companions I always wished farther.
> And now in the desolate night
> I think only of the people I should like to bite.

It was her habit to annotate some of her poems with one-liners, either a terse restatement of the poem's theme, or a new thought, tangential upon either the poem or its illustration. In manuscript, 'The Reason', which begins

> My life is vile
> I hate it so
> I'll wait awhile
> And then I'll go

carries the annotation: 'It will be better later on.'[61] Inscribed like a private afterthought inside the back cover of Kay Dick's copy of *Harold's Leap*, which Stevie gave her, is the familiar saying, 'we shall have tears soon'.

'My whole life is in these poems . . . everything I have lived through, and done, and seen, and read and imagined and thought and argued.'[62] She did not despise the world around her: in 'Distractions and the Human Crowd' it is argued that things 'ephemeral, under time, peculiar, / And in eternity, without place or puff' will never come again and therefore must be studied closely, while we are still alive. But the human crowd, however distracting and enjoyable, could not remove 'the fret and deserts of this world'.[63] One of these was love. 'Le Désert de l'Amour' is the title of one poem, 'the desert of unhappy love', a phrase found in *Over the Frontier*[64] and 'the mirage of the desert of love' a desolating echo in *The Holiday*.[65] Only a person scorched by relationships and in whom unrequited love recoiled with bitter uselessness could begin to tolerate the god-like importance that Stevie accorded death. Reading Winwood Reade's *The Martyrdom of Man*, Stevie noted the page in which he describes the Sahara desert, in terms that evoke the parched isolation she faced.

'The eye is pained and dazzled; it can find no rest. The ear is startled; it can find no sound. In the soft and yielding sand the footstep perishes unheard; nothing murmurs, nothing rustles, nothing sighs. This silence is terrible, for it conveys the idea of death, and all know that in the desert death is not far off.'[66]

CHAPTER 11

Not quite right

'Truly I need a shover,' Stevie remarked to Naomi Mitchison after the publication of *Harold's Leap* in 1950, 'a nice honey-tongued worm, to belly around for me, some pretty young man, eh? with a "theory"?' Janet Adam Smith's rejection of her poems further depressed her: 'Well your old battle-axe on the *New Statesman* won't have me, nor John Lehmann, nor Spender, nor Iain Somebody [Hamilton] at the *Spectator*, nor Ackerley on the *Listener*. Only *Punch* will sometimes if they're funny. Love, Love! And at my age it's tricky!'[1] Poems sent to the *Times Literary Supplement* also came back rejected, as did those which Ruth Landes, on Stevie's behalf, pushed at her editor friends in the States. 'They always say the same thing,' Stevie observed to Kay Dick. 'They are not quite the right mixture and the slant etc. and especially the allusions are far too English.'[2]

The nine poems that appeared in *Punch* between 1953 and 1955 while Anthony Powell was literary editor helped ameliorate her sense of being a literary outcast. More indicative of her future significance was her inclusion in *The Faber Book of Twentieth Century Verse* published in 1953. Edited by John Heath-Stubbs and David Wright, the anthology embodied T. S. Eliot's suggestion that it was time to re-assess non-modernist trends. Its importance lay in its recovery of 'good neglected poets', as the *Time and Tide* reviewer said, adding: 'there are poems here by Edmund Blunden and Stevie Smith which put the selections from, say, Mr Stephen Spender, or Dr Edith Sitwell, in the shade.'[3]

Meanwhile, as a critic, Stevie was steadily gaining recognition; in 1954 she began reviewing novels for the *Observer*. After dining in Stevie's company at the home of Desmond Fitzgerald, editor of *World Review*, Maurice Collis, the author, noted in his diary:

'I dined there and met Stevie Smith, the novelist and reviewer, an amusing odd woman of about forty-eight or so, very human and intelligent, with exceedingly bright eyes and a flow of pleasant conversation. She is the most entertaining reviewer of novels in England. Her reviews contain a humorous malice, but there is no malice in her conversation or apparently in her nature, which is sweet and indulgent, as seen at a dinner.'[4]

His qualification is apt, for on the question of malice there is an alternative view. What is not in doubt is Stevie's generosity to the young and aspiring. She helped assist more than one young woman obtain a start in journalism. Taken to tea at the Strand Palace Hotel where Stevie gleefully consumed a copious cream tea, they were surprised by the ease with which they fell into chatter with this woman whom they had formerly regarded with literary adulation. 'I had the impression,' one recalls, 'even through the fogs of youthful self-centredness, that she was rather lonely.'[5] When the young BBC employee, John Holmstrom, showed some of his poems to Raymond Mortimer and told him of his admiration for *Novel on Yellow Paper*, Mortimer gave him an introduction to Stevie, adding, 'I'm afraid you'll find her a crashing bore'. 'Far from it,' Holmstrom recollects:

'Though nearly as shy as I, she was immense fun (more fun than Mortimer, to be frank) and exactly like the kind of dry, eccentric maiden aunt I adored. She seemed to enjoy talking – I suppose she didn't have too many fans in those days and was generally thought of, if at all, as a quaint relic from the Thirties. She was amused, of course, that I was working for the BBC . . . and pumped me for the latest scandal.

She already had the look of a slightly insecure witch – half alarming, half nervous – but was quite girlish and giggly. The amazing voice came as a complete novelty to me . . . The "refined" vowels undermined by an occasional North London twang was absolutely individual, and riveting.'[6]

Evidence of her generosity is found also in her reviews and in her attitude to the work of her friends. She pressed editors to accept short stories by Inez Holden or reviews by Kay Dick. She urged Helen Fowler to read Inez Holden's novel, *The Owner* (1952) which she extolled as first rate and an alternative to *Brideshead Revisited* in its demonstration of the corruptive influence on a middle-class social climber of a grand house. That same year saw the publication of Betty Miller's life of Robert Browning which showed how, once married, Browning's adulation of Elizabeth Barrett became modified. Having hoped that the excellence of her mind would rule his life and decide things large and small, he was troubled by her indiscriminate upbringing of their son, Pen, her passion for Louis Napoleon and her obsession with spiritualism. He began to obey what he could not respect and after her death knew not only the measure of his loss but also the measure of his gain. Stevie, though still estranged from Betty Miller, was moved to write:

'I have just finished your beautiful and moving and at the same time so wonderfully comical life of Robert Browning and I must say how much I admire it, it is really what one wants in the way of poetical biography, really creative and compassionate – and again oh how sadly comical. I began reading with the prickliest prejudices – to the tune of Oh sickly wife and sickening Mum, Oh follow not the poet home. But how glad everybody must be, and posterity, that you did because there is really a wonderful truthfulness that comes out of it, something for ever valuable. There is such a comical persistent courage running through the beautiful creature's fearful failings – of character, will, purpose and mere manners – there is everything of humanity in it, and the courage most of all. To go on, being so apparently in so many ways "unsatisfactory" (as the Aunt says) and yet to go on. No wonder it is Childe Roland one always comes back to, the startling bravery of the unusual hero, crawling staunchly where others before him pranced knightily – and then the slug-horn and the mere news he had arrived, and what grins from the dark hills, but the last grin his.'[7]

If she identified with Childe Roland as her poem 'Childe Rolandine' suggests, her courage was by this time at a low ebb. Depressed by the rejection of her poems, she told Sally Chilver that she felt her vents had been closed. Failure in other areas counted little when compared with this failure as an artist. When a friend called Margaret Branch introduced her to the writings of St John of the Cross, whom she described as a mystic and depressive who felt cut off from God and Man, Stevie replied that she too felt like that, that she had become cut off from God and now from Man too. This feeling of being beyond reach found creative outlet: in April 1953 Stevie told Kay Dick: 'I felt too low for words (eh??) last weekend but worked it off for all that in a poem . . . called "Not Waving but Drowning".'[8] Her suffering isolation did not go unnoticed: Maurice Cranston told George Buchanan, a journalist and former Newnes employee, that Stevie needed inviting out. It was indicative that she now discouraged her friends from visiting her at the office. To Sally Chilver Stevie remarked rather bitterly of her Newnes colleagues: 'They think I'm funny therefore I'm tempted to horse around.' During the summer of 1953 she stopped telephoning Sally and did not maintain the social contacts that had become an essential part of her life.

She had all the symptoms of the clinically depressed: tiredness, apathy, and irritability. There was often very little to do at the office, and whereas this had in the past enabled her to write letters or get on with her own work, it now meant a lack of distraction that must have been hard to bear. She liked to collect around her in her room small objects of interest, one of which was a paperweight in the form of a seal. When Sir Neville Pearson idly picked up this personal item in the course of conversation, Stevie lost control. What exactly happened cannot now be uncovered. One story that reached Kay Dick was that Stevie lunged at Sir Neville with a pair of scissors. If this was so, she must have turned them on herself after he had left the room and cut one of her wrists. At her request a member of staff telephoned Margaret Branch who left immediately for Newnes. On her arrival she found the small office crowded, managed to extract Stevie and drove her first to Charing Cross Hospital and afterwards, at Stevie's request, to Inez Holden's flat. Inez's own insecurity left her unable to cope with others' psychological problems and she was not sympathetic. Afterwards she told Cecily Mackworth that Stevie's appearance had made her cross and she 'didn't know why she had come'.[9]

Stevie's suicide attempt happened on 1 July 1953. The next day Sir Frank Newnes wrote, urging her to do what the doctor advised and not return to the office until he said she could. She appears to have suffered some kind of breakdown for she stayed in bed three weeks and told Kay Dick: 'I am a Nervous Wreck, it appears, also anaemic.'[10] Olivia Manning and other friends rallied round. In August she was taken to Haverfordwest, from where she again wrote to Kay Dick: 'Heavenly here, very rough seas very rough bathing, but I love it. I feel in the most boisterous good health – and quite *unintellectual.* This is the life I really like, dears, and let Literature go hang.'[11] Despite this quick recovery the decision had been reached that she should not return to Newnes. By the end of August all financial matters had been finalized. Sir Neville Pearson informed her that she would receive her full salary until the end of December and after that £5.10s.od. a week, from pension funds and investments in the firm, a net income which would rise by another £2.2s.6d. when she reached sixty. His inscrutably bland letter begins 'Dear Pompey' and ends with the hope that he would still see her from time to time on her visits to London.

Only to Anna Browne did Stevie give an account of her suicide attempt, in a letter that Anna Browne destroyed, finding it too painful to keep. In this Stevie expressed great contrition, chiefly because of the upset she had caused Aunt. She retained, however, the consolation that death would come, a consolation that made the Christian belief in an afterlife seem profoundly unattractive. At Newnes there was considerable speculation over her sudden disappearance. But to those who had not known her well it was not surprising. She was peculiar: it was to be expected. Stevie, herself, was relieved. 'I have been pensioned off and am so glad. The doctor said "No more" heaven bless him. So now I do nothing but write poems.'[12] The first line of one poem was afforded by an article on river pollution which she found in the *Angling Times* in her dentist's waiting room. She sent a version of this poem to Kay Dick and Kathleen Farrell, inscribed: 'To remind us Literary Chaps that Others, too, have Their Troubles'.

> A dwindling number of ageing fish
> Is all we can present
> Because of water pollution
> In the River Trent
> Because of water pollution, my boys,
> And lack of concerted action
> These fish of what they used to be
> Are only a measly fraction
> A-swimming around most roomily
> Where they shoved each other before,
> And never beefing about being solitary
> Or the sparseness of the fare.
> Then three cheers for the ageing fish, my boys,
> Content in polluted depths,
> To grub up enough food, my boys,
> To carry 'em to a natural death,
> And may we do the same, my boys,
> And carry us to a natural death![13]

Luckily for Stevie her departure from Newnes coincided with an invitation from the *Spectator* to join their rota for novel reviewing. She was one of four regular reviewers, so her hope of getting her friends' books did not always work out. This and other work she did in the dining room, at the back of 1 Avondale Road where the patter of her typewriter was now fairly constantly heard and from where she made regular visits to the newsagents for cigarettes. She was now free of the frustration, tedium and pressure of office life, which in 'Childe Rolandine' waters 'with tears in secret' the tree that bears fruit. Nor need she any longer feel that the sap rising in the dark, desert rose is stolen ('The bold drops ran like thieves').[14] If the poems written at Newnes had grown under cover, in secret and in response to external pressures, she had now to contend with strains and conflicts that lay chiefly within. Chief of these was the pressure of growing isolation.

> I feel a mortal isolation
> Wrap each lovely limb in desolation,
> Sight, hearing, all
> Suffer a fall.

Whereas most silence such feelings for the sake of vanity, sanity, politeness or fear, Childe Rolandine cries 'tell all, speak, speak'.

'Poetry must be based in philosophy and religion', Stevie once averred,[15] and the lightness and humour characterizing her aesthetic cannot for long disguise how intensely moral her verse is. Her familiarity with the Christian religion, her admiration for the Greeks and Hebrew philosophy, and her restlessly inquiring mind left her alert to vice and virtue, the existence of sin and the possibility of good. Her awareness of the need to decide, and decide rightly, underlies all that she wrote. She berated those who wrote for money or worldly success ('the trivial gold, the social pause'[16]) or who allowed journalistic standards to corrupt their use of language. In her view, the poet is under obligation to attend to her or his muse. She would introduce her poem 'My Muse' with the remark: 'Always, against being silent and merely looking at things, the Muse nags and mutters.'[17] Creativity was, for her, associated with pain, grief and joy, with a refusal to opt for soft answers. In 'The Queen and the Young Princess' the mother rebukes her child for remaining content with natural delights:

> Ah my child, that joy you speak of must be a pleasure
> Of human stature, not the measure
> Of animals', who have no glorious duty
> To perform, no headache and so cannot see beauty.
> Up, child, up, embrace the headache and the crown
> Marred pleasure's best, shadow makes the sun strong.

Reviewing the work of others she frequently drew attention to preoccupations that were also hers. 'Kill those dreams of terror, violence and madness,' she warns in one review, 'and the colours will go too. It is like the poem: "Poet, let the red blood flow, it makes the pattern better." '[18] The unattributed line of verse is her own, taken from 'The Lads of the Village'. Aside from this not infrequent habit of quoting her own work anonymously, her reviews have a pronounced absence of verbal display. They contain the unspoken requirement that literature must satisfy the inquiring mind. She praised precision of thought and feeling, courage, wit, intelligence and, whenever she found it, 'a poet's flash and a poet's mastery of words'.[19]

Among the authors Stevie rated highly were P. H. Newby ('an anatomiser of souls' with an even tenor 'inspired and poetical'[20]), Ivy Compton-Burnett and her 'character-stripping conversations',[21] L. P. Hartley, and Anthony Powell beneath whose 'splendid style of elaboration' she perceived a spiritual quest.[22] She could be witty at a book's expense: 'A true blue chip of a publisher's investment, if it is not positively gilt-edged' she said of Enid Bagnold's *The Loved and Envied*, finding its 'easy entertainment' merely 'sad stuff' and containing at times 'the anxious gaiety of a lady who fears the years'.[23] Not concerned to serve fashion, she took up a contrary stand on Angus Wilson's *Hemlock and After* after it had been warmly welcomed by the critics. She suspected that the book's homosexual basis had made the critics determined to appear broadminded. Irritated by what they called its 'deeply moral' view as well as the suggestion that Wilson had bravely uncovered a 'picture of our time', she compared it with books by Aldous Huxley: 'Plainly loving what they profess to hate, their authors heap with affection the details of delinquency . . . with a "heigh-ho, this is how we all are", though it certainly is not how we all are or we should be in the ditch. One prefers the saner hypocrisy of Moll Flanders . . . Sinfulness is always more stimulating to tired readers than virtue, it has the lower flash point they want . . .'[24] Also quick to castigate overt partisanship, she once remarked that it was a rare thing for an English author to be objective without being heartless.[25] One exception was George Gissing, whose *New Grub Street* she read on the advice of her dentist, Wallace Finkel. Of its benighted characters, she said: 'not the angels in their glory are as glorious as these weight-carrying human beings in this glorious book, with their aches and pains of poverty and the fog and cold of their glory fast upon them.'[26]

On one occasion she admitted to Kay Dick that the high standard of novel writing made it difficult to single out the good. But she could also bemoan the fact that most novels were full of thoughts that had been thought a thousand times over. If she could afford it, she told Kay, she would cut reviewing. Her equivocal attitude extended also to her own books. In September 1953 she re-read *The Holiday* in connection with a programme on herself for French radio that Kay was preparing. Her response: 'I think it is perhaps truly poetical because more sustained than the poems . . . it quite ravishes me now again when I read it, and the tears stream down my face because of what Matthew Arnold says, you know?

> But oh the labour
> O Prince, what pain.[27]

A day later she wrote again to Kay: she had totally revised her opinion on *The Holiday* and if given it to review would give it a 'pasting'.[28]

At home Stevie observed the gradual decline of her aunt's health. Often a little comatose, Aunt sometimes dozed off after the introductions to Stevie's friends had taken place. She could also be terse and unforthcoming, making visitors feel they were only moderately welcome. Owing to arthritis in her hip she was now very lame and had difficulty getting up and down stairs, a problem that was aggravated by her weight and swollen legs. Sally Chilver remembers her coming downstairs in obvious discomfort and moving rather painfully from room to room. This friend also noticed that Stevie knew instinctively what to reach for to save Aunt additional effort; and that the sweetness in their relationship was kept in proportion by the Aunt's habit of dismissing as 'silly' anything that smacked of the effusive or sentimental. Her mind was still attached to facts: in one of the school exercise books in which Stevie drafted her poems and which is dated 1956 is the note, 'My Aunt listens with absorbed attention to a talk on the technical values of synthetic rubber'.[29]

Once, when taking her address down over the telephone, Anthony Powell repeated 'Avondale' simply to make sure of what she said. This Stevie, giggling, mistook for contempt for so suburban-sounding a name. Her refusal to leave this remote suburb seemed to many to enhance her eccentricity. It also tried her friends, for after parties she demanded lifts home. One who knew her less well thought she said Parsons Green and was dismayed at the mileage he had to cover to reach Palmers Green. Nevertheless her friends continued to increase, many of them from within the literary world. After reviewing *The Key that Rusts* for the *Observer* in 1954, she received an invitation to lunch from its author, Isobel English, who turned out to be Ronald Orr-Ewing's former wife, June, now married to another writer, Neville Braybrooke and living in Hampstead. Friends of Reggie Smith and Olivia Manning, and of Muriel Spark whom Stevie on at least one occasion met in their home, the Braybrookes enjoyed verbal and literary humour. Stevie at one time considered making Neville her literary executor and had a great fondness for June. She also contributed a drawing to *The Wind and the Rain*, a year book begun in the form of a Catholic, liberal magazine by Neville while he was still a schoolboy at Ampleforth. In 1958 he edited a symposium in honour of T. S. Eliot's seventieth birthday. Stevie contributed an essay on *Murder in the Cathedral* in which she argued that in order to touch 'that Christian nerve which responds so shockingly to fear and cruelty' he resorted to dubious historical and moral assertions. Of all the essays, hers aroused the most response and was, as she admitted, 'a very un-birthday present'.[30]

Whenever Robert Graves was in London, his niece Sally Chilver gave 'at homes' in his honour which Stevie attended. She went also to tea parties given by the biographer Elizabeth Sprigge and the composer Priaulx Rainier, and to parties given at York Terrace in Regents Park by the Marxist architect and sculptor, James Cubitt, to whom she had been introduced by Michael and Anna Browne. Cubitt's wife, Anne Sitwell, was a friend of Rosamond Lehmann and other literary women of a certain class. Stevie mixed easily with these but told James Cubbitt that she never felt part of this society in which an easy familiarity with English literature was expected and unstated assumptions about class prevailed. Few of Stevie's female literary friends, Inez Holden apart, would have shared her pleasure in Brighton. 'I think Aunt dear,' she wrote in August 1955, 'you really ought to come down here some weeks out of season. You would love trotting round the shops hey-ho and you can see everything that's going on from the cliff tops . . . there's rather an endearing festive air about everything. We are now having tea on the pier and reeking of fish and vinegar . . .'[31]

Distrustful of 'abroad', she abjured 'the folly and weakness of foreign travel', concluding: 'We carry our own wilderness with us, our emptiness or our fullness, no matter.'[32] Neither privileges nor holiday distractions could obscure that 'Thou hast been, shall be, art, alone.' Matthew Arnold was a poet she admired and his 'Marguerite' poems describe a state of isolation that Stevie also broached in many of her poems. As with Arnold's 'unmating things', she too took pleasure in landscape and its seasons; likewise his image of 'the unplumb'd, salt, estranging sea' reinforces her own use of the pressure created by watery depths to suggest isolation, oblivion or death. 'And those sweet seas that deepen are my destiny / And must come even if not soon.'[33] In *Over the Frontier* she compares the loneliness of the artist – 'the mind that creates and is aloof and by itself' – with the cold sea 'lapping and sucking beneath the icebound waves of northern Russia'.[34]

Her own isolation was mitigated by her conviction, acquired from the Greeks, that 'there is no part of Nature or the Universe that is not indifferent to Man'.[35] This realization lifted the pressure of loneliness. It is related to the sense of release she got from listening to Fred Hoyle or from thinking about the geological time-scale. 'I like the icy indifferent wind that blows across the flat fields of geological time. I like to think of geological time . . . it lifts the mind, it takes the weight off, it takes the weight off the nerves and the heart.'[36] Another defence against loneliness was writing poems, again for the distraction, solace and release this brought. ('I return to writing poems as if they were toys and I was a child playing alone. You see, there's something unchangeable in all of us.'[37]) Because poetry was her vocation, loneliness became her choice, her 'dark wood', a terrain she would not exchange even in response to those dearest to her.

> Loved I once my darling? I love him not now.
> Had I a mother beloved? She lies far away.
> A sister, a loving heart? My aunt a noble lady?
> All all is silent in the dark wood at night.[38]

No amount of sociability could veil her isolation; her *Times* obituary describes her as 'always in some sense a person apart'.[39] Though tough and realistic, as her friends attest, she lived with her nerves alert to cruelty, both physical and psychological, and took refuge in hilarity partly because life taken too seriously was unbearable. On occasion, when staying with friends, she could exhaust them with her nagging insistence on the unendurableness of life. If those 'tremendously long passages of absolute loneliness', which she described in one interview as a part of her Palmers Green life,[40] had a creative and even enjoyable aspect, they also produced black melancholy. Then, as she told another, being alive was like 'moving in enemy territory'[41] and her sympathy lay with the ghost of Hamlet's father and his desire for revenge.

> All those who go
> In midnight fields of melancholy thought
> Where friends pass distantly and do not speak
> May cry 'Kill, kill' for they are murdered too
> As set upon by Silence and quite killed.[42]

Silence, cold and vicious, drove Stevie to parties with their animated chatter.

> But oh the parties were so beautiful
> And I did not monopolize the faces
> I was only happy to be delivered for a time
> From silence.[43]

Yet, as in *Over the Frontier*, there were times when, in spite of the dear friends, 'loneliness and the fear that waits upon it strikes at the physical heart, so that there is a pain that is physical, with the physical pain of a very extreme icy coldness'.[44] Still more desolate is the poem 'Look!' in which the analogy, which may refer to the creative process, is left open: the pain, however, is specific.

> I am becalmed in a deep sea
> And give signals, but they are not answered
> And yet I see ships in the distance
> And give signals, but they do not answer.
>
> Am I a pariah ship, or a leper
> To be shunned reasonably?
> Or did I commit a crime long ago
> And have forgotten, but they remember?
>
> Into the dark night to darker I move
> And the lights of the ships are not seen now
> But instead there is a phosphorescence from the water.
> That light shines, and now I see
>
> Low down, as I bend my hand in the water
> A fish so transparent in his inner organs
> That I know he comes from the earthquake bed
> Five miles below where I sail, I sail.
>
> All his viscera are transparent, his eyes globule on stalks,
> Is he dead? Or alive and only languid? Now
> Into my hand he comes, the travelling creature,
> Not from the sea-bed only but from the generations,
> Faint because of the lighter pressure,
> Fainting, a long fish, stretched out.
>
> So we meet, and for a moment
> I forget my solitariness
> But then I should like to show him,
> And who shall I show him to?

1955 marks a change in Stevie's fortune. That year David Wright took over the editorship of *Nimbus*, a magazine diverse in its contents and supporting no particular political or ideological stance. It was in general unsympathetic to the Movement and of these poets and writers only D. J. Enright appeared in its pages. Wright was aware that poets of real calibre were having difficulty getting into print and having approached Stevie, was astonished to be sent a batch of some fifty poems which she said no one would publish. *Nimbus* took fourteen, publishing them in Volume 3 No. 2 (1955) generously illustrated with her drawings.

Often it was her drawings that created the stumbling-block. Presented with a batch of her work for possible publication, Ian Parsons of Chatto and Windus approved the poems but found the drawings too comical. Stevie was insistent that the drawings were a part of the verse and must be published with it. She therefore took her work elsewhere, to Mervyn Horder, one of Duckworth's directors. In 1947 he had rejected *The Holiday* but retained Stevie's friendship, an association encouraged by the geographical proximity of Duckworth's and Newnes and frequent teas at the nearby Strand Palace Hotel. He, too, felt the poems unpublishable. 'We cannot see the poems in a selling book,' he told Stevie. 'Their peculiar brand of madness is very elusive, and though the illustrations help to realize it, what is really needed is your presence and voice to recite them.'[45]

David Wright is certain that the appearance of her poems in *Nimbus* led directly to the publication of *Not Waving but Drowning*. A new collection of verse, however, was already being negotiated with André Deutsch before this issue of *Nimbus* appeared. Stevie was by now so demoralized by her lack of success that she was prepared to consider the publication of her poems without drawings. Pleased with the *Nimbus* proofs, even though she saw clearly that her drawing of hands and the back legs of animals was poor, she sent them, on David Wright's advice, to Diana Athill, her editor at Deutsch. These proofs showed how effective the combination of poems and drawings could be; they enabled Stevie to put pressure on the publishers to alter their original contract and by January 1956 they had agreed to include one drawing with every poem.

On first visiting Diana Athill in her office Stevie went pale and announced that unless the print of snakes on the wall was taken down she could not proceed. Thereafter it was removed every time she was expected to visit. This small incident, and the neurosis it revealed, slightly startled Diana Athill who marvelled at the depth of experience Stevie seemed to obtain from living with her aunt in Palmers Green, circumstances that to the younger woman seemed arid and restricting. She never accepted Stevie's invitations to visit Palmers Green and this curtailed their acquaintance. But even slight contact with Stevie introduced one, Diana Athill felt, to a personality that was transparent, honest, entire.

Stevie was not easy to edit. She had lost none of her former uncertainty. There were various delays, some of them Stevie's own making, and the book did not finally appear until the autumn of 1957. 'I hope this won't make you hopping mad,' one of her letters to Diana Athill begins, 'but a book of poems is velly, velly difficult. It's the balance of the thing one can't quite see until one gets the galleys. Will you think it over and if any of the suggested "in" poems seem questionable to you, please do let me know because I want your opinion very much.'[46] As late as April 1957 Stevie decided that certain poems, including 'Jumbo' and 'Magna est Veritas', had been chosen chiefly for their drawings and weakened the book. They were nevertheless retained, for she listened to the opinions of others, and the alternative she had suggested, 'The Light of Life', which, her letter says, had been written the evening before, was also included. When the book finally appeared she was pleased with its format and thought it elegant. It remains the most attractive of all her books.

Not Waving but Drowning opens with the eponymous poem that came to personify her reputation. The sense of alienation and isolation underlying much of her work becomes here a tragi-comic recollection of a man swimming in the sea whose signals for help are misinterpreted and ignored. Just such an experience had occurred to the ex-Newnes-employee-turned-*Times*-journalist, George Buchanan, whom Stevie knew, and whose story is recounted in his autobiography, *Green Sea Coast*. Though this was not published until 1959 he may have given Stevie an oral account of his experience. She, however, is said to have claimed that the idea came from a newspaper story.

'Not Waving but Drowning' displays her ventriloquizing talent: it alternates between commentary and speech, allowing the reader both to share the man's fate and to view it from the outside. The ghost-like speaker overhears the commentary on himself, in the same way that the dying man, in Browning's simile in 'Childe Roland', overhears discussion about his burial. Stevie's clever elision of two different viewpoints helps make this her most memorable poem.

Signals for help are also given from the speaker becalmed in a deep sea in 'Look!'. No previous collection so poignantly evoked an unreachable state. Solitariness leaves the speaker in 'Every lovely Limb's a Desolation' with the feeling that she or he is a prisoner in a passing train behind glass, from which the only release is sleep.

> But I must wake and wake again in pain
> Crying – to see where sun was once all dust and stain
> As on a window pane –
>
> All, all is isolation
> And every lovely limb's a desolation.

Other characters in these poems turn to Death 'as end and remedy'.[47] There is a resistance to sweeter solutions: 'Will Man Ever Face Fact and not Feel Flat', is the title of one poem, and in 'Away, Melancholy' it is suggested that God is man's creation. This poem, in both *Not Waving but Drowning* and as printed in her *Collected Poems*, suffers from a lack of a comma after the word 'god' in the fifth stanza:

> Man of all creatures
> Is superlative
> (Away melancholy)
> He of all creatures alone
> Raiseth a stone
> (Away melancholy)
> Into the stone, the god
> Pours what he knows of good . . .

The absent comma suggests, wrongly, that it is god and not man who does the pouring. The poem argues that man's aspiration to good is enough, that, by implication, the notion of God may be another fairy story.

> Beaten, corrupted, dying
> In his own blood lying
> Yet heaves up an eye above
> Cries, Love, love
> It is his virtue needs explaining,
> Not his failing.
>
> Away, melancholy,
> Away with it, let it go.

Not Waving but Drowning is free of the constriction, slightness and tensity which in places mar her earlier volumes. The sense of greater relaxation arises from the ease with which she slips into narrative and characterization, and the assurance with which she now handles syncopation and half-rhyme. The book contains two comic masterpieces – 'The Jungle Husband' and 'I Remember' – which Stevie was to use regularly at poetry readings. She once said that good writing had to be 'sad, true, economical and funny',[48] epithets that apply also to these poems, especially those which touch on common experience through the use of animals ('The Singing Cat', 'It Filled my Heart with Love' and 'The Old Sweet Dove of Wiveton') and the philosophical comfort observing them can bring. We glimpse her hatred of cruelty, not only in relation to animals ('This is Disgraceful and Abominable'), but also in relation to the mother who 'slew her unborn babe' so that her child would not be born into a world of murder, war and hate ('But Murderous'). She is in addition sharp with parents who send their children to public schools they cannot afford, with literary pundits who form exclusive gangs, with those 'corpse-carriers' who make up the intelligent English upper middle classes, and those who make damaging alterations to Cranmer's Prayer Book.

Though many of these poems invite laughter, they are not frivolous. 'These poems are *déchirant*,' the *Listener* critic observed, 'they are not comfortable at all.'[49] The *Punch* reviewer was 'constantly startled by the intensity of Miss Smith's ideas'.[50] The *Daily Telegraph* reviewed the book alongside Ted Hughes's *The Hawk in the Rain*: 'Where Mr Hughes's words are heavy and burning and sometimes blundering, Miss Smith stabs with a feline but unearthly grace, as disturbing as the first motions of a ship coming into the Atlantic swell.'[51] The book did not emerge unscathed: the *Times Literary Supplement* began on a derogatory note: 'her verse offers somewhat informal commemorations of markedly feminine yieldings' including 'triviality and whimsy, from which it can hardly be said that her little drawings, half wistful and half skittish, help to divert attention.'[52] But it went on to praise her 'searching precision' and the intensity of vision and vigour of language in 'Saint Anthony and the Rose of Life'. Elsewhere, Roy Fuller dismissed her poems outright as lacking in skill and rigour. Ironically, Stevie's harshest critics were often poets, unable, it would seem, to accept her teasing of established rules. When Stevie discovered that Fuller's animadversion had appeared in the *London Magazine*, then edited by John Lehmann, she related his attack to the 'Chatto-Lehmann-John Hayward and I fear also Spender link up',[53] all of whom were by then opposed to her poems. As her absence from various anthologies and literary histories of this period might suggest, her work was and is difficult to pigeon-hole. Her play with a small range of ideas, often repeated, introduces a philosophical element that makes her a kind of lower highbrow, halfway between a solid middlebrow such as Rosamond Lehmann and the sparkling philosophy of Iris Murdoch. In 1957, despite the appreciative reviews, it was evident that literary taste was not yet ready for her.

Though cynical about the advantages of foreign travel – 'How much a dunce that has been sent to roam, Excels a dunce that has been kept at home'[54] – Stevie did go abroad. On the occasion of the 250th anniversary of Rembrandt's birth, she accompanied Armide Oppé to large exhibitions of his paintings and drawings mounted in Amsterdam and Rotterdam. They also spent a half day at Scheveningen where Stevie was aware that for the first time she saw the sun *set* over the North Sea. Abroad, she did not always behave well. She visited Venice in 1962 with Sir John and Lady Lawrence, friends whom she had met through the Brownes, was unwilling to do more than the minimum of sight-seeing and in restaurants demanded traditional English dishes. She had been in Italy once before, in 1957 when she stayed for three weeks and visited Milan, Genoa and Portofino in the company of the musician, Stanley Bate who was married to a Brazilian diplomat, Margarida Guedes Nogueria. 'He and I ran together in the streets, I think / We grew more English with each drink', Stevie afterwards wrote in her misdated poem, 'On the Dressing gown lent me by my Hostess the Brazilian Consul in Milan, 1958' which was not published in her lifetime.[55]

While Stevie was in Italy in 1957 Aunt went to Molly in Aylesbury. By 1962, when Stevie was in Venice, it was no longer possible for Aunt to leave home, and Molly came to Avondale Road. Even visits to the Clutton-Brocks at Chastleton, to the Brownes and Buxtons in Norfolk or to Sir John Lawrence's brother, George and his wife Olga, whose large house near Bath and regular flow of visitors afforded Stevie very congenial hospitality, all now required careful organization on the domestic front. Yet despite the constraints on her life, Stevie was becoming known as a public figure. On at least two occasions she appeared on the popular television programme, the *Brains Trust*. Of the first of these, she wrote: 'I was v. nervous beforehand but when the performance started it was quite fun. But crumbs! how the old hands (Marghanita Laski and Prof. Freddy Ayer) *do go on*.'[56] The medium of television suited her and she 'managed to trip along that tight rope of flippancy and seriousness with great skill', as Inez Holden remarked.[57] Moreover, her remarks on the Poet Laureate brought her a letter of thanks from Masefield himself.

Fortunately for Stevie, her friendship with Professor Hans Häusermann began at a time when she felt bereft of professional support. The introduction came through a mutual friend, Trevor Russell-Cobb, who had for a period worked for the United Nations in Geneva where Häusermann was Professor of English Literature. On hearing that the professor was in London, Russell-Cobb invited him to dinner and asked whom he would like to meet. Hans Häusermann, who took several leading English periodicals and kept files of cuttings by writers he admired, mentioned Stevie Smith and they met on 13 September 1959. The liking was mutual and instantaneous. In many ways Häusermann's views on poetry coincided with Stevie's; he too wanted poetry to be based on philosophy or some faith which, he thought, 'induces the poet who lives in an unpoetic disenchanted world to withdraw more and more from reality'.[58] He had a specialist interest in twentieth-century English literature and English literary criticism, felt close affinities with the thought of Herbert Read and had corresponded with T. S. Eliot since 1934. In his correspondence with Stevie, which began after their first meeting, she wrote more freely about her work than ever before. First, however, she had to convince Häusermann that his high opinion of her was not shared by others. 'You must not think I am accepted,' she told him, after the appearance of *Not Waving but Drowning*, 'though I think sometimes now the younger ones are more favourable to me than my own contemporaries. On the other hand the *Spectator* poetry man, who is young, says that they [her poems] are "old-fashioned", I mean the editor told me he had said so.'[59] In need of critical appreciation, she began to look to this Swiss-German professor, who must have aroused memories of Karl, for encouragement. 'You are a wonderful person to send poems to,' Stevie insisted, 'and I keep reading your comments thereon.'[60] It also pleased her to learn that he wanted to write an article on her novels for the *Neue Zürcher Zeitung*. In turn, Häusermann hoped Stevie would keep him informed on literary matters. Her reply reveals the extent of her disaffection with the literary world.

'I do wish I could help you with up-to-date news of writers and so on but you know you over-rate my innerness – I really am not one of the accepted, far from it, and I don't know or see many writers . . . As a matter of fact I think I have become old without having become famous, always a mistake, and now they want young and famous writers and if they can't find any they invent them. Lit. is awfully racketty, isn't it? At least just now, perhaps it always has been, a lot of shuffling and pushing for place and the publishers and editors, as O.W. [Oscar Wilde] said, knowing everybody's price but nobody's value (or so, naturally, the neglected ones feel). The *Observer* is v. tricky, they only half like me and Terry Kilmartin (the v. nice but timid little lit. ed.) says that my poems have him 'flummoxed' and they do have to be careful not to back the wrong horse, in fact, in their cunning timid way, they really only like to place their bets after the horse is home, ha ha ha . . . somehow the voice of the Ob.[server] is getting far far too much like the voice of the *New Statesman*, the same edgy humourless . . . approach to life, the same nerviness about the awful possibility of slipping behind the fashion line, and all the rest of the silliness that goes on, politically as well as literatureally . . .'[61]

Stevie told Häusermann, as she did others, that her drawings inspired her poems. They captured, ideographically, thoughts, fears, daydreams and arguments. Under the heading 'Beyond Words' she had once made a list of titles and one-line captions, apparently hoping that a book of her drawings could be published. This did not happen until 1958 when Stefan and Franciszka Themerson of the Gaberbocchus Press took up the idea. Franciszka sent off a batch of Stevie's drawings, to be printed slightly enlarged and in grey. On their return Stevie spent a day in Franciszka's studio making a selection from these, arranging them and writing captions, laughing a great deal as she did so. Her humour, in her art as in her life, was rooted in anguish. 'Do not ask for love', is the caption underneath two animals, used here to express human thoughts. 'We all have these thoughts sometimes' is another that voices the book's message. These captions, drawn from her poems, from clichés, questions, exclamations, reflect her admiration for the elliptically suggestive titles used by Goya and George Grosz. The book's title – *Some are More Human than Others* – parodies a famous line in Orwell's *Animal Farm*, replacing political satire with Stevie's belief that the human condition dwarfs politics.

The book's casual appearance and small size may explain why reviewers, for the most part, ignored it. John Betjeman gave it a passing mention in the *Daily Telegraph* where his remark, 'Owes much to Thurber',[62] annoyed Stevie. She admitted that the drawing on the book's cover invited this comparison, but she insisted that she and Thurber were fundamentally different; whereas Thurber deals with social comedy and situations, she pinpoints states of mind. Critics today still tend to overlook the importance of this small book which contains the essence of her art, in content and manner. Its characters and animals are not categorized, politicized or manipulated in such a way as to suit the author's purpose; instead they are observed and described with the same crystalline, detached intelligence that informs her poems, and which gives to both drawings and poems a life-enhancing veracity.

Stevie's blurb for this book, remains its most accurate description: 'These drawings . . . open up a whole world of peculiar experience . . . There is laughter here and depths beneath it, some gaiety, and innocence in depressed circumstances, some cruelty too, perhaps, as if the truths of our world have been trapped off guard. Which are beastly in these drawings, which are human – the sidling animals or the equivocal people? All at least are creatures and have their lives. If sometimes they bite the hand that made them and spit in the eye that beholds, that only shows what strong creatures they are.'

The only piece on *Some are More Human than Others* that interested her was Häusermann's review of it in the *Neue Zürcher Zeitung*. He emphasized the fear of life the book expressed, and the suspicion and defiance this produces, 'particularly in the absolute demands of religion and love'.[63] Stevie responded: 'You are very penetrating and sometimes go further than I had consciously gone. I can't help feeling the whole thing is less under control, more come-by-chance, than you are good enough to allow . . . But the writer I suppose never knows quite what he is up to, or how he will set the echoes flying in the reader's heart.'[64] The arbitrariness she insists on is also evidenced in her occasional use of the same drawing for two quite different contexts. In 1966 she admitted to a publisher that her drawings 'pretty well go with anything'.[65] To her friends she would suggest, perhaps self-mockingly, that her drawings meant more to her than her poems. They captured the first stirrings of an idea, mood or feeling and were drawn on old scraps of paper, the backs of letters, circulars, envelopes and bills, which sometimes made them difficult to reproduce. When one publisher offered to present her with good quality drawing paper, she declared that, with such materials, nothing would emerge.

With Hans Häusermann and the Themersons behind her, Stevie began to suspect that only foreign souls could see the point of her work. *Some are More Human than Others* did not sell. Booksellers were wary of the Gaberbocchus Press, despite its association with Kurt Schwitters, C. H. Sisson and other distinguished names. The Themersons also ran the Gaberbocchus Common Room, an informal club which opened in 1956 and ran for three years. Stevie, who had begun to appear at poetry events, read there twice, on 4 February 1958 and 11 June 1959. The second of these readings coincided with the launching of *New Departures*, an alternative poetry magazine edited by Michael Horovitz who was to involve Stevie in poetry and jazz events in the 1960s.

Right up until the end of the 1950s, however, she was having difficulty in placing her work. In the summer of 1958, whilst doing occasional reviews for the *Daily Telegraph*, she complained she was idle and uninspired. To fill her time and earn a bit of money, she became a reader for the literary agent, Curtis Brown. She went to their offices one day a week and found the job dull and depressing. She still occasionally dreamt she was back at Newnes, and at Curtis Brown she relived her former captivity. Nor did she respect her employers with whom she stayed only six months. 'They, like most publishers, are such embattled middlebrows, so stupid, so conceited, and often, God help us, also so cross! And I won't be badgered and bothered now I don't have to be (shades of a previous office life!) as it's all the same to me whether I have the job or not. Generally they are awfully nice and they do have masses of quarto-sized paper . . . All the same these middle-brows, with their regrettable-deplorable-bounce and energy are England's Bane, the walking illustration of that blood-curdling truth – that the Better is the Enemy of the Good.'[66]

In another letter to Häusermann Stevie declared that, besides writing poems, only Agatha Christie and books on Roman Catholicism could lift her glumness. So regularly were her poems returned, she began to think twice about sending them off. In November 1958 she received a batch from *Encounter*. 'They said they "liked them terribly" but couldn't publish them. How I wish they didn't and would.'[67] Having earlier this year received back from the *Times Literary Supplement* two rejected poems which they had kept a year, she was surprised and pleased when its editor, Alan Pryce-Jones, suggested they should renew relations. This was not the only sign that her reputation was beginning to ascend. She was included in two anthologies that appeared in 1958: *Springtime Two. An anthology of current trends in literature*, edited by Peter and Wendy Owen, and *New Poems 1958*, edited by Bonamy Dobrée, Louis MacNeice and Philip Larkin. Nevertheless, the apathy and despair she suffered at this time seemed to permeate even her relations with Aunt. 'Dear Aunt now has a hearing aid,' she told Häusermann, 'but somehow there doesn't seem much to say.'[68]

Stevie did not visit Häusermann in Geneva in 1959, as he invited her to do, perhaps because Aunt was by then too much of a responsibility. In December of that year his wife died of leukaemia. Eight years later he married his niece, Gertrud Voegeli (née Häusermann) who is not unlike Stevie, in height, build and appearance. She gained an impression that her husband had at one time considered asking Stevie to leave England, something that was never likely, not least because she would never have abandoned Aunt. In their correspondence the mingling of affection and respect is at its warmest during the late 1950s when Stevie's need for appreciation was at its most acute. 'And *do* write,' she ends one letter,[69] closing another long communication with a similar request: 'Write me a *long* letter, this one is abnormal please beat it.'[70]

CHAPTER 12

Fixed on God

If Stevie's appearance in *Nimbus* marked a turning point in her career, it nearly coincided with the re-opening of relations with the BBC. In January 1956 D. S. Carne-Ross, from the Talks department, offered her a fifteen-minute programme. Stevie argued that twenty minutes were needed for an audience to become accustomed to the pattern of her work – 'it is terrifically *worked out*, as you will have noticed'[1] – as well as the differences in metre and mood. The resultant programme, broadcast on 12 April, received an unenthusiastic listener's report: Stevie's manner was found 'somewhat melancholy', her impure vowels, irritating, and her introductions to the poems 'sometimes obscure and often whimsical'.[2] Far from obscure or whimsical was the poem with which Stevie chose to end: 'God the Eater'.

> There is a god in whom I do not believe
> Yet to this god my love stretches
> This god whom I do not believe in is
> My whole life, my life and I am his.
>
> Everything that I have of pleasure and pain
> (Of pain, of bitter pain and man's contempt)[3]
> I give this god for him to feed upon
> As he is my whole life and I am his.
>
> When I am dead I hope that he will eat

Everything I have been and have not been
And crunch and feed upon it and grow fat
Eating my life and all up as it is his.

Afterwards Stevie wrote to Rachel Marshall, asking if she had heard the programme. As an experienced speech and drama teacher, Rachel had earlier advised Stevie on her delivery and was in advance of her time in not trying to impose upon others BBC pronunciation. Of Stevie's first 'Poems and Drawings' broadcast in 1951, Rachel had remarked that there was no audible differentiation between verse and commentary. The 1956 programme she entirely approved:

'It's the best you have ever done. You always have such a distinctive style in reading, detached, rhythmical and perfectly genuine, it is absolute hearts-case after the falsity of most BBC poetry speaking: your voice is fine, low and full without being fruity, and full of individuality, it matched the dry humour of the short links between the poems. You have got your pace just right.'[4]

Stevie was gratified and encouraged. She was 'woefully aware' of her 's's in the broadcast: ' "S" is difficult, isn't it, and there are such a lot of them in the language! I've often noticed it in the theatres when the interval breaks out – it's like the sea rushing in.'[5] Despite Rachel's praise, Stevie's voice continued to worry her. 'What causes a South Kensington accent and is there any way of getting rid of it, oh dear Rachel?' she asked in 1958. 'Whenever I hear my voice on a tape recorder, there that hideous accent is in all its beastliness.'[6] Again, after a 1961 broadcast, she abhorred 'the awful nasalness of my voice', and asked Rachel if there was someone in London who could remedy it.[7]

Her idiosyncratic pronunciation added to the fascination of her readings but it took time for this to be recognized. When later in 1956 Stevie did another programme with the BBC and asked her producer Douglas Cleverdon if she might sing 'Le Singe Qui Swing' he carefully steered away from this idea. The programme, entitled 'Too Tired for Words', focused on the way tiredness, producing despair, hilarity, argument, or religious thought, affects the imaginary people in Stevie's poems. She developed an affectionate respect for Douglas Cleverdon, whose work for the Features department ranged from radio operas to documentaries on folk songs. There existed a particularly good relationship between Features and its writers, facilitated by the George and the Stag, but Cleverdon was exceptional in his desire not to tinker with another's script but to bring out its qualities. He was also extremely professional in the studio and good at rehearsing actors. After rehearsing 'Too Tired for Words', he took Stevie to lunch with his wife Nest, and from then on Stevie was a frequent visitor to their house. Nest Cleverdon's knack of putting people at their ease, her familiarity with the literary world and with English cooking, of the kind Stevie liked, made her entirely sympathetic. Stevie dined at the Cleverdons on many occasions, once in the company of John Betjeman with whom she spent much of the evening singing hymns over the dinner table.

With Douglas Cleverdon, Stevie also made the radio play, 'A Turn Outside' in which the poet Stevie Smith is found in conversation with a mysterious interlocutor. What begins as an interview about her poems and their relation to familiar tunes becomes deliberately spooky when the interviewer, insinuatingly attentive, invites the poet to take 'a turn outside'. Poems and passages from *The Holiday* are worked into the dialogue in which Stevie begins to recognize her interlocutor: it is he who wiped away 'the message of love on the window pane', he whom she rode with in the dark wood and she eventually succumbs to his deathly seductions. Stevie wrote the piece in such a way that certain poems had to be sung, and evidently wanted to sing them herself; but after Cleverdon had warned that 'to be tolerable on the air, female singing voices have to be very good indeed',[8] agreed to record herself singing these poems, her tunes becoming the basis for those used by the actress, Janette Richer, who read and sang the part of Stevie Smith. Hugh Burden took the part of the interlocutor and the programme was broadcast on 18 May and again on 23 May 1959. 'Just to thank you very much again for shaping that ghastly programme so beautifully,' Stevie afterwards wrote to Douglas Cleverdon. 'It was a treat to watch you, and if I fled untimely, snatching the last drink from them as ad earned it, you must forgive me. It was that female character, dear, I could stand no more of! (The one, I wrote, I mean, *not* good heavens, Jeanette [sic], who couldn't be better. Same goes for Hugh Burden. I must say you are brainy about casting.'[9] To another, Stevie admitted that the female character impersonating herself had come across a bit like a dotty deb. An audience report discovered mixed response: one listener thought it 'extremely original' and 'full of pleasant conceits and sly fun'; another complained it was 'too clever, literary and arch'. Janette Richer was praised for 'singing and speaking with an almost schoolgirlish naturalness which developed, as her anxiety grew, into a frenzy of acquiescent despair'.[10]

Stevie had been interested in the performance aspect of her work ever since the reading at Homerton in Cambridge in 1944. The earliest reading of her poems that she herself gave, radio talks apart, was to the Poetry Society at the Oxford Union on 12 November 1957. Eight days later she delivered her lecture, 'The Necessity of Not Believing' to the Cambridge Humanists, received the impression that it was well received and was well pleased to be able to sing some of the poems incorporated into the talk. She hoped this, too, could become a radio programme and asked Anna Kallin if she might send her the text. 'It is partly autobiographical, showing how very religious I was when young . . . and later how I became not religious, but conscientiously anti-religious, with regret because I had enjoyed it so much, especially the morbid hymns like "Days and moments swiftly flying / Blend the living with the dying . . ." etc, but *firmly*, because it was so immoral to believe . . . It is not *at all whimsical*, as some asses seem to think I am, but serious, yet not aggressive, and fairly cheerful though with melancholy patches.'[11] Two days later she wrote again. 'Here is the lecture . . . it is not really a lecture at all but something that is tumbling running and spluttering, as you see.'[12]

Anna Kallin returned it promptly, with the uncharacteristically vague reply that its 'presentation' might cause trouble. Stevie, suspecting that no one else had seen the script, sent it back to the BBC, this time to Dorothy Baker, script editor in the Features Department. Her views on it formed an internal memorandum:

'The essay is eminently readable and proceeds from a naïve and artful beginning to a deeper and more bitter attack on the Christian religion with some excruciating quotations on the nature of hell and purgatory and cutting remarks on ambiguity in the interpretation of the Gospels. She has some very interesting ideas on the reason and nature of goodness and challenges the idea that our age is retrogressive so far as cruelty is concerned . . . It is highly controversial, extremely intelligent up to a point, though I do think that she has overdone the *naïveté* at times. The essay would certainly be provocative and is just as certainly beautifully written.'[13]

Her remark on its *naïveté* was shared by others and the lecture rejected. This was not the only occasion when the BBC refused to handle Stevie's thoughts on Christianity. In 1968 she sent them 'Some Impediments to Christian Commitment', which in its argument and the material used is closely related to 'The Necessity of Not Believing', and again it was returned as 'unsuitable', perhaps because it was too serious and weighty for the Home Service and too much the layman's view to satisfy Third Programme listeners. Both lectures, like Stevie's work as a whole, elude easy categorization and are informed by an uncompromising moral integrity.

Stevie's attitude to the Christian religion, like that of Emily Dickinson, was that of an agnostic who could not entirely abandon belief in a God of Love. She was intensely aware that Christianity involved a commingling of sweetness and cruelty. In 'The Necessity of Not Believing' she instances the hymn, 'Faithful tree above all other' which tells how the tree from which Christ's cross was made must bend its lofty branches so that 'The limbs of heaven's high Monarch / Gently on thy arms extend', the hymn's pastoral sweetness obliterating the suffering of the Crucifixion.

The cruellest aspect of Christian teaching, for her, was the doctrine of hell: while proclaiming a God of Love, Christianity preaches also the severest indictment – eternal damnation. Stevie was not unaware of the various theological arguments surrounding the concept of hell. She knew of Bishop Gore's remark, in his *The Religion of the Church. As Presented in the Church of England*, that 'final moral ruin may involve . . . such a dissolution of personality as carries with it the cessation of personal consciousness',[14] which did not remove her objection. She observed that Christ did not protest against 'this monstrous idea, this crime of hell'.[15] The doctrine of hell, she argues, parts the believers from the unbelievers: 'It is the gateway to the vast emptiness of unbelief.' As she goes on to describe in 'The Necessity of Not Believing', the concept of hell fed her disaffection with the Christian religion, her growing awareness that it bit deeply 'upon the nerve of cruelty that lies in our hearts'; she felt the pull of intellect against feeling and found herself torn between disagreement and approval of a religion she loved dearly, for, owing to her Anglican background, its 'beauties' had become her 'habit'. But alongside her pleasure in the Anglican church strode 'my formidable Conscience, a most practical agent, a really literal creature, full of the plainest common sense and a determination to make words mean what they say'. She also versed herself in the history of the Church and familiarized herself with the Inquisition and with transcripts of its trials: 'Here is the essence of Christianity, here are the harsh bones beneath the soft sweet skin.' With this knowledge it became impossible for her, as it did for Primo Levi after his experience of a concentration camp, to reconcile a belief in Providence or a God of Love with such enormity. Quoting Epicurus, she protests: 'Benevolence would, Omnipotence could, have found some other way.'

'The Necessity of Not Believing' contains a poem, not elsewhere reprinted, which ends:

> Know thy world, Man; through Art or Science, dote on it,
> But do not build a fairy tale upon it.

Aware that religious matters are not open to proof, she saw that belief in others is often at base merely hope, fear or fancy. It had taken her a long time to reach anti-religious conclusions and there was always the danger, as she herself remarked, that she would backslide into belief. Moreover, once firmly outside the fold, cut off from belief in a personal God, her spiritual horizon seemed bleak and empty.

'The path of the unbeliever, especially if he is an unbeliever with a religious temperament, is fraught with the perils of flatness and ennui, and religion, by contrast, particularly the Christian religion, is so dramatic and exciting, with its hazards of eternal life and eternal damnation, its demonic urge to boss, confine and intimidate, and above all, its sweet promise of a heavenly father, oh how sweet that can be, this sweet interest that never fails, even if it damn us. Why listen how sweet it can be, in Isaiah this verse comes: 'I the Lord thy God will hold thy right hand, saying unto thee: Fear not, I will help thee' . . . that so much bears the mark of our humanity – to boss, confine and intimidate, yes, but also to be loved and comforted? *That so much bears the mark of our humanity.* "[6]

The purpose of her lecture was to promote a move from religious darkness to agnostical light, to the recognition of goodness and love in their own right. Though she clung to this argument, she admitted in a radio interview during the last year of her life that she was a 'bad guide for the religious world because my feelings change a great deal. Sometimes I . . . rather think one thing, sometimes another.'[17] She ended the interview with a reading of 'The Repentance of Lady T' which, she admitted, is 'very Christian in its essence'. In content, this early poem finds an echo in 'Mort's Cry' which Stevie sent to the *Observer* in 1967.[18] It begins:

> O Lamb of God I am
> Too sharp; too tired.
> Make me more amiable, O Lamb,
> Less Tired
> No longer what I am

But this yearning for spiritual renewal, and the backsliding it suggests, contrasts with the line she had taken a few years earlier. Interviewed by John Horder on radio in 1963, Stevie argued that man is so lonely he invents God in order to have someone interested in him, in the face of an indifferent universe. When Horder asked what alternative to religion there was, if man is so lonely, Stevie replied there was none; that loneliness was imperative and man must draw richness from that.[19]

Her objections to Christian belief earned her much criticism. She was informed that the line, 'he that believeth not shall be damned' (Mark 16:16), is part of the inauthentic ending to St Mark's gospel tacked on after verse 8 of the last chapter where in the earliest sources this gospel ends. Stevie's reply was one of astonishment that the Bible contained 'forgeries and discrepancies . . . such as would not be tolerated for one moment in an honest human document'.[20] Even annotated editions of the New Testament in use today fail to underline sufficiently how spurious these twelve verses are, possibly out of respect for the Church Missionary Society which has made verse 15, 'Go ye into all the world, and preach the gospel to every creature', a key text.

To a lay person Stevie seems to voice the uncomfortable questions that refuse to go away. To committed Christians her arguments seem inadequate because they remain confined within the arena of rational discourse, whereas many of the religious statements that she is dealing with belong to the language of faith. Moreover those Christians who are not literalists distinguish between biblical authority and personal religious experience. Beginning with the latter, they make a commitment and proceed to an assimilation and examination of the former. Stevie, unable to accept biblical authority on a rational level, refused to make a commitment based on personal experience alone.

The irritation she aroused in churchmen is revealed in the letters printed in the magazine *Gemini* after the appearance of her essay 'The Necessity of Not Believing'. Mervyn Stockwood, then vicar of the University Church, Cambridge and brother of Stevie's friend, Jane, abhorred her use of 'snippets' of Church history and practice and compared her arguments to 'the accounts in Communist textbooks of British colonial rule. The incidents are usually true, but they constitute less than half the story – and the result is travesty, which cannot be treated seriously'.[21] Two other letters, from Simon Barrington Ward, Chaplain of Magdalene College, Cambridge, and John E. Pinnington, likewise criticized her 'hasty and undigested invective', but their wordy replies noticeably failed to answer her objections which, contrary to their criticisms, rested on attentive reading of theological texts and many years of thought and feeling. Stevie's reply to her critics deserves quoting at length:

'Mr Mervyn Stockwood and Mr Barrington Ward imply that this doctrine [of eternal hell] is "one of the mawkish beliefs which Christians hold" and that I am "childish to insist so much upon it".

But are not all Christians bound to believe it, for is it not based on Christ's teaching and taken by the Church to be so based? Mr Pinnington, replying in a letter, says that " 'Orthodoxy' provides no clear idea what these things" (heaven and hell) "are like – a deficiency unfortunately made up by many lively imaginations such as Fr. Faber's quoted in Miss Smith's article". I assure him that Fr. Faber's book is of the highest orthodoxy, bearing the Imprimatur and Nihil Obstat of the Catholic Church. The Rev Dr J. P. Arendzen, writing under the same authority, points the matter and also takes care of Mr Pinnington's historical argument. I quote: "If anyone says or thinks that the punishment of the demons and the wicked will not be eternal, that it will have an end, and that then shall take place a restoration (apokatastasin) of the demon and the wicked, let him be anathemata." Furthermore, though it is not given to men on earth to know which or how many of us are to be damned, it is equally foolish to indulge in facile jest: "I believe in eternal hell, eternally empty." Such words make a mockery of Christ's words to the wicked on the day of judgement: "Depart from me, ye cursed, into everlasting fire, which was prepared for the devil and his angels from the beginning of the world." He goes on: "This Scriptural teaching has been continuously unhesitatingly and emphatically proclaimed by the Church throughout all ages. It would be difficult to find a Christian dogma which, historically speaking, is more undoubtedly an integral part of the Christian revelation than the eternity of punishment for the reprobate." It was the wickedness of this doctrine, and the essential part it has in Christianity, that made me choose for my title "The Necessity of Not Believing". It is a moral necessity . . . If the Anglican Church differs from the Roman Catholic Church in its teaching about hell, I wish they would say so. The slightly equivocal "explanation" so often given – that the damned choose hell – with its inevitable suggestion that choice brings some measure of contentment, is in plain contradiction of the "facts" of hell as found in all "orthodox" writings.

Listen again to Dr Arendzen. "If all that were ever written or painted or carved expressive of the torturing of hell could be brought before us at a glance, it would certainly fall immeasurably short of the truth." He does not exceed his text; Christ said: "where the worm dieth not and the fire is not quenched". The way out of this *impasse* (of reconciling the Christ of Hell and the Christ of Love) seems the way I have taken – to see him as a man, not a god, and so allow him fallibility. I do not think that Christians can take this way."[22]

Stevie was helped to see Christ as man and not God by three books: Robert Graves's *King Jesus*, George Moore's *The Brook Kerith* and D. H. Lawrence's *The Man Who Died*, all of which present a Jesus who is taken down from the cross alive, repents of his earlier beliefs and seeks quietness in the mountains. Stevie was fascinated by this alternative view of the historical Jesus. Graves, using uncanonical sources, constructs a Jesus who is fanatical, deeply versed in rabbinical law and anxious to fulfil prophecies found in Jewish mystical texts. Stevie, on first reading this book in 1947, was impressed by the power of Graves's interpretation. It made her wonder how Jesus, if he had the characteristics Graves described, could have captured the hearts and minds of Europeans for nearly two thousand years: 'What did Europe do to this young Jewish savant to ensure his survival?'[23] Any answer to this question must acknowledge the role played by St Paul, for he, as Stevie perceived, rescued the infant church from the stranglehold of rabbinical mysticism. Because so much hinged on St Paul, the passage in *The Brook Kerith* which haunted Stevie concerned a conversation between Jesus and Paul. Jesus, nursed back to health by Joseph of Arimathea, has gone back to the Essenes to look after his sheep. Paul comes by chance, leaving Timothy at the gate. Jesus speaks with Paul as to a stranger, saying that he has now to devote his whole life to repentance for one great sin – that he claimed to be God. Gradually Paul recognizes that this is Jesus, the one he is preaching and teaching as the Risen Christ. But Paul will not have his vision shattered, shuts his eyes and sets off with Timothy to establish Christianity.

In spite of her unbelief Stevie was captivated by the notion of a God of Love and by Christ whose teaching on love co-existed with the seedy cynicism of the Roman Empire. This teaching, which to her 'burns with such seeming freshness',[24] made Christ 'a person of lofty and passionate beliefs',[25] capable of inspiring Christians and non-Christians. After reading E. V. Rieu's translation of St Mark's Gospel, in his *The Four Gospels* (1952) Stevie wrote 'The Airy Christ'. Her Jesus is not a schemer who repents but a diffident creature who wishes only that others would hear him sing.

> As he knows the words he sings, that he sings so happily
> Must be changed to working laws, yet sings he ceaselessly.

> Those who truly hear the voice, the words, the happy song,
> Never shall need working laws to keep from doing wrong.

If Christ is not God, Stevie wrote, 'he is a human being, a lofty and noble creature, someone we may love and admire and whose words we may sort'.[26]

If, however, Christ is God, Stevie argued, then he is abominable for he is a party to an ignominious bargain, the death of God's Son to redeem our sin, a bargain that imposes an intolerable burden of guilt and gratitude. In addition, if Christ is God his manhood becomes invalid. Stevie once remarked: 'To feel trivial and idiotic and to live with this feeling is to be a hero in a way that no god can be.'[27] She elaborates on this idea in 'Was He Married?' which contains the lines:

> All human beings should have a medal,
> A god cannot carry it, he is not able.

Stevie sent a gloss on this poem to Lyn Newman. 'It's a character poem as well as an argument. Question and Answer. Q. is not very bright. A., a bit shy, is leading him on to see that Christianity (as I think) really contradicts itself. All Q.'s poor predicaments are the result of sin, or failure, or weakness – any way – imperfections, e.g. marriage. If it's such a flop as poor Q. suggests, then it's because of some sort of failure – nerves, selfishness or most likely (Q.'s chief handicap) general feebleness. Even the 'happy' verse – which perhaps doesn't quite fit (". . . find a sudden brightness in everything . . .") ties up with nerves and sin. A. waits until the score has mounted up and then pounces . . . ' "A god is man's doll, you ass" . . . it is left to Q. then to plead that Christianity is at least a move forward. ("He might have made him up worse.") The "medal" that Man carries is the medal of imperfection. Certainly no god can carry it, it would be a contradiction in terms, especially the Christian idea of God – all powerful, perfect, etc. . . . Perfection can never be less than itself. Hence (I think) the awful importance of the lines in my poem. "There is no suffering like having made a mistake, because of being of an inferior make." '[28]

'Was He Married?' explains why Stevie was fond of quoting D. H. Lawrence's remark, that Christ 'ought to have been man enough to be able to come home at tea time and put his slippers on and sit under the spell of his wife'.[29] From 1956 onwards she reviewed few novels and dealt mostly with books with a religious or historical content. She was made very aware that each age has its own Jesus and that in our age he is created in the image of a liberal humanist. Reviewing a book of essays by various authors, *The God I Want*, she observed that English theology was outstanding in its 'amiability and disregard for logic'. She also remarked how curious it was that our age, 'so violent and so devoted to reading and hearing about "evil things", should see Christ only as "kind"'. She adds that it is, of course, also a sentimental age.[30]

In such an age Stevie, who had like her Galloping Cat 'an experienced eye of earthly sharpness', became an important voice. The Revd Gerard Irvine, who got to know her well, rightly insists that her views on Christianity were too cut and dried, dependent more on knowledge than understanding.

But her reviews of theological books acted as a valuable corrective to all that was false or fudged by sentimentality. An instance of her sharp integrity is found in her review of Father D'Arcy's *Facing God*: 'Fr D'Arcy would say: Pray for faith. But what does this mean? We should not pray for what is not true, and if we believe his faith is true, then we already have it. If we pray, we must pray to know the truth. Joyfully Fr D'Arcy will say: There is no distinction. Less joyfully – for it is happier to be settled – we say we think there is.'[31]

Her objections to Christianity, this 'hell-haunted religion',[32] and her awareness of the uncomfortable paradoxes represented in Christ were the subject of 'How do you see?', a long poem commissioned by the *Guardian* and into which, in order to fulfil the required length, she incorporated 'O Christianity, O Christianity'. Published Whitsun 1964, it aroused such controversy that the following Saturday the entire letter page was given over to it. The printed letters represented only a tiny proportion of the total response. Stevie herself was inundated with mail for weeks afterwards, congratulating her, abusing her and much of it concerned to convert her to other views. Like other of her 'argument' poems, 'How do you see?' tends to prosiness and is not one of her best. But as a vehicle for her ideas it communicated widely and created considerable stir.

In spite of her unbelief, Stevie is a religious poet, not only because she deals with the kind of doubt that is a part of religious experience, but also because religious themes and images recur. Moreover several of her poems affirm the existence of a spirit or god to whom we must submit. As Thomas Blackburn has said of Browning: 'It may be a poetry of doubt but it is religious in that it suggests we are involved in many dimensions of existence.'[33] Like other agnostics or atheists, Marlowe, Shelley, Byron, Keats and Arnold among others, Stevie could find no religious certainty in the church and had, in Empson's phrase, to 'learn a style from a despair'.

Like Celia, in *The Holiday*, Stevie's mind was full of biblical tags which sometimes found parallels in the classics. The Latin tag, '*fata nolentem trahunt volentem ducunt*' (the fates drag the unwilling, the willing they lead), seemed to her close in spirit to 'in His will is our peace'. St Paul's 'The evil that I would not, that I do' lay behind her translation:

> The climate of my soul is like a curse
> I see and approve the better and follow the worse.[34]

All three of the above formulations were running in her mind when she wrote 'Recognition not Enough', again compressing complex thoughts into two lines:

Sin recognized – but that – may keep us humble,
But oh, it keeps us nasty.

The narrator and characters in her poems are rarely amoral, but conscious of good and evil, duty and failure. This, again, confirms that she is a
religious poet, aware, as she once said, of 'the lofty idea that a man must
stand alone before the Lord'.[35] When she remarked of Blake that he 'rows
and grumbles at God and nags him . . . he cannot forget Him',[36] she could
also have been speaking of herself. Though irritated by dogma, she was
incapable of denying the spiritual dimension. When in December 1968 she
delivered 'Some Impediments to Christian Commitment' to the St Anne's
Society in London, she asked: 'how can one's heart *not* go out to the idea
that a God of absolute love is in charge of the universe'. Yet she remained in
the world of uncertainty where she insisted there was room enough for love,
joy, virtue, affection and for imagination.[37]

Pulled in two directions, one part of her wanted to turn away from
Christian teaching and practice ('Blow it away, have done with it'[38]) and
another wanted a return to God. Her hankering after a God of Love brings
her close to Matthew Arnold's belief in 'an Eternal not ourselves that makes
for righteousness'. Yet careful always to distinguish between hope and
belief, she urged her readers to 'learn to be good in a dull way without
enchantment',[39] to resist the fairy stories about religion and to love love and
hate hate and not deify them.

There was also a lighter side to Stevie's argument with Christianity for
she was alert to its absurdities. At one party she pinioned a young clergyman
in a corner and was overheard saying: 'But is it really a bird?' Molly's Roman
Catholicism also led to remarks that Stevie would not let pass. 'Molly says
Our Lady has such a sense of humour,' she gossiped to Gerard Irvine.
Then, too, she was stimulated by the 'bright variety'[40] of religious thought
and found many of the books she read on the subject beautifully and
ingeniously expressed. But her remark, that one of the most unattractive
things about Christianity was its belief in an afterlife, was entirely serious.
She did not forget A. J. Balfour's reply, when asked if he would like another
life on earth: 'He said "No" – as the chance of being even *tolerably* unhappy
was so remote.'[41] And when arguing about religion with others, her manner
could become fierce if she felt the other person was glossing over the
argument. On occasion she could get so angry about the cruelty of religion
that she visibly shook and her hearers had the impression that it was not just
human, political or judicial cruelty she abhorred but a cruelty specific to
Christianity. Sir John Lawrence, who once took Stevie and his wife to an

ecumenical conference at Broadstairs, had the feeling that by the 1950s Stevie had closed her mind to theological arguments and clung to views that did not upset her pattern of experience. He also felt that there was something of paradise lost about her attitude to the Church of England, for she more than once exclaimed: 'Why don't I meet those wonderful old Anglican clergy whom I used to know.'[42]

In her attitude to death, Stevie is, it at first seems, at her most unchristian. Talking about the characters in her poems, she commented: 'Seeing sin for what it is, so ugly and nimble, the pilgrim may now and then fall into despair and cry out for death. Not Christian Death, but death in the grand Lucretian sense.'[43] For her death was a scatterer; it brought the best gift of all, a breaking of the whole human pattern, a release that is absolute. She appreciated death for its finality, not as an imaginative experience, as Wordsworth did ('. . . we are laid asleep / In body, and become a living soul'). There is nothing morbid or self-pitying about her attitude. Though she could not share the Christian's optimism, that death is a gateway between earth and heaven, the threshold to the presence of God, her humanist standpoint was nevertheless buoyant: she compared waiting for death to waiting for a train one really longs for to take one away; and she would quote Dryden on its enigma:

> That short dark passage to a future state
> That melancholy riddle of a breath
> That something, or that nothing, after death.

What is remarkable is that she did not fear this enigma and made no attempt to find a formula, defence or answer that would contain or solve it. She bravely confronted what most of us either ignore or harness to a religion. The knowledge that death would come and can be summoned at our will was, for Stevie, 'a fortifying thought, good enough to carry me to a ripe old age'.[44] Death, as Inez Holden once remarked, was the only thing that kept Stevie alive.

Her obsession with death is, however, not unrelated to her desire for a God of Love. Almost certainly her thinking on death was influenced by her reading of J. C. Powys's *The Pleasures of Literature* where he writes of Walt Whitman: 'Death had upon him an effect that resembles the effect of love. It seems the fulfiller of all that is unfulfilled in love, it seems the answer to all that is dumb in love, it seems the grand denouement of love and the rounding off of love's broken circle.' He continues: 'The world hates death. But love does not hate death. Love has something of death in it. Love and death together are stronger than all the meanness and silliness of the world.'[45] Stevie reached a similar conclusion:

'. . . all love seeks its source and its destiny in Love, in the idea of some great Love, that is beyond the human pattern. But that perfect love may be what I have often written of as the greatest of all blessings: Death as a scattering of the human pattern altogether, as an End.'[46]

CHAPTER 13

Frivolous and Vulnerable

A few years after her retirement from Newnes Stevie's life underwent considerable change. She began to notice that 1 Avondale Road had fallen into a state of decline, and in this indirect way she realized her aunt's failing health. 'I don't think the old thing is too well, which is worrying,' she told Rachel Marshall in 1958, 'she is so uncomplaining and sweet, one never knows how she is.'[1] Increasingly Aunt found stairs difficult to negotiate and from 1962 onwards she was confined to the upstairs part of the house. 'You can imagine how boring this is for her,' Stevie told another, 'and what it means . . . in cooking and tray carrying. I camp upstairs with her most of the time, but what one wants always seems to be downstairs, or, of course, upstairs if one is doing out the dustbin.'[2] With Aunt now completely dependent, Stevie took on the role of cook, housekeeper and to some extent nurse. Her friends, appalled at this development, wondered how she would manage. 'I'm having a break from the hoovering,' she gaily announced on the telephone to Norah Smallwood who never once heard Stevie express resentment at this turnabout. She accepted her new role without consideration of alternatives: Aunt had captured her entire sense of duty. Perhaps, too, domestic work came as a relief and a comfort. In a radio interview Stevie insisted that domestic labour satisfied one's creative and destructive urges very satisfactorily. 'I like cooking,' she told an *Evening Standard* reporter, 'I love going out and getting the stuff, and chopping it up, stripping bits off, hacking it up. It's a wonderful way of getting rid of aggression.'[3]

Mona Washbourne's performance of Madge Spear in Hugh White-more's play, *Stevie*, on stage and screen, was admirable but not true to life. Aunt was made of much weightier material, was a stronger and deeper personality. Sweetness of character did not prevent her from making trenchant remarks on anything or anybody whose standards were not quite first rate. She was now under the care of Dr James Curley who noticed that, though deafness made conversation difficult, her questions and remarks were always precise. She would greet Stevie's friends with sweetness and dignity but was also self-effacing. 'You will want to have a talk with Peggy,' she frequently remarked. She had few friends of her own but with Stevie's childhood companion, Olive Pain (née Cooper), enjoyed reminiscing about St John's Church.

Her deafness was to some extent alleviated when she exchanged her ear trumpet for a transistor hearing aid. Dr Curley, on his visits, found her seated in an upright chair in her rather cluttered bedroom, neat, composed and serene. He found her 'formidable in conversation', concerned and benevolent towards Stevie. He also noticed Stevie's way of deferring to Aunt and her habit of saying: 'Aunt would know that.'[4]

Despite the very real affection which made their domestic life possible, Stevie must at times have found the strain intolerable. The business of caring for a severely disabled person in her nineties, the cleaning, launder-ing, cooking and carrying of meals upstairs, day after day, would have fatigued a much stronger person than Stevie, and may explain why she was at this time easily exasperated. Aunt's dependence on her reinforced her isolation, for though a kindly neighbour, Mrs Martin, was prepared to live in when Stevie went away, it was not easy for her to absent herself for any length of time. Having managed to rig up what she called 'quite a presentable little den for the Lion',[5] Stevie more or less lived upstairs with Aunt and only came down to cook or write. The house did not get very well cleaned and after a series of 'fleeting maniacs who favour us',[6] Stevie gave up trying to find domestic help. A district nurse visited regularly and helped bath Aunt, but with no other member of the family near at hand to share responsibility it is no surprise that Stevie once arrived at the home of her near neighbour, Rosemary Cooper, upset because she had slapped Aunt. 'I'm sorry things are not easy,' Molly wrote in August 1962. 'I think probably it is because you are far more "aware" of the old lady's possible difficulties and discomforts than I am. I tend to assume that things are all right with her unless she *says* they aren't – and she probably finds the attitude – though not so praiseworthy – more restful and pride appeasing – after all, she *can talk*, and we both know how ungracious she can be without meaning it. She belongs to the School of Never praise or even acknowledge for fear you may be thought to gush – same attitude which makes her think it "unnecessary" to say "please" to the milkman.'[7]

By 1966 Stevie admitted, 'Everything gets rather *triste*',[8] for Aunt was by then losing her sight and becoming very much deafer. Viewed from another angle this diminishing hold on life had its advantages, as Stevie suggests in an unpublished poem:

> Old age is unbecoming, so they say
> Yes, it is unbecoming, but in this way
> It is an unbecoming of all we've become
> And so it is most becoming and most welcome.[9]

For a period of some ten years Stevie benefited from the advice of a stockbroker, Ladislav Horvat, to whom she had been introduced by Sally Chilver. Horvat estimates that between 1955 and 1965 he quadrupled Stevie's small amount of capital, bringing it up to around £12,000. His letters reflect the meticulous attention he paid to her affairs. She, in turn, claimed that her arithmetic and interest were not equal to the involvement he expected of her, but Horvat disputes this, for her careful accounts were always correct. In fact Stevie so enjoyed her transactions with Horvat that a friendship developed. The terminology of the stockmarket amused her, especially the various terms used to describe the movement of shares. Horvat did not confine his advice to the stockmarket and in 1965 suggested that she should invest her capital in a freehold house in Gloucester Walk. Stevie agreed to this plan but a day or two afterwards backed down, perhaps because even an investment property would have had a destabilizing effect on her life. Horvat, who had by then made an offer for the house, felt her behaviour transgressed the code of behaviour that he followed and abruptly terminated their exchange.

There were other ways in which Stevie transgressed accepted codes and the most noticeable was dress. 'I hate the fashion girl,' Celia announces in *The Holiday*, '. . . the fashion slant is smug, careful, sly, furtive and withholding.'[10] Stevie's own clothes, though picked at random from drawers and cupboards, were always plain, neat and not unelegant. She had a liking for the practical: when Natasha, the teenage daughter of George and Olga Lawrence, made a very short, 1960s shift out of pink calico, Stevie admired it so much she did the same. Hats she bought at church jumble sales or Help the Aged shops, dresses, in C. and A. children's departments or from the trend-setting boutique, Bus Stop, in Church Street, Kensington, which was close to where Anna Browne lived. From this bizarre accumulation emerged a distinctive style, a rightness that made it impossible to imagine her dressed differently.

When the occasion demanded she could, as she admitted, 'posh' herself up, though the effort involved meant that she arrived at the party or event feeling like 'the sheeted dead'.[11] But from her eyes alone it was evident that this small woman with her bird-like movements had great vitality and her presence usually caused a stir. Her beady eyes made memorable her delivery of the biblical tag, 'the truth shall set you free', dropped artlessly into a conversation with Michael Horovitz at the PEN Club. She loved it if she found another guest equally good at the quick riposte. She was sharp, but not relentlessly sharp, and enjoyed jokes about misunderstandings, her humour resting not on ingenuity but on a frank and delighted response to the situation in hand. Occasionally it was tinged with malice: on seeing in a trinket shop in Holt, Norfolk, a terrier in highland dress, she wanted to send it to the poet Hugh MacDiarmid whose nationalism she disliked. Her unexpected angle on things could stimulate a great deal of fun. 'We had a good giggle,' in her terms, meant that the occasion had been a success. The BBC producer, Becky Cocking, once saw her walking down Regent Street apparently 'hopping with joy inwardly'.[12] But her face, and in particular her eyes, could also express the tensions within her. The Revd Gerard Irvine saw that ambiguity informed her whole life, making her at once the sophisticate and the innocent, harrowingly compassionate and acquainted with the glee of cruelty. In a memorial address after her death, he recollected:

'Her appearance manifested the same ambiguity. The old-fashioned strap shoes and knitted stockings; the broad headband; the little girl's white dress: she might look – did, indeed, look – so simple that from a back view you might wonder what so young a person was doing at an adult gathering. But then you saw the wise, sometimes sad, face and the kind eyes, and you knew how wrong you were.'

Gerard Irvine had first been introduced to Stevie by Rose Macaulay at a luncheon party at which the writer and artist, Barbara Jones, was also present. Stevie appears to have seen more of Barbara Jones and Gerard Irvine, with whom she became good friends, as she saw less of Rose Macaulay. The reason for this loss may have been their differing attitudes to religion: Priaulx Rainier recollects that at one of Elizabeth Sprigge's tea parties Stevie and Rose Macaulay pursued a long religious argument, neither shifting one iota in response to the other's views. After Rose

Macaulay's death the publication of her correspondence with the Revd J. H. C. Johnson made public her long affair with a lapsed Roman Catholic priest which had temporarily estranged her from her Anglican faith. Stevie, reviewing this book, felt she romanticized this relationship and criticized her for 'lacking the hard core of experience faced squarely and accepted'.[13] To Terence Kilmartin she repeated this view:

'I can't help feeling that Rose M. though awfully nice, is a bit silly sometimes. The *Letters* (like *The Towers of Trebizond*) get a bit noveletish. Perhaps it's partly that love for the dead man. The awful thing about "love" is that it is easily so completely forgotten, & best so. Because when called up again it is always something false, made up, really. Or sounds so. So the rest does too.'[14]

She felt similar reservations about Antonia White's *The Hound and the Falcon*, letters describing her reconversion to Catholicism: 'Perhaps really letters should not be published, especially letters from people about religion and themselves – I am thinking also of Rose Macaulay's – they are too hungry a trap for romantic egoism.'[15]

Occasionally Stevie's impatience with sentimentality could make her seem hard and intolerant. Moreover, if at a dinner party the conversation did not interest her she simply threw it aside and darted elsewhere or sang one of her poems, her tremulous, atonal chant shattering the ongoing discussion. When her stories went on rather long, in a giggly sort of way, she could be accused of monomania by an unsympathetic listener. Even her friend and admirer, Sir John Lawrence admits: 'She wasn't going to be bored. She wasn't disagreeable about it, but she wasn't going to have it.' He also noticed that, in conversation, she approached nothing in a formal, deliberate way, her thought being sporadic and spontaneous, rarely logical.[16]

The poet Patric Dickinson enjoyed her *non sequiturs* and found her conversation like her poems, funny, macabre and theological. She was fastidious in her choice of words and this, combined with her vigilant curiosity, could make her a ruthlessly observant guest. 'Saw Stevie the other day at a nice grand party,' Barbara Jones wrote to the American poet and publisher, Jonathan Williams, 'and we had a very jolly and very catty giggle, decrying our hosts, the delicious food the champagne and everyone's best frock. What were we both doing there? You may well ask.'[17] Stevie's sharp mind inclined her to flippancy and self-depreciation. When asked by the *Observer* for a paragraph for the annual 'three best books of the year' page, she would ask her publisher of the moment if they had anything on their lists that might do. 'Not poems, heavens, not poems,' she added.[18] This throw-away attitude, however, was related to her firm rejection of self-importance. The soundness of her nature left her distrustful of those who played the Bohemian. When her *Selected Poems* appeared in 1962 she told Anthony Thwaite she found it 'odd being told so often I am eccentric because I never once have felt that I am, but a plain down-to-earther as ever was'.[19]

An increase in weight towards the end of the 1950s brought her up to eight stone. Her love of food reflected the relish of one whose life has been short of luxuries, though she was now occasionally an honoured guest at grand affairs. The Dean of Westminster, Edward Carpenter, invited her to a dinner held in the Abbey's historic Jerusalem Chamber in honour of Sir Huw Wheldon and at which full evening dress was required. Stevie arrived in a short dress, dishevelled, looking tired, distraught and unequal to the occasion. But once the dinner began Stevie coruscated with fun, sarcasm and wit keeping her corner of the table charged with energy. She could so impose herself on others that after dining with her and John Betjeman at Gerard Irvine's, Lady Elizabeth Cavendish left seeing the world 'through the strange and almost dream-like distortion of her imagination'.[20] She could also scintillate at breakfast, and did so at Armide Oppé's flat in Cheyne Walk where she occasionally stayed the night. She also surprised Armide by displaying irritation with those she liked best. But if she could be intolerant, even of those friends who were important to her, she was also spontaneously generous. 'Do write to the old thing,' she urged Cecily Mackworth, after a particular cat belonging to Inez Holden had died. And though in conversation she sidestepped upsetting things, she flung her arms around Doreen Woodcock when on meeting her in the street one day she learnt of her father, Dr Woodcock's death. If a habit of grumbling began with the onset of old age, she approached life generally with grace and understatement. At parties she never disguised her need for transportation and always got a lift home. And at 1 Avondale Road she disappeared, like an animal into its lair.

As a poet Stevie now embarked upon her period of greatest success. She saw her poems published in the *Listener* which, under the literary editorship of Joe Ackerley, had become a prominent vehicle for new verse. Her work also appeared in the quarterly, '*X*', edited by David Wright and Patrick Swift between 1959 and 1962. Wright, in addition, included seven of Stevie's poems in the Penguin anthology, *The Mid Century: English Poetry 1940–60*, which, owing to publishing difficulties, did not appear until 1965. His selection caught some of her best: 'Not Waving but Drowning', 'Away,

Melancholy', 'My Heart Goes Out', 'Songe d'Athalie', 'Childe Rolandine', 'Thoughts about the Person from Porlock' and 'In the Park'.

For the *Observer*'s Christmas books page in 1960 Stevie recommended Minos Volanakis's translation of *The Bacchae*. The year before she had gone to Oxford to see a production of this play, in his translation, with music by Elisabeth Lutyens, and had been profoundly impressed. D. J. Enright has remarked of Stevie's poetic style that it is 'severe, austere, simple, bracing, impersonal',[21] qualities that affirm her debt to the ancient Greeks, an interest which had begun at school and was fostered by her reading of Virginia Woolf's essay, 'On not knowing Greek'.[22] Woolf praises Greek literature for its impersonality and vigour. Stevie, in her reading notebook, had copied out Woolf's statement – 'and it is to the Greeks that we turn when we are sick of the vagueness, of the confusion, of the Christianity and its consolations, of our own age'. Stevie's agreement with this is expressed in her review of Simone Weil's *Intimations of Christianity Among the Ancient Greeks*. Her main criticism of this book was that it looked for certainties where no proof lay. Her review ends: 'And the knowledge we may truly find in the Greeks, glimpsed in their brightest moments and named Necessity, she does not face. It is the knowledge we carry in our own hearts with fear and delight and it is this: there is no part of Nature or of the Universe that is not indifferent to man. There is no love here and little Christianity.'[23]

There was little apparent love in Stevie's own life at this time, aside from that which she exchanged with Aunt. Around 1959 she achieved some kind of reconciliation with Betty Miller. Sarah Miller recollects Stevie once again visiting their house shortly before her mother fell ill with Alzheimer's disease. Eleanor Quass was present on this occasion. Small and fine-featured, precise, urbane and easily amused, Eleanor was, like Betty Miller, married to a man much older than herself, the barrister Phineas Quass. Over tea, as she listened to Stevie and Betty talk, she realized that Stevie's mousey appearance belied her character. She was not aware that she had made any impression on Stevie and was afterwards surprised when, within the space of a week, she received a dozen postcards from Stevie begging for another meeting. Suspecting lesbian inclinations, Eleanor replied to none. If she was correct in her suspicions, this may, paradoxically, explain the disobliging remarks Stevie sometimes makes about homosexuality in her writing. Irritation and sarcasm enter her review of William Beckford's *Life at Fonthill*:

'Just now it is usual to have books indulging sodomites. In "Lord Byron's Marriage" Mr Wilson Knight seems almost to draw Our Lord into their company and hints that normal sexuality is a bar to eminence in the arts. I suppose nobody will ever be able to make a true equation between vice, virtue and art; and why try? . . . Oh leave it, leave it, one feels. Read the stories and poems the sinners write, but leave their private lives (as we should like our own sinning lives to be left – remembering that equation which cannot truly be cast by any human being) to heaven. So one feels. One may be wrong.'[24]

Not only does the equation remain uncast, but even Eleanor Quass's conclusion must be left in doubt, Stevie's action perhaps speaking more of loneliness than sexual inclinations; to Rachel Marshall, she complained about the 'dearth of companionship in Palmers Green'.[25] Nor should the attitude to biography expressed here be taken as final. In other reviews, and in her letter to Betty Miller concerning her life of Browning, Stevie expressed gratitude for biographies, especially those affirming the equivocal nature of human existence.

Her own least satisfactory publication was *Cats in Colour*, published by Batsford in 1959, one in a series of illustrated books that also dealt with ballet, horses, flowers, the zoo, and birds and which were aimed at the popular market. Stevie's task was to provide an introduction and captions to the glossy photographs of prize-winning cats and kittens. She was herself fond of cats and animals in general, as her poems reveal. But in this book her arch chatty captions, inferring human intent from the cat's look or pose, are guilty of that fault which she later condemned. 'I am not very fond of pet books,' she wrote in 1964, 'because I think they get rather neurotic – like pulling creatures over frontiers whither we should not pass. All too often it is cats.'[26] Her introduction to *Cats in Colour*, however, avoids this mistake. It warns against making neurotic wrecks of our pets in our appropriation of them to satisfy human longing or a want of human affection.

'It is we who have made these little catsy-watsies so sweet, have dressed them up and set them up, in their cultivated coats and many markings, and thrown our own human love upon them and with it our own egocentricity and ambition . . . Really to look in an animal's eyes is to be aware of stupidity, so blank and shining those eyes are, so cold. It is mind that lights the human eyes, but what mind have animals? We do not know, and as we do not like to know, we make up stories about them, give our own feelings and thoughts to our poor pets, and then turn in disgust, if they catch, as they do sometimes, something of our own fevers and unquietness.'[27]

She comforted herself with the knowledge that the true nature of animal life remains hidden from us, and we do not, cannot, finally possess them. In this introduction we also discover her liking for Edward Lear's drawings of his cat Foss, are reminded of her familiarity with witchcraft and its history, and are given an unforgettable description of her encounter with a tiger in a glass-bound cage in Edinburgh. So vivid was her account of the tiger's discontent, the zoo complained to the publisher by letter, and Stevie had to ask Helen Fowler and her family, who had also been present, to verify her description and prevent any threat of libel.

Towards the end of 1959 Stevie attended a party given by Maurice Cranston. The publisher, John Guest, director of Longman's, was also present and finding himself crushed in a corner of the noisy room with a small, plain woman, shouted his name. Stevie shouted hers in reply. Guest asked if she was the poet and Stevie affirmed that she was, adding: 'Will you publish my poems?' 'Yes,' John Guest replied, afterwards reflecting that he had never before committed himself to a book with such speed.

A parcel of her poems had reached his desk by 13 January 1960. Simultaneously, the poet Thomas Blackburn, Longman's verse reader, approached Stevie in connection with his anthology, *45–60. An Anthology of English Poetry 1945–60*. The material on John Guest's desk was therefore passed on to Blackburn, for the purposes of his anthology and so that he could advise on what form her new book of poems should take. In May he reported:

'Had a long and most enjoyable session with Stevie, our second long meeting. She is a really remarkable woman. I made it my role to help when she was uncertain about poems, and to put my foot down firmly when she wanted a dud. Otherwise she has done the choosing herself . . . I do feel her work needs a bigger book than we envisaged if it is to make its proper impact. She is not a poet like Ransom or Yeats whose work will stand by a few poems because of it[s] sculptural formal quality. She needs room, makes an accumulative effect. Also she has a number of books out and is towards 60 as such she needs something which surveys the bulk of her poetic life and achievement, like Faber do for their poets at about this time of life.'[28]

The outcome was *Selected Poems*, which incorporated 101 poems drawn from across her entire career including many not previously collected in book form. Cyprian Blagden, who was in charge of Longman's poetry list, acted as Stevie's editor and quickly became a friend. Her intention in this book was to strike a balance between thematic groupings (and which, she told Blagden, composed themselves around religion, arguments, fairy stories, including ghosts and witchcraft) and awkward personal feelings. Owing to the high permission fees demanded by André Deutsch, the number of poems chosen from *Not Waving but Drowning* was kept low. Stevie had no difficulty transferring from Deutsch to Longman's as the former did not wish to do more of her poems, nor the book of drawings she had proposed.

Once again, Stevie revealed surprising uncertainty over her work. She asked Blagden to tell her if he found her punctuation odd and was definite only in her view that an introduction would be a waste of space. In November 1960, by which time the book was well under way, Stevie was sent a volume of E. H. W. Meyerstein's verse, by his executor, Rowland Watson. Reading it without her spectacles Stevie mistook 'The Blade of Grass' for 'The Bridge of Glass' and commented: 'I sort of feel attracted by that, so that's how one poet breeds poems in another, perhaps . . . if I am one, as "collecting" my "poems" for Longmans, I now rather doubt. I know they're *something*, but is it poems??'[29] A similar uncertainty affected her choice of illustrations: many of the poems reached Blagden with alternative drawings attached and the message: 'I should like your help here!'[30] At proof stage she admitted: 'I would never mind cutting a poem to make room for a full-page drawing,'[31] which suggests that for her the visual character of the book had almost more importance than the text.

Whilst plans for this book were in progress Stevie, in January 1961, entered Wood Green and Southgate Hospital to have one of her knee-caps removed. She went in to an 'amenity' ward and had a room to herself. Pleased to find she had fire and radio under her own control and was treated to routine cups of tea, meals and sleeping pills, she told Cyprian Blagden: 'Just the life for your vivacious pal. And as the dear old drug lasts round the clock pretty well, I do nothing but sleep and read and sleep and write letters and sleep again. So I simply never felt better . . . I am writing this in the burst of energy which sometimes arrives after breakfast, it is positively garrulous, eh?'[32] Blagden visited, bringing a bottle of sherry. Aunt wrote regularly. Stevie read many books including Henry James's *The Awkward Age* and *The Wings of the Dove* and was struck by 'how awfully vulgar the Old Thing can be . . . in spite of the beautiful writing'.[33] She kept up with her finances, keeping share certificates under her mattress, as well as several transfers awaiting witness, and apparently wanted nothing. 'How blissful this life is, and not a poem in it, and never would be. Tiredness does seem to be the spur – beastly old tiredness.'[34]

On leaving hospital Stevie went for a brief period of recuperation to Great Missenden, to Edward Hodgkin of *The Times* and his wife Nancy who had formerly been married to Lawrence Durrell. Whilst there Stevie sat to Nancy for a half-length portrait bust. In photograph, the result looks characterful, but as it pleased neither artist or sitter it was eventually destroyed. Before leaving hospital, Stevie had written to a local agency for help with shopping and cleaning. Evidently this failed her because soon after her return to Avondale Road she told Cyprian Blagden: 'I am back now from my travels and happily immersed once more in washing up. Et cetera (see Charladies, Dearth of).'[35] Nine days later she was recording 'A Poet's Reading' for the radio series, 'World of Books' which went out the following day, on 18 March.

At times she must have felt besieged with anxieties over health, her own and that of others. Aunt's infirmities were increasing. Molly, in June 1960, underwent a minor operation to remove a cancerous mole from the side of her nose and which left her face slightly disfigured. Stevie herself continued to suffer from tiredness, to such an extent that in 1964, on doctor's advice, she saw a specialist at Guy's Hospital. What worried her especially, as she admitted to Rachel Marshall, was that when tired after poetry readings she found her 'm's and 'n's began to thicken and the words she spoke echoed in her head. If this was a premonition of her subsequent illness, it was overlooked: Guy's Hospital declared she was in good health with only a slight malformation of the bone in her nose creating a narrow 'air-way' and which explained her nasal speech. Stevie, only partly reassured, quoted 'They murmured as they took their fees, / There is no cure for this disease' to her own doctor, James Curley, who had become a friend and several times invited her to his house. When writing 'Angel Boley', based on a notorious murder case, Stevie used for one evil character the fictional name 'Malady Festing' and asked Dr Curley what it evoked. 'Pustular sores?' he suggested. 'Precisely,' came the reply.

In Dr Curley's garden Stevie proved the success of her recent operation by turning a cartwheel. The operation did, however, at first leave her with much pain. In April 1961 her knee was still so troublesome that on foot she could only get as far as the corner shop or the nearby clinic for treatment. To Rachel Marshall, she confessed: 'I don't know why I feel so awfully off everything really, it's a terrible grind for me to write anything. I'm a "deserter to ill health" ha ha. (My poems always come home to roost – *they* at least know who they were written for!)'[36] In June, when Helen Fowler invited her to dinner in Hampstead, she accepted on the condition that she would afterwards be driven to a tube station on the Piccadilly line.

Her knee helped spoil a holiday she took this year in Devon. She stayed at the New Inn at Hartland in order to be near her friends John and Antoinette Watney and their son Marcus. They had told Stevie that their cottage was only a half-mile from the beach, which it was, but the cove they favoured was some five miles down the coast and involved a bumpy car ride down unmade-up roads through farmer's land. Once there the only way down to the beach was along a rough-hewn path in the cliff side. Stevie insisted she had to be carried, and though happy to be on the beach, was fearful of being left. Then Marcus developed chicken pox and at some point Stevie and John Watney quarrelled. Stevie retired to her bed at the New Inn and scribbled into one of her notebooks sentences that had hurt: 'We thought you might like to take yourself off for bus journeys around Devon' and 'You must not expect us to wait on you all the time.' She complained to Aunt who replied: 'We may be old fashioned but at least we have some degree of good manners and straightforwardness. If Toinette did not want you at the cottage as a guest she should not and need not have kept on asking you to go there ... the whole attitude is unforgivable.'[37] Whilst shut in her room Stevie wrote two poems, 'Saffron' and 'The Holiday', the second of which was printed in the *Observer* a few weeks later.

> Time is passing now
> And will come soon
> When you will be able
> To go home.
>
> The malice and the misunderstanding
> The loneliness and pain
> Need not in this case, if you are careful,
> Come again.
>
> Say goodbye to the holiday, then,
> To the peace you did not know,
> And to the friends who had power over you,
> Say goodbye and go.[38]

Only after the innkeeper telephoned Antoinette Watney in some concern over his guest's behaviour were relations patched up. The Watneys had been staggered by Stevie's ruthless determination to do what she wanted regardless of all else, and remained deeply resolved that she should never again come to stay. When Stevie went into hospital again, in October 1961, Antoinette arrived with a bottle of champagne, but the gesture merely papered over the cracks. The reason for Stevie's return visit to Wood Green and Southgate Hospital was the removal of a cyst. 'I have something they call a BENIGN LUMP – yes, really. It sounds like a fairy godmother beginning to put on weight, but they all agree it has to come out, and in such a dashed hurry that I wonder if it is quite so benign as all that.'[39]

When her *Selected Poems* finally appeared in the autumn of 1962 she worried that glumness prevailed. The collection represented thirty years work and upheld her assertion that her poems dealt with 'universal problems, what most people do feel'.[40] The blend of humour and tragedy that is characteristically hers is established in the first poem, 'Thoughts about the Person from Porlock', which reverses the Person from Porlock's role and finds him not an unwanted interruption, dull reality breaking in on a vision, but desirable, a welcome distraction from the pressure of thought. The poem is cunningly plotted: it opens with a summary of the facts concerning Coleridge and Kubla Khan, proceeds to satirize the inanities of research ('May we inquire the name of the Person from Porlock?'), and then shifts again into a more plaintive mood, as the Person from Porlock is welcomed and the reason why explained:

> I am hungry to be interrupted
> For ever and ever amen
> O Person from Porlock come quickly
> And bring my thoughts to an end.

This poem is followed by 'Thoughts about the Christian Doctrine of Eternal Hell' which she wrote after the debate that followed the publication of 'The Necessity of Not Believing'. This and other titles in *Selected Poems* revealed the extent to which her argument with Christianity had become a major theme. The book, though it contains both Christian and anti-Christian poems, affirms our essential loneliness and in more than one place argues that Man, in his error, invents God. Her ability to press on a nerve of uncertainty allowed these poems, as the dust-jacket rightly states, to arouse 'an immediate and wide response'. It continues: 'But their apparent ease is deceptive; their feather-weight touch is apt to take the reader unawares, to leave an unexpectedly deep and lasting impression of pleasure or of pain.'

Among the fan letters this book brought was one from Sylvia Plath. Plath had admitted her admiration for 'a very great deal of Stevie Smith' in a statement affirming her delight in poets 'possessed by . . . the rhythms of their own breathing'.[41] In her letter to Stevie she declared herself 'a desperate Smith-addict' and expressed the wish that they might meet.[42] Stevie's reply, though warm and grateful, reflects none of the excitement that J. C. Powys's letters had aroused in her. She did not disguise the fact that she had read little of Plath: 'And as for poetry, I am a real humbug, just write it (?) sometimes but practically never read a word. That makes me feel pretty mean spirited when poets like you write such nice letters.'[43]

Honesty is also to be found in her poems, as Elizabeth Jennings observed in the *Daily Telegraph* where she praised *Selected Poems* for asking 'fundamental questions' and thought them 'pared down to a deeply moving and naked honesty'. She added: 'Miss Smith's poems sometimes seem like voices from the edge of a nervous breakdown.'[44] Other reviews were equally good, but the one that changed people's attitudes towards Stevie was that by Philip Larkin in the *New Statesman*.[45] Karl Miller had allowed him to write at length. His article countered the suspicion that her work was dangerously close to light verse by insisting that her poetry was serious and spoke with 'the authority of sadness'. For him her poems had two virtues: 'they are completely original, and now and again they are moving'. Their unexpectedness meant 'that she sees something poetic move where we do not, takes a pot-shot at it, and when she holds it up forces us to admit that there was something there, even though we have never seen anything like it before'. Mixed in with his praise is a vein of puzzlement and complaint; he observed a streak of facetiousness and derogated her drawings: 'a mixture of "cute" and "crazy", they have an amateurishness reminiscent of Lear, Waugh and Thurber without much compensating felicity'. As a knight-errant, anxious to 'correct the bias of general opinion towards the view that she is a light-hearted purveyor of *bizarrerie*', he was singularly ambivalent. When reprinted in his book of essays, *Required Writing* (1983) his qualifications, such as his remark that phrases of hers hang about in one's mind 'long after one has put the book down in favour of Wallace Stevens' seemed gratuitous. And where he describes her mode of writing as '*fausse-naïve*, the "feminine" doodler or jotter who puts everything down as it strikes her', one hears the superior tone of the 'masculine' critic.

Not surprisingly, Stevie preferred Kathleen Nott's review in the *Observer*: 'she does not make me out to be such a tricky character. I got the impression that P. Larkin, though placing us much in his debt, was uneasy, hence shifting around a bit and coming out with the old charge of *fausse-naïveté*!'[46] Larkin was not the only critic shifting uncomfortably in confrontation with Stevie's work: the *Times Literary Supplement* thought the context within which she wrote 'dangerously near the flippant and the facetious', but thought her 'a daring and skilful technician, a human being with a warmth of response that makes all her poems ultimately moving'.[47] The phrase 'frivolous and vulnerable', culled from Celia's sermon in *The Holiday* and heading Larkin's article, had become the accepted view.

Stevie's *Selected Poems* greatly excited the young poet, playwright and storyteller, John Horder, who had graduated from Selwyn College, Cambridge, in 1960 and since then had been suffering from anxiety, depression and panic. Since January 1962 he had been hospitalized in St Luke's, Muswell Hill, but was let out in order to do an interview with Stevie for the radio programme, 'World of Books'. He arrived late. Stevie, meanwhile, had been talking with the producer Helen Rapp who, as the time marched on, broke the rules and got her secretary to fetch Stevie a large whisky. When finally Horder appeared they began without any preliminaries. This proved advantageous, as the conversation that developed was spontaneous and natural. Horder asked Stevie if she had experienced despair. Stevie said she had never succumbed to it and that if she did she would write nothing: it was 'soft melancholy' that drove her to write. She read some of her poems and, looking through the glass panel at the producer, asked if she might sing one. Helen Rapp recalls: 'Her singing was utterly timeless but mesmeric. Later, when I was tidying up the tape, the studio manager who was doing the editing put down his razor and just listened. He then pulled himself together to go on cutting, but said "Who is this lovely person?".'[48]

On 13 September 1963 she was again interviewed, this time by Jonathan Williams, the American poet and founder of the Jargon Society, a small non-profit-making publishing house which promoted artists and writers outside the commercial mainstream. This interview, not published until after Stevie's death, remains one of the most valuable, tapping her views on the origins of her work, her reading and the relationship between her drawings and poems. Williams was at the time lodging in Barbara Jones's Hampstead house and got to know Stevie well. It was he who introduced her work to James Laughlin, head of the New York publishing house, New Directions, which was famous for its poetry list. Williams was not the first to try and interest an American publisher in Stevie's work: the poet Naomi Replansky had previously done so and Stevie's poems had been rejected by Athenaeum, Alfred Knopf and Doubleday. Replansky's familiarity with Stevie's work began when she opened a copy of the *Times Literary Supplement* and read 'Look!' After discovering more of Stevie's work in the anthology, *The Distaff Muse*, she had written to Jonathan Cape only to discover that Stevie's early collections were now out of print. She approached Stevie herself and this began a correspondence that lasted several years and brought Replansky on two occasions to Avondale Road. From her, Stevie learnt that she had in America 'a sort of underground cult ... I say an "underground" cult because you are never mentioned by any of the official critics – but every now and then I run into someone who says "Stevie Smith – oh yes!" and his eyes light up with delight.'[49]

When James Laughlin took up Williams's suggestion and began negotiations with Longman's for an American edition of *Selected Poems*, he discovered Stevie had admirers in Brendan Gill, film critic on the *New Yorker*, and Howard Moss, its poetry editor who, at Laughlin's request, accepted some of her poems. For the American edition of *Selected Poems* Stevie did not object to an introduction and suggested Jonathan Williams should write it. Laughlin wanted to use Ogden Nash. Stevie was obliged to admit that his name would attract readers but felt her poems too sad for him. 'In catty moments I always remember G. W. Stonier wrote some years ago . . . to the effect that I could "drop into poetry" whereas he [Nash] couldn't. (This sounds a bit uppish – not *my* comment . . .) I think he is a superb light poet, but I am not.'[50] In the end Nash's encomium in verse arrived too late to be used as an introduction and was instead printed on a separate card and inserted in the book. It was also used on an advertisement poster, several hundred of which were distributed to the better paperback and poetry bookstores.

James Laughlin did a great deal to promote Stevie in America. He extracted puffs from other poets to print on the back cover of Stevie's book and made every effort to place her poems in periodicals to prepare for, or coincide with, the appearance of *Selected Poems*. Though they met with resistance some did appear, in the *Nation*, *New Yorker*, *Atlantic Monthly*, *Poetry* and the *New York Times Book Review*. Stevie herself wrote the blurb for her book, in an attempt to forestall accusations of *fausse-naïveté*:

'There may be echoes in her work of past poets – Lear, Poe, Byron, the gothic romantics and Hymns Ancient and Modern – but these are deceitful echoes, as her thoughts may also seem deceitful, at first simple, almost childlike, then cutting at depth with a sharp edge to the main business of her life – death, loneliness, God and the devil. Her metric, with its inner rhymes and assonances, and the throw-away line that can seem mischievous, is very subtle . . .'

She also asked that the words 'whimsical' and 'primitive' be removed from the write-up in New Directions' catalogue, as she felt it was handing a gun to the critics and untrue of her tone and metric.

Though she received much praise, the reviews were not uniformly good. On one hand there was an encomium in *Harper's Bazaar*: 'Little flaws in the meter open ugly emotional chasms, minor assonances jar the ear, casual changes in diction set the nerves on edge – and Miss Smith turns out to be writing some of the most violent, bitter, morbid and beautiful poetry now being written in English.' But on the other hand the *New York Times Book Review* thought her drawings pointed up 'a cuteness and coyness that are the exaggerated and corrupting flavour of most of her poems'.[51] When it became clear the book was not selling, Stevie admitted it was a very English mixture and possibly not right for an American audience. She did, however, please Marianne Moore who received a copy of *Selected Poems* from Laughlin and thought it counteracted 'the estranging determination of some writers of prose and verse to obtrude on us their wanton unnatural-ness'.[52]

Stevie's own views on poetry uphold an uncomplicated stance. 'Poetry does not like to be up to date,' she once wrote, 'she refuses to be neat . . . Poetry is very strong and never has any kindness at all . . . All Poetry has to do is to make a strong communication. All the poet has to do is to listen. The poet is not an important fellow. There will always be another poet.'[53] In this view of the poet as merely a channel for communication everything depends on her or his relationship with the muse. Opportunities for distraction Stevie outlined on radio: the danger of being too fêted or promoted, of becoming in turn a promoter, judging competitions, sitting on committees, arranging parties. 'There is also the danger of poets becoming infected with the techniques of the advertising world, and at a still lower level, with the wide boys' cunning. All art is open to these dangers, especially nowadays, because the general public has been made to feel guilty for its past philistinism and is trying to make up for it. But the line between art and pretence, between experiment and fraud, is not easy to draw, so the little criminals creep in. But let no poet concern himself with these matters but just get on with his writing.'[54]

This Stevie did. Her poems began to accumulate at such a rate that by March 1964 Longman's began to negotiate a new collection. At the same time Penguin asked to include her work in their Penguin Modern Poets series. Each book contained a selection by three poets. Stevie did not want to be corralled with two other women, and when asked if she would go in with Denise Levertov replied that she would rather not. However, as only three women poets were included in the entire series, her objection did not prove insuperable. Having herself suggested David Wright, John Heath-Stubbs and Andrew Young as possible stablemates, she was given Edwin Brock and Geoffrey Hill in *Penguin Modern Poets 8* (1966). She now had no difficulty placing her poems which appeared fairly regularly in the *New Statesman*, the *Listener* and the *Times Literary Supplement*. Nor did she need to worry that her creativity would evaporate, for during the last years of her life the 'soft melancholy' that drove her to write did not diminish.

CHAPTER 14

In Performance

Soon after her retirement Molly Smith left Aylesbury for Devon, moving to Buckfast in 1962. The village is famous for its Abbey, built on the foundations of a twelfth-century Cistercian church during the first three decades of this century on the wooded banks of the River Dart. The Abbey has a Benedictine monastery attached, its small community of monks not only serving the religious needs of Catholics in the locality but also engaging in farm work and producing honey and wine. Molly, attracted to the Abbey and the Catholic community that had grown up around it, endured three years of fruitless negotiation before eventually obtaining a small plot on which a bungalow, named Dart St Mary, was built to her design. To make this feasible, Stevie advanced Molly £1,000 against her eventual share in the value of 1 Avondale Road. Though she groaned to others that Molly bungled her finances, created muddle and confusion, Stevie did not refuse her help: in 1964 she lent her an additional £500 and waived the interest on the earlier loan. Her action was probably in response to Molly's misfortune: in December 1963 she had suffered a coronary.

Molly's stroke altered the relationship between the two sisters, as gradually became apparent. At first there was not much Stevie could do to help as Molly was kept in hospital for several weeks, put on a strict diet and forbidden to smoke. But from then on Stevie began visiting Buckfast regularly, staying three weeks in the summer of 1964. To Ronald Orr-Ewing, she admitted feeling contrition towards Molly, whose visits to

1 Avondale Road, Rosemary Cooper avers, she had not welcomed. Up until now, Molly had remained a background figure in Stevie's life and one who invited a mixed response: Sally Chilver found her pleasant and intelligent; Kay Dick thought her coarse and slightly unbalanced; Anna Browne felt she was talking to a woman who had found insufficient outlet for her intelligence and whose loud voice made her seem clumsy; Armide Oppé saw that Molly had little to sustain her in retirement, that she worried incessantly and in Stevie's company quickly became difficult and cross.

Molly made friends at Buckfast, but not easily. At first she seemed rather aloof, a person not easy to know well. Her deep, theatrical voice and caustic remarks could daunt. After her stroke, however, she was obliged to be dependent on neighbours, particularly those 'with little wheels', as Stevie termed car owners. One who regularly shopped and changed library books for Molly was Miss Margaret Miller. She tells how even after subsequent strokes when Molly walked with difficulty, using a three-pronged stick and dragging one leg, and had lost the use of one arm, she never complained of her disabilities. She had never been interested in cooking, and once when Margaret Miller visited she found 'a doleful grey mess' of minced beef and two potatoes boiling together in one saucepan on the stove.[1] Molly grudged money spent on food; she insisted her saccharine tablets should be bought at Boots in Newton Abbot where they sold a couple of pence cheaper than elsewhere, and much of the time ignored hospital advice and lived on jam tarts, milk and milk-chocolate 'Bounty' bars which she asked friends to buy for her by the dozen. Apart from her religion, her life centred on her cat, Ming, and on books. She read voraciously, books piled up around her chair. During her long stint in hospital she had tired of contemporary literature and demanded Chaucer, as more in keeping with her mood. When at the end of her life she moved into a nursing home run by nuns in Torquay, she observed that they did everything for one's body and soul but nothing for the mind.

Her capacity for boredom was another reason why Stevie began to visit, her appearance in Buckfast serving to confirm Molly's eccentric reputation. Few were aware of Stevie's fame and saw only the oddly dressed woman who queue-barged in the Ashburton Co-op and walked the lanes at night when unable to sleep. When the two sisters gave a Sunday morning drinks party all knew that the sherry in the cut-glass decanter was, as usual, bought from a keg in the chemist's. Both benefited from, and were imperious towards, car drivers, Stevie especially expecting to be taken to the shops or the station as and when it suited her. One such who met Stevie off the London train at Newton Abbot was surprised to find her with no luggage:

Stevie explained that she was wearing all her clothes, layer upon layer, and peeled off in the train when she got hot.

At Buckfast Stevie occasionally accompanied Molly to services at the Abbey and came to know two or three of the monks well. As a devout Catholic, Molly was very regular in her attendance at mass, even after the adoption of the vernacular which she hated. As Molly's sister and a regular visitor, Stevie was permitted to go through the Abbey's private grounds on her walks down to the River Dart and on to the moor. One of the monks who, in turn, frequently climbed the hill to have tea at Dart St Mary was Father Jerome. For him Molly would, on occasion, digress on the characters and plot in a Shakespeare play, with such dramatic intensity that he sat listening enthralled. When Stevie visited he was aware of a clash of temperaments, a friction that often characterized the sisters' exchange. Nevertheless Molly shared with Father Jerome her fear that she would be separated from her sister in the life to come owing to Stevie's lack of faith. (Father Jerome, feeling that both were true to their consciences, did not doubt they would be together.) Because in Molly's extrovert and somewhat domineering presence Stevie could seem quiet and withdrawn, Father Jerome was surprised to discover at Dartington, where he accompanied Molly in order to hear Stevie read, how extrovert in performance she became.[2]

By the 1960s Stevie had become an experienced performer. Throughout the 1950s she had been giving occasional readings, to the Hampstead Centre of the Poetry Society, the Kent and Sussex Poetry Society, at the National Book League, to university literary societies at Nottingham, Birmingham and Leicester, at the Gaberbocchus Commonroom, for the 'contemporary Poetry and Music circle' which met on the second Monday of every month in Kensington Road, and in connection with poetry schemes organized by the PEN Club. Poetry readings in the 1950s usually ran on fairly formal lines for the interested few. Stevie, however, altered the tone of these occasions. In October 1960 she appeared in front of an incredulous audience in John Lewis's department store, at a reading organized by David Wright. The listeners were attentive to Dom Moraes, C. H. Sisson, Brian Higgins and Pippa Wright (who read her husband's poems), but it was Stevie, David Wright afterwards told his mother, who 'had them rolling in their chairs and roaring with laughter and astonishment, because no one supposes poetry can be fun'.[3] Wright organized a second reading at John Lewis's in November 1961 and this time paired Stevie with Patrick Kavanagh who, in an inebriated state, sang his poems in a thick Irish accent and overran his time. He and Stevie took an instant dislike to each other and after the reading Stevie declared herself tired to death of 'the owld Irish harp'. John Lewis's, however, had not had enough of Stevie and she was invited back the following year to take part in a general discussion on poetry and literature with Olivia Manning and the poet, Jonathan Griffin.

Those unfamiliar with her poetry were often startled by the contradiction between her dress and her performance; her unfashionable and usually rather sober dress gave no hint of the capering humour her poems proclaimed, her sad eyes failing to prepare onlookers for the mettlesome, contrary stance often adopted. Conversely those familiar with her poetry were sometimes surprised by her appearance; Effie Sinton, a schoolteacher, was astonished when, waiting for Stevie in a hotel lounge near Northampton County Hall, where Stevie read on 5 May 1960, she saw a rather lost, hesitant elderly woman with eyes almost unfocused walk in. At the College of St Mark and St John, Chelsea, in December 1965, where Stevie read at the invitation of the lecturer and composer, Peter Dickinson, the students were made aware that she was less demure than her pinafore dress and white stockings suggested when she read 'Girls!' with the lines:

> Do not sell the pass dear, dont let down the side,
> That is what this woman said and a lot of balsy stuff beside
> (Oh the awful balsy nonsense that this woman cried.)

Owing to the success of these readings and her performances on radio, in 'The Living Poet' series produced by George MacBeth, on 'Woman's Hour' and 'The World of Books', she became in the 1960s a public figure and the invitations to read increased. Gerard Irvine invited her to appear before the St Anne's Society on 30 October 1962. The Society's chairman was then Canon Edward Carpenter and his wife, Lilian, recollects that the reading was held in a very small room. It seemed to her impossible that the mouse-like creature, seated with her skirt above her knees and wearing, as she often did for readings, white lace stockings, would be able to hold the attention of her audience. Yet before long Lilian Carpenter found herself transfixed by 'the incredible power that emanated from this tiny creature'.[4]

The following year she appeared at the Guildhall Art Gallery with Roy Fuller, at the Festival of Poetry which ran for a week at the Royal Court Theatre in July and at the Stratford-upon-Avon Poetry Festival where she was 'The Poet of the Year'. Despite this acclaim and her growing popularity, she remained unceremonious in her approach, though she could not help boasting to an editor at Longman's that at the Royal Court she had sat on stage next to Robert Lowell: 'I thought his poems were most awfully good and he said he liked mine, I mean before I said I liked his . . .'[5]

The growing craze for poetry readings surprised her. In 1965, shortly before taking herself off to Chipping Camden where she was to read to the Society of Industrial Artists and Designers annual conference, she wrote to her editor at Longman's, Michael Hoare, expressing wonder at the 'absolute mania for poetry readings' and doubting if, from the poet's point of view, they were worthwhile, 'as they certainly make one a bit bored with poems and keep one from getting on with that new book'.[6] Yet she almost never refused an invitation to read, perhaps recognizing that poetry readings were helping to create a new climate in which her voice would increasingly be heard. For as the 1960s progressed the ballads and lyrics of the Beatles, Bob Dylan, Donovan and Bert Jansch helped broaden a demand for a fresh, imaginative and popular use of language, and this demand had an effect on poetry readings. No longer were these the preserve of the educated few. In the 1960s people not only left their homes and travelled to a venue in order to hear poetry read, they also paid to get in for it was now expected that poetry readings would not be dull. This development created a space in which Stevie's popularity grew.

Readings took her up and down the country. In November 1965, under the auspices of the Arts Council, she went on a tour of the South-West with Patric Dickinson; conscious of her audience appeal, he always underran the first half so that she could overrun the second. As with any performer, Stevie's success depended partly on her audience and was by no means always assured. One definite fiasco was her visit to Newcastle-upon-Tyne with Elisabeth Lutyens for an evening's entertainment arranged by the Friends of the Laing Art Gallery, with help from the North-East Association for the Arts. For this occasion Stevie dyed her hair, rather badly Elisabeth Lutyens thought, and carried her spare dress in her handbag. That evening, seated on the platform in this blue gingham frock, she looked like a sharp little schoolgirl and puzzled her audience by delivering her poems in such a dead-pan manner that no indication was given whether tragedy or comedy was uppermost. Elisabeth Lutyens, sensing a lack of audience response, whispered, audibly, 'that's enough', and the professional middle-class audience, composed largely of the local medical fraternity, clapped politely. They were still more puzzled when a soprano and rather elderly baritone sang Elisabeth Lutyens's settings of Stevie's poems. Nichola Smith, secretary to the Friends of the Laing Art Gallery, remembers that Lady Ridley, Elisabeth Lutyens's sister who lived near by, made personal comments in a penetrating voice on the performers, all of whom presented a singular sight: 'Rather like the Doyley Carte Opera Group in latter years. One could not imagine these people in ordinary contemporary life, they seemed to belong to another age altogether. One felt that at the end of the evening, they might be folded up and put into a wicker costume basket until the next performance.'[7]

Stevie's refusal to cajole or dictate left her audience free to react. Once it had recognized her humorous, oblique but accessible view of life, the reading was usually an unqualified success. At Eton College, in the library, with the black tail-coated figures of the boys seated haphazardly between the columnar bookcases, Stevie, small and slightly stooped, recited and sang her poems in a strange sing-song voice. At Bryanston School she climbed on a chair to enact one of her poems and wept with laughter at another. At Winchester she also held her audience in the palm of her hand, the pupils surprised to discover that poetry could be so quirky. At the end of one reading at Ampleforth, the English teacher, Ian Davie, felt his pupils would not have been surprised if Stevie had stood on her head.

In performance her use of syncopation became pronounced. A. Alvarez has argued that, read in print, 'her rhythms can seem unsure, the inversions troublesome and the punch lines sometimes flat', but that when performed by her, as recordings demonstrate, the poems take on 'a marvellously shrewd elegance, shifting without effort from solemn to comic, from the grandeur of Victorian romance to owlish bathos'.[8] Because much of the humour resides in the unexpected stress Stevie was often irritated by actors and actresses whose use of more normal standards resulted in a misreading of her verse. Her own reading of her poems clarified its humour and hence its meaning, as she was alarmed to discover: 'Sometimes (at live readings) quite intelligent people come up to me afterwards and say: It puts new meaning into it when you read it. And I say: You are simply telling me you cannot read. The meaning is there on the page. But then I wonder if it is. How is it they always get it wrong? ... I think it's what I said before. Paradoxically – it's the straightforwardness they cannot take.'[9]

In performance, she was a professional, aware that she had something to communicate; she was also remarkably unselfconscious. She had a gift for establishing a rapport, whether it was with the audience who attended the Edinburgh Festival in 1965 or the less specialized gathering who heard her read in a Nonconformist chapel at Cley in Norfolk. In addition she always planned the order of her poems carefully and introduced them with a well-rehearsed patter. She could, however, improvise if the occasion seemed right, and did so at King's College, Cambridge, when she found that she was reading to a very small number of undergraduates, owing to the pressure of essays and other factors. One of her listeners was Norman Bryson:

'She recited her poems in an extraordinary declamatory style, almost singing them, quite high pitched. It was not an easy style to understand. It wasn't a church voice, and it wasn't incantation like Yeats, and it wasn't the alarming voice that might come from behind a mask of Greek tragedy, like Sylvia Plath. There seemed elements of all these in the voice she used, but the dominant tone was of cheerfulness exaggerated, as if the rise and fall of a cheery, vernacular voice were pushed higher and lower and became a stylized sing-song that wasn't cheerfulness but had an alienated relation to cheerfulness. It was remarkably stylized.

The vocal style . . . fascinated me all evening . . . It became tremendous, quite amazing, when she recited not her own poems but border ballads. There is a border ballad called "Twa Corbies" which . . . I happen particularly to like . . . for the way it implies a genuinely terrifying universe at the edges of the poem, without letting you see these terms directly. Stevie Smith's version – her performance – of the "Twa Corbies" was spectacular.

To her normal stylized performing voice she added a middle-English border dialect, with all the sounds made as harsh as possible. Partly this was just to relish the sounds of that kind of middle English. We had been talking about the way nothing in modern spoken English could convey the physicality of words like "tobrosten" in *Gawain*, or certain lines in Chaucer . . . "Twa Corbies" came forward in this conversation as a really good example of this physicality, but when she declaimed it, to illustrate the point, the poem turned into something else.

She introduced into her performance of it extraordinary and inappropriate tones, of sheer disgust – through the clotted words, but it felt almost like disgust *at* the words – and of enormous disappointment . . . It was rather alarming that our conversation about middle English, which had been somewhat polite . . . suddenly produced this drama, this explosion in which the implications of the words grew out of the words, then became stronger and almost crushed the words . . . it was as though she needed a pretext for projecting certain kinds of voice . . . The voices were polyphonic in the sense that they didn't combine – one couldn't see what the cheeriness had to do with the disappointment or the disgust.

The performance was unnerving because it was so excessive . . . The meaning of the words was set aside in the performance. And the *motives* for this were entirely unrevealed: this seemed almost the main point. It was as though what was being dramatized was a state of being so pent up, so much without outlet, that emotions couldn't have, any longer, appropriate objects. Without appropriate objects they went to live in an abstracted world of their own, where they further split up amongst themselves (the polyphony).

Nothing in the world could focus them or make them cohere, or earn them or deserve them.'[10]

Bryson adds that Stevie's dramatic performance ended the moment she finished reciting. Not in the least theatrical in everyday exchange, she chatted lightheartedly with the students.

Stevie's skill as a performer made her a star of the poetry circuit, as Alvarez, with some perplexity, has acknowledged: 'In among all that leather and denim, posturing and self-promotion, she could scarcely have been more out of place.'[11] But she was perhaps not so out of place, in that her poetry abets Michael Horovitz's stated aim – 'to break through the highbrow game reserve'. At his request she took part in at least fifteen of his 'Live New Departures' arts circuses between 1959 and 1968 at which one aim was to bring poetry and jazz into closer collaboration. The poet and poetry editor of *Tribune*, Jeremy Robson, who had taken part in a New Departures event at Oxford, was, though self effacing, another key figure within this development, organizing hundreds of poetry and jazz events in town halls, theatres and for the trades unions' arts festivals organized by Arnold Wesker's Centre 42. Robson's events were more disciplined and formal than Live New Departures which were more involved with and influenced by the international avant-garde, including American 'beat' poetry. Stevie read on three or four occasions, at Robson's invitation, once at the Theatre Royal, Stratford East, on 10 September 1965, with Ted Hughes and Dannie Abse, among others. This may have been the occasion when, as Abse recalls, Stevie threw her book at a persistent photographer while she continued to sing one of her poems.[12] Robson commanded some of the best jazz musicians then playing in Britain, and the fact that poets had to follow their acts encouraged a more relaxed atmosphere than poetry readings had had in the past, and also a more professional performance. Live New Departures also stressed that the delivery of a poem was equal in importance to the writing of it. Together with the Liverpool 'pop' poets, Live New Departures helped redefine the concept of poetry for a young audience. Though Stevie was not uncritical of the verse she now found herself listening to (Roger McGough she dismissed as a 'rhymster'), she recognized and admired the troubadour aspect in Michael Horovitz's role.

Horovitz, with others, was responsible for organizing, at a fortnight's notice, the unprecedented International Poetry Incarnation at the Royal Albert Hall, an event held on 11 June 1965 and attended by nearly eight thousand people. Though three leading communist poets – Andrei Voznesensky, Pablo Neruda and Pablo Fernandez – withdrew at the last moment, the evening was an unparalleled success, its memorability owing much to the appearance of Allen Ginsberg. Horovitz afterwards declared that one of the aims had been 'the transmission, through Ginsberg, of the heritage of Blake'.[13] Adrian Mitchell's 'Tell me lies about Vietnam', one of the poems read, was paradigmatic of the populist political angle Horovitz had in mind. Stevie was not present at this event but she was included in its follow-up, the New Moon Carnival held at the Albert Hall a year later. It was one occasion where she failed to win over her audience and she was subjected to mocking remarks from the floor. As she herself often felt the urge to make disruptive interruptions when she was obliged to sit and listen to other poets, she took her failure in good part.

She continued to appear at workshops and readings, held informally in pubs or at the Refectory at 65 Buckingham Gate where Alasdair Clayre ran music and poetry events on Thursday evenings. She appeared there in 1967 and told an *Observer* reporter that she was using the same script she had used for years. She also admitted that as she herself 'wouldn't cross the road to hear poetry', it always surprised her to find she had an audience. When she read at the Lamb and Flag, in Covent Garden, on 7 December 1968, the upper room nearly collapsed with the weight of her fans. The organizer, Eddie Linden, had met her beforehand at the Arts Theatre Club in Cranbourn Street, Leicester Square, and on arriving at the pub found the manageress complaining that she could not get in to her own flat for the crush of people blocking the stairs. One hundred and fifty people were squeezed into a room that normally only held eighty: Eddie Linden thought it one of the Lamb and Flag's most successful events. On occasions like these Stevie could be a consummate performer: with each poem the delivery of character, intonation and timing were perfect, owing partly to her complete involvement. 'She loved every poem that she spoke,' Douglas Cleverdon has said.[14]

The making of records grew out of her interest in performing. She contributed to 'The Poet Speaks' series, composed of conversations with Peter Orr designed to accompany recordings of contemporary poets reading their own work. The series was produced by the British Council in collaboration with the Poetry Room in Harvard University's Lamont Library. Following this, in April 1967, the Marvell Press issued an LP entirely devoted to Stevie reading and singing her poems with characteristic introductions. As one review said: 'Until one has heard her flat, disenchanted delivery, and the solemn off-key renditions of ecclesiastically flavoured tunes, one cannot fully appreciate the unfacetiousness of her wit.'[15]

The most notorious event Stevie was involved in was the 'A Poetic Show' held in Brussels as part of its British Week in June 1967. Following the success of the poetry events held at the Albert Hall in 1965 and 1966, Walter van de Maele, then affiliated with the Palais des Beaux Arts in Brussels, approached Michael Horovitz and gave him *carte blanche* to put together a programme of radical young poets. Horovitz rounded up twelve poets, including Stevie, Brian Patten, Pete Brown, Alasdair Clayre, Adrian Mitchell and Anselm Hollo. All were young, except Stevie, and unused to the lavish hospitality they were given. By the time they were brought to the Palais in a special coach they were all in loud voice, Anselm Hollo delivering what sounded like Viking battle cries. All were astonished to find that even on stage more refreshment awaited them. From this vantage point, the large audience seemed distant, increasingly so as the evening progressed. Brian Patten fell asleep on stage. Others retain conflicting memories of what actually happened: Michael Horovitz claims that Stevie, though given the bird at the start of her reading, won her audience round; Adrian Mitchell felt the audience failed to understand her. Walter van de Maele was only present for the first and last appearances as he was obliged to transport a theatrical group from Antwerp to Brussels. On his return to the Palais he quickly saw that some of the participants had 'given up' and the audience was losing patience. Under pressure from the Palais direction, he had the lights dimmed and brought the event to an end.[16] To Michael Hoare, Stevie afterwards declared the performance had been 'perfectly frightful'.[17]

This disaster did not prevent her retaining amiable relations with Michael Horovitz and his wife Frances. At mealtimes, during the course of this short visit, Stevie's talk with and encouragement of the others earned her much affection. Brian Patten had met her once before in the company of Michael Horovitz when, crammed into the back of a car, he was surprised by the contradiction between her appearance and her sharp wit. He sat next to Stevie on the flight to Brussels, visibly nervous, and was told by her not to worry, as it was only the landing that was dangerous – a remark he found far from reassuring. Nor did he forget her advice always to insist on payment for his poetry. On another occasion, when both were judges at a poetry competition, Stevie claimed she had forgotten how much she was being paid. Patten thought she was merely fishing to find out if they were all being paid the same.[18] He later wrote an elegy for Stevie – 'Blake's Purest Daughter' – and included it in his book, *Grave Gossip*. Adrian Mitchell also retains affectionate memories of Stevie, even though he was once angered when she remarked in his presence to Michael Horovitz that people should stop writing poems about the bomb.

The climax to the 1960s poetry boom was the Poetry Society Gala Recital held at the Festival Hall on 4 February 1969. It marked the Poetry Society's diamond jubilee and attracted an audience of 2,700 people. Those billed to appear included William Plomer, Hugh MacDiarmid, Brian Patten, Basil Bunting, Tom Pickard, Ezra Pound (whom weather prevented from leaving Rapallo), Spike Hawkins, Christopher Logue, Ted Hughes and Stevie. Yet if anything brought home to Stevie how far she had travelled it was not bouquets of flowers at the Festival Hall but her return to North London Collegiate on 27 October 1970 to give a reading. The uncooperative schoolgirl, 'Peggy', transformed into 'Stevie', was now a person of such prestige that the headmistress, Miss McLaughlan, took hold of her arm, making her feel a piece of venerable antiquity. 'I can't help noticing,' Stevie told a friend, 'my relationship with headmistresses has Changed for the Better.'[19]

As a reviewer, Stevie respected shrewd insight into human character. She believed 'that truth is odd',[20] and liked books which reflected this. The freedom from conventional thought in Marguerite Yourcenar's *Coup de Grâce* caused Stevie to extol it in the *Daily Telegraph* in 1957 and in the *Observer*'s 'Books of the Year' page. Impressed by the 'pitiful subtlety' informing Yourcenar's handling of the relationship between the hero and the young count he loves and the young countess he can neither love nor leave, it made, for her, 'this eerie tale so just and imaginative and so memorable'.[21] She also looked for a freshness in the use of language, and whenever she encountered it praised beauty and simplicity of prose style. Her review of the *New English Bible*, reprinted in *Me Again*, condemned its translators of both the Old and New Testaments for smudging, weakening and betraying the beauty and power of the older versions.

Writing regularly for the *Observer*, *Spectator* and *Listener*, and on occasion for the *Daily Telegraph*, *Evening Standard* and *New Statesman*, she received many letters, welcoming or criticizing her point of view. She abhorred sentimentality. 'Writers whose hearts are better than their heads,' she pronounced, 'often produce sentimental books whose ultimate effect, perhaps paradoxically, is one of heartlessness . . . Sentimental writers can be very cruel.'[22] She placed much estimate on human feelings, those 'problems of heart and conscience', in Maurice Baring's words. And the correlate of this was her distrust of the purely intellectual ('The most educated are so often the most prejudiced'[23]). Nevertheless, her own reviewing was too highbrow for the *Observer*; Terence Kilmartin, under pressure to make the paper more popular and accessible, more 'middle-brow', was asked to terminate her novel reviewing, for she was felt to be too whimsical and esoteric. He fought to retain her but was overruled. Stevie told Kilmartin she felt 'desperate . . . at being told so often I couldn't be understood (both poems and reviews). One feels defeated. *Is* defeated I daresay. Lord God, you may be right.'[24] She was, however, retained as a reviewer of non-fiction and remained on terms on warm friendship with Kilmartin. The switch from fiction to non-fiction was to her benefit for she found ideas for poems in the books sent her, especially those on history and theology which she enjoyed because their content was so different from everyday life. Anthropology was another source of comfort, especially when written by Margaret Mead or Ruth Benedict: 'They lift the weight off the nerves by enlarging the view, and they touch home.'[25] That Stevie found reading a release is also suggested by her piece 'Goodbye to Novels' which brought her stint as a novel reviewer in the *Observer* to a close. Having in her time spotted the talent in Brian Moore's *The Lonely Passion of Judith Hearne*, Norman Mailer's *Barbary Shore* and Muriel Spark's *The Ballad of Peckham Rye*, she ended with an expression of gratitude, 'especially to those strange writers often unfashionable, unliterary and unsung who seem to write from solitude and for themselves alone'.[26]

As a critic of non-fiction, she reviewed biographies and autobiographies with pleasure. She recognized both the craft and limitation of biography. Christopher St John's life of Ethel Smyth she thought 'as good as it could be, that is to say that it gives the facts and the feelings, the press cuttings and the private letters, and the extracts from Dame Ethel's diaries and books, and all with a stylish ease that makes reading a pleasure'.[27] Still more did she admire *Branwell Brontë* by Winifred Gérin ('so scrupulous in mind and heart'). Its detailed accounts of pubs, houses, villages, seaside lodgings, landscapes and sundry figures absorbed her, as did the bitterness of Branwell's life which she summed up as 'the self-destroying need he had (in that house of generous and moral probity), the fear, the slyness and the comicality of his unhappy heart'; all this, she thought, stood out 'most beautifully in this detailed and sympathetic life-history'.[28]

That Stevie herself had an unhappy heart was evident to readers of her poetry. After the *Times Literary Supplement* published 'Exeat', which ends

> Yet a time may come when a poet or any person
> Having a long life behind him, pleasure and sorrow,
> But feeble now and expensive to his country
> And on the point of no longer being able to make a decision
> May fancy Life comes to him with love and says:
> We are friends enough now for me to give you death;

Then he may commit suicide, then
He may go.

she realized what a good circulation this periodical had and that a great many like herself dreaded the thought of old people's homes. 'I keep getting letters from people asking if I will join them in a suicide club. And one lady asked me to tell her how to "manage it" as she couldn't swallow pills. I always write back the most bracing letters telling them to hang on as long as possible as it's absolutely nothing compared with geological time. And that I am afraid it is something they must decide for themselves. I did *not* say, Get your doctor to prescribe it in liquid form! But oh I know the horror they feel at being shut up in some terrible home. I always think I write poems only for myself but I see this may not be so . . . But I do not want to convert anybody to anything.'[29]

She, herself, was detained in this life by, among other things, the prospect of a new book. When her publisher, John Guest of Longmans, had suggested this in February 1964 Stevie had responded with hesitant pleasure; even though her doubts about her own poems had, if anything, increased: 'I might never have written one before and in shame and trembling pack 'em off to the editors, suffering for weeks afterwards those ghastly 4 a.m. waking nightmares for having done so. Do all your poet- authors bore you with these feelings?'[30] Once the contract was signed, the line, 'Songs of deadly innocence', from Ogden Nash's 'Stevie Smith' was suggested by Michael Hoare for the title. Stevie thanked him and objected: 'If a poet said that sort of thing about himself, or allowed it to be said in any circumstances under his control, I don't think there would be much innocence about. And I don't altogether agree anyway – being under the impression (erroneous, I dare say) but I know what I'm doing.'[31] The final book was composed of two halves: sixty-nine new poems and a further selection from earlier collections. Its title, *The Frog Prince*, was taken from a key poem.

In 'The Frog Prince' Stevie twists the Grimm Brothers' fairy tale and makes the frog, not miserable, but enchanted with his spell-bound state. Only when the spell is broken, and he is literally disenchanted, can he become 'heavenly'. Stevie would introduce 'The Frog Prince' as a 'religious' poem, a warning to us in the form of a parable of life that we may become accustomed to mediocre comforts, fail to see what lies beyond and so miss the chance of greater happiness. This reversal of convention is a recurrent tactic. In 'Fish, Fish' the apparently trivial word-play on the phrase 'the fish is on the hook' unexpectedly opens fresh dimensions when the speaker realizes that the fish 'sits *on* the hook / It is not *in* him' and is fatally attracted to it. Enchantment, either good or ill, figures prominently in *The Frog Prince*. In 'I Wish' the speaker, echoing Psalm 55, verse 6, yearns for a wing under which to hide but instead passes through a car's shining hub into another world where there is 'a heavenly sea / A-roll in the realms of light'. Phil in 'Night Thoughts', in order to escape a dull life and imperfect relationships creates for himself in imagination a sea shore where he can walk happily. Other characters fall into a dream, are caught up by a storm or magicked away. Even when the enchantment offers an inspirational experience and is not mere wish-fulfilment it leaves the narrator disenchanted with everyday life, unable to return to the habitual. This idea finds theoretical justification in Paul de Man's essay 'The Sublimation of the Self' in which the plenitude of artistic production is seen to be achieved at the expense or reduction of the self, the artist 'ascending beyond his limits into a place from which he can no longer descend'.[32]

> I went into the wood one day
> And there I walked and lost my way
>
> When it was so dark I could not see
> A little creature came to me
>
> He said if I would sing a song
> The time would not be very long
>
> But first I must let him hold my hand tight
> Or else the wood would give me a fright
>
> I sang a song, he let me go
> But now I am home again there is nobody I know.

Despite the predominance of fairy stories and enchantment, *The Frog Prince* also sounds a note of savage impatience. Words that are banal from overuse here become newly resilient through repetition. In 'Pretty' this word takes on sinister and sarcastic connotations; at times childishly parroted, at others given Swiftian irony, it voices discourses, usually kept separate, in such quick succession that the word 'pretty' is defamiliarized and made unnerving. It ends:

> Cry pretty, pretty, pretty and you'll be able
> Very soon not even to cry pretty
> And so be delivered entirely from humanity
> This is prettiest of all, it is very pretty.

'To Carry the Child' chides those who value the child in the adult without realizing the potentially murderous handicap it creates. 'Under Wrong

Trees' mocks illiberal attitudes towards colonialism, the French terms '*splendide*' and '*stupide*' suggesting both the educated class and the inanity of those whose opinions are satirized. Perhaps the most brutal poem of all is 'V' in which the speaker, in brief conversational phrases, discusses Adela. From the clichés, gaps and implied contradictions we learn that, contrary to what is said, Adela is far from happy.

> Adela is such a silly woman
> Tom says Adela is going off her head
>
> Adela is staying down in the country
> She is v. happy
>
> Dr Not is v. nice
>
> Such a jolly old place quite like home
>
> Dr Not is v. nice
> Adela is v. happy
>
> Adela is Not is
> v. v. happy
>
> With extensive grounds.

The narrative poems in *The Frog Prince* further display Stevie's ventriloquizing talent. In 'I had a dream . . .' the speaker performing the monologue gives to Helen of Troy a gossipy, catty style. 'Mutchmore and Not-So', a mixture of word-play, biblical allusion and genealogy, allowed Stevie to draw upon her experience of Norfolk society, in its tone and subject matter. 'This is just how people talk in the county,' she told Terence Kilmartin.[33] Elsewhere, in 'Phèdre' and 'The Last Turn of the Screw', she revises famous narratives, the first proposing an alternative to Racine's unrelieved tragedy, the second suggesting that the boy, Miles, is tinged with guilt because, taught by Quint, he has learnt 'the process of evil' which for Stevie moved 'from silliness to stupidity, through every malice and vulgarity, through all false values and greed in them, to ultimate absolute cruelty'.[34]

The style of drawing in *The Frog Prince* is more scratchy and sketch-like than in her earlier collections. Often the illustrations convey an impression of character or state of mind; only a few delineate incident or scene. Most have a direct relationship with either the speaker or the poem's subject and help establish its voice, but one arbitrary conjunction slipped in. 'I don't quite see what the bull is doing in the cemetery (p. 182)', Stevie remarked to John Guest, 'but never mind, I am sure people will find some very profound explanation for it.'[35] The casual style of these late drawings belies their sophistication. If the naked woman in a forest illustrating 'Now Pine-Needles' in *A Good Time Was Had By All* is compared with that illustrating 'Saffron' in *The Frog Prince*, the rich suggestiveness of the later drawing makes the earlier seem clipped and formulaic. The gain is a much greater directness. Stevie drew attention to the illustrations in her blurb for *The Frog Prince*. 'This is no time for false modesty,' she warned in a letter enclosing her blurb, a part of which reads:

'There are more drawings in this volume than in previous books, and more drawings than usual of animals, those peculiar, haunted creatures that seem so clearly, as she shows them, to be not only man's friends and servants, but his victims too – and his mirror. Stevie Smith's is a highly nervous talent, one of the most individual of our time; and the laughter that is in it runs often close to panic.'

Praised by John Gross in the *Observer*, by the *Times Literary Supplement*, by Philip Oakes in the *Sunday Times* and elsewhere, *The Frog Prince* received a good press. But the balancing act perceived by Philip Oakes ('she walks a tightrope between McGonagall and Blake'[36]) was not apparent to Bernard Bergonzi. His gendered criticism deliberately belittled an achievement more subtle and less calculating than he suggests: 'She's a clever writer who about 30 years ago adopted the *faux-naif* persona of the wide-eyed, infinitely knowing little girl, and found it so enjoyable that she has kept it up ever since . . . her language, with its false simplicities of diction, insistently draws attention to itself in a coy, self-regarding fashion, and effectively undermines real communication.'[37]

What to Bergonzi were 'false simplicities of diction' seem to other readers the result of a tactical decision to make ordinary words and even clichés fresh and alive. When using hackneyed phrases associated with Christian themes, Stevie could so arrange the words, as in the line

Before Whom angel brightness grows dark, heaven dim,

in 'Why do you rage?' that they acquire a Hopkins-like density. The simplicities of diction are, not false, but sometimes insufficiently burnished into vitality. Stevie admits this in a letter to Hans Häusermann whilst discussing the poems of Herbert Read:

'They fill me with a sort of aching weariness and a desire to be done with words altogether. Yet I think I can feel something of what he is revolting against, something that I think is often a fault in my poems – the too easy, too much trodden over, use of words – having an idea and really shoving it over, as one might in a letter or a talk, without enough care for each word and the life in it . . . I find more in the Joycean distortion of words – Anna Livia Plurabelle etc. – than in Read's stringing of words for richness of sound and association – at least I take it that is his aim.'[38]

Only rarely was she persuaded to read contemporary poetry: she feared that, like the crossing of telephone lines, it would impede her hearing of her own voice. Moreover the critic's habit of bunching poets into groups, and the pack-like identity this suggests, further discouraged her.

She continued to find ideas for poems in the texture of daily life; in conversations overheard; books read, particularly the Bible or Grimms' Fairy Tales; and from within her own mental landscape. Interviewed on radio in 1965, she commented:

'I think if one's writing poetry one's mind is tremendously open to things coming in as well as linking up with what is going on inside one . . . if one's feelings inside for one particular day happens to be fear or horror then one will find that in the outside world too.'[39]

In another radio interview she insisted that her poems were serious without being solemn. 'I really do hate the opposite so much, the poems of people who are solemn without being serious.' Claiming that her own were 'deeply serious' yet 'simply cast', she once again objected to the criticism of *fausse-naïveté*. 'They are not full of tricks. They are quite sort of straightforward with a great deal of thought underneath.'[40]

As her poems now regularly appeared in anthologies, critical opinion was coming round to her view. In 1966 she became, with Ted Walker, a Sussex schoolmaster whose first book of poems had appeared the year before, the first to receive the Cholmondely Award for poetry. In 1967 the Society of Authors awarded her a travelling scholarship which, though it was held in reserve for her, she never used. And in 1968, two years after its original appearance, Penguin reprinted the *Modern Poets* volume in which Stevie's work was included. Financial reward did not equal critical acclaim. When John Guest was approached by 10 Downing Street as to whether Stevie had the necessary qualifications for a Civil List Pension – 'work of a national distinction in the spheres of literature, art or science; and straitened circumstances' – he replied in the affirmative.

'Sorry you are feeling so gloomy,' Terence Kilmartin had written to her in 1965.[41] Her gloom, fortunately, did not enter her reviews which remained gently incisive. 'Differences between men and women poets are best seen when the poets are bad,' she wrote. 'Bad women poets are better characters, they seldom . . . get drunk . . . go to prison . . . shoot the pianist.

Their faults are soulfulness and banality. They like to commune (who does not?) with the Deity, Nature, themselves, but the words they use do not quite carry the traffic. Bad men poets are even more knowing and often they achieve fame as poets by stopping writing and going on committees.'[42] Stevie herself sat on a committee when in 1965 Eric White invited her on to the Arts Council's Literature Panel and Cecil Day Lewis persuaded her to accept. She reckoned she attended only two meetings in three years. At the first of these the panel was invited to nominate judges for a short story competition. When Day Lewis asked Stevie if she would like to suggest a name, she visibly shrank with horror and Eric White saw to it that questions of this kind would not again be directed her way. She did, however, make her presence felt through an occasional explosion of laughter.

In other circumstances she was noticeably lacking in self-consciousness. After appearing at the 1965 Edinburgh Festival she and Auden were filmed talking together over a drink, swapping memories of Germany and vying with each other in the singing of ditties and rhymes. She was equally relaxed with Audrey Insch, a Scottish lecturer in English, who, having invited Stevie to read at Stockwell College of Education in Bromley, took her to tea beforehand in a genteel coffee importers. 'We settled down,' Audrey Insch recounts, '. . . Stevie was shy in some ways . . . and not in others. She was working on a poem which involved a Northumberland/Border voice. We discussed various rhythms and sounds. She became more excited. I encouraged her and – out it came, her attempt at a north country accent as if she were in the Albert Hall . . . The ladies of Bromley clearly thought, by head turns, tight lips, etc. that this rather eccentric looking person should be led off somewhere. The whole thing was glorious. I bought a pair of scarlet jeans specially for the occasion.'[43]

At home, Stevie's routine remained unchanged. In March 1965 she told Hans Häusermann that Aunt was 'blooming' and liked to think this owed much to her cooking. The Revd Clifford Doyle, vicar at St John's, befriended Stevie and found a woman who was prepared to live in when Stevie visited Molly, the Lawrences at Brockham End or the Brownes and Buxtons in Norfolk. The importance these visits had for her cannot be overstressed. 'It's heavenly here,' she wrote from Wiveton to Terence Kilmartin, 'really too marvellous. I do nothing at all but sleep, eat and go for short trots over the saltings . . . I am becoming fat and agreeable and quite incapable of reading Father D'Arcy,' whom she was reviewing.[44] Back home the unspoken misery of her existence was sharply visible to fresh eyes. When Hans Häusermann visited, bringing his second wife, Gertrud, the young woman received an impression of suffocating ugliness and unshifting

despair. The visit began badly. Stevie had intended taking the Häuser-
manns to a nearby restaurant and had forgotten, until the morning of their
arrival, that it was either Sunday or a bank holiday and the restaurant was
closed. Obliged to open a tin of potatoes and a tin of peas, she served a meal
on cracked plates that reinforced the feeling Gertrud Häusermann had of
unbearable sadness. Upstairs, while her husband talked with Aunt, Gertrud
listened to Stevie moving about in the kitchen below. The sighs and
occasional moans that she heard were, she thought, unconscious, a regular
accompaniment to Stevie's household tasks. After luncheon they went into
the front room and Gertrud commented on the watercolours hanging on the
walls. Stevie told her they were done by her mother and added that she
never looked at them. Gertrud thought Stevie saw little of her immediate
environment, with its bleakness and lack of beauty, and lived entirely in a
mental world. On a walk during the afternoon, Stevie grew more animated
in conversation with Hans Häusermann, but his wife observed that her
laugh, though lively, was not gay.

Häusermann evidently felt the need to help Stevie; he approached the
British Council in an attempt to arrange for her a reading tour in
Switzerland. Stevie responded weakly; it was getting more and more
difficult to find someone to look after Aunt as the 'Holy Woman', found by
the vicar, had gone to live in an old people's home. 'One gets into an awful
state of inertia,' Stevie confessed, '. . . and feels one really is not meant to
move and it is better not to try.'[45] Nevertheless she still now and then got
away. After Molly managed a return to Palmers Green in February 1966,
for Aunt's ninety-fourth birthday, Stevie made arrangements to visit
Buckfast that summer. In search of help, she told Olga Lawrence: 'Aunt
needs no nursing, just helping on with her shoes and stockings in the
morning and tucking up at night . . . Nurse comes and gives her a bath once
a week and we have a very nice obliging doctor, so things aren't too bad on
the whole.'[46] When Stevie visited Norfolk for a fortnight in May, Aunt went
into a nursing home that specialized in short stays for the elderly. Nevertheless, Stevie increasingly felt she could not leave home. That August she told
Häusermann: 'Aunt seems very well at present, though the poor darling gets
terribly bored, not being able to see or hear properly, and worrying that she
can't do anything to help etc. I feel a bit delinquent even thinking of going
out of the country.'[47] In February 1967 Aunt spent four days in hospital and
returned home much changed. 'When they carried her upstairs again,'
Stevie wrote a few days later, 'she looked shrunken and defeated – it was
really *awful*. All seems well now.'[48] The following February Madge Spear
celebrated her ninety-sixth birthday. Nina Woodcock brought daffodils and

was surprised when Aunt, who was never heard to complain, remarked, 'I'm going downhill, my dear.'[49]

Given the strain that the Aunt's slow deterioration must have caused Stevie, it is hardly surprising that she herself now showed signs of age. Maurice Collis, seeing her again at a party at the Hanover Gallery in 1965, after a gap of many years, thought she had become 'some sort of extraordinary old insect now, very small, creeping about, and her eye sockets almost as large as saucers. She looks a hundred.'[50] At the same time she was writing poems which, when published after her death, conveyed to John Bayley 'not a relaxation, but a greater quietness and space',[51] and which include some of her best. 'Might one not expect to find something anarchic in the thoughts of the old,' she once asked in a *Spectator* review, 'since they are about to experience the anarchy of death in a natural course, even a positive and malicious pleasure in the possibility of everything they hoped and believed turning out to be not so. . . ?'[52]

News of Aunt's stroke reached her at the Brownes' London house, where she was lunching on her return from a reading at the girl's school, Cranborne Chase. Gerard Irvine had acted as her chauffeur and was on the point of leaving when the telephone rang. He promptly cancelled all appointments and drove Stevie back to Palmers Green. That same day, 10 February 1968, Aunt went into hospital. Fortunately Molly was staying at 1 Avondale Road and had been in the house when the stroke occurred. The next day Stevie, Molly and Revd Doyle visited the hospital. Aunt regained consciousness, recognized her nieces and was given holy oils. After her second day in hospital Stevie wrote to Hans Häusermann: 'Isn't it wonderful, though, that at the age of 96 she can rally round after a severe cerebral haemorrhage? She is a very strong fighting lady.'[53]

From the beginning Stevie realized Aunt would never return home. Her weight made it impossible for Stevie to lift her and, when it seemed that she would survive this stroke, Molly and Stevie began to make arrangements for her to be moved to a home. Then suddenly her strength failed and on 11 March she died. Four days later her funeral took place, Gerard Irvine leading part of the service. Friends were anxious to fill the gap and Stevie was inundated with letters of condolence, telephone calls and invitations to stay. She was also philosophic: 'I know it is best really,' she admitted to John Guest, 'because she would never have been happy or comfortable again, but all the same it is *awful*.'[54] To commemorate Aunt, Stevie and Molly donated a small oak lectern to St John's.

Madge Spear had made Stevie the sole executor of her estate, which, after tax, amounted to £3,698–18s–0d. Some five months before her death she had instructed her solicitor, A. J. Davey, to draw up a fresh will leaving everything to Stevie, giving the following reasons: '(a) because her niece had looked after her for many years (b) had made her loans and paid bills etc. and (c) she had realized that the £2,000 Consols of which she received the income for life would on her death pass in equal shares to her two nieces and would not form part of her estate. Furthermore Miss Spear was aware that her other niece, Miss E. M. Smith owed Miss F. M. Smith £2,000.'[55]

It had always been understood that if anything happened to Aunt, Stevie had a bolt-hole in Norfolk. She spent almost a month there, staying first with the Buxtons and then the Brownes. Nothing, however, could disguise the melancholy that accompanied her return home.

Her friends noticed an increase in loneliness for she had in effect been widowed by Aunt's death. She telephoned them more frequently, often for no other reason than a need for conversation. June Braybrooke received many calls of this kind, brought to a sudden end by Stevie's announcement that she had something urgent to do. Her desolation must partly have been caused by a loss of routine. Her behaviour became more wayward; she developed the habit of sleeping in different rooms, as the mood took her; neighbours were aware that she sometimes did not answer the door. Greater solitude left her more withdrawn, inclined to brood. On one occasion when Helen Fowler visited and they were discussing Antonia Fraser's life of Mary, Queen of Scots, which Stevie was reviewing, Stevie, without warning, broke into tears and admitted that she missed Aunt dreadfully. She had been sufficiently rocked by Aunt's death to return to church, to a communion service, as she afterwards told Gerard Irvine. She also wrote a poem, with eucharistic associations, which was for her 'about bereavement. It is what may be said when human beings lose people they love.'[56] Entitled 'So to fatness come', it was published in the *Sunday Times* on 11 August 1968.

> Poor human race that must
> Feed on pain, or choose another dish
> And hunger worse.
>
> There is also a cup of pain, for
> You to drink all up, or,
> Setting it aside for sweeter drink,
> Thirst evermore.
>
> I am thy friend. I wish
> You to sup full of the dish

I gave you and the drink,
And so to fatness come more than you think
In health of opened heart, and know peace.

Grief spake these words to me in a dream. I thought
He spoke no more than grace allowed
And no less than truth.

The day after this poem appeared Stevie summed up her relations with Aunt in a letter to Hans Häusermann. 'I think in her mind I always remained the rather feeble child I was when she first came to take charge of us all. But I always told her – and how truthfully! – that I depended on her just as much as she did on me . . . I have decided to stay on living here, I really love it, it is so quiet and sweet in a way and I don't feel I want "to get away" and all that – at all. Nor do I feel I want to have anybody else living with me. At least not just yet. Marghanita Laski asked me to go and spend a few weeks with them in the south of France, where they have a house . . . And there was some talk also of my going to Malta with some friends. But I just don't want to go anywhere – except dear old Norfolk, where . . . I am going, yet again, next week for a fortnight to stay with the same long-suffering friends.'[57] When Christmas arrived she was still having to inform friends of Aunt's death, and it was 'still awful'.[58] The same phrase occurs again in a letter she wrote James Laughlin the following spring: Aunt's death had been in some ways a blessing; she had hated her deafness, increasing blindness and debilitation; she had also hated hospital 'and fought most fiercely against it, so that Sister said: Has Miss Spear been always in a Position of Authority?' Though she did not wish Aunt back she admitted that she was making a poor job of living alone.[59]

CHAPTER 15

Black March

The poems Stevie wrote towards the end of her life suggest that the closeness of death made the fabric of everyday life more vivid.

> The grass is green
> The tulip is red
> A ginger cat walks over
> The pink almond petals on the flower bed.
> Enough has been said to show
> It is life we are talking about. Oh
> Grateful colours, bright looks! . . .

The positioning of the word 'life' gives a spring to this poem which characteristically, after the exclamation 'Oh / Grateful colours, bright looks!', suddenly changes in tone: 'Well, to go / On'. For Hermione Lee this poem expresses a belief 'in the objects of the mortal world as the most significant metaphors of, and vehicles for, our spiritual life'.[1] Stevie's poems address the notion of spiritual life as constantly as they voice the stance of an earthy realist and debunker. The cheek, energy and zap of her Galloping Cat who scorns 'all that skyey stuff / Of angels that make so bold as / To pity a cat like me . . .'[2] contrasts with the romantic, expansive evocation of death in 'Black March'. Both are great poems, together encapsulating Stevie's capacity to embrace contrarieties through a multiplicity of voices, simultaneously disparate and unified.

In her late poems her earlier thematics are repeated. An echo of Wordsworth's 'My heart leaps up when I behold / A rainbow in the sky' is heard twice, in 'When Walking' and 'The Word', but in the second of these Romantic optimism is cut off by intimations of mortality.

> My heart leaps up with streams of joy,
> My lips tell of drouth;
> Why should my heart be full of joy
> And not my mouth?

In 'O Pug!' she empathizes with the panic, insecurity and anxiety expressed in the dog's eyes, 'Those liquid and protuberant orbs'. For her, animals too are caught up in a human situation which is half humorous, half tragic and always painful. Only death is offered as a solution to this fear of life. These late poems appeared soon after they were written in the *New Statesman*, *Listener*, *Observer* and *Sunday Times*, and were posthumously collected in *Scorpion and Other Poems*. One of these, 'Oblivion', which appeared in the *Observer* on 3 May 1970, suggests that she came close to committing suicide, for in the same way that the speaker is restrained by 'a human and related voice / That cried to me in pain' ('related' is underlined in one manuscript version of this poem), so Stevie was kept from taking her own life by Molly's need of her.

If her themes had not altered, neither had her poetics. She continued to concertina frontiers, merging genres and their various discourses by audacious juxtapositioning of quotations and half quotations from the Bible, the Prayer Book and Romantic poets with modern colloquialisms. Where her poems can disappoint is when the narrative drive predominates and her rhythms become devitalized. Compared with the sprightly animation of 'The Galloping Cat', the poem commissioned by *Harper's* for their Christmas issue in 1966, 'Saint Foam and the Holy Child', seems poorly coordinated and flat.

That her work is all of a piece and yet uneven was a fact kept in mind by Robert Gottlieb when he set about publishing her poems in America. Associated with Alfred A. Knopf, he had observed her poems in the *New Statesman* and had kept a cutting of 'Phèdre' in his wallet. He approached Stevie in September 1968 and, on her instructions, was sent a copy of *The Frog Prince* by John Guest. Guest told Gottlieb that Stevie had attained a leading place among English poets and, by the standard of poetry sales in Britain, sold well. Both Stevie and John Guest hoped Gottlieb would publish *The Frog Prince* in America but he had other ideas, partly because New Directions' *Selected Poems* had not done well. 'Here is the problem for us,' he told Guest, 'and for *her* in America: Whereas you can without difficulty publish a large book like *Frog Prince*, because you have a famous author with a specific public . . . we are in the business of *creating* that audience . . . A book the size of *Frog Prince*, which has in it works of different levels of quality, will not help Miss Smith here as she deserves to be helped . . . At the moment she has admirers here, but not a public. A new book must be a jewel – and it can be.'[3]

Gottlieb, in pursuit of his ambition, chose the book's title, *The Best Beast*, based on Stevie's poem of that name, and selected its contents. Stevie approved his choice, expressing pleasure that he had picked 'Egocentric' and 'Es war einmal' from her earliest collection, surprise that he wanted 'Piggy to Joey', which she thought slight, and 'The Crown of Gold', which she thought unclear and interesting only to herself. She alerted him to the fact that a number of poems in the earliest collections had not been picked up by Longman's for *Selected Poems* or *The Frog Prince*, nor had many been used from *Not Waving but Drowning* owing to the cost of permission fees, a problem that would no longer arise as *Not Waving* was out of print. Sitting among her books and reviewing their contents, Stevie felt 'absolutely drowned deep in poems' and warned that this was a 'sure prelude to *hundreds* more'. 'You know,' she went on, 'there are really too many. Not too few.'[4] A week later she sent Gottlieb thirty-four new poems for consideration.

Gottlieb had an equally definite attitude towards the drawings. He worried that they put Stevie's work into the category of light verse and decided to use only six, scattered through the book. 'I really do believe,' he told her, '(I know it's heresy) that many of the poems are lessened by their drawings; others, certainly, are complemented.'[5] Stevie, aware that she needed Gottlieb's firm direction as the American edition of *Selected Poems* had not sold well, succumbed.

She was also by now certain that her poems represented a difficult mixture for an American audience. To her surprise *The Best Beast* was well received. Several critics saw that the simplicity of her verse was, not false, but deceptive. One stated: 'The simple forms – frequently rhymes, refrains and short lines like children's verse – and often what would seem to be tame subjects – animals, gardens and so forth – hide (but only for a moment) great power, anger, wonder and love.'[6] Another designated her 'mistress of the dead-pan manner, the flat out, matter-of-fact statement of terrible truths,' and declared 'many of her parables strike a James Thurber note: a child-like innocence of surface which opens to reveal one of life's fundamental ambiguities.'[7]

The strength of her reputation in Britain encouraged Jonathan Cape to begin negotiations in 1968 for the republication of *Novel on Yellow Paper* the following year. With Douglas Cleverdon, Stevie worked on another radio programme, 'Poems and Conversations', in which she read again and introduced her work. It was broadcast on 3 September 1968 and repeated, in revised form, in November. Meanwhile her poems continued to appear in leading newspapers and periodicals and she received several commissions. For the Barrow Poets, who read in pubs and elsewhere, she wrote 'The Galloping Cat' which was both performed by them and made available to their audiences as a printed broadsheet. This demand for her work did not remove self-doubt. She told one reporter: 'There isn't an editor in London who hasn't been asked to collaborate with me. "I enclose the last two verses. Which do you think is better?" '[8] Approached by Ann Thwaite, in connection with her children's annual, *Allsorts* and by the *Daily Telegraph Magazine* which was doing a feature on new nursery rhymes, she began to write verse for children. 'I think it's having rather a bad effect on my poems,' she warned John Guest, '. . . the next book will have to be for Tiny Tots.'[9]

Even before Aunt died, Anna Browne noticed that Stevie's face, now framed by thin and rather lifeless hair, dyed a lighter colour than before, had got sadder. She was easily exasperated and often tired. It is possible that her incipient brain tumour was the cause, as growing intracranial pressure would have caused sleepiness. 'I'm probably a couple of sherries below par most of the time,' she told a reporter.[10] All her life she had been at a low ebb, physically, prone to colds and influenza, headaches and stomach upsets, and from these would emerge looking wan and frail. Her frailty partly explains why she clung to Palmers Green and found it 'very silent, very poetical' and 'quite dreamy'.[11] The character of this suburb had greatly changed, as she recounts in the children's annual, *Allsorts*:

'In one of those parks which is called Grovelands, I spend a great deal of my present time. It has a very large deep lake with an island in the middle. Often I take a boat out and have a picnic lunch, first tying my boat up carefully to one of the trees that drop into the water from the lake's island, which is also where the swans have their house. In winters, if we have a hard winter, the lake will be frozen right across . . .

'Our suburb is now a very-much-alive sort of place; there are clubs and societies for everything . . . There are a great many Chinese, Indian and African people who have come to live here, and that makes it very much nicer, because there is so much variety in everybody's looks and interests, and all of it going on at the same time.

'I do not know many people in Palmers Green very intimately, but I like living here and I like the people to talk to, in the shops and streets, and that is how *they* like it too. There is this politeness I notice. Everybody smiles and is friendly, but it is a sweet distant smile on our faces that we have. In trouble or difficulties we help each other a great deal, and then, when it is over, smile again this sweet distant smile. Sometimes I feel rather peculiar, as if I were looking out through a beautiful window at a distance that is full of amiability, but has cast a spell. I do not mind this; in fact rather like it.'[12]

Away from Palmers Green, at literary parties or in the homes of her friends, her sharp, sometimes malicious, humour and endearing giggle made her very good company. Friends cherished her. She spent Christmas Day 1968 with Douglas and Nest Cleverdon, bringing as a gift a small rocking chair that she had found in a junk shop and thought characteristic of them. On 8 January 1969 she attended the Cleverdon's silver-wedding party, and this time gave Nest a silver bracelet that had belonged to Aunt. Despite the buoyancy that she brought to these occasions, melancholy underlay all that she did. In May she wrote, only half-jestingly, to John Guest: 'I am afraid I am a broken reed, and a neurotic one too – I keep casting loving looks at the gas oven, if only it were more up-to-date, poor darling, something with flashing chromium and dead white hardbake . . . as it is (dated about 1911 I shd. think) I haven't the heart.'[13]

Later that month Stevie was distressed to hear that Molly had had another stroke which at first left her paralysed all down her left side and unable to speak. Stevie went down to Buckfast, put up in Molly's bungalow and was ferried to and from Ashburton Hospital, where Molly remained for the better part of the summer, by friends and neighbours. From Devon she continued her correspondence with John Guest who, at Stevie's request, had considered *The Holiday* for re-publication and now decided against it. Stevie took his rejection without complaint, though she now rated this book higher than *Novel on Yellow Paper*, claiming it 'really beautiful – and awfully but awfully funny'. In this same letter she reverts to her physical tiredness, and the apathy and despair attendant on it. 'I feel quite desperate about it sometimes, like a horse that refuses its hedges, I mean when you said that bit about a valiant heart I thought I've had enough of valiant hearts I don't want to have a valiant heart I just Don't Want to be Here (here, of course, in case once again I fail to make myself understood?) meaning *Alive*.'[14]

Stevie spent three months that summer at Buckfast, managing also a visit to Norfolk. Molly slowly recovered her speech as well as the ability to walk, with the aid of a three-pronged stick, but her left arm remained permanently paralysed. Though she was sent to Newton Abbot three afternoons a week for treatment, shortage of staff at Ashburton meant that she was often confined for long periods to her chair, weeping with boredom and frustration at not being able to move. Prolonged hospitalization left her very depressed and mentally a little unbalanced. Once back at Dart St Mary she was often rude to others and wayward in her behaviour. It seemed unlikely that she would ever live alone again and Buckfast gossip supported the notion that Stevie should now cohabit with Molly and look after her. Stevie had other views, as she told Audrey Insch: Molly 'has built up quite a vivid picture of going down with little sister to the grave hand in hand, after many a long if ageing year closetted à deux! I'm afraid that in this race to the grave little sister wd. have won before Molly left the starting point! But you can imagine how *wicked* it makes me feel and now (I hear, from a Buckfast spy) feeling in that tight little catholic-masochistic society is becoming strongly against me unless I "do my duty".'[15] Instead she made enquiries about Distressed Gentlefolks homes and had Molly's name put on a waiting list. Molly objected, as one of her neighbours reported to Stevie: 'We met one day a monk from the abbey in the village. Molly stopped the car and spoke to him at great length of how she was to be incarcerated in a sort of Belsen, and how you were having a lovely time in Norfolk, making it sound as though you were living it up on the Las Vegas strip. The man did not know her and stood silent in embarrassed amazement. When at last I drove on, she said in terms of ineffable contempt, "He's only a lay brother, anyway".'[16]

While staying at Buckfast, Stevie continued to make poems out of contemporary events, things heard, seen or read. On 1 July 1969 the investiture of the Prince of Wales took place at Caernarvon, surrounded by a fanfare of publicity. Not long after this Helen Fowler and her family visited Buckfast. With them, Stevie went swimming in the River Dart and was moving silently underneath the dark water when she suddenly resurfaced and declaimed:

> We have given the Welsh a most *awfully*
> Nice day out
> And now we never want to hear from them again
> For *years*, and *years*, and *years*,
> And never at all
> *In Welsh.*

('Underlining meant to ensure the drawl'), she told Anthony Thwaite when she sent this same poem ('Soupir d'Angleterre') to the *New Statesman*, adding: 'Here's the nasty poem about the Welsh – poor-things. But I dare say it had better remain unpublished, even if publishable.'[17] Two years earlier *Poetry Review* (Winter 1967) had published 'B.B.C. Feature Programme on Prostitution', another poem fired by crossness, this time with special pleading and self-delusion. 'Un peu de vice', the sub-title of her poem 'Seymour and Chantelle' based on Swinburne's relationship with his cousin, Mary Gordon, also invited sharp treatment. Swinburne's obsession with flagellation, or 'swishing', as he termed it, is exposed as a vicious but immature indulgence. Stevie wrote this poem after reviewing Jean Overton Fuller's biography of the poet for the *Listener* and sent it to Terence Kilmartin at the *Observer*. 'I think the reason I am writing such a lot of poems,' she explained, 'is because I am supposed to be doing something else . . . i.e. collect an anthology for children of other people's poems, not mine of course, and it's such a bore it makes one write.'[18]

The Batsford Book of Children's Verse (1970) provides some indication of her own taste in poetry but has only questionable use for children. An anthology that includes these lines from Sophocles' *Oedipus Colonnus* –

> Not to be born at all
> Is best, far best that can befall,
> Next best, when born, with least delay
> To trace the backward way

– as well as George Darley's 'Deadman's Dirge' firmly rejects the notion that a child's imagination is confined to the sweeter surface aspects of human experience. 'Childhood's thoughts can cut deep,' Stevie announced in the introduction, instancing her own realization, at the age of eight, 'that life lay in our hands'. Nevertheless, when published in America the book bore the title, *The Poet's Garden*, and slight alterations to the introduction removed the suggestion that it was an anthology for children. It is also not entirely trustworthy as a reflection of Stevie's taste, for she followed suggestions made by others including Anna Browne and Sam Carr, the book's editor, who put in Herman Melville's 'The Maladive Shark', Wordsworth's 'The Sun has long been Set' and Pope's 'Engraved on the Collar of a Dog'. The collection as a whole, however, reflects her love of ballads, of word painting, of the sonorous and powerful. Walt Whitman's 'I think I could turn and live with animals' (from *Song of Myself*) could be taken as a manifesto for Stevie's own use of animals in her poetry ('They bring me tokens of myself, they evince them plainly in their possession'). Unfortunately last minute pressure caused Thomas Hardy's 'The Rejected Member's Wife', referred to in the introduction, to be omitted, thereby losing a tragi-comic note closely related to her own stance as poet.

Death, her own and that of those dear to her, pressed more and more insistently on her mind. In September 1968 she had sent an essay on the death of a loved one to the *Observer*, only to have it returned, unpublished. Having mourned her aunt, she offered the following advice for the testing period that arrives some months after the death. 'It is best to pray then, whether your intellect allows it or not, to have love or at least think every night and every morning, in terms as simple and circumspect as possible, about love remembering that self is the great enemy of love and of peace. Remember too that mourning too easily turns upon self, the pain of loss that we feel, and all the rest of the sad feelings we cannot leave, can be selfish . . . one thought that is neither comfortless nor subject to doubts or questioning: You do not mourn if you do not love.'[19] The loss of Aunt had released Stevie from her single most important commitment in this life, leaving death a still more welcome alternative. Interviewed by the *Observer* in 1969 Stevie reaffirmed her belief that death, far from being the greatest calamity, is the greatest blessing. It now seemed to her 'like being drawn into a race of water before it gets to the waterfront. It gets quicker and quicker and more exciting. The older you get the more exciting it gets because the nearer you get to this mysterious end. Oh how mysterious it is!'[20]

One death she had never become reconciled to was that of her mother. In an interview with James Mossman,[21] for the television programme 'Free for All on the Arts', transmitted 16 August 1969, Stevie unexpectedly broke down. Up to that point, the interview had gone well, the discussion having the tone of an intimate chat. But Mossman, who was himself preoccupied with death, having recently lost a close friend and who was himself to commit suicide a year later, began to press Stevie about the passage in *Novel on Yellow Paper* that deals with her mother's final illness. Normally a skilful and sensitive interviewer, Mossman persisted even when Stevie became visibly agitated, as both John King, the producer, and John Drummond, the executive producer, recall. Asked, 'Did you see her die?', Stevie turned her head aside all too obviously in great distress and the interview temporarily came to a halt.

Less painful for all concerned was the ten-minute interview that she had made for a 'Monitor' programme in March 1968. In this she recites her poems and responds to questions asked, though the interviewer, Jonathan Miller, is neither seen nor heard, his role being replaced by a voice-over presenter. Stevie, who did not have a television set, went round to her local vicar, the Revd Clifford Doyle, to watch the result. 'You do look so terribly ill, Stevie,' he commented in the silence that followed. Approached by others in the street with the remark that she was looking much healthier than she did in the film, she reflected they must have a 'permanent picture' of her 'groaning for burial'.[22]

Her visit to Buckingham Palace on 21 November 1969 to receive the Queen's Gold Medal for Poetry has become something of a legend. The extreme absurdity of the situation, combined with the undoubted honour, delighted her as she admitted to Kay Dick: 'I'm sure HM wd. much rather pin it on a doggy-dear than me. Of course I'm delighted but I can't help feeling some of the poems cannot really be what *we* quite want.'[23] Told to arrive at the Palace at 12.40, she arrived too early, went round the Queen's Gallery, bought large numbers of picture postcards and stuffed them into her handbag. She then returned to the Palace and kept a lady-in-waiting and a young man in naval uniform in giggles as she sat waiting her turn and hissed at them one of her poems. In the Queen's presence she was impressed by the monarch's professionalism. But when poetry was mentioned and Stevie began to talk about 'Angel Boley', her poem based on the 1966 murder case in which Myra Hindley and Ian Brady were convicted for the sadistic killings of two children, found buried in shallow graves on Saddleworth Moor, she noticed that the Queen's smile 'got rather fixed'.[24]

By the following November, when Kay Dick made a recording of Stevie talking, her account of the Queen's Medal incident was very well rehearsed. Immediately after receiving the medal, Stevie had joined Cecil Day Lewis, Eric White and Norah Smallwood at L'Epicure in Soho for a celebration meal. Stevie confirmed her enthusiasm for the occasion by ordering oysters and launched into an account of her recent experience. But what began well finished badly. Owing to one bad oyster among the batch available, the head waiter had rejected the lot and sent an emergency runner for more. The delay seemed interminable and, once her initial excitement evaporated, Stevie declared her disappointment by rather petulantly calling for bread and jam. Twelve days later Stevie attended a drinks party given by Cecily Mackworth at Inez Holden's flat, 47a Lower Belgrave Street. Again, Stevie's account of her Palace visit proved hugely entertaining, as Cecily Mackworth recollects. One detail not mentioned in the Kay Dick interview was the Queen's remark that she had been told Stevie lived in a house with nine rooms all on her own. Stevie thought this remark odd, considering how many rooms the Queen lived in, but she replied that it was better for one person to live in nine rooms quite happily than for nine people to live in nine rooms and not get on.

The Queen's Medal brought her much publicity in the form of interviews and articles. The best and longest of these was that Paul Bailey wrote for *Nova*. Drawings used as illustrations for this article went missing. Stevie's annoyance over her loss partly explains why her letter, thanking Bailey for his article, strikes a cantankerous note.

'When I heard from one of those friends who see everything that is published that you "didn't like the drawings", it seemed to make their loss . . . even more pointless and frightful. But after all, why should you like them, a lot of people as you say, don't. And I am not too sure of them myself, or of anything. Anyway it was nice of you to write at such length . . . I have now come to detest *Novel on Y.P.* and to feel it is responsible for the things about my being "a funny little thing who lets things out" as someone said, that get said!'

She corrected a couple of his statements in the article and rebutted a criticism, before reaffirming her gratitude for 'the great care and thought that is in this article and the understanding'.[25]

Displays of irritation were almost certainly related to poor health. Her small size made her seem frailer than she was. Glenda Jackson never forgot her surprise when at a poetry and jazz event at the Aldwych Theatre in November 1964 Stevie got up to read and within seconds had the young audience entirely in her control. This was Glenda Jackson's first and last meeting with the poet she was later to impersonate in Hugh Whitemore's play *Stevie*, on stage and screen. Stevie's performance, for Glenda Jackson, put an end to any notion that poetry had to be read with a BBC voice.

In March 1970 Stevie read at the Crown and Greyhound, Dulwich, where poetry events were a regular fixture, and afterwards fell while crossing the road. The poets Michael Hamburger and Christopher Middleton came to her rescue and more or less supported her as they walked back to Hamburger's house in Herne Hill. There a German professor, Walter Höllerer, interviewed Stevie and others for a film he was making on literary London. Stevie, in considerable pain (she had cracked three ribs and damaged her knee) let no sign of her discomfort appear while being interviewed.

This accident did not prevent her from appearing on Saturday 9 May at the Roundhouse in Chalk Farm, in an event organized by Jeni Couzyn as part of the Camden Festival Fringe. 'Twelve to Twelve', as the event was called, ran from noon till midnight. Twelve names were billed to appear, among them Ted Hughes, Seamus Heaney and Stevie, and in between members of the audience were invited to come up on stage and read. The event was tumultuous; cabbages were thrown and there was much jostling for the microphone. Jeni Couzyn, wearing a feather boa, took charge of Stevie. They had first met at the party following the Festival Hall poetry event in 1969. Jeni Couzyn, astonished by the eccentricity of Stevie's performance, had attempted to express her delight in it. 'Whereupon,' she has written, 'she [Stevie] instantly turned her back on me with a little hiss, and then spent the evening flirting with my escort with the most alarming success . . . That night I realized that the little eccentric spinster was a part played by a highly sophisticated and professional woman. You could admire Stevie Smith, you could be stimulated and surprised by her, you could even dislike her, but you could never, never patronize her.' At the Roundhouse Couzyn experienced other sensations when Stevie, waiting to go on stage, took hold of her arm. By then, as Couzyn has said, Stevie had become for her 'a symbol of that which is most poignant in contemporary woman . . . standing in all her loneliness as one standing on a great height . . . I could find nothing to say to her, but with her thin, claw-like hand clinging to my arm I felt both humble and immensely proud.'[26] It is, however, Seamus Heaney who has best described what happened on stage. Unlike Adrian Mitchell, for example, whose readings insist on audience collusion, Stevie established a more complex, ambiguous exchange: 'her voice pitching between querulousness and keening, her quizzical presence at once inviting the audience to yield to her affection and keeping them at bay with a quick irony'. Heaney also remarks on her singing: 'She chanted her poems artfully off-key, in a beautifully flawed plainsong that suggested two kinds of auditory experience: an embarrassed party-piece by a child half-way between tears and giggles, and a deliberate *faux-naif* rendition by a virtuoso.'[27]

With Molly always now in the back of her mind, Stevie felt the disparity between her fêted life and her sister's severely circumscribed existence. On 7 January 1970 she had read at the London Graduate School of Business Studies, been given dinner and driven home. 'My audience consisted of budding tycoons,' she told Molly's friend, Elizabeth Popley, 'and their awfully nice (I thought) young wives . . . The contrast between my life and poor Mol's makes me sick. I know it's how the luck falls. But goodness, how sad!'[28] To alleviate the situation during the winter of 1969–70 a housekeeper for Molly had been found, an Irish Catholic called Mrs MacLeod who lived in. She began complaining the morning after she arrived, that a house without radio, television or even the morning paper was a morgue. Stevie went down to Buckfast at Christmas and scribbled into her appointment diary: 'Found Molly much better but Mrs MacLeod really *awful.*' Over the page, a couple of days later, she wrote: 'More trouble with Mrs Mac. She is always saying I shall go tomorrow – but she has nowhere to go. In between these brain storms she is quite nice but very fuddled in her mind (rather a lot of "nips" I think plus sleeping drugs) – awfully worrying. Everybody else most awfully nice and lots of visits and parties.'²⁹ Before long Mrs MacLeod was asked to leave.

Back at Palmers Green Stevie continued to worry about Molly. Her difficult character was criticized by others, among them Aylett Hyam, who wrote Stevie letters denigrating her sister. On her visits to Buckfast Stevie had to listen to more fault-finding and at one point, on a visit to Newton Abbot in Aylett Hyam's presence, lost her temper. Aylett complained to Elizabeth Popley who stormed into Molly's bungalow to tell her of Stevie's rudeness. In a letter to Elizabeth, Stevie tried to deal with all the petty slander that had accumulated. Her letter ends: 'To show you how despairing I got ("Upset" I suppose is the Buckfast word!) I now give you some of a poem I wrote, which though rooted in utter despair has alas perhaps come out funny, or *rather* funny. If all your shares are going down the drain, as mine are, keep this, it may be Worth Something some day!'³⁰ There followed the better part of 'Scorpion' which begins:

> 'This night shall thy soul be required of thee'
> *My* soul is never required of *me*
> It always has to be somebody else of course
> Will my soul be required of me tonight perhaps?
>
> (I often wonder what it will be like
> To have one's soul required of one
> But all I can think of is the Out-Patients' Department –
> 'Are you Mrs Briggs, dear?'
> No, I am Scorpion.)

The complete poem, venomous and cajoling, appeared in the *New Statesman* on 28 August 1970 and is another instance of her ability to metamorphose into poetry the miseries of her existence. 'Did you see *Scorpion* in the N.S. a few weeks ago?' Stevie asked Kay Dick. 'My poor beloved unspeakable (just like my turn) Scorpion? It is just what I feel like. Except one feels so much better for having said it.'³¹

She read several mournful poems at the Aldeburgh Festival that year and, more appropriately, at the opening of the exhibition, 'Death, Heaven and the Victorians', at the Brighton Pavilion in May. The exhibition, displaying all the accoutrements associated with mourning in the Victorian period, was richly macabre and nostalgic. A polyphone played hymns in the background, enhancing a mood of sentimental religiosity, and all the costume dummies, whether male or female, bore the face of Queen Victoria. Stevie shuddered on first entering, read her poems to the very smart audience that assembled for the private view, and stayed in the Albion Hotel. The next day she picnicked on Brighton beach with the exhibition's organizer, John Morley, and his wife. A woman friend was also present who, when asked afterwards what her impression of Stevie had been, replied 'a poor thing', adding the prediction that she would be dead within a year.

Stevie herself had a presentiment of death on one of her visits to Norfolk. She was picnicking with the Browne family on Blakeney Point, a spit of land about five miles long which encloses an estuary. When the tide is out it is possible to walk across the channel; when the tide is in a ferry plies its way between the mainland and the Point. Towards the end of the afternoon Stevie wandered across the marshes alone and encountered the boatman who asked if she wanted to be ferried across. Stevie replied in the negative, adding that her friends were still on that side. But in the late afternoon light which brought out the chill and loneliness of the marshes, Stevie saw the scene in terms of Book VI of the *Aeneid*, the boatman transformed into Charon, the channel into the River Lethe, the setting becoming the Stygian marshes and the boatman's question an invitation to cross over to death.

In May 1970 Donald and Molly Everett moved into the bungalow next to Molly's at Buckfast, replacing neighbours who had been unfriendly and unhelpful. Formerly a bank manager, Donald Everett had retired early, for reasons of health, and had an interest in poetry, which he himself wrote. His wife, Molly, painted in a style as direct and exuberant as her character. Both were warned by one of the monks at the Abbey, Father Sebastian Wolfe, that their neighbour was a strong-minded woman. But Molly Smith, even at her most wilful and theatrical, could not offend this easygoing pair who wired up a bell between their bungalow and Molly's so that she could call them in any emergency. They also got on well with Stevie whose reviews they had read for many years in the *Observer*. A great deal of exchange went on between the two bungalows, especially when Stevie visited for she went round each evening to watch the news on the Everetts' television. When *Macbeth* was televised both sisters watched, Molly remarking when Stevie fidgeted: 'the trouble with Peg is she doesn't understand Shakespeare.' On another occasion Molly Smith insisted on showing Donald Everett some poems, liberally sprinkled with classical allusions, which she herself had written as if to prove that she, too, could write.

Stevie spent most of the summer of 1970 at Buckfast, giving a reading at Totnes Castle on 27 July in aid of Shelter and making only brief return visits to London. She found herself watching quite a lot of television and admitted to Anna Browne: 'I don't think I should ever do any writing at all down here, the days rather fritter themselves away.'[32] That year Anna Browne, owing to acute arthritis and the fact that her husband had recently undergone an operation, had to cancel Stevie's summer visit to Wiveton, a decision she afterwards regretted. Stevie was, however, happy at Buckfast if herself not entirely well. On a visit to Dartington with the Everetts, where their daughter Kathy was studying music, Stevie began to faint while they were walking in the gardens and had to be helped inside. On another occasion that summer she returned from a walk covered in mud, having fallen. Aware that something was wrong she saw a doctor whilst in Devon and went to Dr Curley on her return home. She was already taking anti-depressants as well as medication for an intestinal disorder which she could not rid herself of and which, rightly or wrongly, she blamed on the salmon she had eaten at the Royal Academy annual dinner in April 1969.

At the end of September she returned home, to 'my darling old slum',[33] ready to face a busy month. All the invitations she had received to read her poems had been accepted if dates could be fixed within October, leaving her free to return to Molly in November for another long stay. Buckfast had been transformed for her by the arrival of the Everetts. 'It is such heaven having you next door,' she told them, soon after returning home.[34] After the distant politeness of her neighbours at Palmers Green, the Everetts' neighbourliness threw into contrast her isolated existence at Avondale Road. Before a week had passed she was writing again to Molly Everett. 'I do miss you too and all the heavenly ins and outs and to-ing and fro-ing.'[35] Meanwhile poetry readings took her to Cambridge, Newcastle, Brighton and Stroud, making her feel like a parcel in transit; 'I feel rather more scattered than usual,' she told Audrey Insch.[36] At Stroud her reading was a part of a festival, after which she stayed two or three days in the home of its director, the poet and novelist Bryan Guinness, Lord Moyne. She inscribed her poem 'Herzie' in his visitor's book, having been reminded of the trolls in this poem, who steal away a human child, by the sight of two trees in the garden. Exhausted by her performance at Stroud she spent the following day in bed, the writer Paul Jennings seizing the opportunity to tape-record her talking, reciting and singing her poems. 'It is extraordinary going on and on with all this reading,' Stevie told Molly Everett, 'and getting kisses and bouquets and red carpets, it is like a dream specially when I come home again.'[37] She was by now anxious to return to Devon but had still to give two more readings, one in Bromley at Stockwell College of Education, at the request of Audrey Insch, and one at North London Collegiate. She was also waiting for a hospital day visit, in connection with irritable bowel syndrome and intermittent aphasia. Neither prevented her from making a two-and-a-half minute recording of three poems for 'Dial-a-Poem', lunching with Jonathan Williams at the Old Cheshire Cheese in Wine Office Court and giving an interview to Kay Dick which later formed part of her book, *Ivy and Stevie*. Before leaving for Devon Stevie accepted an invitation to become a Fellow of the Royal Society of Literature.

The very last reading that she gave was at Dartington, in the Roundhouse attached to the Barn Theatre. The small room was packed, an overflow of students sitting on the stairs. The occasion was sad and witty, at times savage and moving. Before this she gave readings at Plymouth and North Devon, at the Lobster Pot in Instow. The second of these was organized by John Barnard who was warned that Stevie would need to rest beforehand. She was still suffering spells of giddiness: 'I sort of fade away and the doctors as usual try *lots* of pills, I suppose hoping one will be right.'[38] Barnard took the precaution of offering her a glass 'or two' of sherry beforehand. 'I thought the one "or two" was a particularly nice touch,' Stevie gossiped with Molly Everett, adding, 'should we say "we don't ektually maynd *any* number"?'[39] Peter Kiddle, a young poet and lecturer at Dartington, drove Stevie to Instow and elsewhere on other occasions, and on these drives got much good advice from Stevie. She directed him to Donne's sermons and those of Lancelot Andrewes as well as the lesser known metaphysical poets, advising him to get *The Oxford Book of Metaphysical Verse* for its excellent range. She also extolled Eliot's essay, 'Tradition and the Individual Talent', declared Allen Ginsberg 'hot air' and complained that young poets did not read enough. To Kiddle's friend, the poet Nic Cottis, who had organized the reading in aid of Shelter at Totnes Castle, Stevie expressed a liking for poetry that comes to the lips like conversation, with seeming naturalness, and preferred happy findings of words to literary searchings. Both Kiddle and Cottis were told they did not pay enough attention to rhyme and that their rhythms were slack. Byron's *Don Juan* and Browning's *A Grammarian's Funeral* were advised by Stevie as a remedy and they discovered she knew large chunks of them by heart.

That winter she kept in touch with her publisher John Guest who was planning to reprint *Selected Poems* and *The Frog Prince* in one volume in two years' time. Owing to his encouragement she was also collecting together recent poems for a new collection, the posthumously published *Scorpion and Other Poems*. Over the years Stevie had got to know Guest well and enjoyed his company. In conversation her amusement was sometimes so great that, putting her hands over her face, she rocked backwards and forwards. For Guest, Stevie's most striking aspect was her 'almost permanently anxious look that quickly broke into laughter'.[40] He also saw that her laughter was sometimes very close to tears and that even when laughing her eyes remained wild-looking and sad. 'I hope you are really marvellously well dear John,' Stevie wrote from Buckfast in November, 'and skipping round in a delightful and well-judged and productive way profit-wise *re* publishing.'[41]

That Christmas Stevie sent a postcard of Monet's untroubled 'The Beach at Trouville', in the National Gallery, to Audrey Insch. 'There is not room for horrid *human* details,' she ends, after a brief catalogue of misfortunes, chief of which concerned Molly's cat, Ming.[42] What she omitted to say was that she herself was far from well. One evening, while round at the Everetts', she had almost passed out where she was sitting and when she recovered could not speak properly or finish her sentences. The Everetts and the local GP, Dr Wigram, thought she had had an attack of *petit mal.* She continued to suffer fainting fits and aphasia and on 27 December wrote to her doctor in Palmers Green, James Curley:

'Dr Wigram is wrong when he says the loss of word-control is in the category of "er er" & a slight stammer before being able to go on. It (in my case) is almost a mental black out. One instance I remember – I tried to say to Don [Everett] or someone that I could not find the word I wanted. But instead of "word" I said "milk" first & then "snow". *I refuse to agree that this is in the category of "er er er" i.e. hesitation & a slight stammer.'*[43]

Perhaps hoping to aid diagnosis, Stevie began recording her symptoms in a school exercise book. The fainting, intermittent aphasia and bowel problems continued.

'I go on getting these faint-fits. They only last a few minutes but they are horrible. The mind has a black out but *remembers* forgetting wh. is worse than just forgetting – it is like lots of familiar things getting faster and faster rushing past. Horrid. I sit down and put my head on the table to be low down. All the time there is a ghastly sort of metallic taste coming up very deep from my ghastly tum. Also in my head there is a two-note continuous sound say top *doh* down to la (or is it spelt "lah") I am exhausted practically the whole time. What is the matter? Well, and what would be a good idea to take? I can't say *any* of the innumerable pills, medicines (liquid) etc *is.* Terry [Kilmartin] said in his letter, taking my poem "The Stroke", "Go easy on those pills." Shall I tell Dr Wigram and Dr Moore that the *Observer* has told me not to take what they gave me?? I expect they will recommend the *Sunday Times* as *better.* Go on taking the pills and the *S. Times,* ha ha . . .

Jan 1st 1971. These fits are different now in this way: They come more frequently. In bed at night sometimes when I am awake sometimes in my sleep . . . The fits are like this: they flood my mouth taste and mind with what is like a wash back from a drain pool. Or in me from where it came below.'

After this the purpose of the notebook alters: no longer does it record symptoms of her illness but instead drafts of her poem 'Come Death' appear, its first line emerging naturally from the preceding material:

I feel ill. What can the matter be?[44]

On 6 January a neighbour, Margaret Miller, called in at the bungalow at about eleven o'clock in the morning. She found Stevie sitting at one end of Molly's dining-room table looking extremely ill. 'In front of her was a plate of cold, boiled potatoes and a glass of beer or cider. She was eating bits of cold potato with the aid of her fingers and a knife, drinking gulps of beer and continually repeating, "Oh! I do feel ill." Molly was staring down at her and so was one of the Buckfast monks who had also dropped in to visit Molly and who was propped against the wall by the window . . . it seemed like a terrible stage set . . . utterly unreal.'[45]

Stevie grew worse as the day progressed and was seen by a doctor at ten in the evening. Shortly before midnight an ambulance arrived to take her to Torbay Hospital in Torquay, Molly Everett travelled with her. Molly Smith, not realizing how ill her sister was, thought Stevie was suffering from a stomach disorder combined with a nervous breakdown. At Torbay she was kept in a medical ward for just over a week and given various tests. She could speak, but with difficulty. 'Needles! needles!' she jerked out to Molly Everett, expressing her hatred of injections. Even in a state of disintegration, she retained her humour and an unearthly felicity in her choice of words. 'Lots of love -- my dear,' she ended a letter to John Guest written from hospital, 'I've had lots of every sort you can think of trip-torgen, high hyppers with streen pincers, & etc. & etc. lasting now for 6 days!'[46] As a result of an abnormality appearing in an X-ray, she was moved to the Neurosurgery department in Freedom Fields Hospital, Plymouth, where a biopsy was performed. The tumour it revealed was too advanced to make surgery possible and Stevie was returned to an annex of Torbay Hospital.

Friends visited, among them Anna Browne, Margaret Branch, George and Olga Lawrence and Sir John and Lady Lawrence. The last brought Inez Holden to whom Stevie was able to say, 'I love you', acknowledging a long if imperfect and complex friendship. Helen Fowler found Stevie only able to utter short phrases, neutral conversational openings, which her hearers had no alternative but to ignore: 'The beginnings were so unstressed, so casual. It was as if on the surface of her mind, the detritus of a hundred patterning conversations lay fragmented. Although one leaned eagerly forward each time she began a phrase, one knew that it led nowhere, promised nothing. The nearest to the old Stevie was when once she said, "Hey ho" in a little mocking, sighing way as she always did. Hey ho, indeed.'[47]

On his second visit her executor, James MacGibbon, saw that she would be more comfortable if moved from the sad geriatric ward in Torquay to the cottage hospital at Ashburton. This was easily arranged and Stevie was again in the care of Dr Wigram, the sophisticated Buckfastleigh GP who had been treating her before she went into hospital. Further, MacGibbon had to get power of attorney and this required a doctor's certificate stating that Stevie had complete understanding. Fortunately, in the event, when he and his wife had first visited her Jean MacGibbon had told her that Olivia Manning had telephoned the evening before and her response to the news of Stevie's illness (their relations were cool at the time) was: 'Well, if she's really ill, we'll have to let bygones be bygones.' Stevie, hugely amused, had thrown back her head and laughed. On being told this Dr Wigram took the point and granted the necessary certificate.

Friends found her in a one-bed ward at Ashburton with her head wrapped in a pink turban. Armide Oppé, who had never considered her good looking, was astonished on arriving to see how beautiful Stevie looked. Reminded of John Donne's death mask in St Paul's, James MacGibbon tried to arrange for photographs to be made of Stevie but Molly Smith disapproved and the idea had to be dropped. What Stevie had feared most on entering hospital was a loss of the ability to communicate, as an undated note to Molly Everett reveals: 'I long to die really unless my news of speech gets better. But last evening Dr Richardson told me I should not recover much if any at all.' Another note to Molly, asking for clothes, refers to 'my up to the thing called waist and to feet point' and is accompanied by a drawing of tights.[48]

Before long she became literally 'too far out' for her friends to reach her. She did not even utter the beginnings of sentences. 'This time there was nothing,' Helen Fowler has written of her last visit; 'not even, if one was stern on self-delusion, a gleam of recognition in the dark and still lovely eyes.' She and James MacGibbon took hold of Stevie's hands as they sat either side of the bed, as Helen Fowler goes on to describe.

'We talked to her, reminded her who we were. James was wonderful; kind, loving, patient. He talked to her as if she were listening attentively. He told her what a wonderful smile she had and that was what people remembered about her (for in a sudden illumination, she had smiled and it was like a flash of sun on a dark day), gave her affectionate messages from friends, talked perhaps of some broadcast she had made. The room was full of flowers; outside the window was the hospital garden, wintry still, sodden grass to the hedge and hardly discernible hills under a cloudy sky, inside was the hum of the hospital, voices, footsteps, trolleys wheeled about, dishes clattered. James stroked her cheek, I patted her hand. Suddenly she was restless, fidgety and then was racked with paroxysms of shaking, twisting, shuddering, joking, twitching. We held her in our arms, feeling the light, small body racked and shaken. It was like holding a flailing child in an excess of grief or tantrum, but worse, much worse, for the passion that shook her body was from outside her will. Our eyes met once or twice over her; I know that we were both hoping she would die then at this moment. Incredibly, it seemed, of course she didn't. A nurse brought a feeding cup of tea or orange juice and she had a few sips and lay back on the pillows. We re-arranged her scarf, held her hands again; talked again to her. There was so much to say and no way to say it.'[49]

Before Stevie reached this condition there were days when her speech was relatively free of confusion and blocks. One of these occurred at Torbay Hospital before her biopsy, when Molly Everett brought in 'Come Death' which she had typed at Stevie's request. Stevie sat up cross-legged on her bed and to the astonishment of her visitors and others in the ward performed it there and then without a mistake.

> I feel ill. What can the matter be?
> I'd ask God to have pity on me,
> But I turn to the one I know, and say:
> Come, Death, and carry me away.
>
> Ah me, sweet Death, you are the only god
> Who comes as a servant when he is called, you know,
> Listen then to this sound I make, it is sharp,
> Come Death. Do not be slow.

She read it again to Father Sebastian Wolfe when he visited, astonishing him with her fearless, welcoming attitude to death, an attitude he had rarely encountered even in those whose faith was strong. Inez Holden, in her obituary of Stevie, also recollected that on her visit to the hospital Stevie, though unable to sustain coherent conversation, indicated that she was not daunted by her approaching death.[50] When showing 'Come Death' to

James MacGibbon, Stevie encircled the word 'death', MacGibbon understanding from this that she wished him to obtain for her the means by which
to end her life. He did not do so, but he showed the poem with the encircled
word to Dr Wigram and thereafter Stevie was more and more heavily
sedated. Even before this, she seemed to Sister Hornabrook to be peaceful
in herself, perhaps at last finally disenchanted, for as she had written,
'only / In heaven's permission / Are creatures quiet / In their condition.'[51]
On 7 March she died.

One idea shaping Stevie's attitude to death was the familiar theme of
death as a lover. When Elisabeth Lutyens once suggested that meeting
death might be an anti-climax, Stevie replied, 'you sound rather as if you *had*
met him and found him not quite the dish I thought'.[52] More central to her
thoughts on death, however, was the belief in its finality, that 'in Death's
odder anarchy, / Our pattern will be broken all up'.[53] Death was a firm
dividing line and any attempt on the part of the living to probe the regions of
the dead aroused her distaste. When reviewing Rosamond Lehmann's *The
Swan in the Evening* Stevie dealt severely but equably with the author's
account of her communication with her deceased daughter:

'Miss Lehmann thinks that people who do not wish to traffic with the dead
are cold, careless or timid. They may be more full of love than she thinks.
For if you believe in God, you will let the dying go, glad that the pain of loss
is ours, not theirs. They have finished with the imperfections of human love,
its dark places of egoism, greed and idolatry. And, as even the new-born
baby, with a full span of life ahead, cannot really be said to have to live very
long, is it asking too much that we should love our dead and leave them
alone, waiting for our own deaths to know what it is all about? Or to know
nothing ever again.'[54]

Again, this stance is not wholly characteristic for there are other instances in
which Stevie's concept of death is positively buoyant, death 'bringing
extreme happiness, opening gates, setting us free'.[55] In addition, it was
frequently linked in her mind with the sea. On reaching the low sandhills,
which evoke the Norfolk coastline at Blakeney, and the great seas beyond,
Eugenia, in 'The Ass', having journeyed through evil reaches extreme
happiness. As a parable of life, the poem hints at the transformation death
may bring.

> Oh my poor ass
> To run so quickly as if coming home
> To where the great waves crash.

Now she is gone. I thought
Into her tomb.

Yet often as I walk that sandy shore
And think the seas
Have long since combed her out that lies
Beneath, I hear the sweet ass singing still with joy as if
She had won some great prize, as if
All her best wish had come to pass.

Stevie Smith's published works

FICTION

Novel on Yellow Paper, Jonathan Cape, 1936; William Morrow, New York, 1937; Virago, 1980. Reprinted as *Work It Out for Yourself*, Popular Library Edition, New York, 1976

Over the Frontier, Jonathan Cape, 1938; Virago, 1980

The Holiday, Chapman & Hall, 1949; Virago, 1979

POETRY

A Good Time Was Had By All, Jonathan Cape, 1937

Tender Only To One, Jonathan Cape, 1938

Mother, What Is Man?, Jonathan Cape, 1942

Harold's Leap, Chapman & Hall, 1950

Not Waving but Drowning, André Deutsch, 1957

Selected Poems, Longmans, 1962; New Directions, 1963: includes 17 previously uncollected poems

The Frog Prince, Longmans, 1966: includes 69 previously uncollected poems

The Best Beast, Alfred Knopf, New York, 1969

Two In One, Longman, 1971: reprint of *Selected Poems*, 1962 and *The Frog Prince*

Scorpion and Other Poems, Longman, 1972: Introduction by Patric Dickinson

Collected Poems, Allen Lane, 1975: Introduction by James MacGibbon

Selected Poems, ed. James MacGibbon, Penguin, 1978

EDITIONS

Some Are More Human Than Others: A Sketch-Book, Gabberbocchus, 1958

Cats in Colour, Batsford, 1959

The Batsford Book of Children's Verse, Batsford, 1970; reissued as *Favourite Verse*, Chancellor Press, 1984

COLLECTIONS

Me Again: Uncollected Writings of Stevie Smith, ed. Jack Barbera and William McBrien, Virago, 1981: Preface by James MacGibbon

Notes

INTRODUCTION
1. See Martin Pumphrey, 'Play, fantasy, and strange laughter: Stevie Smith's uncomfortable poetry', *Critical Quarterly*, Autumn 1986, vol. 28, no. 3
2. See Arthur C. Rankin, *The Poetry of Stevie Smith: 'Little Girl Lost'*, Colin Smythe, Gerrards Cross, Bucks, 1985
3. See Jan Montefiore, *Feminism and Poetry: Language, Experience, Identity in Women's Writing*, Pandora, London, 1987, pp. 39, 43–9
4. Martin Pumphrey, op. cit.
5. *The Poet Speaks*, ed. Peter Orr, Routledge & Kegan Paul, London, 1966, p. 226
6. Christopher Ricks, *The Force of Poetry*, Clarendon Press, Oxford, 1984, pp. 246–7
7. *Listener*, 25 September 1975
8. *Stevie Smith: A Selection*, ed. Hermione Lee, Faber & Faber, London, 1983, p. 21
9. Stevie Smith to Hans Häusermann, 19 August 1959, U of N
10. Michael Schmidt, *A Readers Guide to Fifty Modern British Poets*, Heinemann, London, 1979, p. 203.
11. *Listener*, 4 November 1965
12. Martin Pumphrey, op. cit.
13. Adrienne Rich, *Of Woman Born: Motherhood as Experience and Institution*, Virago, London 1975, p. 16
14. *John O'London's Weekly*, 23 July 1949
15. Georgia O'Keeffe, *Georgia O'Keeffe*, The Viking Press, New York, 1976, unpaginated.

1 From Hull to Palmers Green
1. SS to Peter Orr, 16 November 1964: British Council Archives
2. Seamus Heaney, *Preoccupations: Selected Prose 1968–1978*, Faber & Faber, London, 1980, p. 200
3. OTF: 66
4. TH: 188
5. *Listener*, 10 March 1960
6. CP: 390
7. Ethel Smith's birthday book: U of T
8. TH: 37
9. TH: 39
10. TH: 38
11. NYP: 74

12. NYP: 75
13. Kay Dick, *Ivy and Stevie*, (1971), Allison & Busby, London, 1983, p. 64
14. MS notes made by Helen Fowler in conversation with Molly Smith on 14 April 1971. In possession of Helen Fowler.
15. Midland Bank Group Archives (y60/2)
16. See note 14
17. *Ivy and Stevie*, p. 65
18. See note 14
19. *Ivy and Stevie*, p. 65
20. NYP: 76
21. Ibid.
22. Molly Smith's autograph album: U of T
23. OTF: 36
24. TH: 38
25. MA: 83
26. Thomas Burke, *The Outer Circle, Rambles in Remote London*, Allen & Unwin, London, 1921, pp. 129–30
27. MA: 87
28. MA: 84
29. MA: 102
30. MA: 84
31. 'Book of Verse: Thomas Hood', transmitted Eastern Services, 8 June 1946: BBC WA.
32. MA: 102
33. MA: 128
34. MA: 101
35. MA: 99
36. CP: 32
37. MA: 98–9
38. TH: 28
39. TH: 29
40. C. Smith to SS, 17 August 1908: U of T
41. NYP: 156
42. SS to Hans Häusermann, 28 July 1958: U of N
43. NYP: 156
44. Interview with John Horder, *Guardian*, 7 June 1965
45. *Palmers Green High School*, pamphlet published in 1955 on the occasion of the school's fiftieth anniversary.
46. Ann Thwaite (ed.), *Allsorts*, Macmillan, London, 1969, p. 99
47. As listed in the above

48. *Queen*, 20 December 1961
49. TH: 29
50. NYP: 165
51. MS notes made by Helen Fowler in conversation with Molly Smith: H. Fowler
52. Codicil in possession of A. H. Davey, SS's solicitor.
53. CP: 248
54. 'How to read books', *Discovery and Romance for Girls and Boys*, Jonathan Cape, London, 1947, pp. 267–72
55. Ibid.
56. Ibid.
57. *Presenting Poetry: A Handbook for English Teachers*, ed. Thomas Blackburn, Methuen, London, 1966, p. 159
58. See note 54
59. See note 54
60. MA: 94
61. Printed in *The Palmers Green and Southgate Gazette*, 6 March 1931, p. 8
62. Stevie Smith, *Cats in Colour*, Batsford, London, 1959, p. 14
63. CP: 436

2 North London Collegiate

1. Phebe Snow's biographical outline of SS: P. Snow
2. Letter to the author, 5 January 1986
3. Alice M. Head, *It Could Never Have Happened*, Heinemann, London, 1939, p. 16
4. TH: 118
5. OTF: 83
6. Conversation with Miss Winifred Macdonald, sister of Margaret, 5 September 1985.
7. NYP: 137
8. MS of NYP: U of H
9. NYP: 170
10. NYP: 171
11. MA: 33–4
12. 'World of Books: Stevie Smith on Poetry', transmitted 23 December 1961: BBC WA
13. SS to Ethel Smith, 3 May 1916: U of T
14. Ethel Smith to SS., no date [1916]: PGP
15. Ibid.
16. NYP: 158
17. Molly Smith's 1919 diary: U of T
18. NYP: 226
19. MS notes made by Helen Fowler in conversation with Molly Smith: H. Fowler
20. Ibid.
21. Margaret Rolph, letter to the author, 20 May 1984
22. NYP: 173
23. NYP: 173–4

24. R. Meldrum to SS, 23 February 1919: PGP
25. NYP: 177
26. NYP: 228
27. Quoted in Evelyn Waugh, *Ronald Knox*, Chapman & Hall, London, 1959, p. 141
28. Ronald Knox, *A Spiritual Aeneid*, Longman & Co, London, 1918, p. 55
29. Thomas Corbishley, S. J., *Ronald Knox the Priest*, Sheed & Ward, London, 1964, p. 23
30. *Observer*, 8 May 1960
31. NYP: 179–80
32. *Spectator*, 12 September 1958
33. NYP: 174
34. *Gemini*, Spring 1959, p. 41
35. Florence Gibbons to SS, no date [early 1920s]: PGP
36. NYP: 175
37. NYP: 176
38. Conversation with the author
39. *Our Magazine*, No. 134, Vol. XLV, March 1920
40. SS to Hans Häusermann, 17 October 1957: U of N
41. J. I. Monkhouse to SS, 20 April 1937: PGP
42. Letter to the author, 9 December 1985
43. Letter to the author, 4 February 1986
44. MA: 94
45. *Observer*, 21 October 1956
46. NYP: 204
47. Notebook dated 1919: U of T
48. OTF: 92–3
49. *Guardian*, 7 June 1965

3 Bonded Liberty

1. TH: 61
2. SS to Denis Johnston, 4 September 1936: University of Dublin
3. Cancelled pages relating to NYP MS: PGP
4. Phebe Snow biographical outline: P. Snow
5. Ibid.
6. Letter to the author
7. OTF: 85
8. SS to Joan Robinson, no date [February 1939]: KCC
9. OTF: 40
10. NYP: 56
11. OTF: 39
12. NYP: 16
13. NYP: 25
14. SS to Hans Häusermann, 15 August 1958: U of N
15. SS to Hans Häusermann, 17 October 1957: U of N

16. Both now in the Special Collection, U of
T
17. OTF: 121–2
18. Osbert Burdett, *The Beardsley Period. An
Essay in Perspective*, John Lane, London, 1925,
pp. 267–8
19. Ibid., pp. 289–90
20. MA: 74 ff.
21. NYP: 76–7
22. NYP: 64–5
23. Kay Dick, *Ivy and Stevie*, p. 69
24. Florence Gibbons to SS, no date
[c.1924]: PGP
25. Letter to the author, 9 December 1985
26. NYP: 107
27. NYP: 108
28. Gertrude Wirth to SS, no date: PGP
29. Edith Raven-Hart to SS, 10 February
1919: PGP
30. Now, with the rest of SS's library, in the
Special Collection, U of T
31. NYP: 25
32. Conversation with Jonathan Williams,
published in *Parnassus*, Spring/Summer 1974
33. 'Poet's Choice', 2 December 1965: BBC
WA
34. *Tribune*, 28 November 1947
35. 'World of Books', transmitted 23
December 1961: BBC WA
36. MA: 244–5
37. OTF: 32

4 Dear Karl

1. Rosemary Cooper to the author,
interview.
2. NYP: 187
3. NYP: 54–5
4. NYP: 56
5. NYP: 10
6. NYP: 10–11
7. NYP: 9
8. NYP: 11
9. NYP: 60
10. NYP: 62–3
11. CP: 33
12. Letter to the author, 31 December 1985
13. Reading Notebook 1924–27: U of T
14. Ibid.
15. OTF: 46
16. Notes made by Helen Fowler in
conversation with Molly Smith
17. MA: 157
18. Preliminary draft of 'Some Impediments
to Christian Commitment', MS: U of T
19. *The Book of Job*, quoted in Stevie's *The
Batsford Book of Children's Verse* (1970)
20. Preliminary draft of 'Some Impediments
to Christian Commitment', MS: U of T

21. *The Poet Speaks*, ed. Peter Orr,
Routledge & Kegan Paul, London, 1966, p.
228
22. Interview with Jonathan Williams,
Parnassus, Spring/Summer 1974
23. *Observer*, 15 March 1964
24. NYP: 200
25. NYP: 128
26. NYP: 129–30
27. *Spectator*, 10 June 1960
28. *Time and Tide*, 11 January 1958
29. Karl Eckinger to Elfriede Thurner, 15
December 1928: Judith Maravelias-Eckinger.
30. Karl Eckinger to Elfriede Thurner, 12
December 1928: Judith Maravelias-Eckinger.
31. Karl Eckinger to Elfriede Thurner, 24
December 1928: Judith Maravelias-Eckinger.
32. Reggie Smith to the author, interview.
33. NYP: 30
34. NYP: 36
35. NYP: 35–6
36. Karl Eckinger to Elfriede Thurner, 12
February 1929: Judith Maravelias-Eckinger.
37. Karl Eckinger to Elfriede Thurner, 22
February 1929: Judith Maravelias-Eckinger.
38. NYP: 47
39. NYP: 47
40. NYP: 48
41. SS to Hans Häusermann, 17 October
1957: U of N
42. *Queen*, 5 May 1965
43. NYP: 100–01
44. SS to Molly Smith, 5 September 1929: U
of T
45. SS to Molly Smith, 13 September 1929:
U of T
46. Molly Smith to SS, 14 August 1929:
U of T
47. SS to Molly Smith, 12 July 1931: U of T
48. NYP: 100
49. SS to Madge Spear, 16 July 1931: U of T
50. NYP: 48
51. SS to Hans Häusermann, 17 October
1957: U of N
52. NYP: 46
53. Typewritten notes: U of T
54. NYP: 103
55. Kay Dick, *Ivy and Stevie*, p. 68
56. NYP: 49

5 As tiger on padded paw

1. Curtis Brown Reader's Report: PGP
2. NYP: 28
3. 'Thomas Hood', transmitted 8 June 1946
on the BBC Eastern Service and from which
the quotations on Hood are taken: BBC WA

4. Curtis Brown Reader's Report: PGP

5. Questionnaire on her poetry, written in 1952: Phebe Snow

6. Stevie's copy of *The Muse in Chains* is in the Special Collection, University of Tulsa

7. *Observer*, 16 June 1965

8. *Observer*, 18 August 1957

9. 'World of Books', radio programme transmitted 18 March 1961: BBC WA

10. *Observer*, 23 February 1958

11. 'World of Books', 28 January 1963: British Institute of Recorded Sound

12. 'Too Tired for Words', radio programme transmitted 4 March 1957: BBC WA

13. OTF: 88

14. SS to Rowland Watson, 4 December 1956: University of Birmingham

15. OTF: 89

16. OTF: 92

17. Barbara Flower to SS, 29 October 1940: PGP

18. Ibid.

19. H. G. Hilton to SS, 2 April 1930: U of T

20. All remarks made in interviews, except for Joan Prideaux's: letter to the author, 31 December 1985

21. NYP: 223

22. NYP: 234

23. OTF: 41

24. Seamus Heaney, *Preoccupations: Selected Prose 1968–1978*, p. 200

25. NYP: 146

26. NYP: 147

27. NYP: 149

28. NYP: 150–1

29. NYP: 154

30. NYP: 155

31. NYP: 206

32. NYP: 208

33. Typescript: U of T

34. MS of NYP: U of H

35. NYP: 220; MS: U of H

36. NYP: 219–21

37. OTF: 114

38. NYP: 223

39. NYP: 208

40. NYP: 209

41. NYP: 197

42. NYP: 20

43. NYP: 66

44. NYP: 230–1

45. NYP: 229

46. SS to Hans Häusermann, 17 December 1958: U of N

47. Anthony Powell, *To Keep the Ball Rolling: The Memoirs of Anthony Powell. Volume II Messengers of Day*, Heinemann, London, 1978, p. 24

48. Sally Chilver, interview with the author, 13 March 1984

49. Inez Holden, *It Was Different at the Time*, John Lane, London, 1943, p. 9

50. Ibid., p. 20

51. TH: 55

52. TH: 22–3

53. 'Let me tell you before I forget . . .', unpublished autobiographical fragment: Olivia Manning's executors

54. Olivia Manning, *The Doves of Venus* (1955), Virago edition, London, 1984, p. 122

55. *The Doves of Venus*, p. 124

56. Walter Allen, *As I Walked Down New Grub Street*, Heinemann, London, 1981, p. 116

57. Walter Allen, interview with the author, 24 July 1985

58. Olivia Manning to SS, no date [1939]: PGP

59. Louis MacNeice, *The Strings are False*, Faber & Faber, London, 1965, p. 210

60. Allen, *As I Walked Down New Grub Street*, p. 116

61. Olivia Manning to SS, 8 September 1939: PGP

62. Elisabeth Lutyens, *A Goldfish Bowl*, Cassell, London, 1972, p. 143

63. Olivia Manning to SS, 25 September 1942: PGP

6 *Novel on Yellow Paper*

1. SS to Madge Spear, 26 July 1935: U of T

2. OTF: 94–5

3. OTF: 120

4. SS to Hans Häusermann, 17 October 1957: U of N

5. Ian Parsons to SS, 14 August 1935: PGP

6. Ian Parsons to SS, 29 August 1935, copy: U of R

7. SS to John Lehmann, 19 May 1936: University of Texas

8. 'What I Hear' by Audax, *John O'London's Weekly*, 11 February 1938

9. In conversation with Helen Fowler.

10. Ian Parsons to SS, 9 January 1936: U of R

11. NYP: 39

12. NYP: 159

13. NYP: 39

14. Reader's report signed O.W. and J.M.D. on 'Pompey Casmilus', Jonathan Cape Archives: U of R

15. Ian Parsons to SS, 12 February 1936: PGP

16. Hamish Miles to SS, 13 December 1935: PGP

17. Hamish Miles to SS, 17 December 1935: PGP

18. Hamish Miles to SS, 2 March 1936: PGP
19. Unpublished memoir on Stevie Smith: H. Fowler.
20. Virginia Woolf, *The Common Reader*, Hogarth Press, London, 1925
21. Quoted by Woolf in a letter to Vita Sackville-West, in *Leave the Letters Till We're Dead. The Letters of Virginia Woolf*, ed. Nigel Nicolson, Hogarth Press, London, 1980, p. 75
22. MS of TH: U of T
23. Reading Notebook 1928–30: U of T
24. NYP: 115
25. MA: 148
26. Reading Notebook 1928–30: U of T
27. MA: 255
28. OTF: 87
29. NYP: 212
30. NYP: 19
31. NYP: 180
32. NYP: 121
33. Geoffrey Dennis, *Harvest in Poland*, Heinemann, London, 1925, p. 97
34. Neville Braybrooke, 'Stevie Smith's most treasured book', *The Tablet*, 7 November 1987
35. NYP: 104
36. NYP: 107
37. NYP: 38
38. NYP: 78
39. MA: 116
40. NYP: 61
41. *Nova*, November 1969
42. SS to John Lehmann, 19 May 1936: University of Texas
43. *New Statesman and Nation*, 5 September 1936
44. *John O'London's Weekly*, 3 October 1936
45. *Listener*, 16 September 1936
46. Kenneth Clark to SS, no date [1936]: PGP
47. Clive Bell to SS, 11 September 1936: PGP
48. SS to Clive Bell, 16 September 1936: King's College, Cambridge
49. SS to Rupert Hart-Davis, no date [late 1936?]: R. Hart-Davis
50. SS to Rupert Hart-Davis, 3 November 1936: R. Hart-Davis
51. *Parnassus*, Spring/Summer 1974
52. OTF: 108
53. OTF: 25
54. A discussion of her use of this title can be found in Jack Barbera's 'Poetic Intention and Stevie Smith', MLA convention paper, 1986, as yet unpublished.
55. SS to Rupert Hart-Davis, no date [October 1936]: R. Hart-Davis

56. *Observer*, 7 July 1963
57. SS to Rupert Hart-Davis, no date, though internal evidence supplies early October 1936: R. Hart-Davis
58. *London Mercury*, May 1937
59. John Simon, 'The Poems of Stevie Smith', *Canto*, I, Spring 1977
60. Humbert Wolfe, *Dialogues and Monologues*, Gollancz, London, 1928, p. 54
61. *Granta*, 5 May 1937
62. SS to Naomi Mitchison, no date [1937]: National Library of Scotland
63. Naomi Mitchison to SS, no date [c. 1937–38]: PGP
64. SS to Naomi Mitchison, no date [1937]: National Library of Scotland
65. Rupert Hart-Davis to SS, 7 April 1937: PGP
66. In author's possession
67. Unpublished monologues (untitled): King's College, Cambridge
68. Lydia Lopokova to SS, no date: PGP
69. John Hayward to SS, 14 September 1936: PGP
70. John Hayward to R. Lehmann, 2 October 1936: PGP
71. SS to John Hayward, 16 September 1936: King's College, Cambridge
72. Interview with Armide Oppé
73. Quoted in C. H. Rolph, *Kingsley: The Life, Letters and Diaries of Kingsley Martin*, Gollancz, London, 1973, pp. 220–1
74. G. W. Stonier to the author, 30 July 1984
75. Ibid.
76. G. W. Stonier to the author, 18 September 1984
77. G. W. Stonier to the author, 27 August 1984
78. MA: 261
79. MA: 262
80. NYP: 90–1
81. NYP: 225
82. *Now and Then*, Winter 1937
83. Naomi Mitchison, *You May Well Ask*, Gollancz, London, 1979, p. 94
84. MA: 259
85. MA: 258
86. MA: 257

7 The Power of Cruelty

1. Inscribed in Lord Moyne's copy of *Novel on Yellow Paper*: Lord Moyne
2. Roger Senhouse's copy of *Over the Frontier*: U of T
3. OTF: 246
4. Victoria Glendinning, *Times Literary Supplement*, 18 January 1980
5. Reading Notebooks 1928–30: U of T

6. Now at U of T
7. OTF: 16
8. OTF: 17–18
9. CP: 516
10. OTF: 163
11. OTF: 29
12. OTF: 22
13. SS to Rupert Hart-Davis, no date [October 1936]: R. Hart-Davis
14. OTF: 157
15. MA: 270–1
16. *London Mercury*, April 1938
17. OTF: 256
18. MA: 257
19. OTF: 257
20. OTF: 28
21. OTF: 108
22. OTF: 94
23. OTF: 54
24. OTF: 56
25. OTF: 58
26. NYP: 136
27. OTF: 62
28. *Observer*, 4 August 1957
29. MA: 255
30. *Neue Zürcher Zeitung*, 15 December 1957
31. OTF: 135
32. OTF: 220
33. OTF: 271
34. OTF: 272
35. OTF: 210
36. *Listener*, 19 January 1938
37. OTF: 159
38. OTF: 199–200
39. MA: 257–8
40. SS to Rupert Hart-Davis, 24 August 1937: R. Hart-Davis
41. MA: 263–4
42. David Garnett to SS, 21 June 1939: PGP
43. SS to David Garnett, 1 June 1949: Richard Garnett
44. MA: 105. A collection of SS's 'Mosaic' articles for *Eve's Journal* can be found in the University of Hull library.
45. Jane Stockwood, interview with the author
46. Rosamond Lehmann to SS, no date [1937]: PGP
47. Rosamond Lehmann to SS, 19 January [1938]: PGP
48. Rosamond Lehmann to SS, no date [1938]: PGP
49. Rosamond Lehmann to SS, 12 February [1938]: PGP
50. SS to Denis Johnston, 4 July 1938: University of Dublin
51. MA: 266

52. Rosamond Lehmann to SS, 24 November 1938: PGP
53. SS to R. A. Scott-James, 14 October 1937: University of Texas
54. SS to Rupert Hart-Davis, 4 August 1938: R. Hart-Davis
55. MA: 266
56. OTF: 50
57. *Daily Telegraph*, 3 April 1958
58. W. B. Yeats, *Selected Criticism*, (ed. A. Norman Jeffares), Macmillan & Co., London, 1964, p. 79

8 Wartime Friendships

1. SS to Storm Jameson, 5 January 1939: University of Texas
2. Storm Jameson to R. Atkinson, 6 January 1938: PGP
3. Storm Jameson to SS, 3 January 1939: PGP
4. MA: 275
5. MA: 271
6. SS to Joan Robinson, no date [February 1939]: King's College, Cambridge.
7. SS to Joan Robinson, no date [February 1939]: King's College, Cambridge.
8. TH: 28
9. TH: 27
10. SS to Joan Robinson, no date [February 1939]: King's College, Cambridge.
11. *Among You Taking Notes. The Wartime Diary of Naomi Mitchison, 1939–45*, ed. D. Sheridan, Gollancz, London, 1985, pp. 115–16
12. SS to Rachel Marshall, 18 April 1941: Kitty Hermges
13. Inez Holden's diary, 7 December 1941: Celia Goodman
14. TH: 57
15. TH: 55–6
16. Inez Holden's diary, April 1941: Celia Goodman
17. Inez Holden's diary, 6 June [1945]: Celia Goodman
18. SS to Hans Häusermann, 6 April 1959: U of N
19. This and the above letter from Stevie to Orwell, as well as his reply to the first, are quoted in full in Bernard Crick, *George Orwell: A Life*, Secker & Warburg, London, [1980], revised ed. 1981, p. 288
20. SS to John Hayward, 19 November 1942: King's College, Cambridge
21. TH: 69
22. Bernard Crick, *George Orwell: A Life*, p. 289
23. *Other Voices*, 28 January 1955
24. Olivia Manning, *The Doves of Venus*, p. 126

25. *Daily Mail*, 10 September 1959
26. Interview with Kay Dick, 17 March 1984
27. TH: 49–50
28. Essay on Death sent to the *Observer* and returned unused (18 September 1968): PGP
29. T. R. Fyvel, *George Orwell*, Weidenfeld & Nicolson, London, 1982, p. 127
30. Ibid., p. 142
31. Susan Watson, in *Remembering Orwell*, compiled by Stephen Wadhams, Penguin, London, 1984, p. 161
32. TH: 93
33. TH: 97–8
34. OTF: 95
35. TH: 94
36. TH: 95
37. TH: 96
38. Inez Holden's diary, 19 November 1941: Celia Goodman
39. TH: 14
40. TH: 13
41. Joe Ackerley to SS, 2 January 1940: PGP
42. Note in Rupert Hart-Davis's possession
43. MA: 281–2
44. Naomi Mitchison to SS, no date [1941/2]: PGP
45. SS to John Hayward, 2 January 1942: King's College, Cambridge
46. CP: 177
47. Now U of T
48. TH: 183
49. CP: 165–6
50. MS notes: U of T
51. *Daily Telegraph*, 1 January 1943
52. SS to John Hayward, 10 September 1943: King's College, Cambridge
53. Polly Hill to the author, 13 March 1985
54. Cecily Mackworth, *Ends of the World* Carcanet, Manchester, 1987, pp. 111–12
55. MA: 278
56. *Among You Taking Notes*, p. 187
57. Unpublished memoir on Stevie Smith: Helen Fowler
58. Ibid.
59. *Listener*, 25 May 1967
60. *London Mercury*, June 1938

9 Fits and Splinters

1. MA: 276
2. *Modern Woman*, November 1944
3. MA: 177
4. TH: 92
5. TH: 143
6. Quoted in Derek Stanford, *Inside the Forties: Literary Memoirs 1937–57*, Sidgwick & Jackson, London, 1977, p. 95
7. Ibid. p. 95
8. Now in Washington University Libraries
9. SS to Kay Dick, 28 June 1943: WUL
10. SS to John Hayward, 19 August 1942: King's College, Cambridge
11. *Bookman*, June 1949, Vol. 3, No. 9
12. MA: 285
13. SS to John Hayward, 10 September 1943: King's College, Cambridge
14. MS of *The Holiday*: U of T
15. *John O'London's Weekly*, 22 July 1949
16. TH: 92
17. TH: 7
18. TH: 36, 62
19. TH: 53
20. *New Statesman*, 4 May 1979
21. TH: 130
22. TH: 117
23. MA: 285
24. TH: 143
25. MA: 274
26. John Cowper Powys, *The Pleasures of Literature*, Cassell & Co., London, 1938, p. 176
27. TH: 117
28. TH: 43
29. TH: 116
30. TH: 165
31. TH: 50
32. TH: 200
33. TH: 202
34. Aldous Huxley, *Music at Night and Other Essays*, Fountains Press, New York, 1931, p. 102
35. TH: 149
36. *John O'London's Weekly*, 29 August 1941
37. TH: 198
38. TH: 150
39. MA: 274
40. TH: 102
41. *The Nineteenth Century*, August 1949
42. *Britain Today*, October 1949
43. *Listener*, 11 August 1949
44. P. H. Newby, *The Novel 1945–50*, published for the British Council by Longman, Green, 1951, p. 22
45. SS to Hans Häusermann, 17 December 1957
46. Recorded conversation made 1963, published in *Parnassus*, Spring/Summer 1974
47. James Drawbell, *Time on My Hands*, Macdonald, London, 1968, p. 37
48. Madge Spear to SS, 13 May 1957: PGP
49. SS to Anthony Powell, 11 July 1949: Anthony Powell
50. TH: 27
51. MS of *The Holiday*: U of T
52. MA: 302
53. 'The Necessity of Not Believing', *Gemini*, Spring 1958, Vol. 2, No. 1
54. OTF: 29

55. Marguerite Yourcenar, *Alexis*, Aidan Ellis, London, 1984, Black Swan edition, 1985 introduction (unpaginated) and p. 27
56. Reading Notebook, 1924–28: U of T
57. Reading Notebook, 1928–30: U of T
58. *Spectator*, 16 October 1953
59. CP: 242
60. TH: 49
61. Ibid.
62. *Spectator*, 13 March 1959
63. OTF: 152
64. Paul Zweig, *Walt Whitman: The Making of a Poet*, Viking Press, New York, 1985, p. 195
65. Ten are reprinted in *Me Again*, the eleventh, 'Over-Dew' was incorporated into *The Holiday*.
66. *Spectator*, 10 July 1953
67. MA: 50–9
68. Conversation with Jonathan Miller, 30 August 1984
69. Jack Barbera and William McBrien, *Stevie: A Biography of Stevie Smith*, Heinemann, London, 1985, p. 159
70. Betty Miller to SS, no date: PGP
71. MA: 19
72. Ibid.

10 Madness and Correctitude

1. SS to Kingsley Martin, 6 March 1945: City University, London
2. SS to Kingsley Martin, 25 July 1945: City University, London
3. Naomi Mitchison to SS, no date [1942]: PGP
4. CP: 376
5. Oswell Blakeston to the author, 28 August 1984
6. *Modern Woman*, March 1947
7. *John O'London's Weekly*, 3 October 1947
8. Elisabeth Lutyens to SS, no date [late 1940s]: PGP
9. SS to Hans Häusermann, 6 April 1959: U of N
10. SS to Denis Johnston, 28 June 1937: University of Dublin
11. CP: 325–6
12. SS to Anna Kallin, no date: BBC WA
13. TH: 65
14. Interview with Reggie Smith
15. *John O'London's Weekly*, 13 December 1946
16. SS to Kay Dick, 3 March 1948: WUL
17. *World Review*, October 1951
18. *Spectator*, 18 September 1953
19. *Observer*, 23 October 1955
20. SS to Kay Dick, 8 December 1947: WUL
21. *The Windmill*, 1948, Vol. 10

22. *Evening Standard*, 3 December 1969
23. *Parnassus*, Spring/Summer 1974
24. From 'Tradition and the Individual Talent', reprinted in *Selected Prose of T. S. Eliot*, ed. Frank Kermode, Faber & Faber, London, 1975, p. 41
25. 'Books, Plays, Poems: Poems by Living Poets', BBC Home Service, transmitted 15 June 1966
26. SS to Daniel George, 9 February 1951: U of H
27. TH: 60
28. *Stand*, Vol. 13, No. 3, 1972
29. 'Poems and Drawings', transmitted 18 October 1951: BBC WA
30. In *London Guyed*, ed. William Kimber, Hutchinson & Co., London, 1938
31. CP: 294
32. 'Poems and Drawings', transmitted 21 July 1952: BBC WA
33. *Gemini*, Spring 1958, Vol. 2, No. 1
34. Fred Hoyle, *The Nature of the Universe*, Harper & Row, New York, 1950, pp. 14–15
35. *John O'London's Weekly*, 29 August 1941
36. TH: 124
37. J. C. Powys to SS, 30 September 1951: PGP
38. J. C. Powys to SS, 1 November 1951: PGP
39. SS to J. C. Powys, 5 November 1951: The National Library of Wales
40. SS to J. C. Powys, 11 July 1952: The National Library of Wales
41. *World Review*, August 1952
42. J. C. Powys to Mr White, 27 September 1952: PGP
43. SS to Rachel Marshall, 28 February 1944: Kitty Hermges
44. SS to Jack McDougall, 11 February 1949 (carbon copy): PGP
45. Frances Lobb to SS, 12 September 1947: PGP
46. Memo from D. F. Boyd, (Chief Producer, Talks Department) to H. N. Bentinck, 3 March 1949: BBC WA
47. Memo from Anna Kallin to D. F. Boyd, 29 March 1949: BBC WA
48. H. N. Bentinck to SS, 14 March 1949 (copy): BBC WA
49. SS to H. N. Bentinck, 15 March 1949: BBC WA
50. Becky Cocking to the author, undated letter
51. SS to Anna Kallin, 13 June 1949: BBC WA
52. Anna Kallin to SS, 14 June 1949: BBC WA
53. SS to Anna Kallin, 19 October 1951: BBC WA

54. SS to Anna Kallin, 4 June 1952: BBC WA
55. Anna Kallin's memo, attached to SS to A. Kallin, 3 December 1952: BBC WA
56. Talks Proposal form, 3 February 1953: BBC WA
57. SS to Jonathan Cape, 24 July 1950: U of R
58. Joan Prideaux to the author, 31 December 1985
59. Ruth Landes to the author
60. Unpublished memoir: Helen Fowler
61. MS: U of T
62. 'Books, Plays, Poems: Poems by Living Poets', BBC Home Service, transmitted 15 June 1966: BBC WA
63. *John O'London's Weekly*, 11 January 1946
64. OTF: 59
65. TH: 49
66. Winwood Reade, *The Martyrdom of Man*, London: Edinburgh (printed), 1872 p. 17: SS's copy U of T

11 Not quite right

1. SS to Naomi Mitchison, no date [c.1952–3]: National Library of Scotland.
2. SS to Kay Dick, 21 May 1953: WUL
3. *Time and Tide*, Vol. 34, 24 October 1953
4. *Maurice Collis: Diaries: 1949–1969*, ed. Louise Collis, Gollancz, London, 1977, p. 42
5. Jane Barraclough to the author, 16 April 1986
6. John Holmstrom to the author, 19 September 1985
7. SS to Betty Miller, 2 January 1953: Sarah Miller
8. MA: 294
9. Interview with Cecily Mackworth, 13 February 1986
10. MA: 295
11. SS to Kay Dick, 6 August 1953: WUL
12. SS to Rachel Marshall, no date [summer 1953]: Kitty Hermges
13. When published in *The Listener*, 31 March 1966, and subsequently in *The Frog Prince* this poem has 'body' instead of 'number' in the first line and omits the 'And' at the start of the eleventh line.
14. CP: 319. This poem must have been written on or before March 1952 as a manuscript of it, entitled 'St Anthony's Rose', was included in a letter to Naomi Mitchison dated 20 March 1952.
15. Unpublished questionnaire sent SS by Marjorie Boulton: M. Boulton
16. 'My Muse', as printed in *X. A Quarterly Review*, March 1966. This line, in all subsequent printings, was excised.

17. MS: U of T
18. *World Review*, January 1953
19. *John O'London's Weekly*, 28 November 1947
20. *World Review*, June 1952
21. *World Review*, July 1951
22. *World Review*, July 1952
23. *World Review*, October 1951
24. *World Review*, October 1952
25. *Spectator*, 10 September 1953
26. 'World of Books', BBC script, transmitted 18 March 1961: BBC WA
27. SS to Kay Dick, no date, [September 1953]: WUL
28. SS to Kay Dick, 24 September 1953: WUL
29. Notebook dated 1956: U of T
30. SS to Hans Häusermann, 10 December 1958: U of N
31. SS to Madge Spear, 18 August 1955: PGP
32. OTF: 66
33. CP: 562
34. OTF: 63
35. *Spectator*, 3 January 1958
36. 'The Necessity of Not Believing', *Gemini*, Spring 1958, Vol. 2, No. 1.
37. Interview, *Evening Standard*, 24 November 1960
38. CP: 260
39. *The Times*, 9 March 1971
40. Interview with John Horder, 'World of Books', transmitted 28 January 1963: British Institute of Recorded Sound.
41. *Daily Telegraph Magazine*, 1 October 1971
42. CP: 360
43. CP: 358
44. OTF: 120–1
45. Mervyn Horder to SS, 4 January 1955: PGP
46. SS to Diana Athill, undated: André Deutsch files.
47. CP: 368
48. Introduction to Christina Fitzgerald's *Mrs Killick's Luck*, Frederick Books, London, 1960, p. 9
49. *Listener*, 17 October 1957
50. *Punch*, 13 November 1957
51. *Daily Telegraph*, 4 October 1957
52. *Times Literary Supplement*, 4 October 1957
53. SS to Diana Athill, no date [autumn 1957]: André Deutsch files.
54. OTF: 66
55. MA: 246
56. SS to Hans Häusermann, 15 August 1958: U of N
57. Inez Holden to Hans Häusermann, 18 April 1958: Gertrud Häusermann

58. *H. W. Häusermann. Tributes, Assessments and a Bibliography*, ed. G. D. Zimmerman, Geneva, 1972, p. 30

59. SS to Hans Häusermann, 17 October 1957: U of N

60. SS to Hans Häusermann, 1 July 1959: U of N

61. SS to Hans Häusermann, 28 May 1958: U of N

62. *Daily Telegraph*, 12 December 1958

63. *Neue Zürcher Zeitung*, 16 August 1959

64. SS to Hans Häusermann, 19 August 1959

65. SS to John Guest, 8 January 1966: U of R

66. SS to Hans Häusermann, 24 July 1958: U of N

67. SS to Hans Häusermann, 14 November 1958: U of N

68. SS to Hans Häusermann, 12 December 1959: U of N

69. SS to Hans Häusermann, 24 July 1958: U of N

70. SS to Hans Häusermann, 15 August 1958: U of N

12 Fixed on God

1. SS to D. S. Carne-Ross, 13 January 1956: BBC WA

2. Kay Fuller, Listener's report: BBC WA

3. 'Man's' has been deliberately chosen, following a typewritten manuscript in The University of Tulsa Special Collection, and not 'men's' as in *Collected Poems*, p. 339.

4. Rachel Marshall to SS, 5 May [1956]: PGP

5. SS to Rachel Marshall, 8 May 1956: Kitty Hermges

6. SS to Rachel Marshall, 27 March 1958: Kitty Hermges

7. SS to Rachel Marshall, 20 March 1961: Kitty Hermges

8. Douglas Cleverdon to SS, 28 February 1958: BBC WA

9. SS to Douglas Cleverdon, 9 May 1959: D. Cleverdon

10. Audience Research Department report, 9 June 1959: BBC WA

11. SS to Anna Kallin, 21 October 1957: BBC WA

12. SS to Anna Kallin, 23 October 1957: BBC WA

13. Memorandum, 8 January 1958: BBC WA

14. Bishop Gore, *The Religion of the Church. As Presented in the Church of England*, A. R. Mowbray & Co., London, 1916, pp. 91–2

15. This and all following quotations in this paragraph, unless otherwise stated, are from 'The Necessity of Not Believing', *Gemini*, Spring 1958, Vol. 2, No. 1

16. Ibid.

.7. 'Woman's Hour', transmitted 16 February 1970: BBC WA

18. Never used by the *Observer*, it remains in their files and was posthumously published in *Me Again*.

19. 'World of Books', transmitted 28 January 1963: BBC Sound Archives.

20. MA: 160

21. *Gemini*, Spring 1959

22. *Gemini*, Summer 1959

23. *Tribune*, 10 January 1947

24. MA: 167

25. *Gemini*, Spring 1958

26. Ibid.

27. 'World of Books', transmitted 29 February 1964: BBC WA

28. SS to Lyn Newman, 20 April 1960: Margaret Newman

29. D. H. Lawrence, *Fantasia of the Unconscious*, Martin Secker, London, 1923, p. 91

30. *Listener*, 4 May 1967

31. MA: 199

32. *Daily Telegraph*, 2 June 1959

33. Thomas Blackburn, *Robert Browning. A Study of His Poetry*, Eyre & Spottiswoode, London, 1967, p. 85

34. Quoted in an interview, 'The Living Arts', 5 November 1965: National Sound Archives

35. 'Poems and Drawings', transmitted 18 October 1951: BBC WA

36. *Tribune*, 2 December 1947

37. MA: 153

38. CP: 388

39. CP: 517

40. *Listener*, 18 August 1966

41. *Listener*, 22 April 1965

42. Sir John Lawrence, interview with the author

43. 'Poems and Drawings', transmitted 21 July 1952: BBC WA

44. 'World of Books', transmitted 29 February 1964: BBC WA

45. J. C. Powys, *The Pleasures of Literature*, pp. 468–9

46. Unpublished essay on death: U of T

13 Frivolous and Vulnerable

1. SS to Rachel Marshall, no date [June 1958]: Kitty Hermges

2. SS to Rowland Watson, 5 July 1962: University of Birmingham

3. *Evening Standard*, 3 December 1966

4. Dr James Curley, interview with the author

5. SS to Rachel Marshall, 13 December 1964: Kitty Hermges

6. SS to Cyprian Blagden, 10 January 1961: U of R

7. Molly Smith to SS, 7 August 1962: PGP

8. SS to James Laughlin, 27 February 1966: J. Laughlin

9. MS: U of T

10. TH: 123

11. *Evening Standard*, 3 December 1969

12. Becky Cocking to the author, 15 July 1985

13. *Spectator*, 27 October 1961

14. MA: 307

15. *Listener*, 30 December 1965

16. Sir John Lawrence, interview with the author, 30 March 1984

17. Barbara Jones to Jonathan Williams, 17 November 1963: University of New York at Buffalo.

18. SS to Cyprian Blagden, 28 October 1960: U of R

19. SS to Anthony Thwaite: Anthony Thwaite

20. Lady Elizabeth Cavendish to the author, 1 September 1985

21. D. J. Enright, *Man is an Onion: Reviews and Essays*, Chatto & Windus, London, 1972, p. 137

22. Virginia Woolf, *The Common Reader*

23. *Spectator*, 3 January 1958

24. MA: 186–7

25. SS to Rachel Marshall, 13 December 1964: Kitty Hermges

26. *Observer*, 29 November 1964

27. Stevie Smith, *Cats in Colour*, 1959, p. 7

28. Thomas Blackburn to Cyprian Blagden, 16 May 1960: U of R

29. SS to Rowland Watson, 8 November 1960: University of Birmingham

30. SS to Cyprian Blagden, 22 August 1960: U of R

31. SS to Jocelyn Baines, 11 October 1961: U of R

32. SS to Cyprian Blagden, 18 January 1961: U of R

33. SS to Lyn Newman, 2 February 1961: Margaret Newman

34. SS to Cyprian Blagden, 1 February 1961: U of R

35. SS to Cyprian Blagden, 8 March 1961: U of R

36. SS to Rachel Marshall, 14 April 1961: Kitty Hermges

37. Madge Spear to SS, no date [1961]: PGP

38. MA: 229

39. SS to Jocelyn Baines, 11 October 1961: U of R

40. Interview with John Horder, 'World of Books', transmitted 1 April 1963: BBC WA

41. *London Magazine*, February 1962, p. 46

42. MA: 6

43. SS to Sylvia Plath, 22 November 1962: Smith College Library, Northampton, Massachusetts

44. *Daily Telegraph*, 22 March 1963

45. Reprinted in Philip Larkin, *Required Writing: Miscellaneous Pieces 1955–1982*, Faber & Faber, London, 1983, pp. 153–8

46. SS to John Guest, 3 October 1962: U of R

47. *Times Literary Supplement*, 28 December 1962

48. Helen Rapp to the author [Summer 1985]

49. Naomi Replansky to SS, 24 April 1961: PGP

50. SS to James Laughlin, 23 October 1963: New Directions Archives

51. *New York Times Book Review*, 5 July 1964

52. Marianne Moore to James Laughlin, 9 April 1964: New Directions Archives

53. MA: 126

54. 'World of Books', 23 December 1961: BBC WA

14 In Performance

1. Margaret Miller, letter to the author

2. Conversation with Father Jerome, Buckfast Abbey, July 1985

3. David Wright to his mother, 13 October 1960: David Wright

4. Lilian Carpenter, interview

5. SS to Valerie Ripley, 29 July 1963: U of R

6. SS to Michael Hoare, 4 June 1965: U of R

7. Nichola Smith to the author [1986]

8. *Observer*, 3 August 1975

9. SS to Bob Gottlieb, 30 November 1968: Knopf Archives

10. Norman Bryson to the author, 25 February 1984

11. *Observer*, 3 August 1975

12. Dannie Abse, *A Poet in the Family*, Robson Books, London, 1974, p. 185

13. 'Afterwords' in *Children of Albion*, ed. Michael Horovitz, Penguin, Harmondsworth, 1969, p. 337

14. In an obituary on Radio 3, 8 May 1971

15. *Records and Recording*, December 1966

16. Walter van de Maele to the author, 3 September 1985

17. SS to Michael Hoare, 9 October 1967: U of R

18. Brian Patten to the author [January 1987]

19. SS to Molly Everett, 22 October 1970: Molly Everett

20. *Spectator*, 10 June 1960

21. *Daily Telegraph*, 1 November 1957

22. *Observer*, 5 September 1954

23. *Observer*, 22 February 1957
24. SS to Terence Kilmartin, 4 January 1956: *Observer* files
25. *Daily Telegraph*, 20 March 1959
26. *Observer*, 1 January 1956
27. *Spectator*, 13 March 1959
28. *Spectator*, 4 August 1961
29. SS to Francis Stevenson, 21 September 1965: Quentin Stevenson
30. SS to John Guest, 9 March 1965: U of R
31. SS to Michael Hoare, 5 March 1965: U of R
32. Paul de Man, *Blindness and Insight: Essays in the Rhetoric of Contemporary Criticism*, (second edition, revised), University of Minnesota Press, Minneapolis, 1983, p. 47
33. SS to Terence Kilmartin, 24 May 1966: *Observer* files
34. SS to Hans Häusermann, 28 July 1958: U of N
35. SS to John Guest, no date [1966]: U of R
36. *Sunday Times*, 8 January 1967
37. *Guardian*, 16 December 1966
38. SS to Hans Häusermann, 9 March 1965: U of N
39. 'The Lively Arts', transmitted 5 November 1962: BBC WA
40. 'Poet Talking', Woman's Hour, 16 February 1970: BBC WA
41. Terence Kilmartin to SS, 27 March 1965: PGP
42. *Observer*, 19 May 1968
43. Audrey Insch to the author [1985]
44. SS to Terence Kilmartin, no date: *Observer* files
45. SS to Hans Häusermann, no date [February 1966]: U of N
46. SS to Olga Lawrence, 15 March 1966: Olga Lawrence
47. SS to Hans Häusermann, 14 August 1966: U of N
48. SS to John Guest, 3 February 1967: John Guest
49. Nina Woodcock, interview with the author
50. *Maurice Collis. Diaries 1949–69*, ed. Louise Collis, Heinemann, London, 1977, p. 178
51. *Listener*, 25 September 1975
52. *Spectator*, 18 December 1953
53. SS to Hans Häusermann, 11 February 1968: U of N
54. SS to John Guest, 20 March 1968: U of R
55. A. J. Davey's notes, recording his attendance on Miss M. Spear, 30 October 1967: A. J. Davey
56. MS notes: U of T

57. SS to Hans Häusermann, 12 August 1968: U of N
58. SS to Rachel Marshall, 20 December 1968: Kitty Hermges
59. SS to James Laughlin, 7 April 1969: New Directions Archives.

15 Black March

1. Hermione Lee, *The Novels of Virginia Woolf*, Methuen, London, 1977, p. 29
2. CP: 564
3. Robert Gottlieb to John Guest, 14 October 1968 (copy): Knopf Archives
4. SS to Robert Gottlieb, 17 October 1968: Knopf Archives
5. Robert Gottlieb to SS, 6 December 1968: PGP
6. *The Providence Sunday Journal*, 2 November 1969
7. *Christian Science Monitor*, 28 November 1969
8. Interview with John Gale, *Observer*, 9 November 1969
9. SS to John Guest, 15 June 1969: U of R
10. *Observer*, 9 November 1969
11. Interview, *Guardian*, 4 November 1969
12. Ann Thwaite (ed.), *Allsorts 2*, 1969, p. 100
13. SS to John Guest, 15 May 1969: U of R
14. SS to John Guest, 4 June 1969: U of R
15. SS to Audrey Insch, 19 July 1969: Audrey Insch
16. Aylett Hyam to SS, 28 August 1969: PGP
17. SS to Anthony Thwaite, 25 July 1969: Anthony Thwaite
18. SS to Terence Kilmartin, 6 February 1969: *Observer* files
19. Unpublished essay: U of T
20. *Observer*, 9 November 1969
21. Not with Ludovic Kennedy, as stated in Jack Barbera and William McBrien, *Stevie: A Biography of Stevie Smith*, 1985, p. 282
22. Kay Dick, *Ivy and Stevie*, p. 67
23. SS to Kay Dick, 8 November 1969: Washington University Libraries
24. Kay Dick, *Ivy and Stevie*, p. 78
25. SS to Paul Bailey, 28 November 1969: Paul Bailey
26. Jeni Couzyn in *Poetry Dimension I. A Living Record of the Poetry Year*, ed. Jeremy Robson, Robson Books, London, 1973, pp. 83, 85
27. Seamus Heaney, *Preoccupations: Selected Prose 1968–1978*, 1984, p. 199
28. SS to Elizabeth Popley, 7 January 1970: Elizabeth Popley
29. SS's 1969 appointment diary: PGP

30. SS to Elizabeth Popley, 15 June 1970: Elizabeth Popley

31. SS to Kay Dick, 3 October 1970: WUL

32. SS to Anna Browne, no date: Anna Browne

33. SS to Molly Everett, 2 October 1970: Molly Everett

34. Ibid.

35. SS to Molly Everett, 6 October 1970: Molly Everett

36. SS to Audrey Insch, 22 October 1970: Audrey Insch

37. SS to Molly Everett, 22 October 1970: Molly Everett

38. SS to John Barnard, 17 December 1970: the author

39. SS to Molly Everett, 10 November 1970: Molly Everett

40. John Guest, interview

41. SS to John Guest, 24 November 1970: John Guest

42. SS to Audrey Insch, 20 December 1970: Audrey Insch

43. MA: 324

44. Notebook in the possession of Molly Everett

45. Margaret Mills to the author, 17 October 1985

46. MA: 325

47. Helen Fowler memoir on Stevie Smith: Helen Fowler

48. Undated notes in the possession of Molly Everett

49. Helen Fowler memoir

50. Inez Holden, obituary of SS. *Royal Society of Literature Reports for 1970–71*

51. CP: 537

52. MA: 321

53. CP: 535

54. *Listener*, 4 January 1968

55. Stevie Smith in *Let the Poet Choose*, ed. James Gibson, Harrap, London, 1973, p. 147

Index of Works by Stevie Smith

General Index